POLITICS
IN A MUSEUM

Recent Titles in
Italian and Italian American Studies

The Hunchback's Tailor: Giovanni Giolitti and Liberal Italy from the Challenge of Mass Politics to the Rise of Fascism, 1882–1922
Alexander De Grand

Anita Garibaldi: A Biography
Anthony Valerio

Gaetano Salvemini: A Biography
Charles Killinger

POLITICS IN A MUSEUM

Governing Postwar Florence

James Edward Miller

Italian and Italian American Studies
Spencer M. Di Scala, Series Adviser

Westport, Connecticut
London

Library of Congress Cataloging-in-Publication Data

Miller, James Edward.
    Politics in a museum : governing postwar Florence / James Edward Miller.
      p. cm—(Italian and Italian American studies, ISSN 1530–7263)
    Includes bibliographical references and index.
    ISBN 0–275–97231–3 (alk. paper)
    1. Florence (Italy)—Politics and government—1945– I. Title. II. Series.
DG738.792.M55 2002
945'.51092—dc21   2001059084

British Library Cataloguing in Publication Data is available.

Library of Congress Catalog Card Number: 2001059084
ISBN: 0–275–97231–3
ISSN: 1530–7263

First published in 2002

Praeger Publishers, 88 Post Road West, Westport, CT 06881
An imprint of Greenwood Publishing Group, Inc.
www.praeger.com

Printed in the United States of America

The paper used in this book complies with the
Permanent Paper Standard issued by the National
Information Standards Organization (Z39.48–1984).

10 9 8 7 6 5 4 3 2 1

Contents

Foreword *by Spencer M. Di Scala*   vii

Preface   ix

Abbreviations   xiii

Chapter 1   Liberation   1

Chapter 2   Old Wine in New Bottles: From CTLN to Party
              Rule, 1944–1947   15

Chapter 3   Red Flag over Palazzo Vecchio, 1947–1951   31

Chapter 4   Head in the Clouds, Feet on the Ground:
              La Pira, 1951–1954   49

Chapter 5   Building a City on the Hill? 1954–1957   67

Chapter 6   Intermezzo, 1957–1960   83

Chapter 7   The Center Left at Florence, 1960–1965   101

Chapter 8   The Flood   121

Chapter 9   Muddling Through: The Bausi Years, 1968–1974   139

Chapter 10   The Historic Compromise at Florence, 1975–1981   159

Chapter 11   Who's in Charge? The Florentine *Pentapartito*   175

Chapter 12   City of Culture   189

Chapter 13   The Party's Over   205

Chapter 14   Conclusion: Penelope's Spindle   221

Bibliography   227

Index   243

A photo essay follows Chapter 7.

Foreword

Florence is famous as the cradle of the Renaissance and as a "city of art," but few know about its modern history. The postwar capital of the traditionally "Red" Tuscany, province of a state dominated by Christian Democrats, early-twentieth-century Florence was the center of Nationalist thought and during midcentury had a notable Fascist movement. Given this background, it is instructive to follow the city's political and social evolution after World War II as traced by James Edward Miller. During this period, the amazing growth of tourism altered the city's character, but, as Miller emphasizes, Florence is a living city, not a museum. The scale of tourism in Florence presented the medieval city with a unique problem—reconciling the presence of millions of tourists with the conduct of modern life. The city's experience in dealing with mass tourism thus serves as a lesson for other cities struggling with a similar dilemma, if not one on the same scale.

The outstanding characteristic of Miller's book, however, is the way that it describes the interplay of local and national politics, culture, and ideology. He captures the rich and complex recent history of a fascinating city under enormous pressure and suggests a fresh historical perspective. His meticulous study examines an increasingly important question facing the West in the modern world, especially the countries that make up the European Union: What is the proper balance between local autonomy and central control? *Politics in a Museum* discusses the extreme case of a notoriously weak state versus the sophisticated successor of a city-state with a centuries-long history, but it is instructive. It analyzes a major city over a lengthy period characterized by rapid social and economic change and by political turmoil. In doing so, Miller's book serves as a model for the analysis of emerging issues in contemporary politics and society.

Spencer M. Di Scala
Series Adviser
Italian and Italian American Studies

Preface

Firenze da lontano ci parve paradiso
(Florence from afar seems Paradise)

Puccini, *Gianni Schicchi*

On a gray, overcast day in the fall of 1991, Ennio Di Nolfo and I made our way toward his home on the outskirts of Florence. As we talked, Di Nolfo's dark Alfa glided off the ring road surrounding the old city in the direction of Ponte Rosso. We become part of a perfectly choreographed school of fish. In tempo with the cars around us, Di Nolfo repeatedly and sharply changed direction, first one way, then the other, until, finally, we swung onto the via Bolognese and headed up a winding hill and out of town. At this point, my chauffeur, with his customary good-natured malice, inquired: "Is this book going to be something for Americans or for Italians?" A good question that is not easy to address. Architecture questions—how to organize the book, what audience to seek, in sum, what kind of book I could and should write—preoccupied me for months thereafter. I wanted to produce something that would be available to a wider English-language audience while written with a level of sophistication that would meet the requirements of Italian readers.

The vehicle that I have chosen to reach these twin goals is examining postwar Florence's politics as a microcosm of the rise and collapse of Italy's so-called First Republic (1948–1994). Few societies have experienced a more rapid and successful modernization than post–World War II Italy. In 1940 Italy was a largely agrarian society, governed by a repressive regime. By the 1980s through a combination of self-discipline, creativity, and hardheaded political compromise, it was the world's fifth industrial power. Rapid modernization caused many of postwar Italy's political and social dilemmas. Neither of the nation's dominant postwar political cultures—Catholic and Marxist—successfully coped with the social and economic changes that they fostered. Gradually, their hold over postwar Italy crumbled. No new movements arose to seize the opportunities offered by Catholic-Communist paralysis. The existing parties had been too thoroughly integrated into a system of deals and favors. The groups directly challenging the status quo, particularly those on the far left and right, were wedded to antiquated ideologies. An institutional crisis accompanied ideological paralysis. Italy's mass political parties, the institutions that created the nation's constitutional system and mediated its passage into modernity, were unable to meet (perhaps unrealizable) popular demands to build an efficient, all-encompassing, and nonintrusive welfare state. Their attempt to build a welfare state by combining modern techniques of political mobilization with old-time patronage fostered deep and wide-ranging corruption. The parties came to stand for little more than self-preservation. They utilized the state apparatus as a vast cash cow to collect voters. Patronage went mostly to those with economic power: big business, organizations representing smaller industries, big farmers, and cooperatives. No group was more favored than the construction industry.

Modernization meant creating new infrastructure: roads, railroads, airports, housing, factories, offices, and storage facilities. Somehow the new Italy that was rising had to be married to the old. Its medieval cities are home to the greater part of the population and provide the primary attraction for one of Italy's major industries, tourism. Modernizing while preserving these cities has been one of postwar Italy's most tormenting problems. While there have been some notable successes, such as Bologna, the rate of failure has been alarmingly high. Urban policy is one of the clearest cases of the results of permitting the parties to carry out their self-appointed role of mediators. Far from holding the balance between contending interests, the parties generally abdicated responsibility. The modernization of Italy's infrastructure was a triumph for laissez-faire capitalism at the expense of city dwellers. The past, bravely, but ineffectively, defended by small groups with a sense of history or of cultural and environmental preservation, fell victim to the jackhammers of small and large contractors.

Nowhere has the tension between the desire for modernity and the urge to conserve more evident than in Florence. That city has spent a half century in a wearying and, at best, only partially successful effort to protect ancient treasures and achieve individual desires for profit and modern convenience. The Catholic and Marxist parties that led the city in the first twenty years of the postwar era offered programs that defended the interests of the lower classes. They either ignored or failed to discipline extralegal growth that met the demands of an expanding middle class. Postwar Florence's expansion was largely unplanned. Growth became sort of a mantra used by speculators, large and small, to justify their actions.

In the mid-1960s a new generation of pragmatic politicians, markedly lacking a moral compass, largely abandoned the city's commitment to the poor. Responding to demands from a swelling middle class, they accelerated Florence's evolution into a museum city: its historic center hollowed out of population and retrofitted with service industries catering to tourism; its peripheral areas suffering from an accumulation of ills such as exorbitant rents, poorly designed housing, and insufficient, inefficient services. A population that stood at 450,000 in the postwar era declined dramatically. Slowly, Florence appears to be passing along the same path taken by Venice, becoming a Renaissance Disneyland to complement the sad, decadent, and frequently waterlogged *Serenissima*.

This book chronicles that decline, placing Florence's story within the larger frame of postwar Italian politics. It is based largely upon archival sources, public documents and reports, press coverage, and a series of interviews conducted with a representative sampling of Florence's political and cultural elite. It also rests on a group of first-rate books about Italian politics and urban policy. My debts to historians such as Giuseppe Marinini and Patrick McCarthy and to students of urban policy like Mariella Zoppi and Edoardo Detti will be evident to scholars. Above all, I benefited from a more than twenty-year relationship with Nicola Gallerano, whose urbane wit, generosity, and encyclopedic knowledge of Italy's past were all put to service in creating this book. His sudden death in the spring of 1996 was a terrible personal blow. This book is dedicated to his memory.

Like any author, I carry my own share of prejudices to this study. I am, first of all, American-born and cannot expect to comprehend in every instance the full range and subtlety of Italians' responses to their political and urban problems. More fundamentally, I confess to a sympathy for urban planning and environmental and historical preservation. I have tried to achieve a balance by talking with policy makers. While I am frequently critical of Italy's politicians, I have underlined the very real dilemmas that they face.

All writers store up debts that they can never adequately discharge. Among Italian friends, Elisabetta Vezzosi, Ilaria Poggiolini, Ennio Di Nolfo, Tommaso Detti, and Federico and Dolly Romero provided housing, good food, and generous doses of encouragement and criticism. Pier Luigi Ballini used his position in city politics to unlock doors. Paolo De Marco helped to arrange a Fulbright professorship at Naples that provided me both a point of comparison for urban policy issues and extra time for research. Among my Anglo-Saxon brethren, Tom Row, David Ellwood, and Judy Chubb provided critical comment, while Stan Burnette labored over the manuscript with patience, humor, and a keen critical eye. Finally, my students at the Foreign Service Institute endured lectures and slide shows on urban planning and history and responded to the role of captive audience with interesting observations. Subsequently, they have been generous with their hospitality during my frequent visits to Italy. A Fulbright fellowship and a grant from the American Philosophical Society supported research.

Abbreviations

AA BB AA	Division of Fine Arts (Ministry of Education)
ACC	Allied Control Commission for Italy
ACF	Florence Communal Archives
AC/S	Central State Archives (Rome)
ALP	La Pira Archive (Florence)
AMG	Allied Military Government
APC	Communist Party of Italy Archives (Rome)
ASdiF	State Archives of Florence
b.	busta
CTDP	Tuscan Center for Political Documentation (Florence)
CTLN	Tuscan Committee of National Liberation
DC	Christian Democracy
Div.	Division
f.	fascicolo
F.	Fondo
Gab.	Gabinetto
ISRT	Tuscan Institute for the History of the Resistance (Florence)
MI	Ministry of the Interior
MPI	Ministry of Public Instruction (Education)
NA	*Nuova Antologia*
NA	U.S. National Archives
PCI	Italian Communist Party

PdA	Action Party
PLI	Italian Liberal Party
PS	Public Security
PSI	Italian Socialist Party
RG	Record Group
Uff.	Office

Chapter 1

Liberation

Florence is gravely wounded: who knows when we will see it cured, ordered and smiling. Everywhere there are the ruins, everywhere filth and disorder. . . . And hunger, so much hunger. . . . The terror is finished: the drama and suffering of the Florentine people are not.

diary entry, September 4, 1944

Heat, dust, flies, and death. The Tuscan summer of 1944 was harsh and memorable. Allied armies broke the Gustav Line near Naples in May and advanced north. In June they liberated Rome. By late July the Anglo-Americans were poised by the Arno. On July 30, Major Eric Linklater, British 8th Army, and Wynford Vaughan of the BBC made their way along the front lines seeking relief from the heat and a better view of the battle. Spying a stone villa ahead, the two men approached and entered. "We stepped into the quiet hall . . . and then both of us gave a gasp of surprise as we saw on the wall a magnificently painted crucifix. I went hurriedly into the main room . . . that . . . was stacked with canvases . . . the 'Primavera' by Botticelli . . . the chief masterpieces from the Uffizi Gallery, the Pitti, the Academia, and San Marco." Giotto, Cimabue, Rubens, Botticelli, the Lippi, Paolo Uccello, and Raphael were heavily represented among 246 of Western civilization's greatest artworks. An aging custodian appeared and explained to his startled guests that other treasures lay in nearby homes along the battle line. Florence and its art waited helplessly for liberation that summer, exposed to a mounting threat of destruction and possessing the most limited means of self-defense.[1]

FLORENCE AT WAR

On Sunday, June 10, 1940, Florentines crowded the city's piazzas and bars to hear Mussolini broadcast his declaration of war on France and Great Britain. Most had known for days, if not weeks, that war alongside the German ally was inevitable. The majority probably shared the hopes of two Florentines whose letters fell into the hands of Fascist censors: a speedy victory and quick return to peace.[2]

Fascist Italy achieved neither victory nor peace. Military defeat, privation, tens of thousands of casualties, and a devastating Allied aerial bombardment destroyed public support for the regime. When Mussolini fell three years later, Italy was materially and morally exhausted and prey to two massive foreign armies that contested control of the peninsula for another two years.

Florentine morale began to collapse almost as soon as war began. Fascist authorities hoped to provoke public anger against the "barbarian" English, while reassuring Italians that the regime was prepared for enemy attacks. They canceled a major art show, packed up most artworks, and carried them off to safety. Those too big to move and major buildings were strait-jacketed in sandbags and scaffolding. These actions succeeded in heightening public fear of air attacks.[3]

Fascist efforts to keep up public morale were plentiful. Posters and manifestos carpeted the city. Through rubber drives, war bond campaigns, special activities for workers, students, and women, the continuation of the opera and symphony seasons at Teatro Comunale, and major rallies, including a joint appearance of Hitler and Mussolini on October 28, 1940, the regime attempted to build patriotic fervor while maintaining a sense of continuity in daily life.[4]

Despite some successes, official propaganda failed to overcome widespread war weariness and apprehension about Italy's future within the Nazi "new order." Mounting shortages and an accompanying black market, combined with clumsy police efforts to enforce rationing, increased public discontent. Popular belief that party members profited from the flourishing black market created tensions between the rich and poor and between the Fascists and the mass of Florentines. Government decrees then blocked all trading in precious metals and stones and the sales of textiles, staples of the Florentine economy.[5]

By 1942 foodstuffs were so scarce that basic issues of survival dominated Florentine life. The public's obsession with food and its anti-German feelings intersected when the Italian government brought 10,000 Hitler Youth to the city for a "friendship festival," feeding them meat, butter, milk, and a 400-gram daily ration of bread.[6]

The collapse of the regime's support among the mass of Italians opened the way for the growth of a broadly based anti-Fascism. Catholics were among the most active participants. Elio Dalla Costa, Florence's saintly and popular archbishop, carefully followed the lead of Popes Pius XI and XII in opposing German racism. During the first years of the war, the archbishop provided food and other welfare assistance to Florentines and secretly aided Jews and political refugees.

Dalla Costa's principal lay lieutenant, University of Florence law professor Giorgio La Pira, signaled mounting Catholic opposition to the regime in the periodical *I Principî* (1939–1940) and, after its suppression, in essays appearing in the *Settimana Cattolica*. Invited to display his loyalty to the regime by mounting guard over the tomb of a Fascist hero, La Pira willingly agreed but added that he would not carry a rifle: "In front of the dead, I recite the rosary." In January 1942, the city's prefect called the professor into his office for an admonitory chat. At the prefect's "suggestion," La Pira wrote the Fascist federation's secretary a "conciliatory" letter that cleverly lampooned Mussolini.[7]

Local authorities tolerated La Pira's burlesque with ill humor because of his ties to Dalla Costa. Within weeks of La Pira's defiant actions, the police began rounding up suspected Florentine anti-Fascists while informers at the university stepped up surveillance of students and professors. In spite of police repression, the anti-Fascist parties organized and grew as evidence of Italian defeat mounted. Word of plotting by regime stalwarts like Marshal Pietro Badoglio and the king himself spurred the growth of anti-Fascism. By early 1943 representatives of Florence's anti-Fascist parties were meeting regularly at the home of the aging Socialist physician and former deputy Gaetano Pieraccini.[8]

The Fascist regime was in an advanced stage of decomposition. Throughout the peninsula Italians were fleeing the cities in search of safety in the countryside. In May 1943 elite paratroopers and residents of the Santa Croce area fought in the streets, leaving three people dead.[9]

OCCUPATION

The king overthrew Mussolini on July 25, 1943. Jubilant Florentines assembled in Piazza Vittorio Emanuele on July 26 to celebrate the fall of the regime and, they believed, the end of the war. Excited crowds soon filled other streets and squares, destroying symbols of Fascism until the police finally intervened.[10]

As Fascism dissolved at the first blow and its leaders sought safety in flight or through collaboration with the new regime, the leaders of the anti-Fascist parties stepped up their individual and group organizational activities. The parties set up a coordinating committee to establish a common policy toward Marshal Badoglio's new government.[11]

The anti-Fascists had little tolerance for Badoglio's rule. His government was made up of survivors of the old regime, major Fascists were still at liberty, and *La Nazione*, the city's most influential newspaper, remained in the hands of Mussolini's ex-supporters. A second, pressing concern was the government's attitude toward the Germans. Few Italians were aware of the secret negotiations taking place with the Allies, but most could surmise that Badoglio would try to extract Italy from the war. So could Hitler. After a brief hesitation, he flooded northern Italy with fresh troops. Concerned by official passivity, one acute Florentine predicted that in its efforts to save itself, the crown would sacrifice the army.[12]

Florentines reacted with enthusiasm to Badoglio's September 8, 1943, an-

nouncement of an armistice with the Anglo-American allies. Surveying the joy-
ful celebration that greeted news of the agreement, an army officer called out to
some of the revelers: "What are you cheering about? The war has hardly begun."[13]
Rarely has a prediction been so swiftly fulfilled. The king and Badoglio fled Rome
the same night, leaving their military commanders without instructions. Florence's military commander, General Armellini Chiappi, rejected anti-Fascist
pleas to arm the populace and surrendered the city to a handful of German troops
on September 11. The city's vengeful Fascist former rulers returned, and a man-
hunt for leading anti-Fascists began. Representatives of the major anti-Fascist
parties met secretly and created a Tuscan Committee of National Liberation
(CTLN) to organize resistance to the occupation and create a legitimate alternative to an Italian government compromised both by its past collaboration with
Fascism and by its flight from Rome.[14]

Untouched by an air attack for nearly three and a half years, most Florentines
believed that their city would be spared because of its special cultural position.
A September 25 Allied attack ended this comforting illusion. In a pattern that
spread terror, the raid missed its target, the rail yards of Campo Marte. Helpless
civilians living near the yards were the victims of 500-pound bombs dropped by
U.S. Air Force B-26s. The air raid, the first of six that the city would endure
over the next nine months, brought the reality of war to Florence.[15]

Allied raids were only part of the nightmare of German occupation. Repression
and mass murder were staples of the new order. The Florentine Jewish community
was singled out for extermination. Two hundred forty-eight Florentine Jews were
murdered by the occupiers or perished in their death camps.[16]

As the hunt for anti-Fascists became more intense and violent, many of the
best known, including La Pira, fled the city. Others went into hiding. The anti-
Fascist parties organized intelligence services in Florence, stored arms abandoned
by the Italian army, and trained members in their use. The Communists, the best
disciplined and organized, were able to set up small terrorist groups, the GAP
(Patriotic Action Groups), that began harassing and killing Fascist and German
soldiers and police. Simultaneously, in the countryside, the parties organized
larger military formations. The Communists again provided the bulk of these
forces, but both the Action Party and a renascent Italian Socialist Party were
able to field their own military units. By the spring of 1944 the city and surrounding countryside were gripped in a bloody struggle. The Germans and Fascists employed indiscriminate violence to terrorize Tuscany. The anti-Fascists
struck back.[17]

The major parties, Christian Democratic (Catholic), Socialist, Communist,
Action, and Liberal, achieved a high degree of coordination in their battle
through the efforts of the CTLN. From its Florence headquarters, the CTLN
directed both the military and political struggle against Fascism. Through organizational skill, a willingness to stand against oppression, and an ability to attract
Italy's best men and women, the parties acquired a legitimacy that allowed them
to create a postwar Italian state measured to their requirements.[18]

CTLN unity was frequently strained. The Catholics and Marxists had a long history of conflict. The Action Party mistrusted its Marxist rivals on the left and saw the Liberals and Christian Democrats as representatives of an old order that it hoped to abolish. The Communists, often in concert with more conservative parties, acted to contain the Actionists. The refusal of the PCI (Italian Communist Party) to place its forces under the day-to-day control of the CTLN's military committee created severe tactical problems and heightened mutual mistrust.[19]

The CTLN held together because all the parties shared one overriding need: to survive by ridding Italy of its German occupiers and their Italian Fascist collaborators. In spite of major differences over ideology, strategy, and tactics, the parties learned to cooperate. The experience of forced cohabitation probably saved Italy from civil war in the difficult years of reconstruction.[20]

Nowhere was the threat to CTLN unity greater than on the issue of the terrorist tactics of the GAP. The Communists insisted that GAP actions psychologically prepared the people of Tuscany for an insurrection. Cardinal Dalla Costa, taking a stand on the sacredness of human life, called for an end to the cycle of violence and reprisals by both the GAP and the German occupying authorities. Catholics and Actionists shared Dalla Costa's misgiving about this form of resistance.[21]

The issue came to a head on April 15, 1944, when GAP executed the septuagenarian Fascist philosopher Giovanni Gentile as he walked along the Arno. Heated exchanges inside the CTLN ended in deadlock. The city was spared violent Fascist reprisals by the appeals of Gentile's family and, ironically, by the intervention of the German consul.[22]

While a deadly game of hide-and-seek continued, most Florentines sought security in continuation of their regular routine. Fascist authorities encouraged the belief that life could continue as before. The podesta, the city's appointed mayor, called together representatives of the tourist and banking industries to find funding for a projected 1944 edition of the Maggio Musicale festival to include three major operas, a symphonic season, and performances of Verdi's *Requiem*.[23]

Reality overtook these ambitious fantasies in May, when an Allied bomber missed its target, depositing a 500-pound bomb on the stage of Teatro Comunale. The city's food office suspended business because of Allied air attacks. Florence's transportation systems and rail links collapsed. Essential medicines disappeared. Banks no longer made loans to a bankrupt city government, even for essentials such as coal. The Germans refused to assist Fascist officials.[24] In December 1943, Florentine workers joined in a wave of strikes throughout occupied Italy. During January 1944, workers at the Pignone manufacturing complex began a calculated slowdown that denied war production to the Axis. On January 31, Corrado Simone, a PCI activist, set fire to police records in the Prefecture, denying the SS information on resistance members and impeding the shipment of Florentine workers to slave labor camps in Germany. In March the Communist-dominated labor movement mounted an effective general strike. An active clandestine press, widely distributed, provided war news and directives to the populace, while anti-Fascist bands operated with effectiveness on the city's periphery. GAP actions became more daring.[25] The Fascists and Nazis reacted with further doses of terror. In March 1944 five young draft evaders were publicly executed at Campo Marte. The mutilated bodies of captured resistance fighters decorated roadsides as warnings to other "rebels."[26]

By mid-June 1944, most Florentine Fascists recognized that defeat was imminent and fled. Control of the city administration fell to a dwindling band of fanatics and their German SS allies. Fascist and German preparations for withdrawal heightened widespread chaos. A massive flow of refugees from neighboring towns and the countryside swelled the city's population to over a half million. Florence could not meet their needs. The local economy was collapsing as power sources evaporated. The city had little water. Its food stocks were exhausted. Disease threatened as refuse piled up everywhere for lack of transport. Meanwhile, the Germans indiscriminately destroyed immovable property and carried off anything removable of value: trucks, railroad rolling stock, machinery, available food, livestock, and Florence's most treasured possession, its artworks. The CTLN warned the Allies to expect widespread hunger and mass unemployment, serious public health problems, and a paralyzed economy.[27]

OPEN CITY?

The idea of granting Florence immunity from Allied attacks in return for the withdrawal of German and Fascist occupation troops surfaced on a number of occasions after mid-1943. Gerhardt Wolf, the German consul in Florence, urged his government to respect the city's unique heritage in the arts. Cardinal Dalla Costa was another active exponent. Hitler seized upon the concept and milked it for its propaganda value: contrasting purported German respect for "culture" with the primitive destructiveness of Allied bombing raids. The German high command never seriously considered removing its troops or routing supply shipments around Florence. Unilateral German declarations that Florence was an "open city," combined with the staged removal of some headquarters and administrative units, were meaningless propaganda gestures that brought no response from the Allies and infuriated Dalla Costa and Wolf.[28]

The CTLN was equally unmoved. The Communists, in particular, were opposed to the concept of an open city. They aimed at an insurrection and suspected that the church was collaborating with conservative and moderate forces, including parties within the CTLN, in an effort to avoid the swing to the left that would inevitably follow a successful insurrection.[29]

Most moderates and conservatives wanted to avoid an insurrection. However, not even the church endorsed the German proposals. Repeated efforts by Wolf, the Swiss, and Romanian consuls, and Dalla Costa failed to secure the total German withdrawal that would make open city status operative. Fascist city authorities were helpless bystanders, unable to influence German decisions. The CTLN parties remained united in opposition to the open city proposal.[30]

The parties spurned mid-June efforts by survival-minded Fascists to negotiate some form of truce that would permit an unimpeded withdrawal of occupation forces. The CTLN response was swift: prior to any talks, the Fascists would have to secure the release of all political prisoners, including those in German hands; surrender all weapons as soon as the Germans withdrew from Florence; cease all repressive activities directed against CTLN forces; and guarantee adequate provisioning of the city.[31]

While the CTLN took a decisive stand in setting its conditions for talks, the parties reacted differently to the idea of a negotiated withdrawal of enemy forces from Florence. The moderate parties favored discussions, arguing that if the talks simply led to orderly passage of power from the Fascists to the CTLN, the resistance would achieve a central objective and preserve Florence from destruction. In early July, the CTLN again debated the explosive question of the GAP. The Communists, preoccupied that Florentines would passively await liberation, heatedly rejected suggestions that the GAP suspend their attacks.[32]

The resistance effectively took control of the administration of a city still under German occupation on a piecemeal basis. In mid-July, the CTLN ordered Prefect Giuseppe Manna to cease efforts to organize a new police force. It issued warnings against hoarding and speculating in foodstuffs and gave instructions designed to protect existing food supplies from German sequestration.[33]

The effort to safeguard Florence's artistic heritage expanded. Early in 1943, Italian authorities had begun to move many of Italy's most precious art treasures from city museums to safety in villas in the periphery. The transfer of the art was accelerated by experience with Allied "precision bombing." However, the most immediate threat to Florentine art came from Nazi acquisitiveness. Marshal Kesselring, the German commander in Italy, complained about the difficulties of carrying out military operations "in a museum." The Germans initiated a systematic program for removing art treasures under cover of "military necessity." Many masterpieces disappeared into private collections and were not recovered for years.[34]

By mid-June Florence was a temporary deposit point for much of the country's looted art. One senior Fascist leader secured a German pledge to leave all the art—both that already looted and some 300 pieces belonging to local galleries marked for transport north—in the "open city" of Florence. The accord lasted as long as the Germans lacked transport to carry their booty north. By early July they had the trucks and began shipping the artworks to a staging area near Verona.[35]

Mussolini had refused to intervene to gain "open city" status for Florence. He was equally indifferent to the seizure of Italy's artworks. Wolf and a few other powerless German diplomats unsuccessfully sought to stem their government's kleptomania. Fortunately, German looting was widely frustrated by the ingenuity of a handful of Italian art experts and museum custodians, who played hide-and-seek with the Germans, moving major works to secure hiding places.[36]

THE BATTLE OF FLORENCE

The Germans intended to hold Florence for as long as possible to cover their retreat into Appennine defense lines. The CTLN would not permit an orderly, peaceful retreat of German troops from the city. At their July 21 meeting, the five parties agreed that "the CTLN must, by whatever means, make itself master of the city before the Allies arrive; the city must be occupied by our forces." Passively awaiting liberation, as the Romans had, meant that foreigners would decide the postwar organization of the Italian state. Resistance parties that failed to fight would have no claim on popular support. The CTLN took its decision: no negotiations with the occupiers and a no-holds-barred attack on their troops.[37]

The timing of the attack would depend on the Germans. The CTLN military command, with only a few thousand troops, was too weak to attack at will. Moreover, an insurrection could succeed only when the Allies were at hand. Ironically, too rapid an advance by liberating armies would negate Florentine efforts at self-liberation. The CTLN had to speedily seize control of the public administration in the interim between a German retreat and Allied arrival and present their liberators with a political fait accompli: resistance administration of Florence.[38]

In order for the insurrection to succeed, the CTLN had to exercise restraint even as the Germans systematically looted Florence's art heritage and destroyed critical parts of its economic infrastructure. In mid-June the Germans began dismantling the Florentine gasworks in the face of passive resistance by its employees. German soldiers methodically destroyed the city telephone exchanges and water mains. Seventeen water mills and pasta factories met the same fate. German troops seized all available transport, including hearses, and carried away sewer and water system pumps. After repeatedly interrupting the city's electrical supply, the occupiers finally cut it off entirely at the end of July. Heavy, virtually uninterrupted cannon fire from the south could be heard in the center of Florence from July 27 onward. The Germans seemed to respond by redoubling their looting and destructive frenzy. Florentines were imprisoned within their homes for most of the day. The heat was intense. The sewer system backed up into streets filled with refuse and detritus. The dead lay unburied for lack of hearses to transport them to cemeteries. A terrible odor hung over hot and smoldering Florence. Its terrorized populace was nearing its psychological breaking point.[39]

On the morning of July 28, newly awakened Florentines found their streets painted with large arrows designed to guide retreating German troops. At five o'clock that evening the Whermacht ordered civilian evacuation of both banks of the Arno by noon on July 30. Recognizing that a battle for control of the city was imminent, the CTLN assembled 200 partisans to infiltrate the city periphery and prepared for an insurrection.[40]

On August 3, the Germans placed the city under a state of emergency beginning at 3:30 P.M. and ordered the populace to stay inside their homes after 5 P.M.
At midnight they began a systematic destruction of the bridges across the Arno
and leveled medieval buildings on both sides of the river near the still-standing
Ponte Vecchio.

When the Germans acted to hinder an Allied crossing of the Arno, they were
already aware that the Anglo-Americans had decided to envelop Florence precisely to avoid a destructive pitched battle. Their one act of deference toward
the city's artistic heritage was offset by the systematic destruction of the area
around the Ponte Vecchio. Their actions not only destroyed the structural unity
of the area but totally upset its centuries-old economic and social balances, making reconstruction both a physical problem of rebuilding and a nearly insur-
mountable challenge of reknitting a community.[41]

For Florentines, imprisoned in their homes by a ferociously enforced German
curfew, the destruction of the bridges was a terrible psychological blow. Physically, the bridges united the city. Psychologically, the bridges and the surrounding
riverfront buildings were symbols of the city's beauty, its cultural achievement,
its special claim on the respect of humankind. "It's as if a part of me was broken
off forever . . . I feel mutilated from within," one Florentine wrote in his diary.[42]
Jarred awake by the first explosions, Florentines stumbled through dark halls onto
their balconies to witness further explosions, the passage of retreating German
troops, and the rising columns of smoke and debris that marked the end of one
of the city's proudest artistic heritages. Sitting in the hills overlooking the city,
the young Franco Zeffirelli and his fellow partisans watched an awesome pyro-
technic show and wondered what remained of the old city.[43]

The next morning the inhabitants of the southern (Oltrarno) section awoke
to find themselves liberated. The CTLN had established its control overnight.
Its partisans patrolled the streets, setting up checkpoints and exchanging fire with
German and Fascist snipers on the other bank of the Arno. British troops arriving
at Porta Romana met armed Communist partisans who had effective control of
that area. Later in the day, representatives of the CTLN escorted Allied civil
affairs officers to the Pitti Palace, where they got their first taste of the size of the
Florentine problem: an estimated 10,000 refugees were crowed into the palace
and adjacent grounds.[44]

The palace of the Grand Dukes of Tuscany looked like the most crowded slum of Naples.
Mothers, babies, men, boys, with bundles of clothes and mattresses and a few miserable
belongings, lay under the huge arches, swarmed through the courtyard and up the stairs.
. . . Sheets and clothing hung in quantities from every balcony. . . . There was only one
source of water . . . the Romantic walks of the Boboli Gardens were used as a public
toilet.[45]

The British raised the Union Jack over the Pitti, a sign to Florentines across
the river that liberating Anglo-American forces were poised nearby. Freeing the

bulk of Florence from German and Fascist troops took nearly a month. The Allies, determined to avoid responsibility for destroying Florence in a direct assault, left the task of driving the enemy out to the lightly armed forces of the CTLN. Meanwhile, partisan leaders sought Allied recognition. Partisan and Allied representatives met in the middle of a damaged passageway that Vasari built over the Ponte Vecchio in 1565. By August 8, a telephone line through this passage linked CTLN headquarters in occupied Florence with Allied headquarters across the river.[46]

The CTLN established dominance in the occupied zone of the city. It set up a *"giunta comunale"* (city administration) under Gaetano Pieraccini to reestablish city services or keep them functioning, a food commission to protect the city's dwindling food stock from German seizure and provision Florence, a banking commission to reanimate the lifeblood of the city economy, a police organization, public health bodies, and a variety of special organizations to "cleanse" the local government, financial, and cultural bureaucracies of politically compromised employees.[47]

Unable to gain Allied political recognition and believing that another round of explosions signaled German intent to totally and hastily evacuate the city, the CTLN parties launched their insurrection on the morning of August 11. Street battles erupted throughout the old city as the partisans attacked retreating German troops. Early that morning, the CTLN liberated Palazzo Vecchio, installed Pieraccini as mayor (*sindaco*), and took control of the public administration. As CTLN partisans moved through the old city, Florentines, weary from weeks of virtual imprisonment and overjoyed at their liberation by Italian forces, took to the streets and balconies to celebrate their newly won freedom.[48]

The Allies responded to news of the insurrection by sending a representative to the new city government and ordering Col. Ralph Rolf (U.K.) to move his men into CTLN-liberated Florence and establish allied military government over the rest of the city. The Allies waited another three days before sending substantial forces into the old city in order to permit the partisans to mop up a small, but active, group of Fascist sharpshooters. Meanwhile Anglo-American engineers built "Baily bridges" on the ruins of Florence's destroyed masterpieces and began to clear the Ponte Vecchio and surrounding areas for military traffic. On August 14, the first Allied combat units entered the *centro storico* (historic center).[49]

TOTTING UP THE COSTS

The battle of Florence raged along the city periphery for another two weeks. German artillery positioned on the hills intermittently shelled Florence, while small Axis units penetrated the periphery. Sniper fire continued in the old city. The Germans retired at the beginning of September 1944 as the Allies completed their envelopment of the city.

Liberated Florentines again freely circulated in their city, sadly gazing on scenes of massive destruction. "Finally I see up close the horrible destruction everyone is talking about," one Florentine wrote on August 12; "the [Via Por S Maria] no longer exists: it lies under a mass of ruins, at time four to five meters high. Fires still burn from the ruins. . . . The facade of S. Stefano remains standing, but all the rest of the building has fallen. A few walls . . . still stand: but the towers, those beautiful towers, are no more." The short walk from Palazzo Pitti to Palazzo Vecchio was physically impossible because "rubble thirty feet high spilled from the end of via Guicciardini almost to Palazzo Pitti." The Germans had dealt the old city a hard blow: destroying 367 stores, seventy-one artisans' workshops, and 123 other buildings, including ten medieval towers. Other important historical and architectural landmarks suffered varying degrees of damage, as did thousands of shops and private dwellings.[50]

The costs of liberation included over 200 dead and 400 wounded in the August battle. In the weeks following liberation, booby traps sown by retreating German forces killed others. The survivors found their local economy destroyed and transportation, food, water, sanitary services, heat, and light either nonexistent or in short supply. Approximately 150,000 people were homeless. Recovery would be a slow and painful process.[51]

Still, a majority of Florentines welcomed liberation from Fascism and gave overwhelming support to the CTLN parties. Though too weak to effect their military liberation alone, the partisans of Tuscany contributed to Allied victory and provided a war-scarred people with desperately needed psychological reinforcement. Whatever the limits of its military contribution or its ability to rebuild, the Florentine resistance had grasped the moral and psychological high ground for Italy.[52]

NOTES

1. BBC report summary, July 30, 1944, 10000/145/25, RG 331, NA.

2. Aurelio Lepre, *L'occhio del Duce* (Milan, 1992), p. 21; Aurelio Lepre, *Le illusioni, la paura, la rabbia* (Naples, 1989), p. 37.

3. Ugo Cappelletti, *Firenze in guerra* (Florence, 1984), pp. 18, 28; Renzo Martinelli, *Il fronte interno a Firenze* (Florence, 1989), pp. 90, 96–97.

4. Piero Calamandrei, *Diari, 1939–1945*, 2 vols. (Florence, 1982), 1: 244, 322; Cappelletti, *Firenze in guerra*, pp. 40–47, 70–71.

5. Lepre, *Occhio*, p. 47. Martinelli, *Il fronte interno*, pp. 109–10, 128, 188; Cappelletti, *Firenze in guerra*, pp. 104–6; Orazio Barbieri, *Ponti sull'Arno* (Rome, 1975), pp. 8–9; Silvio Lanaro, *Storia dell'Italia republicana* (Venice, 1992), pp. 16–17; Calamandrei, *Diario*, 2: 43.

6. Lepre, *Occhio*, pp. 52–53; Calamandrei, *Diario*, 2: 35; Martinelli, *Il fronte interno*, pp. 171, 203, 233, 239; Giovanni Frullini, *La Liberazione di Firenze*, 2 vols. (Milan, 1982), 2: 9–10.

7. Bruna Bocchini Camaiani, "Ricostruzione concordato e processi di secolarizzazione," in Francesco Margotta Broglio, ed., *Chiesa del Concordato* (Bologna, 1983), 2: 109–10, 159; Marco Palla, *Firenze nell Regime fascista* (Florence 1978), pp. 100–107; Calamandrei, *Diario*, 2: 3, 6; Fioretta Mazzei, *Giorgio La Pira. Cose viste e ascoltate* (Florence, 1980), p. 61.

8. Calamandrei, *Diari*, 2: 7–9, 18–20, 74; Barbieri, *Ponti*, 25–26; Adone Zoli *Discorsi parlamentari* (Rome, 1989), pp. 849–51.

9. Calamandrei, *Diari*, 2: 87; Franco Calamandrei, *La vita indivisible*, ed. R. Bilenchi (Rome, 1984), p. 95.

10. Cappelletti, *Firenze in guerra*, pp. 174–78; Barbieri, *Ponti*, pp. 31–32.

11. Notes on actions of PdA, ISRT, Carte Agnoletti, b 1, f. 2.

12. Calamandrei, *Diari*, 2: 166–67; Lepre, *L'occhio*, p. 218.

13. Piero Pieroni, *Firenze, gli anni terrible* (Florence, 1970), p. 3.

14. Report on the activities of the CTLN, August 9, 1944, ISRT, Fondo CTLN, b 18, f Primi atti; E. E. Agnoletti, "La politica del Comitato Toscano di Liberazione Nazionale" *Il Ponte*, (August 1945), pp. 414–29.

15. Guiseppe Batelli, ed., *Lorenzo Milani, alla mamma* (Genoa, 1990), pp. 52–53; Nicholas *Citta aperta* (Florence, 1945), Nicholas Comene, *Firenze Citta aperta* (Florence, 1945), p. 8; Cappelletti, *Firenze in guerra*, pp. 8–21; Frullini, *Le liberazione*, p. 18; Martinelli, *Il fronte interno*, p. 345; Istituto Gramsci Toscano, *I compagni di Firenze* (Florence, 1984), p. 62; Ennio Di Nolfo, *Le paure e le speranze degli italiani* (Milan, 1986), p. 42.

16. Directive of December 20, 1943, ACF, serie varie, Gabinetto del Podesta, Ebrei; Order from the Ministry of Education, Italian Social Republic, December 1, 1943, ISRT, Carte Fasola, b 1, f 1.

17. Barbieri, *Ponti*, p. 44.

18. Tristano Codignola, *Scritti politici, 1943–1981* (Florence, 1987), 1: 48–115.

19. Calamandrei, *Diari*, 2: 382–83; PdA comments on PLI motion to CTLN, June 5, 1944, ISRT, Fondo F. Lombardi, b 16, f CTLN No. 1; PdA declaration, June 28, 1944, ibid., B 17, f CTLN-Comitato intersindicale; Giovanni De Luna, Piero Camilla and Stefano Vitali, eds., *Le formazione GL nella resistenza* (Milan, 1985), pp. 75–77; Lotti and Dradi, "Partito d'azione," in Ettora Rotelli, ed., *La Ricostruzione in Toscana del CTLN ai partiti*, 2 vols. (Bologna, 1980–1981), 2: 265, 272–74.

20. Pietro Secchia, ed., *Il Partito Comunista Italiano e la guerra di liberazione, 1943–1945* (Milan, 1973), pp. 508–10, 996–1002.

21. Tito Casini, *Elia Dalla Costa* (Florence, 1972), pp. 303–4; Camaiani, "Ricostruzione," p. 173; Orazio Barbieri, *La fede e la ragione* (Milan, 1982), pp. 75–76; Istituto Gramsci Toscano, *I compagni*, pp. 195–219.

22. David Tutaev, *The Man Who Saved Florence* (New York, 1966), pp. 148–49; Giacomo Devoto, *La Parentesi* (Florence, 1974), p. 61.

23. Labroca to Podesta, March 11, 1944, ACF, Varie 1944, Gabinetto del Podesta, 301–400; Minutes of February 21, 1944, meeting, and Labroca to Podesta, April 26, 1944, ibid., Ente Autonomo Teatro Comunale.

24. Note by Podesta, May 17, 1944, ACF, Varie 1944, Gabinetto del Podesta, Ente Autonomo Teatro Comunale; President, Fascist Union of Merchants to Podesta, ibid., 801–900; Promemoria, April 14, 1944, ibid., 501–600; Podesta to Prefect, undated, ibid., 901–1000; Podesta to German Occupation Headquarters, March 1, 1944, ibid., 1–100; Podesta to Prefect, June 6, 1944, ibid., 901–1000.

25. Secchia, *PCI*, 310–313; Barbieri, *Ponti*, pp. 91, 109–14, 232; Cappelletti, *Firenze in guerra*, p. 300.

26. Provincia di Firenze, *Contro ogni ritorno* (Florence, 1972), pp. 106–7; Giulio Villani, *Giorni di guerra* (Florence, 1992), pp. 13–14, 71–72, 74–75.

27. CTLN to Allied Military Command, n.d., ISRT, Fondo CTLN, b 18, f "Primi atti politici."

28. Giulio Villani, *Il vescovo Elia Dalla Costa* (Florence, 1974), pp. 198–99; Tutaev, *The Man*, pp. 120–21, 134–35; Marcello Vanucci, *L'avventura degli stranieri in Toscana* (Aosta, 1981), pp. 189–92.

29. Antonio Roasio, *Figlio della classe operala* (Milan, 1983), p. 265.

30. Tutaev, *Man*, p. 135; Comene, *Firenze*, p. 10; Podesta of Florence to Podesta of Bologna, June 30, 1944, ACF, Serie varie, Gabinetto del Podesta, 901–1000.

31. Giovanni Casoni, *Diario fiorentino, giugno–agosto 1944* (Florence, 1946), pp. 5–9, 17–19, 54, 77–80.

32. Minutes of CTLN meeting, June 23, July 3, 10, 1944, ISRT, Fondo F. Lombardi, b 17, f CTLN no. 2; Casoni, *Diario*, pp. 59, 67; Secchia, *PCI*, pp. 453–54; Roasio, *Figlio*, p. 261.

33. CTLN to Manna, July 19, 1944, ISRT, Fondo CTLN, b 17, f 9; CTLN to Bacchetti, July 23, 1944, ibid; Report of CTLN Food Committee, July 26, 1944, ISRT, Fondo F. Lombardi, b 17 f. CTLN n. 3.

34. Tutaev, *The Man*, pp. 95–97, 120, 179–85; Lynn Nicholas, *The Rape of Europa* (New York, 1994), pp. 229–72.

35. Paoletti and Carniani, *Firenze: Guerra*, pp. 46–48.

36. Siviero, "L'opere d'arte trafugate dall'Italia," *NA* 83 (February 1948), pp. 142–53; Fasola to Siviero, February 20, 1961, ISRT, Carte Fasola, b 1, f 1, Frederick Hartt, *Florentine Art Under Fire* (Princeton, NJ, 1949), pp. 3–4, 76; Nazi plunder included 529 paintings, 162 sculptures, six cartoons, thirty-eight textiles.

37. Minutes of the July 21, 1944, meeting of the CTLN, ISRT, Fondo F. Lombardi, b. 17, f CTLN n. 2.

38. Report to the CTLN by Camillo De Sanctis, July 22, 1944, ISRT, Fondo F. Lombardi, b 16, f. CTLN n. 1; Roger Absolam, ed., *Gli alleati e la ricostruzione in Toscana* (Florence, 1988), 1: 119–21; "Plan for the Organization of Florence and Province," n.d., but July 1944, NARA, RG 331, ACC, 10800/115/321.

39. Tutaev, *The Man*, pp. 204, 224–26; Renato Cassigoli, *Il servizio del gas nella resistenza* (Florence, 1984), p. 41, 44–45; Giovanni Favilli, *Prima linea Firenze* (Milan, 1975), pp. 11–12; Casoni, *Diario*, pp. 189–91; Piero Santi, *Diario 1943–1946* (Venice, 1950), pp. 52–53.

40. Comene, *Firenze*, pp. 47–53; Favelli, *Prima linea*, pp. 13–14; Situation report, nd [July 30, 1944], NA, RG 331, ACC, 10800/115/321; Rosaio, *Figlio*, p. 273.

41. Edoardo Detti, with Tommaso Detti, *Florence That Was* (Florence, 1970), pp. 113–14; Tutaev, *The Man*, p. 246.

42. Santi, *Diario*, 54–56; Hanna Kiel, *La battaglia della colline* (Florence, 1986), pp. 24–25.

43. Favilli, *Prima linea*, pp. 30–31, 52–54; Franco Zeffirelli, *Zeffirelli* (New York, 1986), p. 48; E. E. Agnoletti, "Perche i ponti di Firenze non furono difesi?" *Ponte* (February 1945), pp. 57–63.

44. Absalom, *Gli Alleati*, pp. 225–31.

45. Hartt, *Florentine Art*, p. 38.

46. Absalom, *Gli Alleati*, pp. 355–58; "War in a Museum," *New York Times*, August 8, 1944; Ugo Cappelletti, *Firenze citta aperta* (Florence, 1975), p. 54.

47. Minutes of CTLN meeting, August 5, 1944, ISRT, Fondo F. Lombardi, b 17, f CTLN n. 2; Report: "Activities of Administrative Organs and Technical Commissions," August 9, 1944, ISRT, Fondo CTLN, b 17, f 9; Favilli, *Prima linea*, pp. 40, 50–51; Provincia di Firenze, *Contro ogni ritorno* (Florence, 1972), p. 122.

48. Declaration of the CTLN [insurrection], August 11, ISRT, Fondo CTLN, b 18, f Primi atti; Carlo L. Ragghianti, "Quell'agosto 1944 a Firenze," *NA* 119 (October 1984), pp. 88–95; Orazio Barbieri, *Giuseppe Rossi* (Milan, 1989), p. 150; Favilli, *Prima linea*, p. 56; *Nazione del Popolo*, August 12, 1944; Casoni, *Diario*, p. 267.

49. Notes to Regional Commissioner, 8th Region, August 11, 1944, NARA, RG 331, ACC, 10800/115/321; Cappellini, *Firenze citta aperta*, p. 115.

50. Favilli, *Prima linea*, p. 63; Hartt, *Florentine Art*, p. 44; Piero Calamandrei, *Uomini e citta della resistenza* (Bari, 1977), pp. 198–99; Detti, *Florence*, p. 112; Report of the Superintendent of Galleries of Florence, August 12, 1944, NARA, RG 331, ACC, 10800/145/75.

51. Giorgio La Pira, *Lettere a casa* (Milan, 1981), pp. 174–75; Calamandrei, *Uomini*, p. 140; Ferrovie dello Stato di Firenze, *Ricostruzione di linee ed impianti ferroviari eseguiti della sezione lavori di Firenze dalla Liberazione in tutlo il 1947* (Florence, 1948), pp. 5–6, 14; *New York Times*, December 26, 1944.

52. Arturo Carlo Jemolo, *Italia tormentata 1946–1951* (Bari, 1951), pp. 115–17.

Chapter 2

Old Wine in New Bottles: From CTLN to Party Rule, 1944–1947

We have inherited a strongly centralized state . . . that is difficult to reform. . . . it is difficult to modernize, to really reconstruct: we absolutely have to succeed by working at the local level.
Prime Minister Ferruccio Parri, 1945

An authentic change of regime . . . after 70 years, is bringing about the demise of the state-party model which was introduced into Italy by Fascism and which the Republic ended up inheriting, confining itself to changing a singular [party] to a plural [parties].
Prime Minister Giuliano Amato, 1993

In the late summer of 1945, Giulio Paterno, the prefect of Florence, sent an extremely detailed, "top secret" report to the minister of the interior in Rome. The war in Europe had ended scarcely four months earlier, but already the situation in Florence pleased Paterno. The parties were imposing discipline on a population that "is dominated by a preoccupation for order and the security of their persons and property." While the Communists were powerful, the prefect, a veteran of the Fascist era, approvingly commented that their organization was built around the "principle of hierarchy and obedience." Moreover, Communist power was nicely counterbalanced by a numerous, but badly organized, Socialist Party and by a Christian Democratic Party that Paterno confidently predicted would soon become a "most fearsome enemy of the extremists."

As for the Tuscan Committee of National Liberation, Paterno could scarcely hide his satisfaction. "The prefect" had clipped the wings of this threat to "public order," expelling CTLN appointees from the police force, making short work of its efforts to purge the civil service of suspected Fascists, and cutting off its access to political patronage. Under the watchful eye of Giulio Paterno, the CTLN's subversion of public administration was at its end. The national government's control over Florence and, the prefect might have added, the command of national party headquarters over local organizations had been triumphantly reasserted against the concept of local autonomy embodied by the committees of national liberation.[1]

WHO'S IN CHARGE?

The CTLN had little chance of governing postwar Florence. During the first months of occupation Allied authorities methodically stripped away its powers. Military government officers were under strict orders to assert the control of the national government over the resistance. The Allies had signed the September 1943 armistice agreements with the national government. Enforcing Rome's authority safeguarded the legal basis of the occupation. Latent concern about Communist influence and about the radicalism of the committees of national liberation reinforced this policy.[2]

When the Allies finally handed back full administrative power over Florence and Tuscany to the Italian government in July 1945, the CTLN was a much honored and little consulted advisory body. Occupation authorities speedily disarmed the base of CTLN power, the partisan units. The men of the armed resistance were honored with a parade, offered individual employment, and eliminated as a political factor.[3] The city administration of Gaetano Pieraccini, a government nominated by the CTLN but comprising of representatives of five competitive political parties, increasingly exercised its own judgment, pushing forward the process by which the CTLN became a fifth wheel. As local and national elections approached, the parties broke away from the CTLN straitjacket, seeking political advantage. Simultaneously, they hamstrung a deeply indebted CTLN by limiting their financial support.[4]

Paterno confronted the CTLN over its program of purging local Fascists from the city's administration, economy, and cultural life. The CTLN dismissed a number of Fascist officials and replaced them with its own nominees during the first days of the battle for Florence. By January 1945, 1,509 public officials and 264 separate public institutions had undergone purge procedures. The Allies, who preferred to leave the complicated issues related to the purge in Italian hands, tended to go along with CTLN decisions. This left the committee with fairly wide powers to restructure the city's administrative bureaucracy, and it lost no time in filling these posts with reliable anti-Fascists while returning surviving Florentine Jews to positions that they had lost under Fascist racial laws.[5]

The national government viewed the CTLN-run purge as a direct challenge to its authority. Paterno, with Prime Minister Ivanoe Bonomi's full support, undercut the CTLN's purge program by routinely revoking CTLN orders removing Fascists from their positions. By playing the anti-Fascist parties off against one another, Paterno undercut the committee's authority. Paterno and Bonomi gladly abandoned the chance to punish those responsible for the dictatorship in exchange for curbing the CTLN's threat to central authority.[6]

The city government was Paterno's other target. The Pieraccini administration lost its parallel battle for autonomy. The city government was the creation of the CTLN, and as the latter's power ebbed, Pieraccini's nonelected government lost authority. Paterno insisted on time-consuming reviews of junta decisions before their enactment. Political weakness was accentuated by the financial dependence of the city government. When Pieraccini took control of the city on August 11, 1944, its treasury contained less than 2 million lire ($200,000). The destruction of much of Florence's productive capacity and consequent unemployment of a large part of the citizen body severely diminished Florence's tax base. The Allies and national government had to finance reconstruction and essential city services until Florence's economy recovered. Meanwhile the city bureaucracy was eviscerated in the effort to root out Fascists, just as public demands for its services swelled.[7]

Operating within very restricted parameters, Pieraccini and his colleagues in city government struggled to take the initial steps in rebuilding Florence. On its first day in office, the junta divided the city into three zones and issued instructions for burying war casualties. It repealed Fascist racial edicts and took action to halt summary executions of Fascists. With Allied assistance it maintained public order and reconstituted the local police force (*vigili urbani*).[8]

On January 1, 1946, the junta took over operation of the city's tram and bus services from its private operator, STU, a subsidiary of FIAT, renaming the municipalized transport service ATAF. With funds provided by the national government, the junta expanded employment through public works. Most importantly, the Pieraccini junta began the essential work of rebuilding the destroyed parts of the historic center. The competition for the design of a rebuilt Ponte alla Vittoria was a psychological turning point in the reconstruction of Florence. Beyond the economic need to reunite the two parts of the city, the debate over the artistic merits of the proposals for the first of the bridge reconstructions awakened a war-dazed population and energized the politics of reconstruction.[9]

WORK, FOOD, WARMTH, SHELTER

Florence struggled against problems that were largely outside its control. Its people faced their first winter of freedom cold and hungry. Food supplies and coal were in short supply throughout war-torn Europe. Transportation was virtually nonexistent. Electricity shortages hampered recovery and ground down citizen morale. Natural gas was in short supply. Pipelines needed repair, and few tank trucks survived to transport this vital source of heat and light. Since city markets had no operational refrigeration units, conservation of perishable food was nearly impossible. Even water was scarce as a result of German destruction of aqueducts. Inadequate food and heat contributed to a public health crisis.

Paterno estimated that between 18,000 and 20,000 Florentines were seriously ill during the winter of 1944–1945. Tuberculosis was widespread. Medicines of all sorts were in short supply.[10]

Psychological recovery from the war was equally difficult. "Sadness, sadness, sadness, I don't know how better to define my state of mind," one Florentine confided in his diary, adding, "Now that the danger is past and God has let me remain, I ask myself: for what purpose?"[11]

Yet signs of improvement were also visible. The Allies paid for basic repairs to water and sewer systems, while the CTLN acquired a few trucks to ease the transportation crisis. Repairs of rail lines continued, a couple of rebuilt locomotives entered into service, and the first local trains began to run in the fall of 1944. By winter's end, garbage disposal improved, and the water supply was barely adequate. Local production of electricity increased as the city acquired more coal. Natural gas became available on a limited basis in early 1945. A few bus and tram lines were back in operation. Cars, bicycles, and other forms of personal transportation began to reappear on city streets. City government, with the cooperation of the church and Allied funding, created twenty-two communal assistance sections to provide food, temporary housing, and other forms of aid to about 70,000 people daily.[12]

Florence greeted the end of the war in Europe with a joyous mass public demonstration. Peace, however, brought only limited improvement in essential services. The *reduci* (returnees), demobilized soldiers, former prisoners of war, and survivors from forced labor and concentration camps, began to flood back to the city. The strain created by these new arrivals was particularly evident in food supply and housing. Homelessness continued to rise. The food situation remained too precarious to end rationing, and its inevitable partner, the black market, flourished. Shortages of milk were particularly difficult on children.[13] The Pieraccini junta appropriated 10 million lire for more public works. Electrical power production rose, and the transportation crisis eased slightly.[14]

Florence entered the second postliberation winter with its economy still prostrate. Recovery from the war's destruction remained slow because of continuing worldwide shortages of goods and raw materials and disagreements over priorities between national and local authorities. Nevertheless, the outlines of an Italian-style reconstruction effort were emerging. Government's role was dominant. Every problem, from housing to food supply, from transportation to employment, was in the hands of some Italian state agency. In Tuscany, the government's reconstruction efforts were directed at reanimating small business, particularly artisan-produced handicrafts. Italian officials calculated that the artisans were in the best position to achieve a priority national economic policy objective: acquiring foreign currency, above all, American dollars. While critical to the long-term prospects of the Florentine economy, tourism took a secondary place in early recovery efforts. Italian and Florentine governmental officials had greater success attracting buyers from major U.S. department stores than American tourists. Rebuilding the Florentine tourist industry, important as it was, had to await more basic infrastructural improvements: a revitalized rail service, new airports, the rebuilding of bridges and roads, and the reconstruction of the city center.[15]

Although short of the cash and materials needed to rebuild, the Florentines possessed both ingenuity and an ability to cooperate effectively. Under the direction of the parties, cooperatives sprung up to pool scarce resources. By January 1945, 120 cooperatives were dealing with issues like recreation, transportation, and food supply. Eighteen charity organizations also were operating. Catholics such as Giorgio La Pira played a particularly important role in their operations. Taking advantage of the individual Florentine's famed frugality, the CTLN created a regional savings bank to provide financing for the housing industry.[16]

Reconstruction policy ultimately was a question of financing. Central to the finance question and to the creation of the balanced economy sought by most Florentines was the rehabilitation of the city's limited industrial base. The 643 industries with the city of Florence as their principal seat included both mechanical and clothing firms and employed 8,100 workers. The small size of most of these businesses made individual start-up costs easier to cover for a strained banking system. Key, large-scale industrial complexes (FIAT, Superpila, Manetti and Roberts, Galileo, and Pignone) needed major financial assistance that few local banks could supply. These firms had to resume production if Florence's economy were to recover.[17]

Liberation rekindled long-suppressed antagonisms between labor and management. Tensions were exacerbated by union demands that businessmen who collaborated with Fascism lose their property, by business efforts to escape special taxes imposed for reconstruction purposes, by union calls for job security, and by owners' insistence on the right to dismiss employees.[18]

As the *reduci* flooded the labor market, Florence and Italy entered an era of labor surplus that would enable business to keep wages low, expand its profits, and in the process greatly increase social tensions. The labor surplus undermined the unions' powers and gave management a decisive upper hand. The growth of the Communist Party and a rising crime rate were proof of strong social tensions.[19]

Labor unrest had little evident effect on the efforts of businessmen and city administrators to attract foreign currency. Allied troops were the major source of foreign exchange and of certain noneconomic difficulties. The wartime British complaint that the problem with American troops was that they were "overpaid, oversexed, and over here" applied with a vengeance to occupied Florence. The arrival of the Americans with their seemingly endless supplies of occupation lire stoked the black market. Prices skyrocketed as essential goods grew more scarce. The service sector of the Florentine economy catered primarily to Allied troops. From shoeshine boys to tourist operators and, above all, prostitutes, the Allies virtually monopolized services in a devastated city.[20]

Prostitution was a true growth industry. After nine months of German occupation, Florentines remained favorably inclined to their liberators, but Allied "fraternization" with local women triggered some bad feeling. In the end, economic reality won out. One Fiorentina who supported her family by prostitution was reproached by neighbors. She pointed to her three plump and happy children and replied: "See how they are flourishing."[21]

Reporting on the desperate state of the Florentine economy in the winter of 1945, Consul General Walter Orebaugh advised the State Department that active U.S. intervention was the best way to get Florentine goods on the market. Assistance in procuring raw materials and in finding American markets would permit Florence to create products that would satisfy long-standing U.S. demand and attract tourists. Florentine handicrafts such as copper, pottery, leather, woodworking, art, lingerie, clothing, musical instruments, and straw had traditionally found markets in the United States.[22]

In November 1945, the Department of State organized a meeting in Florence between representatives of the U.S. and Italian Chambers of Commerce. U.S. representatives explained the nature of the American market. Shortly thereafter, financial aid to reestablish the artisan trade arrived from Italian Americans. Florentine businessmen seized the opportunity with their customary innovation, forming consortia to produce and market in the United States. By early 1946, the artisan economy was showing signs of life.[23]

BRIDGES AND BELLINI

Accompanying this slow economic recovery were the first indications that Florentine culture was rising from the ashes of war. One important sign of the resurrection of civic pride was the return to life of the city's musical theater. On October 29, 1944, mobile generators supplied by the Allies permitted Teatro Verdi to offer Puccini's *La Boheme* to an audience that included many American and English soldier-tourists. The following October, a restored Teatro Comunale opened an abbreviated season of opera and concerts.

Paralleling the reassertion of Florence's role as the city of culture came the physical reconstruction of the center. Recovery was symbolized by the spanning of the Arno by first one, then a second and third bridge. Although this process would be completed only thirteen years later with the restoration of the Ponte S. Trinita, the speed with which Florence rebuilt its center gave a critical boost to civic pride, to business, and ultimately to tourism.

Florence's cultural revival owed much to the Allies' belated recognition that they were waging war in a museum. The bombing of the Monte Casino abbey in February 1944 was a public relations catastrophe. Allied commanders belatedly recognized Italy's special cultural status. Experts in the fine arts pressed into duty as military government officials won an influence that greatly outweighed their lowly rank. Lt. Frederick Hartt, a Brown University professor of art, arrived in Tuscany with the first waves of Allied troops. His mission of protecting existing artworks and recovering those seized by the Germans soon expanded. The dry, hot summer of 1944 gave way to an early fall of incessant rain. Water further damaged the many unroofed or partially roofed and generally windowless buildings of Florence. The Arno rose menacingly. Hartt disconsolately watched from the glassless windows of the Uffizi one dark October day: "It seemed as if the whole structure, and indeed the frail city of Florence, would be washed away by the ceaseless downpour."[24]

In the first weeks of liberation, local Allied commanders, using the argument of military necessity, frequently acted without regard for the preservation of art treasures. The CTLN's "Rubble Commission" alerted Hartt that Allied engineers were dumping important parts of the city's architectural heritage together with priceless archives into the river. The Italians recovered many manuscripts and artifacts from the riverbed by hand. Losses, however, were significant.[25]

In September, as the German threat lessened, Hartt employed diplomacy, appeals to the high command, and other forms of suasion to get local commanders to decamp from the landmark buildings that they had expropriated for offices during the first days of liberation. Anglo-American engineers increasingly turned to the monuments and fine arts experts prior to carrying out their critical reconstruction projects.[26]

The CTLN did an excellent job of identifying and protecting art treasures and museums in the first hectic days of liberation. Its efforts were critical to the largely successful effort to safeguard Florence's artistic heritage. Simultaneously, a CTLN commission of architects and engineers, dominated by Action Party activists, began to plan for the reconstruction.[27]

The Allies made two important contributions to the initial work of reconstruction. They financed the emergency repairs that enabled many artworks to survive, and they recovered a majority of the art treasures that the Germans had looted. Armed with detailed lists of artwork compiled with Italian help and intelligence supplied by the Vatican, the CTLN, and other sources, Allied officials followed the trail of the fleeing Germans. Nazi plans to whisk this material out of Italy were largely frustrated when Allied air forces destroyed their transportation. In May 1945, Hartt laid claim to massive quantities of artwork left near Verona and in the Alto Adige.[28] The Allied command skillfully exploited the public relations benefits of the recovery of Florentine art by staging a July 21, 1945, ceremony formally handing back a critical part of the city's artistic heritage to Mayor Pieraccini.

The Pieraccini administration's record in handling architectural reconstruction was mixed. It dealt with the public relations issues in a skillful manner, sponsoring the exhibition *Florence Destroyed*, a photomontage illustrating the destruction wrought by the Germans, to attract foreign investment in rebuilding the city.[29]

The reconstruction debate centered on what architectural style to adopt in rebuilding the bridges and the two zones (Por S Maria and S Jacopo) that fed into the Ponte Vecchio. Beyond the debate over aesthetics lurked the larger question of the ultimate economic and social utilization of the city center.[30]

As befitted a body dominated by art historians and architects, the CTLN set out its position on the political questions involved. The inaugural issue of its

Bulletin of Information featured an essay by architect Ranuccio Bianchi Bandinelli entitled "Rebuilding Florence," outlining the options that the city faced. One was to "indiscriminately" fill the parts of the old city destroyed by the Germans with the "glass and cement" of modern architecture. Another, more likely solution was reconstruction *"com'era"*: rebuilding from photos to exactly re-create destroyed edifices. Neither solution appealed to Bianchi Bandinelli. He argued that Florence needed to employ modern designs that carefully integrated new buildings with existing structures.[31]

Florence's intellectual elite, above all, its Action Party component, saw *com'era* as the momentous and dangerous first step in a process that would turn Florence into a museum city. They insisted that Florence's reconstruction required carefully elaborated plans that would meet the needs of the majority of its citizens by placing emphasis on a careful economic development. A viable mixed economy was the best yardstick for judging the suitability of individual architectural projects. *Com'era* reconstruction would turn the historic center into a large tourist park, drive out nontourist-related businesses, and, by raising property values and rents, force the inhabitants of the center to move to peripheral (and not yet built) housing. While not opposed to tourism or to some *com'era* reconstruction, the Actionists insisted that private profit should not be the yardstick for reconstruction planning.

The Pieraccini administration initially appeared to endorse a reconstruction carried out by capable architects who offered innovative conceptions and shared a collectivist vision of Florence's needs. In January 1945 the city government authorized a public competition for the design of a new Ponte alla Vittoria. The announcement outlining the competition stated that projects must have minimal impact on existing structures and fit into an overall vision of the city that took into account traffic problems and the need for economic balance.[32]

The actual competition revealed the degree of party control over most aspects of public administration. A carefully calibrated sharing of the spoils of office (*lottizzazione*) had already become the norm in Florence. A number of qualified architects were excluded a priori from the contest, and the Action Party was denied representation on the body judging the submissions. The larger parties wanted the patronage that flowed from control of major public works projects. The Pieraccini administration delegated final selection to a subcommittee of politicians, relegating technically competent architects to the role of an advisory committee. Not surprisingly, the Ponte alla Vittoria judging committee voted for a design that had the backing of the mayor and the major parties.[33]

Patronage and party control were only a part of the story. As Bianchi Bandinelli had surmised, the supporters of a *com'era* reconstruction proved to be an especially formidable lobby. Spearheaded by the aged Bernard Berenson, the American art historian, they demanded a widespread restoration of the city's structures "where they were and as they were" (*dov'era e com'era*).[34]

Advocates of a carefully planned reconstruction recognized that for aesthetic and psychological reasons certain structures, above all, the Ponte S. Trinita, had to be rebuilt *com'era*. They hoped to avoid a large-scale reconstruction of "phoney antiquities" that would inevitably reduce the historic center to a single function, tourist attraction. Innovative architectural planning soon collided with the actions of powerful, well-financed interests and with the city government's lack of cash. The reconstruction of the city center was carried out piecemeal. The process oscillated between overregulation and noregulation. It was driven by immediate economic considerations, above all, employment and profit, rather than by aesthetics or longer-range planning.[35]

Business interests organized to make their weight felt in the debate over the physical reconstruction of the center and moved aggressively to protect their economic interests. Shopkeepers on the Ponte Vecchio were repairing their stores even as the city's political leaders debated regulations for reconstruction. The construction industry weighed in with the prefect. Artisans, whose shops had been among the primary victims of German destruction, formed another active lobby. In May 1945 these groups merged into a single business association that won a place on the commission planning the reconstruction.[36]

At the beginning of 1945, the usually cautious Liberal leader Eugenio Artom presented a plan for a locally financed reconstruction. He suggested that the city acquire bank credit and carry forward a self-financed and locally directed program of reconstruction. City efforts to arrange bank loans failed. The banks had little to lend. Only a combination of Italian government and private capital would allow Florence to recover from its war wounds. The political and cultural price for this financing was high: more intervention from the national government and a virtual free hand to individual entrepreneurs to build as they saw fit. The vision of a planned reconstruction that would meet collective requirements gave way to the reality of piecemeal and unplanned development.[37]

The parties had a large interest in involving the national government, as a primary fount of patronage, in reconstruction. By October 1944, the local Christian Democracy (DC) had already contacted its national leadership about creating a government commission to study and finance Florence's reconstruction. In late 1945, the Parri government announced its readiness to take the lead role in the reconstruction process. In August public works minister Giuseppe Romita discussed plans for labor-intensive reconstruction projects with a delegation of Florentine politicians.[38]

The Pieraccini junta turned to the state to finance an increasing number of reconstruction projects, from the removal of antiaircraft shelters, to the restoration of the university and erection of new bridges across the Arno. Many of these projects would, in any case, have involved the national government, but by continually turning to Rome, local administration revealed its inability to carry out a coordinated program of rebuilding. The heavy hand of state regulation simultaneously impeded local reconstruction planning and, because its rules could not be enforced effectively or uniformly, encouraged widespread flouting of the law. Private contractors violated building codes with impunity because they enjoyed broad public sympathy and had friends in power. The reign of the *abusivi* (zoning regulation violators), a hallmark of the postwar republic, began in the first days of the new regime.[39]

Political considerations played an important role in shaping the national reconstruction nonpolicy. The DC was allied with economic forces that feared, with reason, the economic, political, and social effects of a reconstruction carried out according to the collectivist precepts of the left. DeGasperi cooperated with business to scuttle initiatives like the Ministry for Reconstruction and, with it, local and provincial programs for rebuilding Italy that would place strong restraints on private profit.[40]

Operating without effective political constraints and enjoying access to the funds of a government whose laws they flouted, private contractors proceeded to rebuild Florence. Their efforts were aesthetically questionable, but Italy and Florence had to rebuild quickly and grasped the only means available.

BUILDING ITALIAN DEMOCRACY

The resistance was the first step in the creation of a new Italy. The next logical step was writing a constitution to consolidate hard-won freedom. In June 1946, Italians went to the polls to elect the membership of a constituent assembly and simultaneously to decide if Italy would remain a monarchy or become a republic. Among the Tuscan delegation elected to the Costituente, two Florentines played prominent roles. Giorgio La Pira and Piero Calamandrei, committed democrats, personal friends, and legal scholars of recognized competence, represented two fundamentally different visions of Italy's future. Drawing on Cavour's vision of a "free church in a free state," Calamandrei sought a secular republic in which the Catholic Church could carry on its work of religious instruction as one of many contending ethical and social viewpoints. La Pira believed that only Catholic religious and social values could give the new state a solid foundation. In writing Catholic social doctrine into the constitution, the diminutive professor from Florence found powerful allies in places few would have suspected possible. A temporary alliance of Catholics and Communists wrote an Italian constitution that left Calamandrei and others grasping for tools to defend the concept of a secular Italy.[41]

The DC triumphed because it had a much firmer set of objectives than its two principal political rivals. The common goal of the Communists and Socialists was a regime that guaranteed basic freedoms of assembly and political and union organization. For Pietro Nenni and his Socialists, these objectives were summed up in the concept of an Italian republic. Communist Palmiro Togliatti had a somewhat broader vision but was obsessed with maintaining a "unity of action" with the Catholics and Socialists. Both leaders were willing to forgo major social and economic change to win Catholic cooperation.[42]

Ironically, the DC was the weakest of the three mass parties in organizational terms, relying on the church to get out the vote. Moreover, it was under the constant scrutiny of a Vatican and a militant Catholicism that fundamentally mistrusted both democracy and the DC's relations with the Marxist left. The Vatican and Italian bishops viewed the reconstruction as an opportunity to rebuild Italian society on a specifically Catholic model. De Gasperi simultaneously had to satisfy the significant part of his party committed to the creation of a modern, democratic, nonconfessional state and a powerful element that wanted a dominant role for Catholicism and the church in Italian affairs.[43]

The DC's leaders regarded the committees of national liberation as a stopgap to face the enormous crisis created by war and occupation. Once the conflict ended, De Gasperi moved to undermine the already limited authority of these locally rooted challengers to the authority of the central government. The DC briefly supported the government of Ferruccio Parri, a leader who incarnated resistance ideals but also stood for the continuity of the state. It ruthlessly pulled the rug from under Parri in November 1945 in order to claim power for itself. The Socialists and Communists stood aside, expecting to exploit the defeat of Parri and his Action Party.[44] Instead, they were the DC's next victims. In 1947, De Gasperi drove both Marxist parties from power.

Neither De Gasperi nor his fellow Christian Democrats were classic economic liberals. Catholic social teachings stressed that unrestrained capitalism mercilessly (and sinfully) exploited the lower social orders. They joined with the parties of the left to defend the enormous role in the economy that the Italian government had enjoyed since national unification and preserve the state-holding companies that Mussolini created. With aid from the left, De Gasperi laid the basis for the enormous web of patronage that permitted the Christian Democrats to control the Italian state for the next forty-five years.[45]

In rebuilding the authority of the central government, the DC had willing accomplices in the Communists and Socialists. Giuseppe Romita, the Socialist minister of the interior in De Gasperi's first government (December 1945–June 1946), operated with a free hand from the prime minister. His goals were pacifying the country, including the suppression of disturbances caused by former partisans, reaffirming the control of the central government through determined action by the prefects, and preparing for peaceful local and national elections.[46]

Romita and De Gasperi used March 1946 local elections to test the electoral system before the critical June national elections for a constituent assembly. In early 1946 the government purged the prefectural service, eliminating almost all resistance appointees. Romita called Communist labor leader Giuseppe Di Vittorio into his office and instructed him to avoid provocative mass demonstrations by labor during the election campaigns. The republic would be "born in order."[47]

This Catholic-Marxist collaboration continued during the constituent assembly, where the DC secured its objectives at the price of limited concessions to the parties of the left. The Communists, obsessed with reinforcing their legitimacy through collaboration with Catholics, were very malleable, particularly on the primary Catholic objective of inclusion of the Lateran Pacts of 1929 in the new constitution. The corporatist "professors" of the DC's left wing found a large area of consensus with the PCI on basic political conceptions and wrote them into the preamble of the new constitution. This remarkable joint experiment in constitution writing laid the bases for long-term political cohabitation between Catholics and Communists.[48]

The authors of the Italian constitution set a premium on the maintenance of a unitary state. They treated local government with marked suspicion. Italy's republican constitution accentuated the powers of the state against the localism that the communes historically represented. Powers enjoyed by city administrations were delegated directly from the national (and later regional) government that retained extensive jurisdiction to review and approve, amend, or reject the acts of communal government. The republican constitution strengthened the state's stranglehold on public finance. Retention of the prefects and the subsequent refusal of the Italian state to limit its right to govern the communes through the appointment of special commissars further tightened the national government's hold.[49]

Although the Christian Democratic Party successfully took control of the central government, it lost control of many provincial and local administrations. Fearing that its Communist and Socialist rivals would exploit control of regional governments to build up their power and unleash a revolution, the De Gasperi government shelved implementation of regional governments promised by the constitution. A June 6, 1947, law retained the Fascist comprehensive act of 1934 as the basic legislation governing the communes and provinces. Utilizing its wide powers to regulate the operations of communal and provincial governments, Italian prefects continuously cut away at the already limited autonomy that municipalities possessed.[50]

THE COLLECTIVIST ERA

The parties that garnered the largest share of the popular vote in the first years of the republic shared a common conception of the role of the state. During the first two postwar decades, collectivism, whether in its Marxist or its Catholic version, so dominated Italian politics that it was little debated. All major Italian parties shared a vision of a society that was based on major state intervention in social and economic affairs.

Despite De Gasperi's personal reservations, the heritage of united Italy, the extent of war damage, and pressures from both the working masses and Catholic leaders pushed his centrist governments to embrace a strategy of social and economic development based on governmental intervention. The Catholic prime minister and his lay party allies succeeded in placing limits on social engineering projects on a case-by-case basis, aided by widespread popular mistrust of the objectives of the parties of the left. However, Italian reconstruction legislation widened the role of the national government. This development dovetailed with a growing reliance by the DC on political patronage to maintain its control over the state and exclude the left from power.

The speed with which the Christian Democrats first created a constitutional model to their liking and then took effective control of the Italian state startled all of their collaborators. The Communists, who had played the key role in assisting the DC's efforts, paid a heavy price for the cooperation: permanent exclusion from the national government. Increasingly, the DC and the Catholic Church were able to base their claims to a dominant role in Italy on their function as bulwarks against Communism. The parties that allied with the DC in the battle against Communism also paid a heavy price: abandonment of their vision of a secular Italian state. Speaking some years after the Constituent Assembly concluded its work, one of the Liberals' most important national leaders, Giovanni Malagodi, accused the DC of creating a "Marxist-confessional state" that propagated the collectivist values common to both the DC and its two opponents on the left. He added with evident dismay that the DC's right wing did not share the values of secular liberalism but embraced collectivism "no less than La Pira."[51] Stripped of its electorally motivated hyperbole, Malagodi's observation was correct.

As Florence approached local elections in the fall of 1946, a global economic recovery was under way, marked by growing divisions between labor and management. The unity of political action created in resistance evaporated. The dissolution of the CTLN in July 1946 symbolized the end of a brief era of cooperation between essentially antagonistic lay, Catholic, and Marxist parties. Throughout Europe, the unity born of a common struggle against Nazi Germany evaporated, and two hostile power blocs emerged from the wartime grand coalition. The Cold War was beginning in Europe, in Italy, and in Florence.

NOTES

1. Prefect to Ministry of the Interior, September 6, 1945, AC/S, MI, PS-Sezione 1, 1944–1946, b 19 Firenze.

2. James Edward Miller, *United States and Italy* (Chapel Hill, 1986), pp. 137–43; Weekly Report of AMG Florence, August 19, 1944, NA, RG 331, ACC, 10000/115/144.

3. Roger Absalom, ed., *Gli alleati e la ricostruzione in Toscana* (Florence, 1988), 1: 346; Report, October 3, 1944, NA, RG 331, ACC, 10802/110/76; Orazio Barbieri, *Ponti Sull 'Arno* (Rome, 1975), pp. 296–97.

4. Minutes, March 3, June 11, 1945, ISRT, Fondo CTLN, b 36, Verbali. CTLN memorandum, February 2, 1945, ibid., b 49, f. documenti contabili, 1944–1946; Carabinieri Report, April 16, 1945, AC/S, MI, PS, Sezione I, 1944–1946, b. 19, f. Firenze.

5. Piero Calamandrei, *Diari, 1939–1945* (Florence, 1982), 2: 536. *Nazione del Popolo*, September 6–7, 1944; Report, July 10, 1944, ISRT, Fondo CTLN, b 33, f Comitato di cultura; Report on *Epurazione*, January 23, 1945, NA, RG 331, ACC, 10802/110/80.

6. Giacomo Devoto, *La parentesi* (Florence, 1974), pp. 83–84; CTLN resolution, October 2, 1944, ISRT, Fondo F. Lombardi, b 17, f CTLN no. 2; CTLN minutes, December 12, 1944, ibid.; Paterno to CTLN, February 16, 1945, ISRT, Fondo F. Lombardi, b. 16, f CTLN No. 1; *Nazione del Popolo*, October 6, 1944, January 5, 1945; Prefect report, July 4, 1945, AC/S, Presidenza del consiglio, 1944–1947, f 1.1.26/30401, s/f 3; Executive Officer to Regional Commissioner, January 8, 1945, NA, RG 331, ACC, 10800/115/81; Weekly Report, March 1, 1945, ibid., 10800/115/149; Calamandrei, *Diari*, 2: 543.

7. Pieraccini to Prefect, February 1946, AsdF, Prefettura di Firenze, Affari ordinari, 1947, f 89; Treasury report, August 11, 1944, ibid., f 48; Lirio Mangalaviti, *Gaetano Pieraccini* (Florence, 1980), pp. 46–50.

8. Order, August 11, 1944, ACF, varie 1944, Gab. del Podesta, f 1101–1300. CTLN to *sindaco*, August 15, 1944, ibid.; Pieraccini letter, August 31, 1944, ibid.; Division of responsibilities among the junta, October 6, 1944, ACF, varie, Atti 1301–1479.

9. Nicola Cefaretti and Morello Malaspina, *1865–1985. Centoventi anni di trasporti pubblici a Firenze* (Cortona, 1987), p. 295; *Nazione del Popolo*, April 13, August 2, 1946; DeZordo and DiBenedetti, "Piani di ricostruzione," in Pier Luigi Ballini, Luigi Lotti, and Mario Rossi, eds., *La Toscana nel secondo dopoguerra* (Milan, 1991), p. 309. ATAF could be translated as the Florence City Agency for Trams and Buses.

10. Minutes, January 1, 1945, ISRT, Fondo CTLN, b 18, f CTLN Uff. Gabinetto; Florence Province Questionnaire, January 6, 1945, NA, RG 331, ACC, 10800/154/17; Weekly report, December 18, 1944, ibid., 10800/115/145; *Nazione del Popolo*, February 7, 1945; Absalom, *Gli alleati*, pp. 452–453; Andrea Giuntini, *Dalla Lyonnaise alla* (Bari, 1990), *Fiorentinagas*, pp. 144–46; Orazio Barbieri, *La fede e la ragione* (Milan, 1982), p. 93; Davis Ottati, *L'acquadotto di Firenze dal 1860 ad oggi* (Florence, 1983), p. 226.

11. Piero Santi, *Diario, 1943–1946* (Venice, 1950), p. 56.

12. Estimate of repairs, March 8, 1945, NA, RG 331, ACC, 10800/150/431; Glenn to AMG, March 29, 1945, ibid., 10800/142/3300; Absalom, *Gli alleati*, pp. 469–71; Minutes, March 24, 1945, ISRT, Fondo CTLN, b 34, verbali; *Nazione del Popolo* January 13–14, February 6, 1945; Comune di Firenze, *Firenze: Rassegna del Comune, 1944–1951* (Florence, 1951), pp. 89–90, 106–107; Renato Cassigoli, ed., *Il servizio del gas nella resistenza* (Florence, 1984), pp. 70–84; Cefaretti and Malaspina, *1865–1985*, pp. 294, 478–79.

13. Sindaco to Prefect, July 3, 1946, ASdiF, Prefettura di Firenze, Affari ordinari, 1946, f 29; *Nazione del Popolo*, April 28–29, August 30, 1945; Memo, February 23, 1946, ISRT, Carte Traquandi, b 3, f Anona; Letter, June 5, 1946, ASdiF, Prefettura di Firenze, Affari ordinari, 1946, f 29; Ministry of Public Work to Genio Civilie, November 6, 1946, ibid.

14. *Nazione del Popolo*, April 18, May 17, 30, June 6, August 23, September 7, 11, 1945; Orebaugh to Department of State, June 11, 1945, NA, RG 84, Florence Post, 815.3.

15. Paterno to Ministry of Interior, September 21, 1945, ASdiF, Prefettura di Firenze, Affari ordinari, 1945, f. 45; Memorandum, November 23, 1945, ISRT, Carte Traquandi, b 3, f. Anona; Report, January 27, 1946, ISRT, Fondo CTLN, b 49, f 8579, 1946; Orebaugh to Department of State, January 15, 1946, NA, RG 84, Florence Post, 842; Industry and Commerce Division, ACC, to AMG, Florence, November 20, 1944, NA, RG 331, ACC, 10802/161/89; *Nazione del Popolo*, September 8 and 23, November 21, 28, December 15, 24, 1945, January 1, 4, 8, 17, 1946.

16. *Nazione del Popolo*, January 23, April 26, May 6, 1945, April 4, 1946; Minutes, February 14, March 17, 1945, ISRT, Fondo CTLN, b 34, verbali; Paolo Paoletti and Paola Torrone, *Firenze anni '50*, 2 vols. (Florence, 1991), 1: 66, 70.

17. Minutes, August 28, 1945, ISRT, Fondo CTLN, b 34, verbali; Minister of Industry to President of Council, September 12, 1945, AC/S, Presidenza del consiglio, 1944–1947, f 3.1.7/45069; Prefect to Ministry of Transportation, September 26, 1945, ibid.; *Nazione del Popolo*, May 23, 1945; Carlo Sorrentino, *Firenze* (Rome, 1990), pp. 24–26; "Promemorium of the Industrial Situation in Florence Province, January 1945, NA, RG 84, Florence Post File, 850.

18. "Norms for the Reprise of Labor Activity," July 10, 1944, ISRT, Carte Martini, b 1, f. 4–DC; Accord between industrialists and labor leaders of Florence, September 30, 1944, ISRT, Carte Collini, b5, s/f CdL di Firenze 1947–1953. *Nazione del Popolo*, October

2, 1944; Ferrero to CTLN, October 4, 1944, ISRT, Fondo CTLN, b 48 f. 8424–8594; Zeffiro Ciuffoletti, Mario Rossi and Angelo Varni, *La Camera di Lavoro di Firenze* (Naples, 1991), pp. 28–35.

19. Minutes, July 26, October 4, 6, 1945, ISRT, Fondo CTLN, b 34, verbali; Union Committee of the PSIUP to Executive Committee, undated but c. June 18, 1945, ISRT, Fondo F. Lombardi, b 10, f PSI-Federazione Fiorentina; Questura Report, July 1946, NA, RG 84, Florence Post Files, 800.

20. Ugo Cappelletti, *Firenze in guerra* (Florence, 1984), p. 428; Devoto, *La parentesi*, pp. 80–81; Paolo Paoletti and Paola Torrini, *Firenze anni '50* (Florence, 1991), 1: 17–18.

21. AMG report, March 29, 1945, NA, RG 331, ACC, 10800/143/15; Calamandrei, *Diari*, 2: 554.

22. Orebaugh to Department of State, August 21, 1945, NA RG 84, Florence Post, 850.102.

23. Minutes, undated, NA, RG 84, Florence Post Files, 600; Orebaugh to the Department of State, August 7, 1945, ibid., 843 Amici d'Italia; *Nazione del Popolo*, October 20, 1946.

24. Frederick Hartt, *Florentine Art Under Fire* (Princeton, NJ, 1949), pp. 51, 56.

25. Ibid., pp. 49–53; Philippe Dubois, ed., *Eduordo Detti architetto e urbanista* (Milan, 1993), pp. 72, 75.

26. Hartt to AMG, 5th Army, September 4, 1944, NA, RG 331, ACC, 10800/145/56; Pratt to Walker, ibid., 10800/144/35; Hartt, *Florentine Art*, pp. 6, 26, 53–54.

27. Report, August 29, 1944, ISRT, Fondo CTLN, f "10911–10988–1944"; Absalom, *Gli alleati*, pp. 257–258; *Nazione del Popolo*, September 5–6, 7–8, 1944.

28. Hartt to AMG 5th Army, November 30, 1944, NA, RG 331, ACC, 10800/145/58; Hartt to 2677th Rgt, OSS, March 22, 1945, ibid., 10800/145/56; Regional Commissioner's Report, July 1944, ibid., 10800/115/254; Hartt, *Florentine Art*, pp. 16, 20–21, 67–70, 79, 96–97, 102–05; *Il Ponte*, May 1945, pp. 141–46.

29. Paolo Bagnoli, "I giorni di Firenze (politica e cultura dal 1944 al 1974)" *Citta e regione* 7 (April 1981), p. 83; *Turismo a Firenze*, p. 186.

30. *Il Ponte*, April 1945, pp. 1–3; Giacomo Becattini, "Introduzione," Ettore Rotelli, ed., *La ricostruzione in Toscana dal CTLN al partiti* 2 vols. (Bologna, 1980–81), 1: 55; Dubois, *Eduardo Detti*, p. 43.

31. CTLN Bulletin, August 15, 1944, ISRT, Fondo F. Lombardi, f CTLN no. 3, s/f 6; *Nazione del Popolo*, August 31, 1944.

32. *Nazione del Popolo*, September 4–5, 1944, January 17, 1945; Minutes, March 3, 1945, ISRT, Fondo CTLN, b 34, verbali.

33. Memorandum, February 19, 1945, ISRT, Fondo F. Lombardi, b 16, f CTLN no. 1; Martini to Poggi, December 13, 1944, ibid., Carte Martini, b 1, f Democrazia Cristiana; *Nazione del Popolo*, February 16, April 3, 1945; Minutes, February 22, 1945, ACF, Uff legale, filze speciale, b. Commission Concorso, f Concorso P. Vittoria; Mariella Zoppi, *Firenze e l'urbanistica* (Rome, 1982), pp. 8–10.

34. *Il Ponte*, April 1945, pp. 33–38.

35. Bandinelli, "Come non ricostruire la Firenze demolita," *Il Ponte*, May 1945, pp. 114–18; Zoppi, *Firenze*, pp. 17–18.

36. *Nazione del Popolo*, September 27, 1944; Communication, May 25, 1945, ASdiF, Prefettura di Firenze, Affari ordinari, 1949, f 50; Letter, April 12, 1945, ISRT, Fondo CTLN, f. 10693–10767–1945.

37. Gaetano Salvemini, *Lettere dall'America*, 2 vols. (Bari, 1967–1968), 1: 27, 28, 35; CTLN to Banca di Roma, April 5, 1945, ISRT, Fondo CTLN, f. Emissione buoni del

tesoro; Prefect to AMG, April 5, 1945, ibid.; *Nazione del Popolo*, February 8, November 17, 1945.

38. DeGasperi to Martini, October 3, 1944, ISRT, Carte Martini, b 1, f Democrazia Cristiana; Minutes, January 20, August 9, 1945, ibid., F CTLN, b 34, verbali; Resolution, July 5, 1945, APC, f Firenze 1945; *Nazione del Popolo*, August 3, 1945.

39. Sindaco to Prefect, January 12, 1946, ASdiF, Prefettura di Firenze, Affari ordinari, 1949, f 50; Guirati to Prefect, March 12, 1946, ibid., 1946, f 29; ACS, MPI, AA BB AA, Divisione II, 1945–1955, b 46, f Ponte alla Grazia; *Nazione del Popolo*, February 19, September 21, 1946; Hartt, *Florentine Art*, p. 50.

40. Zoppi, *Firenze*, p. 22.

41. Giorgio La Pira, *La casa comune* (Florence, 1979), pp. 109, 141; M. Glisenti and Leopoldo Elia, eds., *Croniche sociali*, 2 vols. (S. Giovanni Valdario, 1962) 1: 100–07; Giorgio Galli and Paolo Facchi, *La sinistra democristiana* (Milan, 1962), p. 352.

42. Furio Columbo, ed., *In Italy* (New York, 1981), pp. 73–74; Giuseppi Romita, *Dalla monarchia alla repubblica* (Milan, 1973), p. 7; Barbieri, *La fede*, p. 69; Pietro Secchia, *PCI* (Milan, 1973), pp. 1054–60; "Promemoria," in Enzo Collotti (ed.), *Archivio Pietro Secchia* (Milan, 1979), p. 197.

43. Bruna Bocchini Camaiani, "Ricostruzione Concordato e processi di secolarizzazione" in Francesco Margiotta Broglio, ed., *La chiesa del Concordato*, 2 vols. (Bologna, 1983), 2: 217; *Atti e documenti della DC*, 1: 102, 261–63; Pietro Scoppola, *La repubblica dei partiti* (Bologna, 1991), pp. 26, 184, 228–29, Letter, October 2, 1944, ISRT, Carte Martini, b 1, f Democrazia Cristiana.

44. Giulio Andreotti, *La Democrazia Cristiana 1943–1948* (Rome, 1975), pp. 28–29; Rugger. Orfei, *L'occupazione del potere* (Milan, 1976), p. 61.

45. Giulio Andreotti, *De Gasperi e la ricostruzcone* (Rome, 1974), pp. 67–69, 75–80; Andrea Damiliano, ed., *Atti e documenti della DC*, 2 vols. (Rome, 1968–1969), 1: 230–54; Mario Martini, *La missione sociale e politica della Democrazia Cristiana* (Rome, n.d.), pp. 37–49; Resolution, February 1947, AC/S, MI, Gabinetto, fascicoli permanenti, b 184, f 5919P, DC-Firenze.

46. Romita, *Dalla monarchia*, pp. 28–34.

47. Robert Fried, *The Italian Prefects* (New Haven, CT, 1963), p. 224. Romita, *Dalla monarchia*, pp. 65–78, 93–94.

48. Camiaini, *Ricostruzione*, p. 234. Giovanni Di Capua, *I professorini all costituente* (Rome, 1989), pp. 20–23.

49. Massimo Teodori, *Costituzione italiana e modello americano* (Milan, 1992), pp. 138–39, 147; Francesco Malgeri, ed., *Storia, della Democrazia Cristiano* (Rome, 1987), 1: 123–24; Giorgio Colzi, "La provincia ed il comune," in Piero Calamandrei, ed., *Commentario sistematico alla Costituzione italiana* (Florence, 1950), 2: 381–429; Arturo Caro Jemolo, *Questa repubblica* (Florence, 1981), pp. 12–13; Attilio Piccioni, *Scritti e discorsi* (Florence, 1967), 1: 117–36; S. Bartole et al., "Le regioni, le provincie, comuni," in Giuseppi Branca, ed., *Commentario della Costituzione* (Bologna, 1985), pp. 3, 8, 10–11, 232–34, 299, 392.

50. Percy Allum, *Italy—Republic without Government?* (New York, 1973), pp. 216–17; Fried, *The Italian Prefects*, pp. 234, 238, 254–55; *Studi sull'organizzazione comunale*, pp. 12–13; *Dieci anni dopo, 1945–1955* (Bari, 1955), pp. 27, 209, 220, 234–35, 244–45; *Processo a De Gasperi*, p. 449.

51. Ennio DiNolfo, *Le paure e le speranze degli italiani* (Milan, 1986), pp. 201–2; Orfei, *L'occupazione*, pp. 10–11; Malagodi quoted in Gianni Baget Bozzo, *Il partito cristiano e l'apertura a sinistra* (Florence, 1977), p. 65.

Chapter 3

Red Flag over Palazzo Vecchio, 1947–1951

Today by popular will, the representatives of the poor have assumed the administration of the city. . . . The red flag waves over Palazzo Vecchio.

Vasco Pratolini, 1946

In his June 1945 final report, the Allied regional commissioner for Tuscany described the situation in Florence as a dormant volcano. The end of the war screwed political tensions among the parties to new heights. While the parties, the Allies, and the Italian government maneuvered over the question of timing and sequence of local and national elections, local party organizations filled their war chests, formed alliances, and sought control of the press.[1]

Florence's local elections followed the June 2, 1946, national vote. A Socialist Party circular of July 31 admonished its members to prepare for a hard electoral campaign fought along class lines. PCI leader Giuseppe Rossi reminded his militants that conquest of Florence would give the Communists complete control of Tuscany. The unions marched into Florence's piazzas in coordinated protests against rising prices and the policies of the De Gasperi government. These demonstrations turned ugly when a mob of urban poor invaded the city market, grabbing food and beating up farmers accused of price gouging.[2]

The November 1946 city council elections turned into a plebiscite on the performance of the DC-led national government. The left ably exploited popular discontent with a painful reconstruction. Meanwhile, all national party headquarters, whether on the left or right, tightened control over their local organizations. Local autonomy, the proclaimed objective of all resistance parties, shrank under the demands of political necessity.[3]

Reporting on the hard-fought Florentine election, one interested observer, U.S. Consul General Walter Orebaugh, was both impressed and disturbed by the activities of the PCI. The left excelled at grassroots organization. Its promise of a "Socialist" city government mobilized voters. Fearful businessmen sought to buy protection from the PCI. The fragmentation of the center and growth of the Uomo Qualunque (UQ—Common Man) movement on the right were equally disturbing to Orebaugh. Burdened by the unpopular policies of the national government, the Florentine DC was on the defensive.[4]

TRENCH WARFARE

On November 10, 1946, the PCI and its ally, the Italian Socialist Party (PSI), captured control of Florence's city government. The Communists with twenty-one seats and the Socialists with thirteen held an eight-vote majority in the sixty-man body. The Christian Democrats, with a respectable showing of fifteen seats, and UQ, with a surprising eight, were the main parties of opposition. The jubilant Communists hoisted a red flag over Palazzo Vecchio and began an exhausting Cold War confrontation with the Christian Democrats.

On both the local and the national level the PCI sought to conciliate its powerful Catholic rival. DC leaders, with more foresight, recognized that political cohabitation with the Communists was not only unworkable but counterproductive. Clashes between the United States and the Soviet Union were intensifying, polarizing the international scene. Italy would have to make a choice of foreign alliance. Moreover, the Vatican strongly opposed continued cooperation with the Communists. DC dependence on the church for voter mobilization was too strong to defy the desires of the fiercely anti-Communist Pope Pius XII and the Italian bishops. The fall election results demonstrated that, by remaining in coalitions with the left, the DC would lose support to right-wing movements like UQ and the neo-Fascists. The Christian Democrats employed confrontation to establish the party both nationally and locally as the primary bulwark against the left. The Florentine DC rejected a Communist offer to participate in the new junta on December 20, 1946. Eight days later, Mario Fabiani took his oath of office as mayor. In a conciliatory address, he called for cooperation in rebuilding the city. In response, DC leader Adone Zoli offered to work for the common interest but reiterated his party's opposition to the left's program for Florence.[5]

The first Cold War confrontation in Florence was for control of the major daily newspapers. Fabiani fired the director of the DC-dominated *Corriere di Firenze*. The DC loudly protested. The left already controlled *Nazione del Popolo* and Tuscany's only local radio station. Fabiani's action threatened to create a left-wing monopoly of the local media. The De Gasperi government, through the prefect, intervened in support of the center parties. Reprimanding Fabiani for violating laws governing replacement of city employees, the prefect oversaw a division of the media among the major parties. The DC took over *Nazione del Popolo* and promptly rebaptized it *Il Mattino*. The three left parties gained *Il Corriere*.[6]

The skirmish over control of the press underlined a critical weakness of Florence's left-wing government. Its freedom of action was tightly constricted by an existing web of law. The Christian Democratic-dominated national government repeatedly employed these regulations to frustrate Communist-Socialist initiatives. The prefect played the role of watchdog. Left-wing city administrations like Fabiani's faced constant harassment not only from political opponents but from the massive state bureaucracy.[7]

Moreover, division of newspapers intensified discord within the PSI. Months earlier, then-Mayor Gaetano Pieraccini had warned that joint editorship would reinforce the Florentine PSI faction supporting fusion with the PCI. Recognizing that they had lost control of the press, Florentine reformist Socialists joined Giuseppe Saragat's defection from the PSI in January 1947.[8]

The split in the PSI seriously weakened the position of the left throughout Italy. The Socialists lost a large number of seats in parliament to defecting reformists. A weakened PSI became even more dependent on the PCI. The forces favoring fusion with the Communists grew stronger, provoking further divisions among the Socialists. Florence Federation secretary Jaures Busoni warned national headquarters that a badly disoriented local PSI faced the defection of a large number of intellectuals and professionals.[9]

On the national and local levels, the PCI exploited Socialist divisions to establish a dominant role on the political left and among the working classes. However, the overall effect of Socialist schism was to weaken the left. Within six months of the split, De Gasperi ejected the PCI and PSI from the national government. Togliatti was unsure about how to react to De Gasperi's maneuver. He was concerned about his ability to maintain control of a still-expanding mass party, had to fend off pressures from more radical leaders, such as Pietro Secchia and Luigi Longo, for risky and probably violent action, and had to determine his party's attitude toward the rules of democracy from the new and uncomfortable position of opposition. The PCI was politically paralyzed. Finally, in the late summer of 1947, Stalin intervened. He summoned Italian and other Communist leaders to a special meeting in Poland designed to create a unified party line and coordinate a mechanism to oppose the Marshall Plan. This firm shove in the direction of hard-line opposition to the De Gasperi regime gave the Italian Communists a policy.[10]

The PCI's Florentine Federation mirrored the general malaise of Italian Communism. Extremely successful at recruitment and mass mobilization, the Florence PCI also possessed a large arms cache and was capable of unleashing an insurrection. The Florentine Communists, however, lacked any firm direction, and, acting under orders from national party headquarters, their leaders were busily disciplining radical elements among the rank and file.[11]

Stalin's more aggressive line produced positive effects in Florence. National headquarters softened the harshness of the Soviet critique of PCI performance and the hard-line measures that Stalin demanded in the report that it made to the rank and file. The Italian party presented the new policy as a "tactical revision" of Togliatti's existing strategy. Morale rose as the PCI began an aggressive attack on the policies of the De Gasperi government and on the American-financed Marshall Plan.[12]

The PCI's recovery came at a critical point. National elections loomed, and the Left was badly equipped to contest them. The PSI was divided and disoriented. The reformist Socialist Party (PSLI) was drifting toward collaboration with De Gasperi and the DC. The constituent parts of the Action Party continued a confused search for a position on the political spectrum.

The electoral campaign of 1947–1948 demonstrated the capabilities of the PCI's mass organization. Rooted in the urban working masses and among Tuscany's landless sharecroppers and building support among the lower middle classes, the PCI mobilized a formidable electoral machine during the winter of 1947–1948, financed by an ample treasury (partially supplied by the Soviet Union). The cash-strapped PSI had to rely on the PCI to turn out crowds and to get the message of the left into print. Increasingly, the Socialists abandoned efforts to organize among the working classes. The Popular Democratic Front, the joint slate that the PCI–PSI presented for the 1948 election, was the fruit of Socialist weakness.[13]

The PCI's mass mobilization was no match for the De Gasperi government's combination of propaganda, patronage, and police, aided by the United States, which intervened with a massive public relations campaign and, ultimately, provided secret funding to the parties of the center. In Tuscany, as in the rest of Italy, the elections of April 18, 1948, were a net refutation of the left. The DC leaped from 28 percent (June 1946) to 46 percent of the vote. Although the PCI actually picked up support, its advance was at the expense of the PSI, which, together with the small parties, paid a heavy price for political polarization.

The April 1948 victory was the signal for a much more aggressive stance by the DC. Hard-line politics had improved the party's position, DC leaders reasoned, and should be intensified to exploit PCI weakness and drive it from power in the next elections.[14]

The Florentine PCI was again on the defensive. Defeatism was widespread after the crushing psychological setback of April 18. A sense of isolation grew as the DC unleashed its repressive actions. Nursing grievances over the wartime and postwar behavior of the left parties, conservatives made common cause with ex-Fascists to seek revenge. Repression of the left became a central feature of politics during the next five years. The government sought to weaken the PCI, the PSI, and their key supporting organizations, the unions and the national partisan association.[15]

The constituent elements of the left, the parties, organized labor, and the ex-partisans failed to develop an effective strategy to counter the DC. Socialist resentment of the PCI and that party's chronic disorganization had the effect of increasing the PCI's isolation.[16]

Disagreements over the future of the *Nuovo Corriere* played a special role in poisoning a deteriorating PCI-PSI relationship. Daily newspaper sales, in decline before the vote, spiraled downward after the election defeat. A powerful, well-financed, and politically independent paper, *La Nazione*, resuscitated by conservatives in 1947, overturned the party press monopoly and cut deeply into the circulation of all other papers. An April 1948 accord between the Communists and Socialists, designed to save *Nuovo Corriere* through the infusion of 4 million lire in new capital, almost collapsed. When the Socialists could not raise the 2 million lire that they had pledged, the Communists demanded editorial control. The two parties eventually agreed to a compromise that made the PSI a junior partner in the paper's administration. PCI editor in chief Romano Bilenchi ignored Socialist demands for a share in editorial control, openly challenging his putative allies to do something about it. A financially strapped PSI nursed its grievances.[17]

Growing realization of the costs of dependence on a powerful PCI further fragmented the PSI. Centrist factions, determined to avoid fusion with the Communists, took control on the national level and in the province of Florence in mid-1948. Torn between rejection of PCI hegemony and a desire to retain the unity of the left, they were unable to fashion a viable program. Nenni and his left-wing allies regained control but were equally incapable of resolving the party's fundamental dilemma.[18]

The mostly spontaneous mass uprisings that accompanied news of the July 14, 1948, assassination attempt on Togliatti provided a frightening display of the insurrectionary potential of the left and gave the forces of the right an excuse to unleash the police. While party leaders appealed for calm, angry PCI militants filled the streets of Florence, harassed and beat up political opponents, and set up roadblocks before the leadership regained control of the situation. The local labor movement split. The Christian Democrats withdrew in protest over Communist–Socialist actions. The Italian government increased police measures against the left. Frequent, widespread, and generally unverified reports of PCI coup plots, dutifully relayed to Rome by the prefect, provided a convincing justification for further government action.[19]

During the next three years, Florence's Cold War continued with little respite. The PCI solidified its control over the local labor movement and directed a number of bitter, usually unsuccessful strikes. Its membership continued to grow, and its ability to mobilize mass demonstrations in protest against government actions remained impressive. Business and the Italian government, however, held the initiative. The Socialists were sullen. The DC and other parties of center and right were hostile. An isolated PCI governed Florence.[20]

THE MAN IN THE MIDDLE

In the winter of 1947, as the national election campaign entered its critical phase, the prefect of Florence requested that the city's Communist mayor participate in ceremonies welcoming the "Friendship Train," a U.S.-backed project designed to assist needy Italians and not so subtly to reinforce public recognition that economic recovery was tied to support for the pro-American Christian Democrats. Two months later, with the electoral campaign at a fever pitch and his own party accusing the United States of massive, unwarranted intervention in Italy's domestic affairs, Mayor Fabiani appeared with U.S. consul general Walter Orebaugh at a ceremony dedicating a statue to George Washington and eulogized the first president and his country. In polarized Cold War Italy, Fabiani attempted to govern by finding common ground among Italy's battling political parties.[21]

Small, gaunt to the point of emaciation, with piercing eyes and a shy, but appealing, smile, Mario Fabiani looked like a survivor of one of Hitler's death camps. Physically, he appeared to mirror the Italian people's hard experience of war and reconstruction. Thirty-four years old at the time he assumed control of city government, Fabiani was a very different type of Communist politician. He had been a party activist since the late 1920s. In 1932–1933 he spent eighteen months studying Leninism in Moscow. Shortly after his clandestine return to Italy in 1934, he was arrested and imprisoned. Liberated at Mussolini's fall a decade later, he returned to Florence and became active in party operations, playing a key role in organizing strikes against the German occupiers. After liberation Fabiani served as vice mayor in Pieraccini's junta.

The Moscow experience was critical in forming Fabiani. It made him a dedicated anti-Stalinist who never abandoned his faith in Communism or his opposition to the Soviet dictatorship. Fabiani was a predecessor to the Berlinguer generation of PCI leaders, whose post-1968 effort to square the circle between democracy and Communism sparked the party's gradual rejection of Leninism and eventual transformation.[22]

In the Stalinist Italian Party of the 1940s, Fabiani occupied an extremely exposed position. He operated with great caution and never publicly challenged official adulation of the Soviet dictator. His presence in the leadership of the Florentine party owed as much to this circumspection as to an extraordinary personal appeal to voters.

With a fragile majority in the city council, Fabiani regularly reached out to the opposition. He recognized that reconstruction was impossible without the support of both the DC-dominated national government and the Florentine business community. They had the money and the political and administrative power that he lacked. They, too, needed a successful reconstruction. Businessmen wanted to prosper. Christian Democrats could hinder basic reconstruction only at their political peril. Moreover, Fabiani could count upon support for many of his projects, above all, those dealing with hunger and housing, from the dominant, socially concerned left wing of the Florentine DC and Cardinal Dalla Costa. Ultimately, the effort to create common ground drove the Fabiani administration to accept limits on its reform objectives that fatally weakened it.[23] The mayor had no realistic alternatives.

Fabiani assumed office at a difficult moment. After nearly two years of peace, Florence still faced massive unemployment, food shortages, power outages, and rampant inflation as well as mass demonstrations, strikes, and a widespread public pessimism. One conservative Florentine diarist complained of "the immorality of this post war" rooted in a collective mental illness. "Many young men and women do not seem to enjoy their bodies. They give them without joy or interest." Compounding these problems was a continuing migration from the Tuscan countryside. Ultimately, this influx of new labor fueled economic expansion, particularly light industry and construction. Initially, the new migrants overwhelmed both city services and the housing market.[24]

Fabiani's government sought to meet these problems by encouraging investment, expanding services, improving city administration, building new housing, and relaunching the tourist industry. This ambitious program required major and expanding new sources of revenue. The search for financing was a constant theme of Florentine politics under Fabiani.

In December 1946, shortly after his inauguration, Mayor Fabiani set out for Rome to make contact with senior government officials and to present Florence's case for special assistance from the national government. Communist and Socialist members of the De Gasperi government assisted the youthful mayor, and a week later he telegraphed the city council news of grants of 100 million lire for housing and a further 70 million for the construction and repair of classrooms. The following month, Fabiani fulfilled one of his election promises, winning state funding to build new apartment blocks on the periphery.[25]

The collapse of De Gasperi's DC-PSI-PCI coalition government cut off easy access to public funding, forcing the city administration to find new revenue sources. The city's taxing authority was very much restricted. New levies needed approval from the prefect and his principal advisers, the Provincial Administrative Junta (GPA). Bank loans were hard to acquire, given the city's existing indebtedness. A cumbersome review process required GPA approval for every loan request. Property rental or sales, while a useful cash source, did not produce the kind of funding needed to launch major new projects.[26]

In spite of fiscal and political pressures for economic belt tightening, Fabiani had to try to expand both revenues and services. The city's needs were pressing. Moreover, the left had come to power on a platform of expanded government activism. The Communist-led administration was under constant pressure from party sections to meet public demands for services. They insisted that the city find food and housing for displaced party members on a priority basis. Communists also expected preferential treatment in the issuance of permits and in the use of public property for party functions. PCI-supported organizations demanded city action on questions of labor relations, pensions, benefits, and employment far beyond its competence. One party section urged Fabiani to raise parking fees and weekend bus rates in order to strike at the middle classes. Party leaders, in another small example of their class warfare mentality, complained that public urinals on the periphery were not as clean as those provided to tourists and the bourgeoisie in the city center. Hard-pressed by his own comrades, Fabiani begged for patience as he struggled to meet a myriad of small demands that, taken together, put great strain on a city administration trying to establish its priorities and conduct a major reconstruction of Florence.[27]

Fabiani and other city administrators believed that increased local autonomy offered the best chance to meet constituent demands and to carry out a successful reconstruction in the face of government hostility. On February 4, 1947, Fabiani hosted a meeting of the Tuscan mayors, whose objective was creating a section of the National League of Italian Communes. Mayors from forty-nine communes passed contradictory resolutions demanding more local autonomy and a 50 percent increase in the funding that they received from the national government. Their wish list also included easier terms from state-run credit institutions, resumption of the purge, limits on the prefects' scope for action, and a greater say in national government decisions affecting their cities.[28]

The National League of Democratic Communes provided little practical aid to the Fabiani administration. The De Gasperi government ignored its demands, while Prefect Paterno treated it as another potential subversive organization. PCI national headquarters tended to view the league and its sections as part of its electoral machine. Coordination among communes proved very elusive even when they were governed by the same parties. It became nearly impossible when the left ruled in one commune and the DC in another.[29]

The Fabiani administration's first and most basic problem was ensuring an adequate food supply for a growing population. The prefect and mayor clashed repeatedly over control of SEPRAL, the provincial food supply mechanism. Bread rationing continued into 1947. As late as 1949, SEPRAL was still functioning, and food supplies were still limited. Milk prices rose steadily as the result of price gouging by local suppliers. Fabiani's efforts to increase supply and control prices through the creation of a communal diary met with fierce opposition from the suppliers, the prefect, and the DC. The De Gasperi government intervened to protect the operation of market "mechanisms."[30]

Transportation policy was the hair shirt of city administrators. ATAF, the municipalized city transportation service, was a large and continuing drain on finances. The debt-ridden company lacked vehicles, necessitating major outlays. It was also labor-intensive, and its many semiskilled jobs were a magnet for out-of-work PCI members. A Communist-led administration could not regard ATAF simply as an economic problem. The PCI–PSI junta recognized that public transportation was a social issue and a political flash point with its voters. Encouraged by a DC that hoped to reap political benefits from support of major investment in city transportation services, the Fabiani government struggled to keep basic fares low, offer special group fares, and simultaneously improve the quality and quantity of services.[31]

The inevitable result was a mushrooming deficit. By mid-1947, ATAF's debt was 216 million lire. The company turned to banks for additional loans to cover existing expenses and to the state for cash assistance to finance improvements. In February 1948 Fabiani requested a government-financed bailout. The city abandoned plans for special discounts and raised fares. The DC was able to capitalize on ATAF's financial difficulties, opposing fare increases while simultaneously arguing that an "independent" agency like ATAF had to balance its budget.

The opposition accused the city of maladministration, and payroll padding and added charges of pork barrel politics when the junta handed out free bus passes to its supporters.[32]

As a part of general belt tightening that took place in the last two years of Fabiani's administration, ATAF's budget was pared and brought closer to balance. The ambitious, socially oriented programs of the mid-1940s gave way to austerity imposed upon the city by the Italian government and by an opposition that had skillfully exploited the issue of deficit spending to deflect ambitious social programs and to undercut the Fabiani administration's support among important sectors of the public.[33]

The ATAF case proved to be a model for other Fabiani social service programs. Conceived to deal with the needs of the mass of Florence's citizens, they proved too costly to carry through, particularly in the face of national government opposition. Meanwhile, other public services suffered from underbudgeting. The water and sewer systems were particularly inadequate. Outbreaks of typhus and tuberculosis underlined the problem in a city where six out of ten homes lacked indoor plumbing. Florence's schools were housed in antiquated buildings and lacked equipment. Outdoor illumination was inadequate. Street cleaning was pathetic. The opposition pounced upon these defects, pointing out that the lack of adequate services hampered efforts to attract tourism, further slowing the pace of economic recovery.[34]

Efforts by the city administration to meet the lower social classes' fundamental need for housing faced an uphill battle. In 1946, the Fabiani administration, aided by the Communist-Socialist presence in the national government, won a 100 million lire state grant that enabled it to rebuild about half of all damaged buildings. Thereafter, the pace of repairs and new housing starts slowed, while the population grew, and homelessness increased. Funding for publicly financed housing was at a premium. Aided by La Pira, Fabiani was able to requisition a number of school buildings for homeless shelters. Unfortunately, this form of emergency action was essentially self-defeating, given the city's need for classrooms. Evictions rose because the unemployed were unable to cover their rents. Owners began rehabilitating their property to provide apartments to wealthier citizens. Opposition parties hammered away at the housing crisis. Fabiani's truthful rejoinder that he was powerless without government assistance ran thin as a defense. By late 1947, the De Gasperi ministry was formulating a national strategy to deal with the housing crisis that allowed it to seize the political initiative and to claim the lion's share of the credit.[35]

In an effort to break the deadlock created by massive reconstruction problems and the tight credit policies of a hostile government in Rome, the left tried to attract new investment. An effort to woo FIAT failed when the auto company rejected city terms. Lacking domestic investment capital, the Fabiani administration began to look abroad, particularly to the citadel of capitalism, the United States, for markets that would spark sustained economic growth.[36]

As part of the effort to attract foreign capital, the Fabiani administration strove to revive the tourist industry. In addition to economic considerations, broad public support existed for reviving "cultural tourism." A well-managed cultural program gave the working-class parties the chance to demonstrate their support for the arts in a concrete manner. Fabiani personally controlled cultural policy from the start of his administration.[37]

As always, Fabiani's ability to carry off a large-scale cultural program that promoted tourism depended on the willingness of the national government to provide assistance. The De Gasperi administration carefully distinguished between repair projects for the city's cultural monuments, which it lavishly financed, and the exhibits and performances promoted by the commune, which it frequently underfinanced. This policy contributed to the slow recovery of tourism without affecting the DC's public image.[38]

Fabiani lobbied hard to attract major directors to film and to premiere their works in Florence. Political leaders discussed possibilities of a Florence film festival. The PCI-led city administration sponsored major art shows and restored the popular annual *calcio in costume* (medieval rugby) program.[39]

The proudest claim of the Fabiani administration was its rehabilitation of the Teatro Comunale and re-creation of the Maggio Musicale festival. The city acted under considerable pressure. In the summer of 1947 Parise Votto, the Communist superintendent of the Teatro Comunale, warned Fabiani that Milan's La Scala appeared ready to create a rival spring festival. This spur to local pride came just as the Cold War reached new heights of intensity. Arguing that too much city money was being spent on politically motivated meetings and shows aimed at groups that were incapable of assisting the overall recovery of tourism, critics, both cultural and political, scanned every musical program presented by the city for signs of propaganda.[40]

In attempting to rebuild Florence's premier cultural institution, Fabiani faced his constant burden: a lack of funding. With Florence's main theater out of commission as a result of errant Allied bombs, the musicians and stagehands of the theater chafed at their limited employment and low wages. The city had to lay off a number of theater employees, creating problems with the unions. Fabiani found himself appealing once again to Rome, to tourism undersecretary Giulio Andreotti, for special funding to rebuild the Teatro Comunale.[41]

Not for the last time, Fabiani's deus ex machina was Giorgio La Pira. The Christian Democratic law professor and constitution maker intervened with Andreotti to secure a 20 million lire grant that permitted the city to mount a 1948 Maggio Musicale festival. Other special funding enabled the city to repair the Teatro Comunale for the 1948 season.[42]

Overcoming limited resources, the PCI-run Teatro Comunale managed to put on an imaginative and increasingly broad cultural program during the last three years of the Fabiani administration.[43] Votto was a capable administrator. The city government supported his initiatives with others that won the grudging admiration of hostile observers. However, the cultural program was unable to rebuild the city's tourist economy or to silence Fabiani's critics. In May 1949, the British magazine *Fortnightly* reported that Florence's intellectual and cultural life was vital, but its physical surroundings were depressing; the city was poor, many of its galleries were partially closed, and long stretches of the Arno remained in ruins. Overall, Florence was far from the ideal place for a vacation.[44]

Tourism, moreover, was a battlefield in the Cold War confrontation between the DC and local Communist administrations in Italy. While the PCI dominated the provincial "ente" (administration) for tourism (EPT), the state and business put most of the funds into the prefect-administered "Autonomous" tourist agency (AAT). Cooperation between these two bodies was difficult, and, as a result, Florence lacked a coordinated program for attracting tourists and their capital. The AAT, whose budget was largely derived from special taxes on Florence hotel owners and a required contribution from the city government, spent without reference to the wishes of the Fabiani administration. City officials, while obviously irked by its noncooperative attitude trod lightly in their criticisms of a body that was part of the prefect's administration.[45]

The Fabiani administration's ambitious programs fell victim to its lack of money. The opposition was able to exploit the question of Fabiani's fiscal management to devastating effect. They made the annual presentation of the city budget the centerpiece of the assault on the Communist-Socialist junta. Liberal Eugenio Artom led the attack, accusing the city of wasting its limited resources and warning that its growing public debt was unsustainable.[46]

Ultimately, the opposition made deficit financing politically unsustainable. In its 1949 budget submission, the Fabiani administration introduced a package of major increases in city consumption taxes. Simultaneously, Fabiani announced that lowering the city deficit had become a major priority. In 1951, the mayor presented a balanced budget.[47]

The political price of this policy was enormous. The workers' government had accepted the political agenda of the middle classes. Squeezed between a hostile national government and a combative local opposition, Fabiani's politics of conciliation ran aground. As the fall 1951 elections approached, the government of the left had exhausted its political capital.

Fabiani's achievements were a product of his tenacious reformism. The city had a manageable public debt. In five years his administration had managed to construct enough housing units to replace those destroyed by the war. It had improved the quality of life: better public health services, expanded public transportation and housing, and enlarged after-school programs for children. It presided over the passage of Florence from an artisan- to service sector-based economy, and, in its final months of life, the junta tackled the festering question of Florence's long-term development.[48]

A CITY PLAN

The housing crisis, tight money, and the concomitant need for support from both the local opposition and the De Gasperi government help to explain the slowness with which Florence's government took on the politically sensitive issue of a general zoning and reconstruction plan. While the city's leading architects and urban planners urged implementation of such a plan, Fabiani was listening to the demands of the middle classes, strongly backed by the DC, who wanted maximum control over their property. As a result, the reconstruction was carried out by private capital on a piecemeal basis. The city adopted a series of localized plans for reconstruction in war-damaged areas and then fought over their content with a DC-dominated Superior Council for the Fine Arts in Rome. It surrendered to the basic demand of middle-class property owners by expanding the commercial zone in the center and building new housing on the periphery. What one critic called "tepid" *com'era* construction triumphed in the center, while more commuters added to the city's growing traffic congestion.[49]

By late 1946 a number of groups were beginning to have second thoughts about the shape of the reconstruction. Merchants from the Ponte Vecchio area were not happy with either the aesthetics or the economic consequences of the construction that was rising to replace war-destroyed property. The politically influential architects of the University of Florence continued to agitate for a single, all-encompassing plan. The larger property owners of the area emerged as the villains, attacked by both left and right for seeking quick profits without regard to considerations of aesthetics or of the social and economic requirements of old neighborhoods.[50]

Emboldened by growing public support for more coherent reconstruction and modernization planning, the Fabiani administration organized design competitions for rebuilding the center. Fabiani personally chaired the opening session of the committee drawing up rules for the competition. Its recommendations and the subsequent proposals made by local architects were the seedbed of a general city plan. By focusing attention on interrelated issues such as traffic, space utilization, the linkages between the two sides of the Arno, and environmental concerns, the Ponte Vecchio reconstruction project sparked a wide and better-informed discussion of the future of the city.[51]

The city council took up the plan at its March 17, 1948, meeting. While all sides agreed that the plan presented by the government was a good basis for the reconstruction of the city's historic center, they sharply disagreed on the particulars of reconstruction planning, especially architects' plans for pedestrian zones and for covered walkways. Pressed hard by the DC, Fabiani agreed to go forward with the right bank part of the program, leaving the left bank for further study. At its May 4 meeting the city government conceded more ground to the opposition, who represented the views of shop owners, by dropping the proposal for covered walkways.[52]

Having rejected more innovative architectural concepts, the city council was able to agree on a plan for reconstruction of the left bank in 1949. It also authorized completion of a plan for rehabilitation in the S. Croce area.[53]

Gianfranco Musco, the assessor of urban planning in the Fabiani administration, subsequently gave the Ponte Vecchio reconstruction a mixed review. He noted that the decision to save the city's remaining medieval towers helped to give the area definition but also made erecting compatible new structures difficult. This encouraged a good deal of *com'era* building. Fortunately, the new construction was low-rise, protecting the panoramic views that are available from the hills and larger buildings like the Duomo and Uffizi. Widening the streets improved lines of sight, and the reconstruction preserved the centrality of Ponte Vecchio. Unfortunately, higher rents drove out the zone's traditional economic backbone, artisans.[54] Moreover, as even the most casual visitor to the zone can observe, the new buildings are, like most modern Florentine ceramic production, serviceable replicas, lacking any innovative design.

The Fabiani administration's ability to control reconstruction policy was sharply limited. On Florence's periphery, private builders continued to throw up structures that violated city codes. Merchants in the center were powerful enough to force through reconstruction projects that ignored norms for historic preservation, and the Italian government continued to intervene, imposing its will on the city.[55]

The center of the struggle of local versus national authorities was the replacement of the bridges destroyed by the Germans. The city pressed forward with plans for a *com'era* reconstruction of Ponte S. Trinita that enjoyed extremely broad popular support. Arguing that the bridge was, in fact, a major piece of sculpture and pointing to the steady accumulation of fragments, Fabiani's administration proposed to utilize massive archival documentation to carry out an artistic restoration. The national government's experts insisted that the bridge pilings could not support this form of reconstruction. The result was a deadlock during which no work was carried out. During the long years of stalemate, the city slowly collected the money needed to carry out reconstruction, primarily from private donors.[56]

Local autonomy suffered a humiliating blow in mid-1949, when the Italian government intervened to reject the prizewinning design for the reconstruction of Ponte alla Carraia. The city had let contracts when the Ministry of Public Works announced that it would oversee the selection process. An angry Fabiani went to Rome to protest, but to no avail.[57] During the spring of 1950, the fine arts office of the Ministry of Public Instruction intervened to assert its control over local plans for the ongoing reconstruction of the area around Ponte Vecchio and to reconfirm its opposition to a reconstruction of Ponte S. Trinita *com'era*.[58]

In spite of these setbacks, Musco appointed a special committee of six influential city architects to draw up a general zoning plan (PRG—*piano regolatore generale*) in March 1949. The planners were asked to draw up a plan that would take into account both the changing nature of the Florentine economy and the relationship between the city and neighboring communes. Special stress was laid on the growing problem of traffic into and inside the city, a reflection of the rapid motorization of Florence.[59]

The commission's report was laid before the city council in April 1951. Musco, in his presentation, noted that post-Risorgimento Florence had expanded like an oil stain—in all directions and without great regard for aesthetic or environmental issues. Post–World War II Florence could no longer follow this course. Areas for expansion within its territorial limits were rapidly being exhausted, and, unless rational choices were made, the remaining land would be exploited by private investors to the long-term harm of the city. An orderly and successful expansion of roads and new industrial development required cooperation with neighboring jurisdictions, above all, Prato.[60]

The draft plan foresaw the creation of new industrial zones in the northwest of the city, together with housing for those employed there. Construction in other zones would be halted. The city would build new parks in the northwest and would expand the Cascina park and the Campo Marte sports facility. The plan called for widening of existing roads and new construction designed to link Florence more securely with Prato and other neighboring communes. Finally, a general rehabilitation of the historic center would permit an orderly expansion of the tourist industry, while providing improved housing to inhabitants of the zone. By moving industrial and much commercial activity outside the center, planners hoped to preserve the specific characteristics of older zones, protect the remaining greenbelt in the hills, and reinvigorate the city by restoring the balance between commercial, recreational, and residential utilization of space.[61]

The 1951 PRG was a typical product of Fabiani's "big tent" approach to politics. It appealed to both intellectuals and working class because of a stress on planning that would protect their interests and take another step toward an egalitarian society. Simultaneously, the city pledged to carry out the plan through private investment and development. Fabiani observed that the plan was organic and thus subject to frequent revision and that it was gradual, allowing for the preservation of private interests. Politically, this approach worked. The city council unanimously approved the 1951 PRG. It would be the last achievement of the Fabiani administration.[62]

NOTES

1. Report, June 1–19, 1945, NA, RG 331, ACC, 10800/115/268.

2. *Nazione del Popolo*, September 10, 22, 1946; *Toscana Nuova*, October 27, 1946.

3. Frida Zampella, "L'amministrazione Fabiani, 1946–1951" (Tesi di lauria, University of Florence, 1986–1987), pp. 47–48; Notes 1946 administrative elections, ISRT, Carte Collini, b 6, f. Materiale PCI.

4. Roger Absalom, ed., *Gli alleati e la ricostruzione in Toscana*, 2 vols. (Florence, 1988), 1: 332; Police report, November 10, 1946, AC/S, MI, Gab., Partiti Politici, b 68, f. 200/8/31.

5. Serena Innamorati, *Mario Fabiani* (Florence, 1984), p. 131; *Nazione del Popolo*, November 21, 29, 1946; Zampella, "L'amministrazione Fabiani," pp. 13–14.

6. Prefecture to Fabiani, January 29, 1947, ACF, Gabinetto del sindaco, Atti 201–500.

7. Zampella, "L'amministrazione Fabiani," pp. 214–17.

8. Pieraccini letter, April 4, 1946, ISRT, Fondo F. Lombardi, b 11, f PSI-Firenze 1946; Foscolo Lombardi to Jaures Busoni, November 23, 1946, ibid.

9. Busoni to Lombardi, January 26, 1947, ISRT, Fondo F. Lombardi, b 11, f. PSI-Firenze, 1947.

10. Nicola Gallerano and Marcello Flores, *Sul PCI* (Bari, 1992), pp. 98–99, 124, 127; Enzo Collotti, ed., *Archivio Pietro Secchia* (Milan, 1979), pp. 194, 204–5, 208–9, 611–27.

11. Resolution, February 7, 1947, APC, f Firenze 1947, 141/1674–1679; Letter to PCI Headquarters, ibid., f. 141/1682; Report, March 7, 1947, NA, RG 84, Florence Post, Classified General Records, 800; Reports, July 11, 30, 1947, ibid., 350 Political Reports, 1947–1948; Police report, September 2, 1947, AC/S, MI, Gab., Partiti politici, f 161, P/31-PCI-Firenze.

12. Minutes, October 22, 1947, APC, f Firenze 1947, 141/1695; Report, December 24, 1947; ibid., f 141/1664.

13. Lombardi to "Giovanni," March 22, 1948, ISRT, Fondo F. Lombardi, b 17, f Il Nuovo Corriere no. 3.

14. Innamorati, *Mario Fabiani*, p. 132.

15. Ruggero Orfei, *L'occupazione del potere* (Milan, 1976), p. 121; Silvio Lanaro, *Storia dell'Italia repubblicana* (Venice, 1992), p. 185; Serena Innamorati, *Per la unita della resistenza* (Milan, 1990), pp. 49–50.

16. Letter, May–June 1948, ISRT, Fondo F. Lombardi, b 17, f Nuovo Corriere, no. 3.

17. Lombardi to PSI members, May 8, 1948, ISRT, Fondo F. Lombardi, b 17, f Nuovo Corriere, No. 3; Lombardi to Busoni, May 21, 1948, ibid.; Bilenchi to Lombardi, June 9, 1948, ibid.; Basso to Lombardi, June 16, 1948, ibid.; Lombardi to PSI Direzione, July 2, 1948, ibid.

18. Lombardi to Pertini, November 11, 1948, ISRT, Fondo F. Lombardi, b 13, f PSI-Firenze; Tristano Codignola, *Scritti Politici, 1943–1981* (Florence, 1987), 1: 214–24.

19. Consular reports of July 16 and 30, and September 18, NA, RG 84, Florence Post, 350 Political Reports, 1947–1948; Prefect to MI, July 12, 1948, AC/S, MI, Gab., Partiti politici, f 161, P/31-PCI-Firenze; Prefect to Ministry of Interior, January 13, 1949, ibid.; Prefect to Interior Ministry, March 15, 1949, ibid., P/19-PCI; Prefect to Ministry of Interior, April 24, 1950, ibid., P/3/31, PCI.

20. Report, December 12, 1948, APC, f. Firenze 1948, 0244/4121; Notes on Party Day, July 17, 1949, ibid., f. Firenze 1949, 0302/0138; Prefect to MI, October 24, 1949, AC/S, MI, Gab., Partiti politici, f 161, P/31 PCI-Firenze; *Toscana Nuova*, April 29, 1949, March 5, 1950.

21. Pavone to Fabiani, December 30, 1947, ACF, Gabinetto del sindaco 1947, Atti 1801–220; Orebaugh to Department of State, March 25, 1948, NA, RG 84, Florence Post, 820.7–45.

22. Innamorati, *Mario Fabiani*, pp. 17–20; Gianni and Giorgio Giovannoni interview, Florence, May 25, 1993.

23. Zampella, "L'amministrazione Fabiani," pp. 104, 134–45; *Nazione del Popolo*, December 11, 1946; Dalla Costa to Fabiani, January 1, 1947, ACF, Gabinetto del sindaco 1947, Atti 1–200.

24. Piero Santi, *Diario, 1943–1946* (Venice, 1950), p. 104; Questura report, December 30, 1946, NA, RG 84 Florence Post, 800 Pol. Beccatini, *Sviluppo economico*, pp. 17, 70–71; Zeffiro Ciuffoletti, Mario Rossi, and Angelo Varni, *La camera di lavoro di Firenze* (Naples, 1991), pp. 36–37.

25. *Nazione del Popolo*, December 11, 18, 1946; Mariotti to Musco, January 20, 1947, ACF, Gabinetto del sindaco 1947, Atti 201–500.

26. Fabiani, letter, July 1, 1947, ASF, Gabinetto del sindaco 1947, Atti 801–1300; Fabiani to Prefect, October 18, 1947, ibid.; Zampella, "L'ammistrazione Fabiani," p. 104.

27. See letters in, ACF, Gabinetto del sindaco 1947, Atti 1–200, 501–800, 800–1300 and ibid., 1948, Atti 1–200; Memoranda of January 18, February 1, 13, 1947, ibid., 1947, Atti 1–200; Zampella, "L'amministrazione Fabiani," pp. 134–136; Fabiani to Buggiani, January 7, 1947, ACF, Gabinetto del sindaco 1947, Atti 1–200, for the mayor's plea for patience.

28. Memo of the *sindaco*, January 28, 1947, ACF, Gabinetto del sindaco 1947, Atti 1–200, s/f Convegno provinciale sindaci; Police report, February 17, 1947, AC/S, MI, Gab. Fascicoli permanenti, b. 277 bis, f 661/E/31, Lega comuni democratici.

29. Prefect to MI, September 9, 1948, AC/S, MI, Gab., Fascicoli permanenti, b 277, f 661/E/31, s/f Lega comuni democratici; Osti to Fabiani, July 5, 1948, ACF, Gabinetto del sindaco 1948, Atti 601–800.

30. *Toscana nuova* March 28, 1947; Prefect to Fabiani, September 2, 1947, ACF, Gabinetto del sindaco 1947, Atti 1301–1800; Giuseppe Pozzana, *Tra pubblico e privato* (Florence, 1985), pp. 78–85.

31. Zampella, "L'ammistrazione Fabiani," pp. 89–90; Nicola Cefaratti and Morello Malaspina, *1865–1985. Centoventi anni di trasporti pubblici a Firenze* (Cortona, 1987), p. 420.

32. Fabiani to Prefect, February 3, 1948, ACF, Gabinetto del sindaco 1948, Atti 1–100, s/f ATAF; ACC 1948, pp. 291–302, 307–15; ACC 1949, 1: 99, 228, 264–73; 2: 944–66.

33. ACC 1951, pp. 307–17.

34. Minutes of Council of Administration of the University of Florence, January 7, 1947, ACF, Gabinetto del sindaco, Atti 1–200; Prefecture to Fabiani, June 28, 1947, ibid., Atti 801–1300; Assessore of Public Instruction to Fabiani, August 25, 1947, ibid.; Fabiani to Simonetti, September 1, 1948, ACF, Gabinetto del sindaco 1948, Atti 801–1000; ACC 1950, pp. 100–110, 606–9, ACC 1951, pp. 10–12; Davis Otatti, *Firenze pulita* (Florence, 1990); p. 116.

35. Innamorati, *Mario Fabiani*, pp. 47, 78; Press release of IACP, September 15, 1947, ACF, Gabinetto del sindaco 1947, Atti 1301–1800; Fabiani to La Pira, December 18, 1947, ibid., Atti 1801–2200; ACC 1948, 36–38, 121 ff.; IACP to Ministry of Public Works, August 2, 1947, ACdiF, Prefettura di Firenze, Affari ordinari 1948, f 55; Monthly reports of Commune of Florence on housing, January, February, October, 1948, ibid.; Giulio Andreotti, *De Gasperi e la ricostruzione* (Rome, 1974), pp. 90–92; Aurelio Lepre, *Storia della prima repubblica* (Bologna, 1993), pp. 150–51.

36. ACC 1948, p. 607; Letter to Fabiani, February 9, 1948, ACF, Gabinetto del sindcao 1948, Atti 101–400.

37. Report, February 28, 1949, NA, RG 84, Florence Post, 350 Political Reports 1949; Fabiani to Ambassador of the USSR, December 16, 1946, ACF, Gabinetto del sindaco 1947, Atti 501–800, s/f settimana europea.

38. Director General of Culture to Fabiani, February 11, 1947, ACF, Gabinetto del sindaco, Atti 501–800; ACC 1950, 430–35; Guido Gonella, *Cinque anni al Ministero della pubblica istruzione* (Rome, 1982), 3: 13–14, 31–32, 267–68.

39. Mariella Zoppi, *Firenze e l'urbanistica* (Rome, 1982), p. 27; Madori to Votto, Sep-

tember 21, 1948, ACF, Gabinetto del sindaco, 1948, Atti 1001–1400; Fabiani to de Sica, December 28, 1948, ibid. Atti 1401 al fine.

40. Leonardo Pinzauti, ed., *Il maggio Musicale Fiorentino dalla prima alla trentesima edizione* (Florence, 1967), p. 100; Report, January 31, 1949, NA, RG 84, Florence Post, 350 Political Reports 1949.

41. Fabiani to Andreotti, January 21, 1948, ACF, Gabinetto del sindaco 1948, Atti 1–100, s/f Teatro comunale.

42. Report on Proposed Special Law for Florence, April 14, 1948, AC/S, Ministry of Industry and Commerce, Gabinetto, b 15, f. schema D.L. concessione Firenze.

43. Report, July 18, 1949, NA, RG 84, Florence Post, 350 Political Reports 1949; ACC 1949, 1: 595–612.

44. "Florentine Letter," *Fortnightly*, May 1949.

45. Zampella, "L'amministrazione Fabiani," p. 187; ACC 1949, 1: 24–25, 427–33, 560–67; ACC 1951, pp. 157–63, 472–74.

46. ACC 1948, pp. 349, 363–64.

47. ACC 1949, 1: 278–304; ACC 1951, pp. 383–93.

48. Zampella, "L'amministrazione Fabiani," p. 177; Mario Rossi and G. Santomassimo, "Il PCI," Pier Luigi Ballini, Luigi Lotti, and Mario Rossi, eds., *Toscana nel secondo dopoguerra* (Milan, 1991), pp. 440–43.

49. Zampella, "L'amministrazione Fabiani," pp. 115–19, 125–26; Zoppi, *Firenze*, pp. 13–14; ACC 1949, 1: 44–50; ACC 1950, pp. 789–90.

50. Augusto Boggiano, ed., *Firenze: La questione urbanistica* (Florence, 1982), pp. 42–46, 54–57; Pro-memoria, c. January 15, 1947, ACF, Ufficio legale, filze speciale, b Comitato gestione, f v. Por S. Maria.

51. Zoppi, *Firenze*, pp. 13–14.

52. ACC 1948, 139–51, 211–29, 234.

53. ACC 1949, 1: 382–86.

54. *Firenze: Questione urbanistica*, pp. 58–61.

55. Paolo Paoletti and Paola Torrini, *Firenze anni '50* (Florence, 1991), 1: 254–58, 298–99; ACC 1949, 1:10 ff.

56. Zoppi, *Firenze*, p. 19; Paolo Bagnoli, "I giorni di Firenze (politica e cultura dal 1944 al 1974)" *Citta e regione* 7 (April 1981), p. 92; *New Republic*, April 4, 1949.

57. ACC 1950, 9–14; Paoletti and Torrini, *Firenze anni '50*, 1: 214, 252–53.

58. Minister of Public Instruction to Fabiani, April 15, 1950, AC/S, MPI, AA BB, division II, 1945–1955, b 46, f. Firenze; Decree, April 3, 1950, ibid., Ufficio conservazione monumentale, 1953–1959, b 59, f. P. S. Trinita.

59. ACC 1949, 1: 421–23; Zoppi, *Firenze*, pp. 29–33.

60. ACC 1951, pp. 322–30.

61. Boggiano, *Firenze: questione urbanistica*, pp. 49–53, 97–102, 104–6, 143–45, 160–68; Philippe Duboy, ed., *Edoardo Detti, 1913–1984: architetto e urbanista* (Milan, 1993), pp. 14–16.

62. ACC 1951, 322–30.

Chapter 4

Head in the Clouds, Feet on the Ground: La Pira, 1951–1954

Put aside some time for Florence: Here we are conducting a "model" social experiment that merits particular attention.

La Pira to Giulio Andreotti, October 1, 1952

Change the laws. I can not change the gospel.

Giorgio La Pira, c. 1952

November 7, 1977. In the midst of mounting social and political unrest, Florence buried Giorgio La Pira with dignity. Thousands crowded peacefully outside the church of S. Marco for the last rites. Prime Minister Giulio Andreotti traveled to Florence to honor the man and his achievements. Reflecting upon their political conflicts, Andreotti mused: "La Pira was certainly a saint . . . but also a hard nose [duro]." Another La Pira acquaintance, director Franco Zeffirelli, recalled: "[H]e had that sort of holy madness that grips some very devout people, yet he was not a holy fool—far from it, he was exceptionally clever, and it was this combination of worldly intellectual and holy simpleton that made him so unnerving yet so fascinating." Small, slender, bespectacled, dressed in suits that threatened to devour him, a jovial Giorgio La Pira mixed sermons and arm-twisting in about equal proportion in his crusade to reshape Florence, Italy, and the world. He dominated nearly every aspect of the city's life for fifteen years.[1]

CRONACHE SOCIALI

La Pira emerged as a leader of the Christian Democratic left in the mid-1940s. A decade earlier, Giuseppe Dossetti, a university professor and fervent Catholic, organized a group of students and teachers at Milan's Sacro Cuore University.

La Pira made contact with these Catholics, who shared common values of Christian social activism and anti-Fascism. In the late 1930s and early 1940s, these young intellectuals met at seminars organized by the Catholic University Students Federation (FUCI), which evolved into concrete political action.

Dossetti, a hero of the resistance, was the natural spokesman and leader of a postwar movement that sought to aid the poor and working classes through the exploitation of state power. "The Professors"—La Pira, Dossetti, Amintore Fanfani, Ezio Vanoni, Aldo Moro, Giuseppe Lazzati, Giuseppe Glisenti, Gianni Baget Bozzo—sought to influence other members of the nation's elite, leaving the task of organizing Catholic workers to labor leader Giovanni Gronchi and his followers. Orthodox Catholics, they were nonetheless eager to reach out to the leaders of the Marxist left in a common effort to build an Italian welfare state. Idealists, they were less flexible on matters of "principle" than De Gasperi and his lieutenants. A battle with distinct generational overtones broke out between the Dossetti–La Pira forces and the older Catholic leaders, survivors of the pre-Fascist Popular Party (PPI).[2]

Gifted, fractious, impatient with an older leadership incarnated by De Gasperi, the Professors scored their greatest success at the Constituent Assembly, where their rhetorical skills and conviction helped them shape the new republic's basic law. Their efforts to widen Catholic-Marxist dialogue inevitably strained relations with De Gasperi and were a catalyst solidifying conservative factions within the Christian Democratic Party.[3]

De Gasperi later described their relationship as "oil and water." Dossetti clashed with the prime minister over his policy of DC neutrality in the referendum on a republic or monarchy. The Professors' decision to publish their own journal, *Cronache Sociali*, in May 1947, was a direct challenge to De Gasperi's leadership. The DC's leader responded to this open challenge to party unity with disciplinary actions. De Gasperi could isolate the Professors; he could never bring them to heel. He alternated concessions and discipline to keep them in his coalition.[4]

Long-term collaboration was difficult. The Professors' objective was a radical reconstruction of Italy's political and social fabric, inspired by the Scriptures and mixing a modernized corporatist vision with economic theory enriched by the work of John Maynard Keynes. Vanoni argued that the state had responsibility for harmonizing economic activity to promote the common good. Public and private economic activity must combine to create employment, strengthen the family, encourage the development of the individual, and provide a just salary. Tax policy, Vanoni told the third DC national congress (1949), had to be based on the principle that the rich pay their fair share. De Gasperi backed the "protected" free market economics of big business and of the conservative wing of the DC. La Pira, who admired De Gasperi, was conviced that the DC's leader was in the hands of entrenched wealth.[5]

Ultimately, the Professors discovered that they lacked the political weight of the business right and had no friends on the left. Togliatti, making an exception only for La Pira, branded them hypocrites. The church wanted to put a stop to further flirtation with the left. Nevertheless, it acted with restraint. The Professors were reliable allies on issues such as divorce, religious training in schools, and the defense of the concordats. Nothing restrained the business community that funded their opponents within the DC and fiercely attacked the Professors' economic theories.[6]

Nevertheless, the Dossetti group was strong enough to force De Gasperi into two major compromises. First, he invited them into the government after the DC's April 1948 triumph, appointing Fanfani minister of labor and La Pira his deputy. Second, the astute De Gasperi, seeking to reinforce his government's anti-Fascist pedigree and to keep the Gronchian left at bay, adopted a key element of the Professors' program. In 1949 parliament approved the Fanfani Plan, a program for public housing that expanded employment, created low-cost homes, and established state controls over the construction industry.[7]

The Professors viewed the Fanfani law as the first step toward both a full employment policy and a reorientation of Italian politics that placed the needs of the masses at the center of government concern. Neither the collectivist vision embodied in their approach nor their continuing efforts to "moralize" the DC sat well with De Gasperi and his collaborators or with the business community. The prime minister and the conservative majority of DC parliamentarians were ready to support a concrete program of public employment that would address key infrastructural problems and widen political patronage. They drew the line at committing the DC to either greater collectivism or to a "moralization" that would mean control by the Professors. Thus, after a brief truce, factional warfare again broke out within the DC in early 1949.[8]

La Pira stepped forward as the principal spokesman for the Professors' economics of full employment and as the lightning rod for opponents' criticisms. In November 1949 he and Fanfani resigned to protest the conservative direction of De Gasperi's economic policy. In the December 1949 essay "The Government of the Possible," he argued that through a Keynesian policy of deficit financing the De Gasperi ministry could dramatically boost employment, production, and consumption and effect an equitable redistribution of wealth. The tools were at hand in the form of Italy's large public sector economy. Four months later, in "The Expectations of the Poor," La Pira combined biblical imagery and more Keynesian economic theory to castigate Italy's government and the well-to-do social classes that it backed for failing to meet their Christian social duty.[9]

Business and its economists counterattacked. They found La Pira a particularly inviting target since he seemed to combine the odor of the sanctuary with the appearance of ingenuousness toward the Marxist left. The Dossetti group nurtured strong misgivings about the United States and its "materialist" values. The publication of La Pira's essays followed full-blown debate over Italian participation in the North Atlantic Treaty Organization (NATO) that found the Professors lined up with the Communists in opposition to the treaty and exposed the strength of anti-Americanism in their ranks. It preceded by just two months the Korean War, a conflict that finalized the division of Italian politics along pro- and anti-American lines. The Professors found themselves on the wrong side of the divide.[10]

In addition to their suspect ideas on foreign policy, the Professors were open to attack on two critical issues of domestic policy. The first was their emphasis on the needs of the working class as the matrix of public policy. The DC's majority had already condemned "classist" politics within its ranks. The church, too, had a strong objection to any public policy that exalted the interests of one class over the other.[11]

The second weakness of La Pira's economics was a subordination of the economy to noneconomic objectives. La Pira simply grafted Keynes to his biblically based political agenda. Opponents, who included De Gasperi's powerful treasury minister, Giuseppe Pella, blasted away at the simplicity in this approach to a mechanism as complex as the Italian economy. Although La Pira demonstrated a solid grasp of economics in the successive debate and, in the view of at least one sympathetic Catholic economist, had the best of the technical issues, he could never shake off the charge of shaping his economic analysis to conform to his religious objectives. The cautious De Gasperi was unlikely to embrace the economics of a holy man.[12]

In any case, by 1950 De Gasperi was thoroughly exasperated with the Professors. In January of that year he complained to Nenni that he was fed up with the "revolt of the saints" against his leadership and party discipline. A brief effort to fold the Professors into the majority collapsed. Pella demanded assurances of full support for the interests of the business community, threatening to resign if the government adopted the deficit financing projects of the DC left. The treasury minister found plenty of support within the government, the DC, and big business. The prime minister made one final effort to find a modus vivendi with the Professors, which included the passage of a new development law for the south. De Gasperi then came down firmly on the side of conservatives. Dossetti recognized the handwriting on the wall and abandoned politics for the seminary. La Pira had already decided to carry on his political crusade at a different level.[13]

Defeated, the Professors nevertheless had a permanent impact on Italian politics. The Fanfani Law and southern development fund (Cassa per il Mezzogiorno) were major steps along the path that turned the Italian state into a massive patronage machine controlled by the Christian Democrats. Dossetti and his allies provided the ideological justifications for the all-embracing Italian welfare state. They laid the basis for an eventual rapprochement between the DC and the parties of the left, starting with the Socialists. Finally, in the person of Amintore Fanfani, their heritage was direct and immediate. After abandoning the ideological "excesses" of "Dossettianism," the politically supple Professor Fanfani emerged in the early 1950s as the man who put the ideas of the left at the service of the right, fashioning the basis of the decades-long Christian Democratic hegemony in Italy.[14]

THE KING OF FLORENCE

Before it could impose its hegemony, the DC had to change its leadership. By the spring of 1951 the DC's hold on power was threatened by the lackluster performance of the De Gasperi governments. The economy was recovering, but slowly. Unemployment remained high. Land reform was limited. The PCI was exploiting worker and peasant discontent. The governing coalition was rent by deep disagreements over policy. In a January 1951 report to the DC's national council, Dossetti urged the party to expand its hold on local government as a means of "stabilizing" democracy. Interior minister Mario Scelba told the cabinet that the government could win back a number of major cities from the left if it speedily enacted the proper election law.[15]

The key to success for the Christian Democrats was a local election law that would simultaneously force and entice the smaller parties of the center and right to coalesce with the DC. In early 1951, the government adopted a reinforced proportional representation law that achieved these goals. Under its provisions, the parties ran independent slates but could sign an agreement committing themselves to govern together. The law assigned a "prize" of two-thirds of the seats in the local assembly to the party or coalition of parties that won an absolute majority (50 percent plus one) of the vote. The two-thirds of seats on the city council assigned to the winning coalition would be divided proportionally on the basis of the number of votes that each collected.[16]

The 1951 electoral law was carefully crafted to meet the needs of minor parties for an expanded role in city government and to reduce the power of the Communists in local administrations. Ultimately, however, its success depended on the DC's ability to find allies and present a slate of candidates that would appeal to voters. Above all, the party needed a prestigious candidate for mayor to head its slate. For the Florentine DC, the choice was clear: Giorgio La Pira. Giovanni Giovannoni, then a youthful leader of the DC left, recalled: "To defeat Fabiani . . . the Christian Democrats needed a man who was . . . above all a man of the left."[17]

In early 1951 the Florentine Party and Cardinal Dalla Costa made their desires known to La Pira. For La Pira, election as mayor of Florence offered the chance to build a model state on a small scale and export it to the rest of Italy. Democracy, not theocracy, was La Pira's objective, a democracy guided by the teachings of the Roman Church.

Giorgio La Pira was forty-seven years old when he first ran for mayor of Florence. Born in Pozzallo, Sicily, in 1904, he moved to Florence as a student and graduated with a degree in Roman law from the University of Florence in 1926. He immediately began teaching and by 1934 held the chair in Roman law at his alma mater. La Pira began to openly challenge the Mussolini regime in 1939. After the war he won election first to the Constituent Assembly and then, in 1948, to the first parliament of the new republic.

La Pira's political objectives were grandiose. First, he wanted to carry the

Catholic Church into an unequivocal embrace of democracy. Second, he wanted to give democratic politics a firm base in Christian doctrine. Third, he aimed to find a common area in which Marxists and democrats could live and collaborate until the eventual triumph of Christianity over Marxism. La Pira never doubted that Marxism was a mistaken doctrine but was equally insistent that most individuals who followed this philosophy did so in good faith. Areas of common interest existed and had to be exploited: peace, the well-being of the poor, expansion of the protective role of the state.[18]

Florence became the springboard for the realization of these goals. Its vocation was to be a "city on a hill": a model society that would inspire and guide humankind. La Pira's vocation was to make the practical decisions and arrangements that would equip Florence for its world role.[19] In *Le Citta Sono Vive*, La Pira explained that the city was central to people's needs and to God's plan. He outlined and prioritized his objectives: "In a city there has to be a place for everything: a place to pray (the church), a place for love (the home), a work place (the factory), a place to think (the school), and a place to heal (the hospital)."[20] A Christian city must be organized and centered around its churches, which provided divine inspiration for people's actions. Placing Christianity back at the center of politics meant first dealing effectively with the immediate needs of the poor for work, food, shelter, and dignity. "I see no benefit at all in politics unless they benefit the poor," he told one American journalist. Simultaneously, La Pira wanted to reassert the spiritual values of society: "art and beauty, . . . a country's traditional values, but above all grace and prayer."[21]

At the heart of La Pira's vision of the city was the medieval model. The city must be a community of faith, founded on the family. The role of the state was that of protector and intermediary. La Pira sought to promote corporatist models of mutual cooperation among individuals and families. He rejected Marxism because it denied freedom to the individual. He was equally hostile to free-market capitalism because it trampled on the poor in the name of individual freedom.[22]

On a practical level these views made La Pira deeply suspicious of urban planning. He would utilize the power of city government to nurture and protect the poor but limit its intervention in the other areas of the economy. In an essay in Fanfani's *Iniziativa*, the newly elected La Pira evoked the parable of the servant who failed to exploit the money entrusted to him to proclaim that his administration would look to the needs of citizens, not the requirement of a balanced budget, as its objective. Public spending would take into account first the needs of Florence's citizens—jobs, homes, assistance. Insistence on a balanced budget as the first priority of government was "cowardly, lazy," and "out of touch with reality."[23]

At the heart of his program to "spiritualize" Florence was another "medieval" event. The Council of Florence (1439) briefly brought unity to the Roman and Greek Churches. According to La Pira, Florence's global "mission" was to provide both a model for Christian response to the problems of the city and a place where diverse religious faiths and atheists could meet and work toward a peaceful reconciliation of their differences and, ultimately, produce the proper, spiritually rooted response to the various economic, social, and political problems that troubled humankind. Out of this vision would emerge the "*convegni*" (congresses). These meetings ultimately attracted participation from both Christian and non-Christian societies, including the Soviet Union and Communist China.[24]

POLITICS IN THE SPRING OF 1951

Clerical and secular conservatives tended to downplay La Pira's more radical social and political views as they joined forces to wage a fiercely anti-Communist campaign for the city election of 1951. La Pira enjoyed the full confidence and support of the ecclesiastical establishment. Cardinal Dalla Costa shared the Professors' outlook on social issues, agreed with his approach toward the Marxist left, and recognized that La Pira was fully committed to protecting the interests of the church. Dalla Costa was concerned that the anti-Communist stance adopted by the church went beyond its role in a democratic state and, while obeying guidance from the Vatican, sought to ameliorate its tendency to extremism. Recognizing La Pira's need for autonomy, Dalla Costa provided consistent, but understated, backing to him as the DC candidate and as mayor.[25]

Campaigning on the issue of Communism presented no problems for La Pira. He regarded the Communists as wrong on the philosophical level and dangerous on the practical plane. The Fabiani administration was an inviting target. Its generally positive record was obscured by the actions of the local and national PCI. The party, following its usual practice, sacrificed the interests of local administrators to its recruitment and foreign policy ("peace") initiatives. Fabiani's effort to build a record of service to the entire Florentine community was consistently undercut by the actions of his own party. As election day approached, the PCI's campaign accentuated class differences, anti-Americanism, and anticlericalism, while affirming loyalty to Stalin. PCI tactics attracted more members to its ranks but scared away many moderate voters. Fabiani angrily protested to both the local and the national leadership, without success.[26]

The outcome of spring 1951 local elections left both sides unhappy. Putting the best face on an ambiguous situation, the left's *Nuovo Corriere* headlined "Popular Forces Victorious in Many Communes." The PCI had increased its total vote. The left had done very well in the first elections for provincial governments. The capture of Florence province helped to offset the loss of the city administration. The PSI-PCI coalition managed to hold on to control of most Tuscan local governments. In Florence, Fabiani actually outpolled La Pira in total preferential votes. But Florence and many other major cities ended up in the hands of the DC and its allies. Moreover, the PCI's success at the ballot box came at the expense of its coalition partner, the Socialists, further fraying ties with the PSI.[27]

While officially welcoming its limited successes and rejoicing in victories in Florence, Milan, Genoa, and Venice, the DC's outlook was as somber as that of the PCI. It won with a rigged election law while polling 2 million fewer votes than in the 1946 local elections. The slight decline in the left's overall vote was offset by rising support for the parties of the extreme right. Christian Democracy was still weak at the grass roots and profoundly divided on economic policy. As a result it offered only the most tepid reformism to Italian voters, who were sick of the restrictions imposed by reconstruction policies and ready for more dramatic action. Anti-Communism had lost much of its edge as an electoral tool.[28]

Recognizing that the party was paralyzed between aging leaders and an increasingly isolated opposition, Fanfani mounted a bid for leadership. In late June 1951, he deserted Dossetti and, in collaboration with other younger DC party chiefs, set up a new group, "Iniziativa democratica." Fanfani championed greater government intervention in the economy, but with the dual objectives of strengthening the hand of the party and promoting economic growth in partnership with business. By strongly supporting NATO and the alliance with the United States, Fanfani made his candidacy more attractive to large constituencies within the party.[29]

GOVERNING FLORENCE

The DC clearly needed a new direction. While Fanfani proposed to provide it on the national level, La Pira was busily crafting a new politics in Florence that prefigured events in the rest of Italy. Their common past experience and interest in redirecting the DC created an odd alliance. While Fanfani marched further away from the moral basis of Dossettianism, he remained a firm believer in governmental action. La Pira, whose ties with the DC's national leadership were almost exclusively personal—he never bothered to join the party—relied on Fanfani to mediate with the power brokers and to use his party and government powers to support reform in Florence.[30]

"La Pirism" in practice was action-oriented government with little reference to political theory. La Pira used city government as a tool to effect change. He quickly outflanked the opposition on the left and his allies on the right, laying the basis for a rapprochement with the Socialists. In doing so, he moved toward an "opening to the left" that Fanfani would subsequently champion but also undercut his own four-party governing coalition. By 1956, La Pira had isolated himself and soon was forced from office. His return to power had to wait upon the slower rhythms of national political life.[31]

Following the elections, the victorious DC formed a coalition with the Liberals, Republicans, and Social Democrats, expanding its majority. Mayor La Pira introduced his program in an October 3, 1951, statement to the city council. It echoed that of Fabiani five years earlier in offering cooperation with the opposition. The left, adopting the 1946 strategy of the DC, immediately attacked the "fraudulent" electoral law that put La Pira in power. Fabiani was inaugurated president of the PCI-led province of Florence a few days after La Pira was elected mayor. He used the occasion to challenge DC control of Florence, projecting his

administration as the alternative center of local government. In subsequent statements to the city council (of which he remained a member), Fabiani attacked
La Pira's management of the budget, correctly accusing him of running up huge
deficits, and pointed to the city's housing crisis as the issue that would define the
success or failure of the new mayor.[32]

The PCI played into La Pira's hands. By embracing budgetary austerity and
ridiculing La Pira's visionary politics, the men of the left played the role of the
conservatives with self-destructive skill. In the role of fiscal watchdog, the opposition warned that La Pira could not pay for a school free milk program and
suggested that distribution be limited to poor children. The city administration
responded that all children needed milk, irrespective of class. Later, when La
Pira moved to create a city-run milk production facility, an idea that Fabiani had
championed as mayor, the left offered technical objections and invoked free
enterprise! By attempting to substitute provincial for city administration under
the banner of local autonomy, the PCI and PSI invited the national DC both
to limit their access to funding and to expand La Pira's. By defining housing as
the central issue, they handed La Pira a ready-made catalyst to justify large-scale
funding from the DC-led national government.[33]

Pira learned from Fabiani's experience to deal aggressively with a myriad of
small problems affecting the voters of Florence. On the negative side, this meant
attacking noise, air, and water pollution in the city center through traffic control,
improved sanitation, and cleanup projects. On the positive side, it meant more
athletic and cultural activities for the young, improved city gardens, and better,
cheaper milk.[34]

La Pira succeeded in winning money from Rome by mixing a kind word with
political blackmail. In thanking Finance Minister Vanoni for a grant of 3 million
lire for housing, La Pira proclaimed that he was "fighting the great Christian
battle" in Florence and asked for 1.25 million lire more. Two months later La
Pira complained to Interior Minister Mario Scelba about limits on his spending,
reminding the minister that "the bureaucracy is at the service of our social goals."
Scelba diplomatically suggested that La Pira rein in his spending demands. Florence's mayor shot back that he would either get the cash or resign, handing the
city over to the Communists. He demanded that Scelba and his colleagues in
government "keep your promises." Failure to deliver money was the sure road to
defeat in national elections. Post and Telecommunications Minister Merlin
plaintively reminded La Pira that even God took seven days to create the world,
while promising to do more.[35]

Such tactics might have backfired without La Pira's enormous moral force and
the political connections that he built during his years in Rome. Nor would the
pipeline of funding have remained open for so long had La Pira not shown skill
at using the funding both to reach his goals and to reinforce the position of the
DC in Florence. The DC patronage system (La Pira dubbed it the creation of
the "Christian face of Florence") had one of its first successful tryouts in Florence.

The mayor demonstrated that a DC willing to spend without regard to financial restraints could remain in power indefinitely.[36]

La Pira had access to money because he had a clear agenda. The city had to deal with unemployment through public works projects, build low-cost housing, drastically improve the availability of water to an expanding population, modernize its transportation system, and, to prosper, revitalize the tourist industry.[37]

In October 1951, shortly after the presentation of La Pira's first budget, an awed and worried ally, city councillor and, Liberal leader, Fossimbroni, noted that the mayor had nearly doubled Fabiani's last budget and had found the money to support his proposals. By early 1952, Florence became a vast public works project as La Pira pushed one spending bill after another through the city council. Although La Pira continued to raise money at a spectacular rate, the city was forced to increase its indebtedness. Fabiani built up a 2.5 billion lire public debt in his five years. La Pira created an additional debt of 3 billion lire in his first few months in office. As the left predicted, the inclusion of all classes in La Pira's social welfare programs drove the deficit skyward.[38]

Housing, the largest item in the city budget, provided La Pira's greatest political opportunity. A successful construction program would undercut the left's position with its main voting bloc by demonstrating that Christian Democracy was a party committed to the interests of the average citizen. While all social classes required new housing, the need was most severe among the urban working classes. Property owners, seeking a higher return on their investment, were busily filling the streets of Florence with low-income renters. In 1950, the city witnessed 437 evictions. The number rose to 799 the following year. By June 1952, a further 666 lost their homes, and 800 more cases were being processed.[39]

To confront this crisis, La Pira developed a broad program of public housing, secured financing from public and private agencies, and stopped the evictions. Viewing the housing crisis as both a practical and a moral challenge, he moved with speed and persistence. Leaning heavily on his political contacts, La Pira tapped every available source of public funding, created a program of emergency housing (the *case minime*), and secured a freeze on evictions. The first La Pira administration built 3,500 new homes.[40]

In this struggle La Pira had some of his finest moments. His deep concern for the homeless was evident. Frustrated by bureaucratic inaction and the resistance of wealthy property owners to lease unused space to the homeless, La Pira boldly seized their property and provided shelter for hundreds. He pressed the Italian army to turn over unused barracks, with limited success. Most importantly, through the *case minime* program, he was able to create enough housing to alleviate the shortage.[41]

La Pira's pump-priming of the home-building industry with public funds stimulated a boom in construction of private housing, further alleviating the crisis and expanding employment. It was not without its costs to the city. The *case minime* were controversial. Critics charged that their construction was substandard (and were proved correct), that they were inadequate to the needs of the families that inhabited them, and that their placement on the city periphery accentuated the physical isolation of the poor.[42]

La Pira's defense was that he acted in the interests of the poor, as even his harshest critics admitted. Still, as one of his severest critics, Edoardo Detti, noted, charity without planning did considerable long-term harm to the city: creating ghetto housing and encouraging substandard construction.[43]

For all the energy that he poured into resolving the housing crisis, La Pira revealed another side of his personality. He was no administrator. He tended to delegate actual responsibility for achieving his goals to others, concentrating on fund-raising from the Rome government. The result was considerable delay in start-up for the *case minime*.[44]

La Pira's shortcomings as an urban planner were shared by his primary Christian Democratic collaborators. Their policies opened the city to a decade of unplanned growth. On the national level, the party consistently backed private development, cutting back subsidies for public housing after 1951. The right wing of the Florentine DC, whose spokesperson was the city's cultural assessor, Piero Bargellini, viewed private construction as a good in itself and promoted modernization and economic growth as necessarily complementary to aesthetic values. Bargellini's *Splendida storia di Firenze* (1969) proudly defended the city's unplanned reconstruction.[45]

The left shared responsibility for unplanned growth. Having passed the outline of an urban plan in 1951, the Communists and Socialists conspicuously failed to promote or defend its basic concepts. The left, above all the PCI, centered its criticisms on two aspects of La Pira's urban policy: its costs (they suggested spending less) and the poor quality of the product. They unconvincingly attacked La Pira for doing too little. Major construction projects, whether private or public, offered employment to working-class constituents. Thus, while lamenting La Pira's performance, the PSI and PCI were not interested in stopping the building boom.[46]

Surveying Florence's postwar reconstruction, one prominent architectural historian labeled it the worst in Italy, adding that the performance of its political leaders called into question the city's "capacity for renewal." The consensus that reconstruction was at its heart a jobs creation program was so broad that the city defied stop-construction orders from a central government more concerned about historic preservation than Florence's political elite. Horrified by the piecemeal reshaping of the city by a combination of small contractors, real estate speculators, and Roman bureaucrats, Florence's leading architects, urban planners, and art historians vainly protested against widespread violations of construction codes and common sense. By 1954, while still reaping big profits in new construction on the periphery, contractors and developers were eyeing a large-scale rehabilitation of the city center.[47]

Despite some notable successes in city planning and historic preservation (pressuring the Italian army into abandoning historic buildings in the center, reclaiming the scenic Forte da Belvedere, rehabilitating city markets, and accelerating the reconstruction of Ponte alla Grazia), La Pira only gradually recognized the need for coherent urban planning. Artom, the assessor of urban planning, attempted to win the mayor's approval for stiffer resistance to unregulated construction. Opposition architects and art historians like Ragghianti and Detti kept up their efforts to educate La Pira. In 1954 La Pira took the first halting steps toward the implementation of a program for historic preservation, seeking consensus with the national government on a plan for the Por S. Maria area. The mayor began to stress the role that the "bellezza di Firenze" must play in the city's universal mission.[48]

Unfortunately, La Pira's newly found zeal for beautifying the Florentine environment did not extend to the periphery, where he continued to pursue schemes for "satellite cities" that fulfilled the dreams of real estate speculators while destroying the natural beauty, green spaces, and splendid vistas offered by the hills surrounding the city. Plans for a massive, modern, middle-class satellite city in the Sorgane area, drawn up by Florence's leading architect, Michelucci, ignited a political explosion. Sorgane became an isolated, economically unconnected, and architecturally sterile bedroom community.[49]

La Pira's management of Florence's acute water resources problem was, as he admitted, a failure. In spite of broad support and the availability of state funds, the mayor failed to push forward a plan for new dams to control the Arno and greatly increase the drinking water supply.[50]

He did somewhat better in handling the burgeoning problems of traffic and public transportation: modernizing the bus fleet, improving administration, and briefly holding out against fare increases. Under La Pira Florence became the first Italian city to completely suppress its energy-efficient tram system in favor of diesel-powered buses. The decision, made for aesthetic reasons (ridding the historic center of obstructing wires), as well as to modernize city services at the lowest possible cost, contributed to the center's worsening pollution.[51]

City government improved the quality of roads and expanded paved streets to the new housing developments on the periphery. It introduced one-way streets in an effort to speed up the flow of traffic in the city center but failed to address the serious problems posed by the massive growth of privately owned vehicles (94,000 by 1954). By removing trams and repaving the roads, the city encouraged ever more Florentines to abandon public transportation for their cars, expanding traffic jams, increasing pollution, and snarling public transportation. In 1952 *Holiday* compared the swarming traffic of city rush hours to a hoard of "cockroaches." When pressed about the issue, the assessor of traffic, Francioni, replied that the public was not concerned and asked why the government should be.[52]

Meanwhile, La Pira reaped political capital for the DC by securing government approval for the reconstruction of Ponte S. Trinita. In an October 1951 statement to the city council the new mayor took his stand: the bridge would go up *dov'era* and *com'era* (where it was and as it was). The council backed him in a bipartisan vote. The wily mayor outflanked the state bureaucracy by appealing directly to "friends" in Rome. In 1954 Rome agreed to reconstruction *com'era*. La Pira and Florentine artistic self-determination had triumphed.[53]

La Pira's first administration coincided with a sudden spurt in tourism throughout Italy. Postwar tourism was vastly different from the prewar version. The old mix of Italians and well-heeled foreigners gave way to the American middle classes. U.S. tourists were rarely deeply informed about the artistic heritage of the city, were anxious to cover as much ground as possible in the few vacation days allowed by their employers, and were looking for comfortable, well-appointed hotels that featured the latest conveniences, especially private baths. Their children formed the "Europe on Five Dollars a Day" group interested in economical accommodations and possessing enough spending power to attract the attention of merchants, artisans, and small hotel owners. As Western Europe grew prosperous, most European tourists would conform to this pattern. The era of the grand tour was over. Florence would have to fight for its share of a highly mobile tourist industry by creating a modern infrastructure of hotels, public transportation, banking, information, and mass cultural events.[54]

La Pira was the ideal mayor to relaunch Florentine tourism and turn it into a mass phenomenon. It appealed to his vision of the city as a center of civilization and his ability to raise money. The mayor used Florence's central role in the national tourist industry as leverage to extract aid from Rome for related industries. By one of those nice ironies of history, Pope Pius XII's designation of 1950 as a "Holy Year" launched postwar Florentine mass tourism. The Holy Year attracted millions of pilgrims to Rome. Many traveled to Florence to enjoy the splendors of the Renaissance. Christian tourism inspired La Pira to hold a series of conferences on issues of faith and critical foreign policy questions, designed to promote international understanding and showcase Florence as a unique cultural center. Major exhibitions on Florentine art and history appealed to the less devout.[55]

Recognizing that the Maggio Musicale and Teatro Comunale were major assets in promoting tourism, La Pira pushed the tourism vice minister, Giulio Andreotti, for money to turn Florence into a showcase of the arts. Andreotti agreed with Florence's mayor that the DC needed a cultural policy and came up with extra funding. Upon learning that the government was proposing a "special" law to assist that other treasure house of the Renaissance, Venice, La Pira immediately demanded similar treatment for Florence. He eagerly sought foreign funding for various activities, suggesting that West Germany use its economic might to buy post-Nazi respectability.[56]

La Pira's courtship of the Americans was carefully reasoned. The United States had a great affinity for small-business people entrepreneurs and was a primary export market for Florence. In addition, it was the center of both technology and the money needed to bankroll new investments. The American tourist dollar was extraordinarily attractive to a city trying to relaunch one of its principal service sector industries. The mayor assiduously courted representatives of the U.S. government.

The U.S. press and American officials in Italy were initially attracted to La Pira. They admired his hands-on leadership style and his commitment to reforms that benefited the poor. In the eyes of American journalists and government officials, La Pira's major charm was his reputation as "the Christian Conqueror of a Red City." Ambassador Clare Boothe Luce told La Pira: "We are aware in America of your own inspiring and noble work in Firenze—especially the tireless way you have fought to bring the healing spirit of Christ into the red battlefield of politics."[57] The Eisenhower administration's enthusiasm for La Pira cooled as it became aware of some of his ideas. The United States continued to assist Florentine exports while using its considerable economic leverage to oust Communists from key positions in city unions and factories.[58]

CHARTING A NEW COURSE

The year 1953 was a watershed year for the DC and for Italy. Cold War conflicts reached a boiling point in the spring as the government and the left squared off in a national election campaign. The death of Stalin and the rapid policy reversal executed by his successors appeared to open the way to a general reduction of tensions between East and West. After eight hard postwar years of painful economic reconstruction and political polarization, Western Europeans were, in the main, eager to take the new Soviet policy at face value. The United States was skeptical, viewing the "new course" as window dressing behind which the USSR would continue its pursuit of world revolution and hegemony. De Gasperi and the older generation of DC leaders shared American convictions. The prime minister was concerned about the social and economic views of the younger generation of DC leaders, which he believed dangerously collectivist. Finally, De Gasperi had to deal with an increasingly reactionary Pius XII, who threatened to provoke a split within the DC. The prime minister told Scelba that a government hard line against the Communists would prevent the Vatican from wreaking havoc on the DC.[59]

Challenged on both the right and the left, De Gasperi opted for a reform in the electoral law similar to the 1951 communal version that brought La Pira to power in order to preserve his center coalition. Simultaneously, he attempted to weaken the left and the extreme right through rigid application of "special laws" that widened police powers.[60]

De Gasperi misjudged the temper of swing voters. His hard-line anti-Communism ran into both widespread popular desire for an end to political polarization and concerns about the authoritarian methods of the government. The De Gasperi coalition was further discredited by its failure to carry out major reform or to foster wider economic prosperity. In June 1953, De Gasperi and his coalition partners failed to reach the 50 percent plus 1 vote needed to trigger automatically the "prize" of extra parliamentary seats. Although the workings of the reinforced proportional representation law left the center with a slim majority in parliament, De Gasperi was finished as leader of the DC and of the nation.

In early 1954 Amintore Fanfani took over as party secretary. He shrewdly concentrated on reshaping the DC and building a power base. Fanfani completed the reconfiguration of the DC into a party rooted in clientelism and began a gradual movement toward a more conciliatory and pragmatic relationship between government and the parties of the left that ultimately permitted the Socialists to join the majority.

Having provided a model for successful Christian Democratic patronage politics, La Pira was to take a leading role in the "opening to the left." His ties to Fanfani remained strong, based on friendship and mutual need. Fanfani could provide financial assistance and other forms of patronage to La Pira. The DC's secretary needed strong alliances with local party leaders as he tried to reshape Christian Democracy.[61]

La Pira was aware that powerful enemies within the DC's national leadership regarded him as dangerously radical. In 1952, when they pushed through a law that forced him to choose between being a parliamentary deputy and mayor of Florence, La Pira protested heatedly and then made a virtue of necessity by announcing: "Better king at Florence than number one in Rome."[62]

As La Pira steered toward a new relationship with the left, he found willing interlocutors. By mid-1952, the Florentine PCI recognized that confrontation with the La Pira government had failed. Preoccupied with "our weakness in the city of Florence," the PCI was ready to cooperate on issues of mutual interest. Florence's Cold War was ending.[63]

NOTES

1. Giulio Andreotti, *Diari, 1976–1979* (Milan, 1981), pp. 137, 145–46; Franco Zeffirelli, *Zeffirelli* (New York, 1986), p. 257.

2. Paolo Pombeni, *Il gruppo dossettiiano e la fondazione della democrazia italiana, 1938–1948* (Bologna, 1979), pp. 42, 132–43; Paolo Pombeni, *Le Croniche Sociali di Dossetti* (Florence, 1976), pp. 3–4, 10; Giuseppe Rossini ed., *Alcide De Gasperi e l'eta del centrismo* (Rome, 1990), p. 260.

3. Bruna Bocchini Camaiani, "La lezione," in Giuseppe Rossini, ed., *Democrazia Cristiana e costituente nella societa del dopoguerra* (Rome, 1980); Giorgio Galli and Paolo Fracchi, *La sinistra democristiana* (Milan, 1962), p. 325.

4. Maria Romana De Gasperi, *De Gasperi scrive* (Brescia, 1974), 1: 287–91, 303–4; Pombeni, *Croniche sociali*, pp. 58, 225; Giorgio La Pira, *Lettere a casa* (Milan, 1981), p. 179.

5. Enzo Vanoni, *La politica economica degli anni degasperiani* (Florence, 1977), 22–32, 222–23; Piero Roggi, *I cattolici e la piena occupazione* (Milan, 1983), pp. 2, 94–95; Fioretta Mazzei, *Giorgio La Pira Cose viste e ascoltate* (Florence, 1980), pp. 76–77.

6. Palmiero Togliatti, *Opere*, 5: 406; M. Glissente and L. Elia, eds., *Croniche sociali, 2* vols. (S. Giovanni Valdorno, 1962), 1: 108–9, 165; Pombeni, *Il gruppo dossetti*, pp. 13–14, 218–19.

7. Giulio Andreotti, *De Gasperi visto da vicino* (Milan, 1986), p. 142; Giorgio Galli, *Fanfani* (Milan, 1975), pp. 29, 37–38; Andrea Damiliano, ed., *Atti e documenti della DC*, 2 vols. (Rome, 1968–1969), 1: 381–82.

8. Glissenti and Elia, eds., *Croniche sociali* 2: 800–801, 906, 927–28, 921, 924–25; De Gasperi, *De Gasperi scrive*, 1: 296–303, 2: 229.

9. Giorgio La Pira, *L'attesa della povera gente* (Florence, 1997), Francesco Malgeri, *Storia della Democrazia Cristiana*, 5 vols. (Rome, 1987–1989), 2: 92–98, 265, 511; Galli and Fracchi, *La sinistra democristiana*, p. 27.

10. Glissenti and Elia, eds., *Croniche sociali*, 1: 130, 144, 310; Pombeni, *Il gruppo dossetti*, pp. 164–65; Rossini, *De Gasperi*, p. 193.

11. *Atti e document della DC*, 1: 409.

12. Roggi, *I cattolici*, pp. 78–85, 240–49, 278–88; De Gasperi, *De Gasperi scrive*, 1: 316–17.

13. Pietro Nenni, *Tempo di guerra fredda. Diari, 1943–1956* (Milan, 1981), pp. 503–4; De Gasperi, *De Gasperi scrive*, 1: 220–23, 227–29, 403–4; 2: 275–84, 296; Alcide De Gasperi, *Lettere al presidente* (Milan, 1964), pp. 208–10; Roggi, *I cattolici*, pp. 27–28, 168–77.

14. Galli, *Fanfani*, pp. 46–47; Galli and Fracchi, *La sinistra demo cristiana*, pp. 118–19.

15. *Atti e documenti della DC*, 1: 500–501; Minutes, March 29, 1951, AC/S, Presidenza del consiglio, verbali, b 35; Minutes, November 24, 1950, APC, Firenze 1950, 0326/2236–45.

16. *Atti e documenti della DC*, 1: 503; De Gasperi, *De Gasperi scrive*, 2: 236–38; Norman Kogan, *The Government of Italy* (New York, 1962), p. 151.

17. Giovannoni interview, Florence, May 25, 1993.

18. Bruna Bocchini Camaiani, "L'apporto di La Pira" in Fondazione La Pira, *La Pira Oggi* (Florence, 1983), pp. 141–61. A good introduction to La Pira is his *Premesse della politica e architettura di uno stato democratico* (Florence, 1978).

19. Mazzei, *Giorgio La Pira, Cose*, pp. 74–91; Amintore Fanfani, *Giorgio La Pira* (Milan, 1978), p. 73; Bruna Bocchini Camaiani, "La chiesa di Firenze," in A. Riccardi, ed., *Le chiese del Pio XII* (Rome, 1986), p. 290.

20. Giorgio La Pira, *Le citta sono vive* (Brescia, 1978), p. 37.

21. "The Mayor of Florence," *Commonweal*, May 1, 1953.

22. Giorgio La Pira, *Premesse della politica e architettura di uno stato democratico* (Florence, 1978), pp. v–xvi; Fiorillo Lilia, "I fondamenti teorici dell'impegno politico di Giorgio La Pira (1926–1945)," in Giovanni Invito, ed., *Novecento minore* (Lecce, 1977), pp. 182–83; Giorgio La Pira, *La casa comune* (Florence, 1979), pp. 73, 76, 82–83, 89, 95, 104–5.

23. Giovanni Galloni, ed., *Antologia di Iniziativa* (Rome, 1973), pp. 70–71.

24. Mazzei, *Giorgio La Pira, Cose*, 91; La Pira, *La citta*, p. 70.

25. Bruna Bocchini Camaiani, "La chiesa di Firenze"; Mazzei, *Giorgio La Pira, Cose*, pp. 29, 35; Bruna Bocchini Camaiani, "Ricostruzione concordato e processi di secolarizzazione," in Margiotta Broglio, ed., *Chiesa e concordato*, 2 vols. (Bologna, 1983), 2: 131, 244–45, 329.

26. De Gasperi, *De Gasperi scrive*, 1: 312–313; Giorgio La Pira, *Lettere alle claustrale* (Milan, 1978), pp. 54–55; Minutes, August 1, 1950, ACP, Florence Federation, 1950, 0326/2159–72; Minutes, October 18, 1950, ibid., 0326/2178-89; Fabiani letter, May 21, 1951, ACF, Gabinetto del Sindaco, Atti 1101–1300.

27. *Nuovo Corriere*, June 13, 1951; Report on June election, APC, f. Firenze 1951, part 2, 0337/1760.

28. Minutes, May 30, 1951, AC/S, Consiglio dei Ministri, verbali, b 35; *Atti e documenti della DC*, 1: 512; De Gasperi, *De Gasperi scrive*, 1: 233, 251–52.

29. Malgeri, *Storia*, 2: 124–25, 138, 555; Roggi, *I cattolici*, p. 136.

30. Mazzei, *Giorgio La Pira*, pp. 74–75; Gianni Baget Bozzo, *L'elefante e la ballena* (Bologna, 1979), pp. 77–79.

31. Fioretta Mazzei interview, Florence, May 19, 1993.

32. ACC 1951, pp. 434–37, 459–63, 483–96.

33. ACC 1952, 1: 68–91, 178–79; ACC 1954, 1: 88–99; La Pira to De Gasperi, November 10, 1951; ALP, b 64, Comune di Firenze; Giuseppe Pozzana, *Tra pubblico e privato* (Florence, 1985), p. 46.

34. Del Giudice to La Pira, July 12, 1951, ASF, Gabinetto del sindaco, Atti 1601–1800; La Pira to Guintoli, July 17, 1951, ibid.; La Pira to Scelba, c. September 20, 1951, ALP, b 64, Comune di Firenze 1951; Indecipherable to La Pira, October 23, 1951, ibid.; ACC 1952, 1: 25–42.

35. La Pira to Vanoni, September 12, 1951, ALP, b 64, Comune di Firenze 1951; La Pira to Scelba, November 16, 1951, ibid.; Scelba to La Pira, November 22, 1951, ibid.; La Pira to Scelba, November 24, 1951, ibid.; Merlin to La Pira, December 31, 1953, ALP, Comune di Firenze, Subject file, b 68, Case minime; Campilli to La Pira, January 21, 1952, AC/S, Carteggio Campilli, b 1, f 103.

36. La Pira to Scelba, n.d. (but c. September 20, 1951), ALP, b 64, Comune di Firenze 1951.

37. La Pira to Aldisio, January 8, 1952; ALP, b 64, Comune di Firenze 1952; La Pira to Tucci, October 8, 1951, ibid., b 69, cantieri; Cenni su un piano di assorbimento della disoccupazione, n.d. [late 1951], ibid., b 64, Comune di Firenze 1951; La Pira to Romani, September 20, 1951, ibid.

38. ACC 1951, p. 471; ACC 1952, 1: 424–75, 639–51, 717.

39. Alex Fubini, *Urbanistica in Italia* (Milan, 1979), p. 198; La Pira to Gargiulo, June 5, 1952, ALP, Comune di Firenze, Subject File, b. 68, Case minime.

40. Mazzei, *Giorgio La Pira, cose*, p. 102; La Pira to Guala, July 8, 1953, ALP, Comune di Firenze, Subject File, b 68, f. Case mimime; ·Ministry of Public Instruction to La Pira, April 15, 1953, ibid.

41. La Pira to Prefect, [February 1952], ALP, Comune di Firenze, Subject Files, b 68, f case mimime; La Pira to Zoli, July 8, 1952, ibid.; Decrees, January 12, February 21, 1953, ibid.; Military Commander, Florence to La Pira, June 13, 1953, ibid.

42. Gargiulo to Minister of Industry and Commerce, April 18, 1952, ASdiF, Prefettura di Firenze, affari ordinari, 1952, f. 73; *Firenze, questione urbanistica*, pp. 107–11, 156–59.

43. Phillipe Duboy, ed. *Edoardo Detti, 1913–1984: architetto e urbanista* (Milan, 1993), pp. 14–16; Edoardo Detti, with Tommaso Detti, *Florence That Was* (Florence, 1970), p. 126.

44. Fanfani to La Pira, November 13, 1952, ALP, Comune di Firenze, Subject File, b 68, Case minime; La Pira to Fanfani, ibid.

45. Corrado Giustiniani, *La casa promessa* (Turin, 1981), pp. 52–53, 59–60, 78–79; Piero Bargellini, *La splendida storia di Firenze* (Florence, 1969), 4: 242.

46. ACC 19852, 1: 539–43; *Unita*, January 25, 1952; *Toscana nuova*, February 22, 1953; Minutes of meeting of Federation Committee, October 2, 1952, APC, f. Firenze 1952, 0346/0382.

47. Giovanni Fanelli, *Firenze* (Bari, 1980), p. 236; Superintendent to Ministry of Public Instruction, June 16, 1952, AC/S, MPI, AA BB AA, Div II, 1945–55, b 46; Report, 1954, ibid., Ufficio Conservazione Monumenti, 1953–1959, b 74; Firenze Palazzi. A. Boggiano, ed., *Firenze: Questione urbanistica*, pp. 112–19.

48. La Pira to Taviani, August 29, 1953, ALP, b 64, Comune di Firenze 1953; Valle

to La Pira, September 9, 1953, ibid.; Piero Baldesi, *Un 'esperienza liberale* (Livorno, 1985), pp. 104–5; ACC 1953, 1: 235–37; ACC 1954, 1: 75–76; Mariella Zoppi, *Firenze e l'urbanistica* (Rome, 1982), pp. 46–49.

49. Zoppi, *Firenze*, pp. 59–64; Detti, *Florence*, pp. 125–26.

50. Davis Ottati, *L'Acquedotto di Firenze dal 1860 ad oggi* (Florence, 1983), pp. 235–39; Report, July 25, 1952, ALP, b 64, Comune di Firenze 1952; La Pira to Aldisio, [July 1952], ibid.; *La Nazione*, July 11, 18, 1952.

51. La Pira to Villani, July 5, 1952, ALP, b 64, Comune di Firenze 1952; Guinti to La Pira, October 1, 1952, ALP, Comune di Firenze, Subject File, b 68, ATAF; Reports, January 28, February 20, 1952, ibid.; Cefaretti and Malaspina, *1865–1985: Centoventi anni di Trasporti pubblici a Firenze* (Cortona, 1987), pp. 300–304, 311–12.

52. Centro Studi Pistelli, *Firenze uno due* (Florence, 1967), pp. 34–35; Cefaretti and Malaspina, *Trasporti*, p. 311; *Holiday*, October 1952; ACC 1952, 1: 570.

53. ACC 1951, pp. 513–15; ACC 1952, 1: 63–68, 188–89; La Pira to Aldisio, March 3, 1952, ALP. b 64, Comune di Firenze 1952.

54. *Turismo a Firenze*, pp. 16–17; Paolo Paoletti and Paola Torrini, *Firenze anni '50* (Florence, 1991), 1: 335; Vannini and Pareti to La Pira, December 4, 1952, ALP, b 64, Comune di Firenze 1952; ACC 1953, 1: 379–82.

55. Azienda autonoma del Turismo di Firenze, *Tourismo a Firenze* (Florence, 1972), p. 184; Zoppi, *Firenze*, p. 39; La Pira to Malvestiti, October 1, 1952, ALP, Comune di Firenze, Subject Files, b 68, ATAF; La Pira to Pella, September 4, 1953, ibid., b 64, Comune di Firenze 1953.

56. Guido Gonella, *Cinque anni al Ministero della pubblica istruzione*, 3 vols. (Rome, 1982), 3: 13–14; Leonardo Pinzauti, *Il maggio Musicale Fiorentino dalla prima alla trentesima edizione* (Florence, 1967), p. 127; La Pira to Andreotti, July 3, 1952, ALP b 64, Comune di Firenze 1952; Andreotti to La Pira, August 6, 1952, ibid.; La Pira to Piccioni, July 8, 1952, ALP, Subject File, b 69, f. leggi speciale.

57. *Saturday Evening Post*, November 15, 1952; *Commonweal*, May 1, 1953; *New Republic*, July 6, 1953; Luce to La Pira, February 25, 1953, LC, Luce Papers, Ambassadorial File, 1953 Lap-Laz.

58. Reed to Department of State, October 23, 1951, NA, RG 84, Florence Post, 510.23 Trade Complaints; Embassy in Italy to the Department of State, May 19, 1952, ibid., 510.21; ACC 1952, 1: 721–31.

59. De Gasperi, *De Gasperi scrive*, 1: 114–16, 149–53, 209–10.

60. Giancarlo Scarpari, *Democrazia cristiana e le leggi eccezionale* (Milan, 1977), pp. 58–59; De Gasperi, *De Gasperi scrive*, 1: 195–99, 210–11; 2: 60–65.

61. Galli, *Fanfani*, pp. 22–23, 29, 42–46; Piero Ottone, *Fanfani* (Milan, 1966), pp. 80–81; Malgeri, *Storia*, 2: 555.

62. Ugo De Siervo, Gianni, Giovannoni, and Giorgio Giovannoni, eds., *Giorgio La Pira sindaco*, 3 vols. (Florence, 1988–1989), 1: 197–98; Mazzei, *Giorgio La Pira, cose*, 92.

63. Report, July 1952, APC, Firenze 1952, 0348/0280–88; Undated report, ibid., 0340/0249–69; Minutes October 27, 1952, ibid., 0364/0433; Minutes July 7, 1953, APC, Firenze 1953, 0405/0764–87.

Chapter 5

Building a City on the Hill?
1954–1957

A city on the hill, like an ancient lighthouse of grace and beauty for the entire human family . . . Florence.

La Pira, June 1959

I will not leave the weaker part of the city without a defense: [the victims of] factory closings, firings, and evictions will find in me a dike that can not be easily broken. . . . All real politics is based on this: defending the bread and home of the majority of the Italian people. . . . Bread (and therefore work) is sacred; the home is sacred: no one can touch the one or the other with impunity! This is not Marxism: it's the gospel.

La Pira to Fanfani, 1955

Giorgio La Pira needed a miracle. Rallying support among allies in the church and the DC, he stymied efforts by the owners of Pignone to break up a months long strike and factory occupation. Florence's mayor, however, could not convince a stubborn management to rescind orders laying off hundreds of workers or to agree to resume production. In the summer of 1954 the company was ready to shut down Pignone for good. Then the mayor had an inspiration. He called the most influential state sector manager and DC power broker, Enrico Mattei. La Pira's message was brief and direct: "Buy Pignone." Recovering from his initial surprise, the National Oil Agency's (ENI) chairman patiently explained that purchase of the company was a bad investment. Nevertheless, La Pira responded, ENI would buy the company: the Holy Spirit had appeared to him in a dream the previous night, assuring him that Mattei would act. "Then the Holy Spirit has made a mistake," Mattei responded dryly and hung up.[1]

Within a week Mattei bought the company. ENI's chairman had created an efficient and profitable state sector. To protect and expand his power base, Mattei set up links with a DC left whose corporatist outlook included the protection and expansion of the state's role in the economy. In supporting La Pira, he took a calculated economic and political risk in order to shift the axis of Italian politics leftward. Setting strict terms that included layoffs, Mattei provided the infusion of cash and the linkages to the international economy that Pignone needed. La Pira's miracle owed as much to calculation as to divine intervention, but the mayor had won another round against conservative foes inside and outside his coalition who found his politics increasingly radical and threatening to their interests.

A WIDER VISION

Giorgio La Pira's view of his own role and that of Florence evolved during his first term as mayor. In the early days of his administration, the effort to feed and house the poor meant attention to concrete economic needs. As early as 1952, however, La Pira was looking beyond the city's immediate requirements and developing a more inclusive vision of Florence's role in Italy and in the world. Florence, he wrote Fanfani, had to serve as a center both of culture and of an effort to unite the peoples of the world. For La Pira, these two roles were not exclusive but rather mutually supportive. At the center of this vision were the "*convegni*" (congresses), which La Pira defined as "meetings of peace and Christian civilization, inseminating the world with theological and historical hope for peace."[2] Meetings on East-West relations, the future of the Mediterranean, and the problems of Latin America illustrated the mayor's ability to grapple with the real political and economic issues of the Cold War era from a different perspective. In seeking to make Florence a center for international cooperation, La Pira developed a more integrated view of the city. While never abandoning the idea that he must serve and protect the interests of the poor, La Pira increasingly focused on making Florence a city where all social classes and all peoples could find inspiration. Practical improvements, such as new housing, better roads, more water, streetlights, public parks, artistic restoration, sports, summer activities for the young, and improved public transportation services, were part of a mosaic that would enable Florence, "the pearl of the world," to carry out its wider mission for all humankind.[3]

Culture in its broadest sense moved to the center of La Pira's preoccupations during his first term as mayor. He was aware of the declining importance of Florence in Italy's contemporary arts and sought to revive the city's major cultural institutions: book publishing, its orchestra, the visual arts, architecture, and artisan industries. Ultimately, it dawned on the mayor that a city plan would enable him to carry forward all of these projects. The conversion was slow, but it proved an essential element in the creation of a new governing coalition for Florence.[4]

Tourism and culture moved from distinctly secondary to primary positions as the mayor recognized their value in both creating wealth and providing the proper environment for the citizens. La Pira won cooperation from DC-dominated governments to carry out major exhibitions, reclaim areas like the Forte da Belvedere, and bring to completion building projects like Ponte alla Grazia and Ponte S. Trinita. In areas of its specific competence, the city dealt with small, but annoying, problems like controlling tour guides and interpreters. In one of their more memorable sessions, red-faced city fathers tackled a lack of rest room facilities for women that had produced tragiccomic consequences for female tourists.[5]

Florence's revived cultural program got rave reviews in middle America but faced a considerably harsher judgment closer to home. The PCI charged La Pira with catering specifically to the despised Americans and their fellow Italian cultural lowbrows at the expense of true (high) culture and failing to spend on the infrastructures needed to support tourism and gloomily prophesied that the city would lose the tourist lire to rivals such as Rome.[6]

La Pira's hair shirt was the jewel of Florentine high culture, the Teatro Comunale with its supporting orchestra and its spring arts festival, the Maggio Musicale. Upkeep and repairs on the theater steadily drained the cultural budget and required major subvention from Rome. La Pira managed to increase state contributions considerably, but Florence remained a distant fourth when the government allocated its funds. Parise Votto, the Teatro's Communist holdover director, outlined the problem in an April 1954 memorandum to the mayor: in spite of La Pira's success in doubling the size of the state assistance and increasing local contributions by 90 percent the cultural program lost money. Poor administration and bad performance choices damaged city finances. During the 1954 Maggio festival, a production of the opera *Agnese Hohenstauffen*, attracted fifty paying customers. The 1954 concert and opera season (including the Maggio) cost 427 million lire to mount. Gross receipts amounted to 70 million.[7]

A NEW GENERATION

After Fanfani captured the Christian Democratic secretaryship, factions on the party's left and the right tried to block his efforts to reorganize the DC. In the subsequent jockeying for power, the enemies of one day became the allies of another. Fanfani built a massive and effective patronage system; he never succeeded in giving the DC a disciplined organization like that possessed by its Communist rival. His attempt to lay a basis for an alliance with the Socialists alarmed more conservative Christian Democrats.[8]

Opposition to Fanfani within the DC right coalesced quickly around a group of "notables," senior De Gasperi lieutenants who favored a continuation of conservative economic policies and hard-line anti-Marxist politics. On the left, Giovanni Gronchi emerged as Fanfani's principal opponent. In 1955 anti-Fanfani forces of the left and the right coalesced in support of Gronchi's successful bid for the presidency of the republic, placing a major roadblock in Fanfani's path. Throughout the mid-1950s the DC's secretary brought important parts of a badly

divided DC left into his camp by a combination of policy concessions and patronage.

The coalition that supported Fanfani was as diverse as the opposition. It included De Gasperi, who, in the last year of his life, favored mixing more radical
economic ideas with the DC's traditional anti-Communism. Fanfani built alliances with Paolo Bonomi, head of the powerful Christian Democratic small farmers organization (Coldiretti), with oil magnet Enrico Mattei and, with La Pira's
help, added the DC's Tuscan left to his existing power base in the south of the
region. He also found friends in the Sicilian DC, including the Mafia. Taking
advantage of his control of the major state-owned companies, Fanfani ladled out
jobs and contracts to backers, consolidating their loyalty, and accelerated the
passage to a DC-run welfare state.[9]

La Pira remained attached to Fanfani, who delivered funding for the mayor's
projects, shared, in a carefully moderated way, La Pira's insistence on programs
that would eliminate poverty, and was ready to use the power of the DC's patronage machine to co-opt the PSI. La Pira played a key role in neutralizing a
new challenge from the left to Fanfani. In the early 1950s a "third" generation
of Christian Democratic leaders emerged and, in the wake of the DC's 1953
election setback, made a strong bid for leadership roles inside the party. Picking
up many of the rallying cries of the "Professors," these young men demanded that
the DC break its ties with the nation's conservative economic elite and, shifting
its axis to the left, become a truly democratic mass party. Christian Democracy's
natural partner, third-generation leaders argued, was the Italian Socialist Party,
which shared common values of political and social democracy. At the 1954 DC
national congress at Naples, Fanfani emerged as undisputed leader of the DC's
majority by moving rightward and drove the third generation into the arms of
Gronchi. They joined a new faction, the Base, that enjoyed the financial backing
of Mattei, securing dominating positions within it.[10]

The Base was strong in a number of northern areas, especially in Tuscany and
Florence. Nicola Pistelli, a recent University of Florence law graduate, was the
outstanding Florentine leader of the movement. As a student activist, he had
edited *San Marco*, a publication that carried on an active dialogue with the
Marxist left. While insisting that the DC retain its characteristics of a multiclass
party and bulwark against Communism, Pistelli argued that Catholic social doctrine was at root anticapitalist and that the DC could create areas of mutual
cooperation with the left, even as it rejected the philosophical and moral outlook
of Marxism.[11]

Cooperation between La Pira and Pistelli was natural. In 1955 the older leaders
of the Tuscan DC aided Pistelli and his youthful associates in the takeover of
the provincial Florentine Federation. La Pira effected a truce between his ally
Fanfani and the Tuscan Base.[12]

La Pira needed the backing from both. He faced increasing hostility from both
secular and Catholic conservatives. By supporting various left-wing currents
within the DC and by opening to the Marxist left, however cautiously, the mayor

of Florence struck a nerve at the Vatican. On the religious level, the curia was concerned with the growth of innovative Catholic movements, such as one in La Pira's satellite city of Isolotto, that challenged the church's traditional administrative and disciplinary structure. On the political level, Pope Pius XII was alarmed at the growth of Catholic–Communist dialogue in Florence. In 1953, he publicly took La Pira to task for developing a "new social theory" that the pontiff feared created confusion among Catholics about the dangers of Marxism. Two years later, *La civilta cattolica*, the Jesuit review that frequently served as the Vatican's spokesman, blasted La Pira's *convegni* for undermining the basis of Italian security, its ties with the United States.[13]

Only Cardinal Dalla Costa's continued backing protected La Pira and the various Catholic left projects that he encouraged from a more severe censure. Dalla Costa's enthusiastic support of the *convegni*, in particular, proved essential. However, the primate of Florence was aging and in 1954 requested and received an adjutant, Cardinal Ermenegildo Florit, a bishop of considerably more conservative political and social views, to help him administer the diocese. La Pira's political base in the Florentine church weakened as Florit expanded his day-to-day control of the diocese.[14]

PIGNONE

While fending off conservative critics, La Pira confronted the challenge that redefined his administration. Pignone, one of the city's major industrial employers, had a long tradition of quality production and major labor unrest. Bombed and badly damaged during the war, the company, its plant, and its workforce passed from CTLN control to ownership by the textile manufacturer SNIA-Viscosa in 1946. The new owners determined to modernize plant and at the same time to reduce a labor force that had grown to over 2,000 during the war-induced production boom. This decision put SNIA-Viscosa on a political collision course with the left. The common corporatist outlook of the Catholic left and Marxists made full employment the keystone of national reconstruction. The left briefly succeeded in enforcing a ban of firings in the months immediately after the war. By 1946, De Gasperi had lifted the freeze. Striving for competitive advantage, employers throughout Italy reduced their labor force. Communist-dominated unions resisted, and in the polarized politics of postwar Italy the issue of employers' right to reduce their workforce became intertwined with the right's growing campaign to destroy the political power of the Communist-Socialist alliance. For companies like Pignone reduction of the workforce was both good economics and effective political action.[15]

Following the DC's decisive triumph in the 1948 elections, Pignone management fired 150 additional workers in economy moves. Continuing consolidation of the workforce sparked an eighty-three-day strike in 1950. After government intervention, another 158 employees lost their jobs in a settlement made on company terms. Labor–management relations remained tense. SNIA-Viscosa was determined not simply to rationalize its operations but to break the Communist-dominated union. It sent an intransigent ex-Fascist to manage its Florence operation with instructions to root out Communist activists. In 1953 Pignone announced that it would fire fifty senior employees and lay off an additional 300. The workers reacted by occupying the factory. La Pira intervened and elevated this local crisis into a defining event in national politics.

La Pira's concern with issues of employment was well known. Until 1953 he relied on increased public spending to create jobs. Avoiding direct intervention in local labor-management disputes, La Pira cited the need for negotiation and suggested that the best place to work out these issues was at the national level through the action of the Italian government.[16]

Pignone's February 1953 layoff announcement came at a particularly bad moment for the local economy. La Pira was taking emergency steps to deal with rising homelessness. In spite of its state contracts, the Galileo optics factory had announced that it would fire 800 employees. La Pira caustically inquired if De Gasperi normally prepared for national elections by increasing unemployment and demanded government action to head off firings at both plants. La Pira called on allies inside the De Gasperi ministry for help, warning that Florence would vote for the left in national elections. De Gasperi, under pressure from a coalition of conservative interests, including business and church, refused to intervene.[17]

The DC's defeat in the June 1953 parliamentary elections opened the way for the party's left to rally to La Pira and turn Pignone into an issue of national significance. At La Pira's urging, interior minister Fanfani seized the passport of SNIA owner Franco Marinotti and, utilizing information supplied by La Pira, implicated Marinotti in a major scandal that simultaneously brought down the minister's party rival Attilio Piccioni.[18]

Harassment failed to bring Marinotti to his knees. Big business rallied in support of SNIA-Viscosa while the left lacked the leverage to force concessions from a management that had dug in its heels. In late November 1953, minister of industry and commerce Piero Malvestiti wrote DC party president De Gasperi that the difficulties in forging a compromise were a direct result of "La Pira's actions," adding: "Who would be willing to open a plant in Florence with this type of mayor [in power]? All producers have concluded it's a city to be avoided." As if to drive home businesses' resistance to La Pira, the ceramics maker Richard-Ginori, another pillar of the Tuscan economy, announced in January 1954 that it would close its Florence plant.[19]

The deadlock continued another six months before La Pira managed to prompt "divine" intervention. A Mattei-brokered compromise ensured that the company, renamed Nuovo Pignone to stress its break with its antilabor past, would continue to operate but at the cost of layoffs. The subsequent expansion of the Italian economy and Mattei's clever exploitation of Nuovo Pignone's skilled labor force enabled most redundant employees to find employment as independent subcontractors. Mattei reinforced his public image as the friend of the little man by breaking with his fellow captains of industry. He improved the parent company's international position by concocting a barter scheme involving the trade of Nuovo Pignone's finished goods for Soviet oil. On both internal and international planes Italy's politics had been nudged leftward.[20]

La Pira had a major victory and a powerful ally in Mattei and, to the satisfaction of both the Catholic and the Marxist left, made a significant dent in the concept of private property. Moreover, he had attracted the support of the Socialists while isolating the Communists. In May 1954, the Socialist contingent on the city council announced its full backing for the mayor's Pignone actions. A few weeks later Nenni met privately with "the point man of the Catholic left." While wary of dealing with "a 'saint' who does not disdain the temporal," Nenni was drawn to La Pira's plan for "an encounter of Socialism and the Church that would break political confines," creating repercussions "from Rome to Moscow."[21]

The PCI was left out. It gave La Pira's efforts short shrift. At the 8th Federation Congress the following spring, keynote speaker and PCI vice secretary Luigi Longo told delegates that while La Pira had done the right thing, he failed to understand the national and class context of the Pignone battle. Mocking La Pira's "medieval" economic theory, Longo predicted that the mayor would be reined in by the antiworker majority that elected him and would carry out their reactionary politics. The Communists lost on two fronts. A July 1954 Florentine Federation report to PCI headquarters admitted that the Pignone compromise had pleased all sides and was supported by labor unions that, in spite of strong PCI membership, simply did not listen to the party. PCI conduct reconfirmed the Base's assertion that the party was an unsuitable partner for reformists.[22]

La Pira's triumph carried certain costs for the mayor as well. Italian conservatives refused or failed to recognize how skillfully La Pira had isolated the PCI. They found confirmation of their long-simmering fear that the mayor was a Communist sympathizer. Pignone was the critical step in the unraveling of Florence's governing coalition.[23]

Moreover, the Pignone deal affected national politics negatively. As historian Silvio Linaro pointed out, the Pignone crisis provided a model for state intervention. In the name of controlling the excesses of private industry, the national government increased party patronage. Over the long term, expanded state control of the economy, with its concomitant of maintaining labor-intensive but inefficient industries in operation, undercut Italian competitiveness in critical industrial sectors while inflating the budget deficit.[24]

BUILDING THE CITY ON THE HILL?

Emboldened by success, by the prospects of a new social coalition, and by a sense of duty to the city's poor, La Pira plunged forward with further reforms. The mayor saw the city's future threatened by challenges to the basic element of social organization, the family. Unemployment, housing shortages, and a continuing lack of basic services all damaged family cohesion. La Pira wanted to respond with an aggressive and extensive program of public spending. Introducing the 1955 budget to the city council, the mayor did not mince words. Florence was going into debt to meet these needs and its other critical requirements: beauty, culture, and its dignity as a city.[25]

At the center of La Pira's plan was the passage by parliament of a "special law" for Florence. The mayor had been lobbying both the DC and the government for a law since early 1953. In July 1954 the city council, with the PCI in support, passed a resolution outlining a six-year, 30 billion lire project that included large investments in improved water supply, education, sanitation, urban renewal, and historic preservation. However, the December 1954 bill introduced by DC parliamentary deputies authorized spending at limits far below what was required to realize La Pira's ambitious agenda. The mayor and his allies would have to find another way to build a new Florence. Parliament subsequently defeated special legislation for Florence, a clear sign of La Pira's declining influence within the national DC.[26]

While waiting for parliamentary action, La Pira guarded the gains already made in a manner certain to outrage propertied interests. In November 1954, he intervened to win a settlement of a threatened gas strike, pointing to potential damage to the local economy. In February 1955, citing the threat to the city economy and provisions of the Italian constitution, he ordered the requisition of the Fondiaria *officina* (factory) and handed over management to a cooperative composed of its workers, fixing the monthly repayment to be made to its "former" owners at 300,000 lire per month.[27]

La Pira was on a collision course with local business, the conservative wing of his coalition, and the national government. The mayor, as always, stood in an exposed position. For all his rhetorical flights, La Pira was a reformer, not a revolutionary. He proposed to destroy the worst excess of capitalism, not replace it with socialism. Large elements of the secular left viewed him with suspicion, especially the influential intellectual elite that was contemptuous of the theological underpinnings of his program. At the same time, his more radical social prescriptions, above all, his desire to restrict the rights of private property, alienated conservatives who, having backed the mayor to defeat the left, saw fewer reasons to support him once they had secured this objective.[28]

A decade after its liberation, Florence was a vastly changed city. Thanks to the efforts of Fabiani and La Pira, the city's reconstruction phase was nearly completed in a physical, economic, and psychological sense. The local economy was growing rapidly. Certain sectors led the way: ceramics, transportation, and tourism. Others were undergoing painful transitions as a result of national and international competitiveness, particularly larger, highly skilled sectors such as optical (Galileo) and mechanical (Pignone) industries, with accompanying job losses. Agriculture, too, was shedding unnecessary labor. The landless unemployed flooded Italy's cities, including Florence. Nevertheless, the outlook was good, as a vibrant commercial sector absorbed more unskilled and semiskilled labor while personal consumption mushroomed. Rising incomes, in turn, boosted the entertainment sector, and Florence enjoyed a boom in sales of sports and movie tickets, televisions, and, most significantly, automobiles.[29]

Along with prosperity came social and political conservatism. Fewer Italians were ready to engage in major experimentation. Treasury minister Ezio Vanoni, La Pira's longtime ally, put forward his proposal for a five-year economic plan in 1953, arguing that democracy was best served by government planning that achieved a full employment economy. Vanoni's proposal met with determined resistance. Conservatives loudly criticized planning as a threat to the market economy. In Florence, a growing middle class of small entrepreneurs was particularly upset by La Pira's frequent recourse to indirect taxation, in the form of service fees, as a drag on economic growth. They claimed that the mayor had saddled Florence with the highest per capita taxation rate in Italy. The mayor needed new allies if he were to continue to promote the interests of the city's poorer classes. This meant that the Socialists would have to be brought into government and that the parties of the right would leave the coalition.[30]

Regrettably, the Socialists of Florence were a most unappealing potential partner. After nearly a decade as the junior partner of the PCI, the PSI on both the local and national level was badly divided, and bankrupt and still lacked a program that would give it a separate political identity. Nenni, who belatedly recognized the need for a new direction, was just beginning to feel his way toward an alliance with the center. Slowed by remarkably durable ideological blinders, he fumbled about in search of contacts. In-mid 1953 he was counting on Communist support for Socialist participation in a government. Initially, he believed that the PSI could join the DC in governing the country without paying the price of fundamental changes in its foreign and domestic policy outlook. In early 1955, Nenni helped secure the election of Gronchi, the most outspoken supporter of an opening to the Socialists, but soon discovered that this tactical victory had divided the Christian Democrats and pushed back indefinitely his strategic aim of PSI membership in a government. Seeking to smooth the way to an alliance, the Socialist leader journeyed to Moscow to request Soviet backing, seemingly innocent of the effect that this action would provoke within the DC and with their American allies.[31]

Florence's PSI was in shambles. The local party's financial condition had gone from bad to worse in the early 1950s. At the beginning of 1953 the Florence Federation was 3 million lire in debt. The national party intervened, replacing local federation secretary Luigi Mariotti with the youthful Alfio Dini. The new leader had trouble putting together an electoral slate and equal difficulty raising money for the campaign. The following year the Florentine Federation was begging for special contributions just to keep operating. In an October 1955 confidential analysis of the local party, veteran Socialist leader Foscolo Lombardi confessed that the cash-strapped Florentine PSI lacked leadership, activists, and influence, was out of contact with the national party, and was incapable of mounting an effective public relations effort.[32]

Worse was to come. In January 1956, the party discovered that federation secretary Dini, with the apparent knowledge of other key Florentine Socialists, had skimmed over 300,000 lire from party funds. The press and opposition had a field day with the case. Ultimately, the national party had to intervene to replace Dini after local Socialists, displaying Mafia-like *omerta*, refused to move against him. Subsequent inquiries into federation finances uncovered a debt more than triple that reported by Dini, about 21 million lire.[33]

Extraordinary efforts by national headquarters resuscitated the Florentine operation, but the local PSI still lacked leadership. Its best hope for survival lay in a coalition with the small, but capable, group of Socialist intellectuals, survivors of the Action Party (PdA), whose latest effort to build a political movement, Unita Popolare (UP), predictably lacked a mass base. If the PSI was a ship without a captain, Calamandrei, Tristano Codignola, Detti, Enriquez Agnoletti, and Alberto Albertoni were officers without a crew. Both PSI and UP shared the belief that the 1953 national elections had opened the possibility of breaking the DC's stranglehold on government. Each hoped to create an autonomous and democratic political force to the left of center.[34]

THE COALITION COLLAPSES

Increasingly, La Pira's programs for Florence relied on the votes of the PCI and PSI for passage. The left parties began to demand what one of their spokesmen described as "de-escalation" of the confrontation between the city government and opposition.[35] The Italian Liberal Party (PLI) meanwhile moved into the ranks of the opposition. Eugenio Artom, the Liberals' most commanding public personality, was appalled by La Pira's inability to carry forward a coherent program for city development. He resigned as assessor of urban planning to protest the mayor's continued support for the concept of satellite cities over a coherent citywide plan. La Pira concluded negotiations with the national government for the completion of his pet project, the satellite city of Isolotto, without the participation of either his urban planning assessor or chief architect.[36]

Political calculation played an equal role in the Liberals' defection. An anti-communist identity was central to the PLI's position in the national government. Liberals generally were sincere opponents of the PCI. They were very upset when the PCI-dominated League of Democratic Communes endorsed La Pira's 1953 ordinance requisitioning private property. This administrative law confirmed their worst suspicions about the mayor's political direction.[37]

The PLI also objected on principle to La Pira's deficit spending. The rising indebtedness of ATAF was a sore point for the Liberals, who proposed that the city cut its outsized budget deficits by privatizing both its transportation and cultural operations. In December 1953, the PLI briefly pulled out of the ruling coalition to protest La Pira's decision to municipalize street-cleaning services. The confrontation was papered over, but Liberal discontent with the junta's basic policy was on record.[38]

By late 1954 the PLI was one of La Pira's harshest critics. The Liberals attacked the man, his style, his program, and his vision. The final straw was the mayor's decision to issue permits for a PCI-sponsored "Unity Festival" (Festa dell'Unita). The PCI had been holding these annual festivals in the Cascina since 1947. In the 1950s they were massive, ideologically charged displays of Communist political muscle. Middle-class voters resented the heavy-handed propaganda that issued from the Festa and were disquieted by repeated displays of Communist discipline and paramilitary organization. Ignoring the limits that La Pira placed on PCI use of the park, the PLI denounced the mayor and withdrew from the governing coalition in September.[39]

La Pira's major opponents on the right united over the Cascina permit issue. Playing upon fears of Communism, they charged that La Pira was being duped by the PCI and that his programs increasingly were indistinguishable from those of the "subversives." The attack, spearheaded by *La Nazione*, enjoyed the full support of the PLI, many church officials, the Catholic right, major industrialists, and other social conservatives, as well as the neo-Fascists.[40]

Ironically, the Cascina issue was moot by the time that the PLI broke with the government. The questor of Florence, the state's senior law enforcement official, banned the entire Festa dell'Unita. In so ruling, he handed the left an issue, suppression of the basic right of assembly, that it gleefully exploited. While the PLI celebrated its triumph by moving rightward and losing influence, La Pira, relieved of the incubus of conservatives, tacked left, further outraging his conservative critics.[41]

The mayor moved forward with municipalization of sanitation services and expanded Florence's city pharmacy program. Ignoring the rising municipal transportation deficit, the La Pira administration increased bus service, buying eighty new vehicles. La Pira reinforced contacts with both the local chamber of labor and partisan groups that had ties to the left parties. He attempted to impose price controls on heating fuel. With Dalla Costa's enthusiastic backing, La Pira hosted the second of his *convegni*, an October 2–5, 1955, meeting of mayors on the theme of "friendship, hope, and peace." Participants came from Moscow and other Communist bloc cities.[42]

THE ELECTIONS OF 1956

La Pira's opening to the left forced his Marxist opponents to reevaluate their electoral strategy. The PSI hoped to build on its success in the 1953 national election. Given its financial problems and internal divisions, the party was beginning to see participation in governing coalitions as a panacea. The PSI's electoral criticism of the mayor was moderated in tone. La Pira, it suggested, was frequently well intentioned but needed the discipline that a Marxist party could provide. Running a joint slate with the intellectuals of UP, the PSI came down hardest on La Pira's management of urban planning.[43]

The PCI's response was complex. The "Little Mayor" had repeatedly bested the Communists. Party leaders recognized the benefits that they gained from improved relations with the La Pira and were looking for ways to expand the dialogue. After misplaying the Pignone crisis, PCI leaders would never again underestimate Florence's mayor. In periodic meetings Fabiani and La Pira explored the areas of agreement on specific issues. The mayor and provincial president agreed on many national and international issues, including antinuclear politics and the need to support peace demonstrations. Both were hostile to the policies of the U.S. government. La Pira sought the involvement of the left in planning for the annual commemorations of the resistance and liberation. In his final statement to the city council prior to the 1956 elections, the mayor was generous in praising the role of the opposition in the legislative process, recalling that its votes at times pushed forward government initiatives.[44]

The PCI's position was too tenuous to permit it the luxury of going easy on La Pira. Success in the 1953 national elections had not translated into membership growth in successive years. Party leaders had been perplexed by their inability to turn the Pignone crisis into a major propaganda or recruitment success. In spite of an extremely varied and intense program of public events, participation in PCI-sponsored activities was declining, as was party membership. Party militants blamed television's growing popularity together with a government program that reclaimed the property occupied by PCI "people's houses" (*Case dei popoli*) since the war for breaking down contacts with the masses. While true, the analysis missed the point that expanding economic prosperity was at the root of the PCI's gradual decline.[45]

The party's pressing problem was the impact that revelations of Stalin's reign of terror had on the morale and discipline of its members. Details of Khrushchev's February 1956 "secret" speech to the 20th Congress of the Soviet Communist Party, initially reported to local Communist organizations in a bowdlerized version, soon became generally known, creating widespread disorientation and revulsion. PCI headquarters, concerned about dwindling membership and drooping morale, determined to replace the faithful Stalinist Mazzoni with the more popular Fabiani. The move's potential benefits were offset by full revelation of Stalin's crimes and by subsequent Soviet actions in Poland and Hungary.[46]

The PCI's long and well-rehearsed criticism of the La Pira government included attacks on his one-man style of government, on the weaknesses of his programs for infrastructural improvements, on rising taxes and unbalanced budgets, and on the junta's cultural programs. It derided the mayor's vaunted ties to the Rome political establishment, underlining the declining benefits that these ties provided the city. The Communists charged that La Pira's satellite cities programs had created working-class ghettoes with substandard services. In contrast to the free-spending, well-meaning, undisciplined La Pira administration, the PCI offered Communist-run Bologna as the model of efficient, cost-effective government.[47]

In addition to a PCI thirsting for electoral success to overcome its internal problems, La Pira faced harsh criticism from the right and from the center. The

PLI's no-holds-barred attack on the mayor was designed to discredit La Pira personally. Initially, PLI leaders hoped to force the DC to withdraw the mayor as a candidate as a prelude to returning to the government. When the Christian Democrats rejected this suggestion, the Liberals stepped up their criticism, with the objective of denying the DC enough city council seats to permit La Pira reelection as mayor. The Liberals accused La Pira of violating property rights, maladministration, cohabitation with the Communists, and, in an odd twist for members of a secular party, deviating from correct Catholic doctrine. The crusade picked up some useful support when the Republican Party denounced the mayor and offered to work with the PLI in defeating him. It enjoyed the backing of *La Nazione* and many members of the business community. Pistelli charged that the "Masons" were out to get La Pira, employing their positions inside the state bureaucracy to clamp down on the mayor's initiatives.[48]

Even progressive Catholics were becoming critical of La Pira. In an essay in the left Catholic journal *Il Mulino*, political scientist Alfonso Prandi warned that the mayor of Florence was losing his international appeal. Praising the achievements of La Pira's administration, Prandi questioned whether the mayor's management style was creating an unhealthy alliance of church, state, and party.[49]

Pistelli commented that La Pira and Dossetti (who reentered politics to run for mayor of Bologna) had to demonstrate that the DC left stood for creative use of public power while simultaneously displaying anti-Communist credentials. The radical policies that split his coalition undermined La Pira's credibility with many electors. He needed to refurbish his image with a coherent program of government and governing partners. The coalition that had backed him since 1950 clearly could not be resurrected.[50]

Further complicating La Pira's 1956 campaign was the new law on local elections that reinstated strict proportional representation. The revised rules favored both the right and left at the expense of the DC. La Pira faced an uphill struggle to maintain a DC majority in the city council.

La Pira entered the campaign with a united party but one that took divergent positions. In publicly endorsing La Pira, DC party president and fellow Florentine Adone Zoli was fulsome in his praise for the mayor's social initiatives but pointedly added: "In defending La Pira we are defending our only 'opening,' the evangelical opening." DC secretary Fanfani warned that the party would use its influence to dissolve any postelection city administration based on coalitions between the DC and Marxist parties. The party's right succeeded in placing its members on the DC slate while excluding a number of La Pira's allies, including Pistelli.[51]

La Pira responded with a carefully crafted mix of the practical and the visionary. The first step in his election strategy was a last-minute orgy of pork barrel politics. In the days before its dissolution, the city council passed a number of public works programs designed to generate jobs and appease a restless electorate.[52]

In his initial election address, April 22, the mayor, with a supportive Fanfani seated beside him, picked up the pork barrel theme, reminding voters of his ability to bring back aid from Rome, sketched the large infrastructural, cultural, and employment producing programs of his administration, and promised more.[53]

Cardinal Dalla Costa provided an enthusiastic endorsement of the mayor and his social policies, effectively smothering charges that La Pira was out of step with the church. La Pira sought to make the distinction between his social Catholicism with its religiously based vision of the city and the values of atheistic Communism. He underplayed his own centrality as an election issue, insisting that voters had a more fundamental choice to make: the contrasting visions of the city's future offered by the DC and the PCI. A vote for La Pira was a vote for Florence: "The city of God, the city of Mary, the mediatrix of people, the depository of values, the sister of cities, [and] the beacon of culture."[54]

NOTES

1. Piero Ottone, *Fanfani* (Milan, 1966), pp. 100–01; Ruggero Orfei, *L'occupazione del potero* (Milan, 1976), p. 142.

2. Amintore Fanfani, *Giorgio la Pira* (Milan, 1978), pp. 110–11; Giorgio La Pira, *Lettere alle claustrali* (Milan, 1978), pp. 161–69, 189–98; Gianni Conti interview, Florence, May 26, 1993.

3. Commune di Firenze, *Firenze nella vita e nell'opere, 1951–1956* (Florence, 1956).

4. ACC 1954, 1: 262–65, 305–6, 596; La Pira, *Letteer alle claustrali*, pp. 75–76; Ugo De Siervo, Glanni Glovannoni, and Giorgio Giovannoni, eds., *La Pira sindaco*, 3 vols. (Florence, 1988–1989), 2: 329–32.

5. Scelba to La Pira, July 16, 1952, ALP. b. 64, Comune di Firenze 1952; Colombo to La Pira, December 30, 1954, ibid.; Gargiulo to La Pira, April 8, 1952, ibid.; Questore to City Government, August 25, 1952, ibid.

6. *Saturday Evening Post* (January 21, 1956); Partito Comunista Italiano, Federazione Fiorentina, *Resoconto del VIII Congresso provincale* (Florence, 1954), pp. 132–36.

7. Votto to La Pira, April 20, 1954, November 20, 1954, November 4, 1955, all ALP, Subject Files, b 70, Teatro comunale.

8. Cf. the comments in Cyrus Sulzberger, *The Last of the Giants* (New York, 1970), pp. 516–17.

9. Giorgio Galli, *Fanfani* (Milan, 1975), pp. 49, 62–63; Francesco Malgeri, ed., *Storia della Democrazia Cristina* (Rome, 1987–1989), 2: 267–69; 3: 6; Judith Chubb, *Patronage, Power, and Poverty in South Italy* (New York, 1982), pp. 61–80.

10. Galli, *Fanfani*, pp. 68–70; Pietro DiLoreto, *La difficile transizione* (Bologna, 1993), p. 124; Giovanni Tassani, *La terza generazione* (Rome, 1988), pp. 40–41, 109, 222, 227–28.

11. Giovanni Di Capua, *Nicola Pistelli* (Florence, 1969), pp. 12–13; Merli, *Antologia di San Marco*, pp. 13–14, 19–21, 30–38, 43–44; Tassani, *Terza generazione*, pp. 111, 224.

12. Giovannoni interview, Florence, May 25, 1993.

13. Ibid.; Bruna Bocchini Camaiani, "Ricostruzione concordato e processi di secolarizzazione," in Francesco Margiotta Broglio, ed., *La chiesa del Concordato*, 2. vols. (Bologna, 1983), 2: 341.

14. Ibid., 336–37; Comunita di Isolotto, *Isolotto sotto processo* (Bari, 1971), pp. 18–19.

15. Francesca Taddei, *Il pignone di Firenze, 1944–1954* (Florence, 1980); Nicola Pistelli, *Scritti Politici* (Florence, 1967), pp. 3–34.

16. La Pira to Campilli, October 16, 1951, AC/S, MIC, Carteggio Campilli, b 1, f 69; ACC 1952, 1: 107–9, 550–52.

17. *Libro Bianco Sulle Officine Galileo* (Florence, 1959), pp. 111–13; La Pira to Campilli, April 7, 1953, AC/S, MCI, Carteggio Campilli, b 1, f 69.

18. Galli, *Fanfani*, pp. 54–55; Vittorio Gorresio, *L'Italia a sinistra* (Milan, 1963), p. 20.

19. Alcide De Gasperi, *Lettere al presidente* (Milan, 1964), pp. 308–10; *Toscana Nuova*, January 17, 1954.

20. P. H. Frankel, *Mattei* (London, 1966), pp. 22–23, 98–99, 139.

21. Prefect to MI, November 10, 1953, AC/S, MI, Gab, Partiti politici, b 34., f. 165/P/31-DC-Firenze; La Pira to Nenni, November 16, 1953, Fondazione Nenni, Archivio, serie C, Carteggio La Pira-Nenni, Pietro Nenni, *Gli anni del Centro Sinistra. Diari, 1957–1966* (Milan, 1982), p. 622; Alfio Dini, *La mia pietra* (Livorno, 1985), 2: 72–73; *Mondo Operaio*, January 23, 1958, pp. 1–4, 8–10.

22. PCI, Federazione Fiorentina, *Resoconto del VIII congresso*, pp. 234–40; Report to Direzione, PCI, July 24, 1954, APC, f. Firenze 1954, 0419/1635; Luca Merli [Giovanni Di Capua], ed., *Antologia della Base* (Rome, 1971), pp. 209–22.

23. Paolo Bagnoli, "I giorni di Firenze (politica e cultura dal 1944 al 1974)," *Citta e regione* 7 (1981), pp. 72–97, 211–242, 149–79; *La Nazione*, November 24, 17, 28, 1953; Giovannoni interview, May 25, 1993.

24. Silvio Lanaro, *Storia, dell'Italia repubblicana* (Venice, 1992), p. 285.

25. *La Pira sindaco*, 2: 63–66; Conti interview.

26. Comune di Firenze, *Proposta di legge speciale a favore di Firenze* (Florence, 1954); ACC 1954, 2: 847–56; Cf. ALP, Subject File, b 69, f. leggi speciale.

27. *Libro Bianco*, pp. 114–15; ACC 1954, 2: 1061–74; *La Pira sindaco*, 2: 27, 29–39.

28. *The Reporter*, October 6, 1955; Franco Boiardi, *Dossetti e la crisi dei cattolici italiani* (Florence, 1956), pp. 214–17; Pistelli, *Scritti*, pp. 752–57.

29. Piero Barucci, *Profilo economico della provincia di Firenze* (Florence, 1974), pp. 100, 113, 122, 142, 163–64, 179, 193, 204.

30. Enzo Vanoni, *La politica economica degli anni degasperiani* (Florence, 1977), pp. 314–20; Prefect to MI, May 29, 1954, AC/S, MI, Gab, Partiti politici, b 39, f 170/P/31-PLI-Firenze.

31. Nenni, *Anni*, pp. 567–68, 580 passim.

32. Lombardi to Dini, October 18, 1955, F. F. Lombardi, b 11. PSI-Firenze 1955; Dini, *La mia pietra*, 2: 66–68, 75, 94–95.

33. Dini, *La mia pietra*, 2: 135, 146, 193, 212–14; Police report, c. February 1956, AC/S, MI, Gab, Partiti politici, b 44, f 175/P/31-PSI-Firenze.

34. Piero Calamandrei, *Lettere, 1916–1956* (Florence, 1968), 2: 366–68; Maurizio Degl'Innocenti and Stefano Caretti, *Il socialismo in Firenze e provincia* (Pisa, 1987), pp. 181–82; Lelio Lagorio interview, Florence, October 4, 1995.

35. ACC 1954, 2: 1033–39; ACC, 1955, 1: 817–20.

36. Mariella Zoppi, *Firenze e l'urbanistica* (Rome, 1982), pp. 49–59.

37. ACC 1954, 2: 950–60; Pier Luigi Ballini, Luigi Lotti, and Mario Rossi, eds., *Toscana nel secondo dopoguerra* (Milan, 1991), p. 462.

38. ACC 1953, 2: 1255–93; *La Nazione*, December 21, 1953.

39. ACC 1954, 2: 889–93; Prefect to MI, June 7, 1955, AC/S, MI, Gab, Partiti politici, b 39, f 170/P/31-PLI-Firenze.

40. Pistelli, *Scritti*, pp. 575–64; *La Nazione*, August 13–15, 1954.

41. Prefect to MI, February 13, 1954, AC/S, MI, Gab, Partiti politici, b 39, 170/P/31-PLI Firenze; Pistelli, *Scritti*, pp. 749–52.

42. ACC 1954, 2: 1238; ACC 1955, 1: 705, 727, 817–20; 2, 1306; ACC 1956, 1: 699–723; MI to President of the Council, June 24, 1954, AC/S, Presidenza del consiglio, 1951–1954, f 1.6.1/81346; Prefect to MI, July 6, 1955, AC/S, MI, Gab, Fascicoli permanenti, b 259, f 266/E/31, IACP; Prefect to MI, July 7, 1955, ibid.

43. Nenni, *Gli anni*, p. 732; PSI, "Per il comune libero e democratico," ISRT; Fondo F. Lombardi, b 14, PSI, Firenze, f. 47, s/f Elezione amministrative 1956.

44. *La Pira sindaco*, 2: 173–75.

45. Federation Reports, November 2, 1953, APC, Firenze 1953, 0405/0819, and February 6, 1954, APC, Firenze 1954, 0419/1209–57; Notes on Work Plan for 1956, December 6, 1955, APC, Firenze 1955, 0429/2706; Minutes, April 16, 1955, ISRT, Fondo F. Rossi, b 1, f. Federazione PCI, zona industriale.

46. Orazio Barbieri, *La fede e la ragione* (Milan, 1982) pp. 150–54; 0445/0711. Minutes, June 17, 1956, APC, Firenze 1956, 0455/0713–16.

47. *Toscana Nuova*, October 12, 1952, January 16, April 3, November 27, 1955; "Per la soluzione dei problemi piu urgenti della citta," n.d. APC, Firenze 1954, 0419/1671–80; "Case minime ma non umane," n.d., ISRT, C. Collini, Materiale PCI-Firenze, 1947–1956.

48. Pistelli, *Scritti*, pp. 764–70; ACC 1955, 1: 820 ff., 2: 1203–20; Prefect to MI, October 6, 1955, March 1, 1956, both AC/S, MI, Gab, Partiti politici, b 68, f. 200/P/31-PRI-Firenze.

49. *Il Mulino* 5 (April 1956), 267–75.

50. Pistelli, *Scritti*, pp. 40–43.

51. *La Difesa*, April 27, 1956; Prefect to MI, January 9, 1956, AC/S, MI, Gab, Partiti politici, b 34, f. 165/P/31-DC-Firenze.

52. ACC 1956, 1: 157–284; 2: 940–1063.

53. *La Pira sindaco*, 2: 177–78.

54. Ibid., 2: 189–202.

Chapter 6

Intermezzo, 1957–1960

At Florence they have reached agreement on a junta: La Pira will be mayor, comrade Agnoletti will be vice mayor. A Catholic idealist and a lay and socialist idealist. Something interesting ought to come from this.

Nenni, diary entry, February 17, 1961

The 1956 elections at Florence were waged over Giorgio La Pira. His personality, his style of government, and his vision were the center of debate. Ironically, the object of so much adulation and scorn was absent for much of the campaign. Feeling ill, La Pira retired to bed and stayed there, "with the covers pulled up to his nose," surrounded by his friends. This unorthodox campaign style was a success. La Pira got 34,000 preference votes, while the DC with over 100,000 votes confirmed its standing as the city's first party. The Communist vote dropped, the right declined, the centrist Republican Party disappeared, and the PSI–UP–Social Democratic vote total increased.[1]

La Pira's personal triumph left the city in a political no-man's-land. Running under a strict proportional representation system, the DC emerged as the largest party but, with only twenty-five seats, lost the majority that it had held since 1951. Moreover, the increase in Socialist support strengthened pressure for a center left government based on the DC and PSI. Neither the church nor the Christian Democratic leadership would endorse such a coalition. Completion of the alliance with the PSI would require more than four years because of hardline Catholic opposition to any collaboration with the "Marxists."

SEARCHING FOR A GOVERNING FORMULA

A number of Italian cities faced the dilemma of creating an effective coalition government after the June 1956 vote. At Venice, the DC could govern only in coalition with parties of the left. Cardinal Angelo Roncalli, the patriarch (and future Pope John XXIII), acting on orders from the Vatican, staunchly opposed any alliance with the left. In July the DC and PSDI formed a minority government with the "external" support of the PSI. The Socialists would vote for the government and support its policies but agreed not to seek any seats on the city council. The church grudgingly accepted the "Venice formula." The Socialists offered to apply the formula to cities like Florence. Caught between the conflicting demands of the PSI and his major allies, Fanfani and the church, La Pira had limited room to maneuver. When he proved unable to square the circle of governing in cooperation with the PSI, the national government intervened and placed the city under a prefectural administration that lasted four years. In the interim, the national political situation evolved toward the center left formula. La Pira could then take up his reform agenda, but in vastly changed political and social circumstances.[2]

Fanfani could convince neither his party's powerful conservative wing nor the Vatican of the wisdom of a center left alliance. Pope Pius XII, in particular, was adamantly opposed to including any leftists in government. This sentiment was shared at the U.S. Embassy in Rome, where Ambassador Luce refused to admit that any significant differences existed between PSI and PCI. While the influence of the Americans in Italian politics was declining, they still constituted an important factor in Italy's complex game of power. The DC right was happy to exploit their views.[3]

While eager to govern and to push the political axis leftward, La Pira, as a dutiful Catholic, conformed to the desires of the church. Although he had engaged in heated private disputes with Fanfani, La Pira was determined to avoid embarrassing or undercutting his most important national ally. La Pira would not go beyond a governing formula that created a DC–Social Democratic junta with external support ("case by case") from the PSI.[4]

La Pira stood by as Fanfani successfully undercut the elements of the Florentine DC favoring a center left government. Employing the newly elected secretary of the provincial DC, Edoardo Speranza, as his agent, Fanfani divided the Base. Pistelli was booted off the provincial council and suspended from the party for revealing information on the situation in Venice. His monthly, *Politica*, lost its status as an official party publication and an accompanying financial subvention.[5]

In the weeks following the June elections, La Pira searched for a formula that would permit him to govern with the support of the PSI and at the same time avoid any ties to that party. His efforts failed when the Social Democrats decided to enter a coalition with the DC only if the PSI joined and the DC's National Council passed a resolution opposing any deals with the Socialists. *Nuovo Corriere* accurately defined the resolution a "closure to the left."[6]

The Socialists and Social Democrats rejected La Pira's initial proposal for a DC minority government with external support from both parties. The Socialists insisted that their expanded representation on the city council gave them the right to participate in government. Their spokesman, Raffaello Ramat, bluntly informed the city council that centrism was dead. The PSI was ready to deal with the DC, but only on a basis of the creation of a center left government.[7]

Calamandrei declined to form an interim city administration in early August. The DC and PSI faced off over the election of a new mayor. After two inconclusive ballots, La Pira and Ramat finished the third vote in a dead heat. The rules governing the election of a mayor gave the victory to La Pira as the elder of the two. The Liberals and the neo-Fascist Italian Social Movement (MSI) abstained, and the Social Democrats' (PSDI) support enabled the DC and Social Democrats to elect a slate of councilmen as the new junta. La Pira was mayor again but at the head of a minority government with no immediate prospect of creating a majority.[8]

After a summer recess, the city council reconvened in October 1956. Citing the positive tone of the mayor's program speech, the Socialists announced that they would back the government on a case-by-case basis. Socialist spokesman Alberto Albertoni (UP) attacked the junta's competence, criticized La Pira's administrative style and "cult of personality," and demanded careful control of the junta's spending. Detti added that the opposition would focus its attention on La Pira's management of urban planning issues, particularly his willingness to adopt a new city plan.[9]

The mayor reinforced his personal standing with the left through his willingness to consult them on issues. He won further praise by blocking a plan to send a small, but important, collection of Florentine art to the United States. His efforts to extract more funding for the Maggio from a reluctant national government got positive reviews. As a result the minority junta managed to govern through the winter of 1956–1957.[10]

Clouding the La Pira government's future was the outcome of DC and Social Democratic Party congresses. When the DC's national congress failed to approve a center left government for Florence, Guido Maier announced that on orders from his national headquarters, he and his fellow Social Democratic assessors would resign.[11] In late April 1957 the PSI and Social Democrats used a budget issue (significantly, urban planning) to topple La Pira's minority government.

"The living saint . . . has resigned," crowed the right-of-center *Il Mondo*. Satisfaction over the end of La Pira's flirtation with the center left was widespread. Communists joined Liberals and Christian Democrats in applauding the La Pira junta's fall. Following his resignation as mayor, La Pira and the entire DC group of councilmen resigned from the city council. This act of party discipline permitted the DC-led national government to impose a prefectual commissioner, a special official charged with administering the city until new elections. Normally, the commissioner was expected to govern for a few months. In the case of Florence, Prefect Lorenzo Salazar would hold his post for four years in order to preserve DC unity.[12]

STALIN AND HUNGARY

Italian-style consensus building was never more evident than in the long march toward a government of the center left. From the time when Nenni first proposed a Socialist-Christian Democrat government in 1954, to the formation of Aldo Moro's first ministry, a decade elapsed. In that period, the opening to the left won the grudging acceptance from the DC's right wing. The church ended its opposition. The United States abandoned its anti-Socialist position and engaged in a paralyzing interagency debate that rendered it irrelevant to the final outcome. Over the same decade, the center left concept lost much of its innovative thrust. Increasingly, the real objective of the PSI was simply getting into government, not reforming it. Would-be allies on the DC left never won control of Christian Democracy. DC secretaries Fanfani and Moro regarded the center left primarily as a tool in their interparty power struggle.[13]

The complexities of building the center left were illustrated by the impact that the 1956 Khrushchev secret speech and subsequent Hungarian revolution had on Italian politics. In the summer of 1953 Pietro Nenni had a conversation with De Gasperi about Socialist participation in government. The prime minister laid out his party's position succinctly: the Socialists would not enter a coalition as long as they retained their ties with the PCI. Nenni responded that the PCI was no longer a revolutionary threat, that it had lost its ideological edge, and that the PSI could never divide the Italian working class. Nenni, in fact, hoped to convince the PCI to back its bid for membership in a coalition.[14]

Nenni's search for a path to Socialist participation in power included many forays into the Catholic world. He found support from Gronchi and a degree of understanding among the Jesuit fathers of *Civilta Cattolica*. Nenni also recognized that the most direct road to governmental responsibility ran through the Social Democratic Party. Support for the Socialists' application from this staunchly anti-Communist party would instantly give the PSI the bona fides necessary to join a government.[15]

The PSDI leadership wanted Socialist reunification, and they were willing to back PSI participation in the ruling coalition, on their terms. In August 1956, Nenni and the PSDI's leader, Saragat, met at Pralognan, France, to survey the possibilities of cooperation. Saragat's terms were simple: the PSI must distance itself from the PCI.[16]

The first steps toward reunification with the Social Democrats unleashed a flurry of activity at the local levels of the two parties. Socialist electoral strategy in 1956 was to form local administrations with any political forces ready to cooperate. This meant coalitions with both the PCI and the DC as well as experiments in governing with the smaller parties when the possibility arose. In Florence, the search for coalition partners was also a search for unification of the various "Socialist" movements into a single party. In June 1956, Tuscan Socialists of differing political persuasions met informally in Siena to commemorate reformist Socialist Giacomo Matteotti, the staunch opponent and early victim of

Fascism. They agreed to meet the following month in the working-class Florentine suburb of Rifredi for discussions about both practical cooperation and party unification.[17]

The July 13, 1956, meeting at Rifredi took the first halting steps toward Socialist reunification at Florence. Delegates from four Socialist movements agreed to tone down their mutually damaging political attacks, to seek to develop a common platform, and to postpone discussion on practical steps toward reunification until they had secured agreement from their respective parties that political unity was their goal. A second meeting at Rifredi, September 9, helped to define the objectives of the participants more clearly. It also focused attention on the relationship of Socialists with Communists.[18]

By September 1956 that relationship was extremely troubled. The full text of Khrushchev's February denunciation of Stalin reached the West, jolting Communist rank and file. The PCI's Florence Federation held a series of meetings to discuss and explain away Khrushchev's revelations. Previously steadfast party intellectuals were badly shaken by these revelations and the PCI's effort to suppress part of Khrushchev's speech. Togliatti came to Florence to quiet unrest in a profoundly divided and demoralized party.[19]

The secret speech delivered a coup de grâce to the possibility of further collaboration between PCI and PSI. In July, shortly after it became public, Togliatti and Nenni met. The PCI leader was furious with the Soviet party chief. Attempting to make the best of a bad situation, Togliatti suggested that the PCI would welcome a Socialist-Social Democrat rapprochement. However, the Communist leader insisted that the PSI balance off moves to the right by renewing the Communist-Socialist unity of action pact. Nenni responded that while the PSI wanted to retain ties to the Communists, it needed more freedom of action.[20]

Nenni's first halting steps away from the PCI reflected the continued hold that the idea of working-class unity had on Socialist leaders. At a July 6 meeting, senior party leaders were highly critical of the Soviet Union but still unwilling to accept the Social Democrats' position that the price of cooperation and possible reunification was a total break with the Communists. Latent opposition to any deal with the Social Democrats bubbled over at the September 29 leadership meeting. When Nenni subsequently met with Togliatti (October 5) to discuss the terms of a renewal of political cooperation between the two parties, he discovered that the PCI had sprung a trap. By leaking information on the meeting to the press, the Communists calculated that they could derail any deal with the Social Democrats and force the Socialists to renew the PCI-PSI unity of action pact.[21]

Togliatti's ploy worked. The Social Democrats immediately and publicly warned Nenni that renewal of the unity of action pact meant the end of any possibility of Socialist collaboration or reunification. Nenni grimly admitted that his tardy denunciation of Stalin's crimes coupled with the accord with the PCI sowed confusion in Socialist ranks. The Florentine PSI complained that the PCI-PSI-PSDI showdown provided opponents with a propaganda field day without clarifying the nature of relationships between the parties. Members were confused. Their leaders waited on events.[22]

Ironically, the apparently unworkable strategy paid huge dividends. Within weeks, the PCI faced a crisis that effectively settled the issue of Communist-Socialist relations. In late October 1956, the Hungarian people rose against Communism. Soviet troops intervened in early November, crushing the revolt.

Soviet actions devastated the PCI. The Hungarian revolution demonstrated that the Stalinist system had not died with Stalin. Togliatti and his lieutenants consistently followed the Soviet line, thereby dramatically refuting their claims to represent a new approach to Communism. Thousands of disillusioned members left the PCI in the weeks after the Hungarian revolution. Florentine party membership dropped by about 9,000 after the Soviets' Hungarian intervention. PCI officials had great trouble recruiting young members. Losses were particularly heavy among the intellectuals, many of whom would become persistent critics of the PCI for decades to follow.[23]

The Florentine PCI suffered severely from Togliatti's decisions. Togliatti cut financial support to *Nuovo Corriere* when editor Romano Bilenchi broke with the party over Hungary. The paper went out of business, and the local PCI lost a major public relations tool. The ninth congress of the Florentine Federation, November 1956, was an open battle between a "renewal" faction that wanted profound change and the party's nomenklatura, standing firmly on the positions outlined by Togliatti. The federation's new leader, Fabiani, had the unhappy task of trying to maintain unity. He launched a biting dissection of La Pira's administration to rally the party.[24]

Nenni belatedly recognized the true colors of the Soviet system. "Internationalism has become colonialism," he noted in his diary. As the PCI dug in, providing full support for the Soviets, "an abyss" opened between the two parties. On November 6, Nenni stood before the Chamber of Deputies to make a "discourse of rupture" with the PCI. Infuriated Florentine Socialists denounced both the Soviets and the PCI.[25]

The end of the alliance with the powerful PCI opened the way for PSI collaboration with the numerically weak Social Democrats. On October 25, 1956, Nenni and Saragat met again and agreed to move toward unification. They spoke hopefully of creating a Socialist alternative to DC rule, even as the PSDI continued in its coalition with the DC, and the PSI with equal pragmatism held on to many local alliances with the PCI. The statement of the tenth congress of the PSI Florentine Federation accurately mirrored the contradictory objectives of the party. The Florentine Socialists pledged to break with the discredited strategies of the DC ("centrism") and the PCI ("frontism"). They would avoid class provocation but promote workers' internationalism. The party embraced "the end of the blocs" in foreign policy. It would cooperate with the PCI on issues of interest to the proletariat while extending its hand to Catholic workers' organizations. The ultimate objective of the PSI, either in collaboration with the DC or as an alternative governing party, would be to give Italy a democratic, anticapitalist policy.[26]

AT A SNAIL'S PACE

Between 1957 and 1960, the three major protagonists in the center left drama moved with an agonizing slowness toward the completion of a political realignment that the events of 1956 had made inevitable. The PSI was too weak to force its entry into the ranks of the governing parties and paid a high price in the form of concessions on program and principle to the Christian Democrats for its eventual participation in power. The DC, meanwhile, continued its internal struggle over the center left idea. The right remained the dominant force within the party, eventually ousting Fanfani. His replacement, Aldo Moro, achieved an alliance with the Socialists, but one almost totally void of the reformist thrust that Italian society needed. The Communists licked their multiple wounds, hardened their position of opposition, and carefully rebuilt their damaged political machine.

The PSI had no alternatives to a deal with the DC, essentially on Christian Democratic terms. The mirage of reunification with the Social Democrats evaporated shortly after the 1956 elections. The PSDI demanded concessions on domestic and foreign policy issues that the PSI was not disposed to make, especially to a smaller party. At a November 1956 meeting of PSI and PSDI chiefs in Florence, Social Democratic spokesmen reaffirmed that the price of unity was a reversal of its line on NATO, the alliance with the United States, related defense issues, and total rejection of cooperation with the PCI. The following April, Saragat engineered the substitution of his protégé Mario Tanassi, a hard-line anti-Communist, for the pro-unity party secretary Matteo Matteotti.[27]

With reunification on the shelf, Nenni sought renewed contact with those favoring the center left. In May, the Socialist leader rendezvoused with La Pira at Rome's Ponte Garibaldi. The Florentine brought assurances from Fanfani that the DC secretary aimed at parliamentary cooperation after new elections. La Pira assured Nenni that cooperation was "an historic design of providence." Nenni made no effort to hide his skepticism about Fanfani's ability to deliver.[28]

Given the weakness of his party in both organizational and financial terms, Nenni waited on developments in the DC. The Florentine PSI exemplified these weaknesses. It supported few activities, was only minimally in evidence outside the city of Florence, and lacked strong leaders. Its organizations atrophied, and recruitment stagnated. In spite of its 1956 success at the polls, the PSI lost about 2,000 of its approximately 14,000 members the following year. Its average monthly deficit was nearly 2.5 million lire, a small, but persistent, leak that drained its vitality.[29]

Nenni's triumph at the PSI's October 1957 national congress at Venice seemed to open the way for a deal with the DC based on a concrete platform of reforms that addressed the effects of Italy's "economic miracle" (1955–1964). The PSI received a welcome infusion of talent when *Unita Popolare* finally agreed to a merger in November 1957. The intellectuals of UP allied with the "autonomist" faction within the PSI and at the 1958 federation congress wrested power from the ineffective left.[30]

The autonomists believed that they could put enough pressure on the DC to force it to shed its past links to the right (Monarchists, Liberals, and MSI). They looked to the DC's left wing to take firm command of the party. The PSI left, with more realism, warned that the DC left was too weak to carry out the role assigned to it by the autonomists.[31]

The DC's left, in fact, was in a particularly difficult position. It was under constant attack for religious deviation. The party's right pinned the label "white Communists" on the Base. The 1956 local elections, which marked an impressive advance for the PSI, placed the DC on the political defensive and made it less disposed to a deal with the Socialists. Fanfani, reacting to the mood of the party, set tougher conditions for alliance with the Socialists. Even when resuscitating the center left formula at the DC's July 1957 national council meeting, Fanfani repeated that a deal with the PSI had to await the results of parliamentary elections.[32]

The left's position was difficult even in its Tuscan power base. Provincial party secretary Edoardo Speranza, Fanfani's chief ally, handily defeated Pistelli at the local party congress. La Pira maintained his popularity with Florentine voters but could not escape buffeting from both the DC right and senior churchmen. His *convegni* were targets of fierce criticism for their supposed pro-Communist bias. The powerful Cardinal Alfredo Ottaviani, head of the Vatican's office on religious orthodoxy, made the former mayor of Florence a principal target of attacks aimed at derailing a center left government.[33]

The 1958 parliamentary elections resulted in advances for both PSI and DC. Fanfani, whose party restructuring was widely credited with improving DC fortunes, push forward the idea of a center left. Pistelli and other Base leaders felt they had no alternative but to support their old nemesis in hopes of finally arriving at a deal with the Socialists. The PSI lacked reliable interlocutors inside the DC.[34]

The continuing inability of the PSI and DC to reach an accord was good news for a PCI that slowly rebounded after the disasters of 1956. Togliatti capitalized on these setbacks to reaffirm his control of the party. He pushed a number of older, more radical Communist leaders, including his former deputy Pietro Secchia, out of leadership positions, replacing them with younger, more politically moderate bureaucrats. Secchia grudgingly admitted that the PCI's chief had carried out a "masterpiece of duplicity": placing the blame on the old left, pushing them from power, and retaining the undemocratic party structure that ensured his personal control.[35]

Togliatti's reshuffling of personnel was an effort to deal with the PCI's reputation for playing a "double game." By packing off the old left in favor of younger, moderate cadres not associated with the resistance, Togliatti accentuated the party's break with its paramilitary and rhetorically radical recent past. To underline this break, the PCI disbanded its remaining cells, introduced measures favoring internal democratic dialogue, always under strict controls, and gave more power to its federations. Without abandoning democratic centralism, the PCI softened its public image.[36]

Togliatti continued his approaches to the Socialists. Nenni flubbed his chance to collect the majority of dissident ex-Communist intellectuals and, with them, a dominant role in Italian culture by aggressively pursuing reunification with the Social Democrats. Freed from concern about a Socialist challenge on this level, determined to avoid isolation, and hoping to utilize the PSI as its entrée into government, the PCI briefly assented to Nenni's approach to the DC. That tolerance evaporated as the Socialist leader increased the distance between the two parties to win DC approval. In October 1958, Togliatti accused the Socialists of apostasy. He defended the Soviet Union as reformable in spite of Stalin's "errors." Stressing his party's democratic objectives, Togliatti left the door open for an eventual rapprochement, suggesting that the Socialists ultimately would recognize that their Communist rivals had successfully married full democracy with Leninism and the "revolutionary vocation" through a strategy of first replacing the old ruling class through free elections and then proceeding to Socialism. Subsequently, he warned the PSI that in alliance with the DC or Social Democrats, it would be forced to accept terms that fundamentally divided the working classes.[37]

The Florence Federation followed the lead of the national PCI, offering to open dialogue with all comers in a bid to reduce its isolation. The Communists repaired their internal divisions, reached out for allies among all classes, expanded their cultural program, and tried to rebuild ties to the PSI and other left-of-center parties, using the Florentine section of the National Partisans Association (ANPI) as their vehicle. Fabiani, ever the realist, warned that possessing power on the local level was inadequate to the party's needs. As long as the province remained in debt, it would be dependent on the DC-led national government and possess only a strictly limited autonomy.[38]

The Tuscan party was able to avoid isolation, but only by abdicating its traditional role of leader in causes associated with the left. In 1957 it played a distinctly secondary role in ANPI efforts to launch a national protest march on Rome. In early 1959, it was on the sidelines as La Pira and the Florentine Church battled to save the Galileo factory. The company's owners, the Venetian corporation SADE, decided on a major downsizing, announcing plans to fire over 500 workers. La Pira and Dalla Costa swung into action, mobilizing local opposition and pressuring the government to intervene. After a factory occupation and violence, a government-mediated agreement saved the company, but at the cost of layoffs. Its rivals again won the laurels, and the PCI played the role of spear-carrier.[39]

Nevertheless, the prospects of the center left appeared dim. In the wake of his May 1958 electoral victory, Fanfani formed his second government. As prime minister, he displayed the same dynamism that marked his party secretaryship: an activist foreign policy accompanied his schemes for bringing the PSI into the government. Party opponents capitalized on both. By January 1959, Fanfani was isolated within the governing coalition and within the DC. Neither the Liberals, the Social Democrats, nor DC conservatives backed his plans for opening to the PSI. Hoping to save his political program, Fanfani resigned as prime minister on January 26 and gave up the secretaryship on January 31, confident that President Gronchi would give him a new mandate to form a government. Gronchi, however, doubted that Fanfani could build a center left majority. The situation called for a mediator rather than a forceful leader to cut a deal.[40]

A center left government would have to wait until that mediator emerged. Gronchi turned to the conservative Christian Democrat Antonio Segni to form a new government. Pistelli compared Fanfani's fall with the coup de main that ousted Mussolini. The right had control of the party and the government. Asked a few months later about the center left, the new prime minister responded: "The problem—as such—does not exist."[41]

Actually, the problem was growing on the local level, where more radical versions of the center left appeared. No acceptable alternative coalition formula existed in Florence, Venice, or Naples. In Sicily, a faction split from the DC and joined with the Communists and other parties to form a regional junta. Moreover, neither Fanfani nor his former allies on the DC left were ready to concede defeat and abandon the center left idea.[42]

DC conservatives, in fact, inadvertently laid a fresh basis for a center left when at a March 1959 meeting at the convent of S. Dorotea, outside Rome, they made Aldo Moro their candidate for party secretary. Moro, the master of the elliptical phrase, was a self-contained, deeply fatalistic southerner whose talent for mediation was matched by a remarkable capacity for political analysis. Convinced that the DC could continue to govern only with cooperation from the left, he methodically moved toward a center left government. Recognizing that party unity was equally critical to continued DC dominance, he made the concessions needed to carry the party's right wing along. At the DC's October 1959 congress, held at Florence, the coalition supporting Moro easily defeated both Fanfani and the Base. The congress adopted a platform that called for a center left but conditioned by so many demands that Nenni immediately rejected the offer. Moro's October 24 address to the congress stressed that the DC would continue to govern with the Social Democrats but would leave the door open to alliance with the PSI when it judged that the Socialists were reliable partners.[43]

Moro's policy line was a shrewd jab at the solar plexus of the PSI. Nenni faced as much internal opposition to a deal as Fanfani and Moro. Moreover, the Socialist leader continued to create doubts about his reliability as a coalition partner with public statements that attacked the church's role in society, the capitalist economy, and the alliance with the United States. Nenni also had to contend with near-bankruptcy of the party daily, *Avanti!*, an entrenched PSI bureaucracy dominated by left-wingers fiercely opposed to the center left idea, and the continued paralysis of the party's local organizations.[44]

Florence remained a prime example of paralysis. The local party was divided on the issue of cooperation with the DC. Federation secretary Raffaello Ramat shuttled between his job at Salerno and duties on the city council and with the party. The entry of the former UP group produced positive results at the polls but deepened existing party divisions. The rising generation of Socialist leaders, Foscolo Lombardi complained, were political pragmatists with little commitment to Socialist traditions. The party lacked a strong base of militants.[45]

CREATING A FLORENTINE CENTER LEFT

The economic expansion of the late 1950s increased the well-being of most Italians but created serious structural problems. Continuing migration from countryside to city provoked housing and classroom shortages and played havoc with local government efforts at rational city development; inadequate roads and public transportation constricted economic growth; the growth in automobile ownership had a serious, negative environmental impact. Italy's entry into the common market (1958) spurred further growth and accentuated many of these structural problems. A widespread consensus that growth needed a guiding hand led Nenni and the DC left to argue that the country would be better positioned to deal with its problems if its government included representatives of the working classes ready to pursue serious reforms in collaboration with other social groups.[46]

By early 1960 economic and political pressures for coalition with the PSI built within the DC. In spite of heated opposition from conservatives within the church, Gronchi pushed forward his preferred candidate to lead the center left, the ambitious, lackluster Christian Democratic warhorse Ferdinando Tambroni. In February 1960 the DC's leadership issued a policy declaration on the organization of a national government that laid out terms for Socialist entry. While its demands were fairly rigorous, including "absolute loyalty" to NATO and a declaration of opposition to the PCI, they also included a paragraph that endorsed an expanded government role in economic management.[47]

With the Republican Party in the hands of forces favorable to the center left and the DC apparently ready for some sort of experiment, prospects for passage to a Socialist-DC government seemed good. Then blunders by Gronchi and Tambroni resulted in a minority DC government's relying on neo-Fascist votes for its survival in parliament. The tragicomedy continued when the government issued a permit for an MSI party congress in Genoa, one of the strongholds of the resistance. Mass demonstrations in the streets of Genoa forced the neo-Fascists to flee and Tambroni to resign. The DC displayed the dexterity that enabled it to govern for forty-five years by closing ranks around Fanfani, who formed his third ministry in late July.[48]

Tambroni's defeat helped launch the center left on the local level. Speaking shortly after Fanfani formed his government, Nenni pressed for speedy local elections. Fanfani and the DC were eager to test their strength, and the government introduced a bill reforming the local election system that appeared to boost Socialist chances for expanded representation in city councils. The government announced that normally scheduled local elections would take place that fall. The announcement meant the end of prefectural rule in Florence and offered new possibilities to Giorgio La Pira.[49]

La Pira had stayed at the center of local politics throughout the four years of prefectural rule. His *convegni* kept the publicity spotlight on the "saint." They played an important role in the city's tourist initiatives, and even a decidedly unenthusiastic Prefect Salazar provided public support. In spite of his worsening relationship with Archbishop Florit, La Pira maintained his influence within the church, in part by bombarding successive popes with advice-filled letters. (The new pope, John XXIII, privately urged him to "write a bit less.") La Pira moved onto the international political stage, garnering full press coverage for an August 1959 Moscow visit.[50]

La Pira remained the most important Christian Democrat in Florence on the basis of his showings in 1956 local and 1958 parliamentary elections. He would be the DC's candidate for mayor. However, winning the backing of a coalition oriented toward the left required La Pira to recast himself politically. The issues that had brought him to power in 1950 still had resonance. Housing had to be approached in the context of the type of overall planning that the former mayor always avoided. Transportation issues, too, necessitated careful and detailed study. Laissez-faire was no longer acceptable as city policy. La Pira would emerge as a center left reform mayor by adopting planning approaches favored by his Socialist partners.

During the 1950s, Edoardo Detti and other activists pushed the issue of a coherent city plan to the center of political debate. Initially, they utilized the city council as the bully pulpit for denouncing rampant speculation and the lack of city planning. Pointing to the haphazard growth on the periphery, one council member remarked that Florence was a great place to live for those in the center but a mess on the periphery. Detti and Fabiani exposed La Pira's mismanaged Sorgane project.[51]

After the city council's mid-1957 suspension, proponents of effective planning staged a series of effective media events to keep their concerns before the public. In mid-1957, Carlo Ragghianti lent his prestige to a "trial" of leading architects and public officials involved in the creation of "urban disorder." The "jury" decided that the leading culprits were Giorgio La Pira and his junta. Simultaneously, proponents of planning made their case against haphazard zoning in major journals, appealing to city elites to mobilize against the destruction of their artistic heritage and protect their economic future. The Socialist Party of Florence, rising from its torpor, adopted the cause of urban planning, making it a central demand for coalition with the DC.[52]

The efforts of urban planning proponents prodded Prefect Salazar to produce a new PRG for the city in 1958. The regulatory project, drawn up by Michelucci, the bête noir of the planners, received derisive reviews and further fueled opposition.[53]

Although the planners were winning the battle for public opinion, they were losing the battle to reshape the periphery and preserve the historic center. The economic boom that began in the mid-1950s fueled itself on new construction on the periphery and on reconversion in the center. The Salazar regime, like the La Pira administration, failed to regulate the building industry effectively. Review by the central government remained haphazard at best. As a result, new construction that largely ignored existing building codes and zoning regulations mushroomed, while a progressive reconfiguration of the center for the tourist trade went forward.[54]

Tourist-related issues surfaced as major factors in the battle over urban planning. Traffic, parking, road utilization, noise pollution, and public illumination all emerged in the mid-1950s as significant issues because of the congestion created when armies of tourists and masses of Florentines congregated in the old city. One solution, increasingly favored by urban planners on both sides of the debate, was moving a number of government and commercial functions out of the city center. The 1958 PRG contained plans for the creation of a commercial zone (porto) located about five kilometers from the old city along the rail and road lines leading to Prato as the new business and administrative center of Florence.[55]

Road construction was critical to the city's economic expansion and management of its burgeoning tourist industry. By 1958, with Ponte S. Trinita back in operation, the city's north and south banks were completely reunited, facilitating both tourism and trade. Access to Florence from the outside remained a problem. While most planners and businessmen agreed on the need for an air link, they were divided on the location of a city airport. Business interests favored rehabilitating the small Peretola airdrome on the city periphery, arguing that a close-in facility would encourage tourism. Detti and other urban planners responded that activating Peretola would only increase congestion in an area that was already scheduled for major development. They proposed building a provincial air hub at the nearby town of S. Angelo a Lecore.[56]

Accord existed on the need to tie Florence to expanding national and international markets by superhighway. However, the urban planners were outraged by a decision of the La Pira junta to support building the national superhighway, the Autostrada del Sole, close to the city. The opposition contended that a highway built close to the city would increase crowding and constrict new construction. Completion through the rugged Apennines of the Florence–Bologna leg of the autostrada (a true engineering marvel) brought new wealth and increased congestion.[57]

As in the past, the dividing line between right and left was the role of government in designing and regulating the expansion of Florence. Business, particularly the construction industry, wanted to proceed with an essentially

laissez-faire model. The left responded that the state and city paid for most of
the infrastructural improvements and shouldered the bulk of the costs for rehabilitation of older structures. They had a responsibility to oversee a carefully
planned construction in both the old and new zones of the city that would respect
architectural values and provide balanced growth.[58]

A NEW JUNTA

The local elections of 1960 were fought over planning and local autonomy.
The PCI, DC, and PSI adopted campaign platforms that stressed these issues,
albeit with subtle differences in tone. A second issue was the creation of center
left local administrations. The PCI opposed them, the PSI endorsed them, and
the DC avoided a definitive statement. La Pira gave the DC's platform a theological spin and came down firmly in favor of an urban plan. He also promised
further economic investment, increased cultural activities, and an expansion of
the city's international contacts.[59]

November 1960 elections produced a result that conditioned the formation of
center left juntas in the DC's favor. The Socialists, whose public battles over
alliance with the Catholics soured voters, lost seats. The PCI picked up support
with its call for a "Turn to the Left" (*svolta a sinistra*). The DC gained seats at
both the provincial and local level and was strongly positioned to demand its
price for coalition with the Socialists. The election's outcome seemed to call for
serious reevaluation of PSI strategy. However, Nenni and the majority of Florence's Socialists were eager to consummate a deal. They ignored the implications
of the election setback in their haste to join a government and launch the center
left at the local level.[60]

La Pira encouraged this haste. On November 17, "feverish about again being
mayor," he met with Nenni to lay out his plans and, more importantly, to assure
the Socialist chief that his candidacy had the support of Fanfani and Mattei.[61]

Nenni began sounding out DC leaders over the prospects for coalitions in
Florence, Milan, and Genoa, three cities where both electoral arithmetic and
left-wing political traditions would encourage alliance. His interlocutors demanded a high price for Socialist entry into power. On November 23, the DC's
Directive Committee opened the door to collaboration with "reformist elements"
but set as its basic condition the dissolution of existing political alliances between
the PSI and PCI. The party gave itself some maneuvering room by permitting
Moro to decide "difficult cases."[62]

The battered state of the DC left further complicated Nenni's efforts. It consisted of three weak and quarreling factions, without attractive ideas or power
positions within the party machine. Thus, when Nenni and Moro met in December, the DC secretary spent most of his time outlining all the difficulties
standing in the way of a deal. Moro's position included a bit of give over Florence,
where he suggested that the DC might be willing to permit formation of a center
left government even if the PSI remained part of a provincial government with

the Communists. Nenni felt that he had to have Socialist-Catholic coalitions in Milan and Palermo as well. He saw few positive signs of a deal that would lift his party's sagging fortunes. He had to calm down the impetuous La Pira, who had returned from a pilgrimage to the Holy Land, "more feverish than ever." Contrasting La Pira's haste with apparent DC lethargy, Nenni commented acidly: "Strange that he has never understood that the DC is a machine for losing time."[63]

In the end, Moro made just enough concessions to permit negotiations to move forward on Genoa, Milan, and Florence local administrations. Carefully briefed by the national parties, Socialist, Social Democratic, and DC negotiators began writing up programmatic accords in January 1961. Milan formed a center left government on January 21, and Genoa followed on February 6. Florence put together its government on February 17.

The sticking point at Florence was over who would get the assessor of public instruction. La Pira insisted that education must remain in Catholic hands. The PSI demanded the position for nearly two weeks before capitulating. The Socialists, fearful that failure to reach an accord would lead to a second prefectural regime, gave on this issue as well as on the DC's insistence that La Pira lead the government.[64]

Italy took a first halting step toward the governing majority that reformers had envisioned for nearly a decade. While Nenni staked his party's future on the belief that the DC contained a rank and file eager for major reform of the state, Moro, more realistically, drew the PSI into power as a means of reinforcing the existing DC-dominated system. For the PSI leader, the opening was a change in direction (*svolta*); for the DC secretary, it was an "experiment." Moro's evaluation proved correct. Lacking unified support in both the DC and PSI, the center left experiment reinforced the existing power structure, without providing the basis for major reform, as Giorgio La Pira and his colleagues were about to discover.[65]

NOTES

1. Fioretta Mazzei, *Giorgio La Pira. Cose viste e ascoltate* (Florence, 1980), p. 78.

2. Giovannoni interview, Florence, May 25, 1993; *Nazione*, June 7, 1956.

3. James Edward Miller, "Roughhouse Diplomacy: The United States Confronts Italian Communism, 1944–1958," *Storia delle relazione internationale* 5 (Fall 1989).

4. Nicola Pistelli, *Scritti, Politici* (Florence, 1967), pp. 772–778; Gianni Baget Bozzo, *Il partito cristiano e l'apertura a sinistra* (Florence, 1977), p. 68; Giovannoni interview, May 25, 1993.

5. Di Capua, *Nicola Pistelli*, pp. 48, 51; *La Difesa*, April 15, 1957; Giovannoni interview, May 25, 1993.

6. *Nuovo Corriere*, June 5, 7, 1956.

7. ACC 1956, 2: 1078.

8. ACC 1956, 2: 1112–13.

9. ACC 1956, 2: 1376–49 and 1251–53; *La Difesa*, April 15, 1956.

10. Ugo DeSeviero, Gianni Giovannoni, and Giorgio Giovannoni, eds., *La Pira sin-*

daco, 3 vols. (Florence, 1988–1989), 2: 247–56; ACC 1956, 2: 1295–1308; ACC 1957, pp. 9–36.

11. ACC 1957, pp. 196–99, 204–6, 214–15.

12. *Il Mondo*, July 9, 1957.

13. See Gianni Baget Bozzo and Giovanni Tassani, *Aldo Moro* (Florence, 1983). On the U.S. side, see *Foreign Relations of the United States*, vol. 27 (1955–1957), vol. 7 (1958–1960), vol. 13 (1961–1963). Also Roger Hillsman, "U.S. Policy," in Giovanni Austin Ranney and Giovanni Sartori, *Eurocommunism* (Washington, DC, 1978).

14. Pietro Nenni, *Gli anni del Centro sinistra. Diari, 1957–1966* (Milan, 1982), pp. 548–49, 736; Enzo Collotti, ed., *Archivio Pietro Secchia 1945–1973* (Milan, 1979), p. 736.

15. Nenni, *Gli anni*, pp. 661–62, 713–14.

16. Ibid., pp. 737, 748–49.

17. *Mondo operaio*, June 1956, p. 337; Foscolo Lombardi to Lucaccini, June 21, 1956, ISRT, Fondo F. Lombardi, b 14., f 48, s/f Convegno di Rifredi, 1956; Lombardi to Targetti, September 4, 1956, ibid.

18. Minutes, July 13, 1956, ibid.

19. Circular, July 9, 1956, ISRT, Fondo F. Lombardi, b 12, f. PSI-Firenze 1956; Orazio Barbieri, *La fede e la ragione* (Milan, 1982), pp. 150–54.

20. Nenni, *Gli anni*, pp. 740–741.

21. Ibid., pp. 742, 751–53.

22. Ibid., pp. 740, 753.

23. Furio Colombo, ed., *In Italy* (New York, 1981), pp. 117–18; Nicola Gallerano and Marcello Flores, *Sul PCI* (Bari, 1992), pp. 115–16; Barbieri, *La fede e la ragione* (Milan, 1982), pp. 150–54; Fabrizio Bagatti, Ottario Cecchi, and Giorgio Van Stratten, eds., *Autobiografia di un giornale* (Rome, 1989), p. 17; ACC 1956, 2: 1514–16; Report to PCI Direction, May 25, 1957, APC, Firenze 1957, 0450/0383; "Situation of Membership" n.d., ibid., 0450/0403.

24. Bagatti, Cecchi, and Van Stratten, *Autobiografia di un giornale*, pp. 14–15; Barbieri, *La fede*, pp. 150–54; Minutes, November 1956, APC, f. Firenze 1956, 0445/0795–0871; Report, December 10, 1956, AC/S, MI, Gab, Partiti politici, b 4, f 161 P/31-PCI-Firenze.

25. Nenni, *Gli anni*, pp. 755–56, 758, 760; Circular, November 6, 1956, ISRT, Fondo F. Lombardi, b. 12, f. PSI-Firenze 1956.

26. Nenni, *Gli anni*, pp. 755–56; Policy statement, n.d., ISRT, Fondo F. Lombardi, b 15, f 53, Xo congresso provinciale.

27. Prefect to MI, November 19, 1956, ACS, MI, Gab, Partiti politici, b 42, f 171/P Partito Radicale; Nenni, *Tempo di guerra Fredda*, p. 751; Nenni, *Gli anni*, p. 10.

28. Nenni, *Gli anni*, p. 13; La Pira to Nenni, June 18, 1958, Fondazione Nenni, Archivio, serie C, Carteggio La Pira-Nenni.

29. Paper: "Guidizi politici," n.d. [c. July 1957], ISRT, Fondo F. Lombardi, b 12, f. PSI-Firenze 1957; Foscolo Lombardi to Nenni, April 15, 1959, Fondazione Nenni, Archivio, serie C, Carteggio Nenni-Foscolo Lombardi.

30. Tristano Codignola, *Scritti politici: 1943–1981* (Florence, 1987), pp. 447–448; Giuseppe Tamburrano, *Storia cronaca del centrosinistra* (Milan, 1971), p. 100; Lelio Lagorio and Giorgio Morales interviews, Florence, October 4, 1995.

31. Draft policy paper, January 1958; ISRT, Fondo F. Lombardi, b 12, PSI-Firenze, 1958; Circular, January 1958, ibid.; Tiziana Borgogni, "Il PSI a Firenze tra il 1956 e il 1960: alla ricerca di un'identia autonomista" *Citte e regione* (December 1981), Lagorio interview.

32. Francesco Malgeri, ed., *Storia della Democrazia Cristiana*, 5 vols. (Rome, 1987–1989), 3: 99–100, 108, 427–72; Luca Merli (Giovanni Di Capua), ed., *Antologia della Base* (Rome, 1971), pp. 81–85; Pistelli, *Scritti*, pp. 96–109. Giovannoni interview, May 23, 1993.

33. Prefect to MI, January 4, March 4, 1958, ACS, MI, Gab, b 274, f 16995/31; Piero Bargellini, *La splendida storia di Firenze* (Florence, 1969), 4: 247; Silvio Lanaro, *Storia dell'Italia repubblicana* (Venice, 1992) p. 399; "Lo Svizzero," *La Pira e la via cattolica al comunismo* (Milan, 1964), pp. 163–69.

34. Malgeri, *Storia*, 3: 133, 141; Giorgio Galli *Fanfani* (Milan, 1975), pp. 72–73.

35. Massari, "Federazione" in Massimo Ilardi and Aris Accornero, eds., *Il Partito Comunista italiano* (Milan, 1982), p. 142; Collotti, *Archivio Pietro Secchia*, pp. 275, 320–21, 339–43.

36. Collotti, *Archivo Pietro Secchia*, pp. 330–34, Massari, "Federazione," pp. 127, 146, 173–75.

37. *In Italy*, p. 119; Collotti, *Archivio Pietro Secchia*, pp. 270–72; Palmiro Togliatti, *Togliatti e il Centro sinistra*, 2 vols. (Florence, 1975), 1: 3–24, 113–33, 165–71.

38. Amministrazione provinciale di Firenze, *Mario Fabiani* (Florence, 1975), pp. 52–53; Prefect to MI, November 29, 1956, ACS, MI, Gab, Partiti politici, b 4, f 161, P 31 PCI Firenze; Police report, February 26, 1957, ibid., b 53, f 12010/31; Prefect to MI, March 27, 1957, May 26, 1959, ibid., b 22, f 11080/31; ANPI circular, July 13, 1960, ISRT, Fondo F. Lombardi, b 18, f ANPI, s/f 1960; Barbieri, *la fede*, p. 236.

39. *Mario Fabiani*, pp. 107–12; Piero Meucci, *Giornalismo e cultura nella Firenze di dopoguerra, 1945–1965* (Florence, 1986), p. 89; Giovanni Contini, *Memoria e storia* (Milan, 1985), pp. 23, 71–72. Comunita di Isolotto, *Isolotto, 1954–1969* (Bari, 1969), p. 133. Togliatti, *Centro sinistra*, 1: 191.

40. Malgeri, *Storia*, 3: 180–81, 187, 203; Gianni Baget Bozzo, *Il partito cristiano e l'apertura a sinistra* (Florence, 1977), pp. 163–64; Nenni, *Gli anni*, p. 31.

41. Pistelli, *Scritti*, 115–19. Cyrus Sulzberger, *The Last of the Giants* (New York, 1970), p. 590.

42. Andrea Damiliano, ed., *Atti e Documenti della DC*, 2 vols. (Rome, 1968–1969), 1: 1004; Pietro DiLoretto, *La difficile transizione* (Bologna, 1993), pp. 303–4; Sulzberger, *Last*, pp. 591–92.

43. Malgeri, *Storia*, 3: 196, 212; Pietro Scoppola, *La repubblica dei partiti* (Bologna, 1991), p. 331; Nenni, *Gli anni*, pp. 79–80; Pistelli, *Scritti*, pp. 145–150.

44. Nenni, *Gli anni*, p. 23, 52, 67; Pietro Nenni, *La battaglia socialista per la svolta a sinistra nella terza legislatura* (Milan, 1963), pp. 11–13, 17; Sulzberger, *Last*, 519; Lanaro, *Storia*, p. 88; Foscolo Lombardi to Nenni, October 25, 1958, Fondazione Nenni, Archivio, serie C, Carteggio Nenni-Foscolo Lombardi.

45. Lombardi to Ramat, July 8, 1959, ISRT, Fondo. F. Lombardi, b. 12, f. Firenze-PSI 1958; Lombardi to Lombrato, February 12, 1959, ibid., PSI-Firenze 1959; Circular, June 25, 1959, ibid.

46. Giuseppe Tamburrano, *Pietro Nenni* (Rome, 1986), p. 307; Nenni, *Gli anni*, pp. 106, 112–13.

47. Nenni, *Gli anni*, pp. 69, 92–94; *Atti e Documenti della DC*, 1: 1058–60; Tamburrano, *Storia e cronaca*, p. 28.

48. Nenni, *Gli anni*, pp. 102, 109, 114, 128, 135; *Atti e Documenti della DC*, 1: 1107–09; Di Loreto, *La difficile*, p. 375.

49. Nenni, *La battaglia*, pp. 89–90; Spencer Di Scala, *Renewing Italian Socialism* (New York, 1988), p. 121; Baget Bozzo, *Il partito*, p. 280.

50. Prefect to MI, March 4, 1960, ACS, MI, Gabinetto, b 274, f 16995/31; Giuseppi Batelli, ed., *Lorenzo Milani alla Mamma* (Genoa, 1990), p. 311; Bruna Bocchini Camaiani, "La chiesa di Firenze fra La Pira e Dalla Costa" in Andrea Riccardi (ed.), *Le chiesa di Pio XII* (Rome, 1986), p. 296; Giorgio La Pira, *Lettere alle claustrale* (Milan, 1978), pp. 204–19; Antonio Lugli, *Giorgio La Pira* (Padua, 1978), p. 53.

51. ACC 1955, 1: 34. ACC 1957, 40; Mariella Zoppi interview, Florence, May 27, 1993.

52. Augusto Boggiano, *Firenze: La questione urbanistica* (Florence, 1982), pp. 216–25, 226–38, 253–55; Lombardi to Mariotti, February 10, 1960, ISRT, Fondo F. Lombardi, b. 12, f. PSI-Firenze 1960; "Il piano di Firenze," *Urbanistica* 26 (March 1959), pp. 19–22.

53. *Firenze: La questione urbanistica*, pp. 244–52; Mariella Zoppi, *Firenze e l'urbanistica* (Rome, 1982), pp. 74–77; *Firenze: studi e richerce sul Centro antico* (Pisa, 1974), p. 149.

54. *Firenze: La questione urbanistica*, p. 257; Zoppi, *Firenze*, pp. 78–80; Philippe Dubois, *Eduardo Dettti architetto e urbanista*, p. 19; Alex Fubini, *Urbanistica in Italia* (Milan, 1979), p. 243; Zoppi interview.

55. ACC 1954, 2: 1079–83; ACC 1955, 1: 8–9, 46, 104; 2: 1175; Edoardo Detti, with Tommaso Detti, *Florence That Was* (Florence, 1970), p. 132; F. Indovina, ed., *Citta fine millennio* (Milan, 1990), p. 80.

56. Zoppi, *Firenze*, pp. 59, 87.

57. Pier Luigi Ballini, Luigi Lotti, and Mario Rossi, eds., *La Toscana nella seconda dopoguerra* (Milan, 1991), pp. 266–67; Despatch 100 from Florence, June 12, 1959, NA, RG 84, Florence Post, Acc. 68 A 1814, 504.1 Public Works.

58. Gianni Cavallina, *Firenze universita e centro storico* (Florence, 1976), pp. 28–31; *Firenze studi e ricerche sul centro antico*, pp. 16–20, 24–25.

59. Togliatti, *Centro sinistra*, 1: 549–79; Nenni, *Gli anni*, p. 140; *Rinascita*, October 1960, pp. 783–86, 824–28; *Atti e documenti della DC*, 1: 1116–17; La Pira, *Lettere alle claustrali*, pp. 240–67.

60. Nenni, *Gli anni, Centro sinistra*, pp. 145–46; Togliatti, *Centro sinistra*, 1: 591–593.

61. Nenni, *Gli anni*, p. 148.

62. Ibid., pp. 151–52; *Atti e documenti della DC*, 1: 1128–1129.

63. Pistelli, *Scritti*, pp. 185–96. Nenni, *Gli anni*, pp. 152–54, 159–60.

64. Order of the day, November 14, 1960, ISRT, Fondo F. Lombardi, b 12, PSI-Firenze 1960; Circular, December 1960, ibid.; Nenni, *Gli anni*, p. 164; Malgeri, *Storia*, 3: 249–52.

65. Baget Bozzo, *Il partito*, p. 322; Scoppola, *La repubblica*, p. 345; DiScala, *Renewing*, pp. 103–4; Cf. the comments in "La nostra opposizione," *Rinascita*, February 1961, pp. 92–94.

Chapter 7

The Center Left at Florence, 1960–1965

Looking at the city today one realizes how little has remained. Open spaces have been filled; [the center] . . . reconstructed; the countryside is increasingly threatened by new developments, while Florence continues rapidly to lose any sense of relationship with the other cities of the [Tuscan] plain. Monuments, palaces, churches and museums almost disappear in the frantic traffic snarl. The old slogans "cradle of art" and "city of culture" [are] used as advertising gimmicks for mass tourism . . . [a]ccompanied by an ignorance and inadequate understanding of the city's drama by its own citizens.

Edoardo Detti

They were Florence's political odd couple. La Pira, small, delicate, smiling, was a mystic brimming with optimism. His endorsement of collectivism was hedged by profound concern for the rights of the individual. The taller, broad-shouldered Detti, a descendant of poor, strongly individualist mountaineers, was a pessimist by nature and, perhaps as a result, a convinced social planner. While La Pira's vision of society was rooted in the church fathers, Detti's had been shaped in the Florentine resistance. Strongly suspicious of the church and its political party, Detti nevertheless viewed politics as a moral exercise. During the early 1960s this lay "Calvinist" joined in partnership with a profoundly spiritual Catholic to remake Florence.[1]

In the spring of 1961, the two men began a collaboration that was increasingly grounded on respect and friendship. Detti came to admire the "semicrazy holy man" whose honesty and desire to improve the lot of the poor mirrored his own concerns and character. They were thrust together in the government of Florence as much by the persistent weakness of the local PSI as by design. Detti, forceful and organized, provided the city government with a concrete program of urban reform and renewal that would be the major achievement of the center left at Florence.[2]

CREATING A PROGRAM

The center left experiment took place in a rapidly changing city and province. The plain that connected Florence to the sea was becoming a single economic unit whose communes knitted themselves together in a web of mutually supporting productive activities. Detti recognized that Florence had to seek the fullest possible cooperation with other localities' governments, with provincial authorities, and with a network of semiautonomous institutions such as the universities to achieve its economic and social objectives. By 1961, over one-third of the province's 1.1 million citizens lived in Florence, and the influx of new inhabitants from the countryside continued unabated throughout the decade. Florence's stores, factories, and workshops provided employment to commuting workers from neighboring communes. The artisan sector of the economy grew robustly. The province had 35,000 artisan shops and the highest sectoral growth rate in Italy (150 percent) for the decade 1957–1968. By 1968 artisans composed 39 percent of the local economy. Heavy industry grew as well. In 1964, one prominent economist concluded, the city and province were well on the way to the levels of employment and output present in northern Italy. Economic expansion and accompanying intellectual ferment created a palpable sense of public optimism. The men of the center left capitalized on these feelings, offering to resolve the social strains that rapid expansion created. In their collectivist vision of Italy, this well-being had to be linked to leveling class distinctions based on wealth.[3]

Togliatti and others harshly criticized Italy's growth as uneven, dismissing its "economic miracle" as a "capitalist phenomenon" that would create more problems than it solved. Education statistics indicated that Italy lacked the skilled professionals needed to thrust its prosperity forward. In the spring of 1961 demonstrations at the University of Florence challenged an authoritarian administration, classroom overcrowding, and inadequate facilities. At the same time, the first signs of mass marketing were appearing in Italy. In June 1961, Alessandro Pintacuda, of "Supermarkets, s.p.a.," applied to La Pira for a zoning exception, promising that his stores would offer Florentines lower prices and greater customer convenience.[4]

Emboldened by the evidence of growth and concerned by inadequate past efforts to confront the city's festering urban problems, La Pira and his Socialist allies embarked on a two-front offensive: seeking major government financing for badly needed immediate infrastructural improvements while creating a consensus for a bold city plan that would discipline growth for the common good.[5]

As usual, La Pira was the point man for dealing with the national government. Despite growing signs that he was out of touch with changes inside the party, La Pira could still count on powerful support from Mattei and Fanfani and from the skillful mediation of an increasingly influential Nicola Pistelli. Prime Minister Fanfani journeyed to Florence in September 1961 and attended a city council meeting to display his support for La Pira. Mattei continued to put his wealth and influence at the disposition of the mayor. Pistelli, parliamentary deputy, vice secretary of the DC, and alderman in the La Pira junta, had concluded a new alliance with Fanfani. The mayor sought collaborators on the DC's right, offering an alliance with Defense Minister Andreotti to "utilize the human talent" of Florence fully.[6]

Ironically, La Pira's past success in winning funding for his local administration haunted him during the center left experiment. By 1960, Fanfani had molded the DC into a vast patronage machine with limited resources. Thousands of DC-led communal governments were emulating La Pira by demanding special assistance for their problems. The state treasury was strained to its limits. La Pira would win assistance, but never at the levels that he needed. The city would go deeper into debt as the mayor pressed on with his costly programs.[7]

Spending rose inexorably because the Socialists had extracted a major concession from La Pira during negotiations on forming a junta. The mayor agreed that the city needed a single, well-articulated, and detailed urban development plan (PRG). Detti, with Pistelli's support, demanded immediate realization of the mayor's commitment. In an April 24, 1961, memorandum to La Pira, the new assessor of urban planning minced no words: the city had suffered from a "confused and disordered" development in its center. The private contractor-driven city expansion of the 1950s complicated the job of imposing a coherent and effective plan. Moreover, a PRG would succeed only if Florence collaborated with the Communist-run local administrations of its communal neighbors. A new plan had to be drafted and approved speedily.[8]

La Pira adopted Detti's concepts with enthusiasm and sought the support of his major national allies for the Detti program. Typically, he found the divine hand in the urban plan. In an April 28 letter to Mattei, the mayor passed along Detti's memorandum, emphasized the necessity of ordered expansion, and urged the business chief to become the "point of force" for realizing a new Florence. Earlier, in a letter to Fanfani, La Pira argued that the success or failure of the Florentine center left experiment would have a major impact on both domestic and international politics.[9]

Detti's conception included new business, public administration and university zones, an airport, a massive expansion of primary and secondary classrooms, extensive construction of public housing, new industrial development, rehabilitation of the ancient city center, an expanded network of roads, a reorganized freight and passenger rail system, a vastly improved water supply, more parks, a carefully designed and regulated tourism, and the imposition of a cap on Florence's total population. Key to the entire plan was a wide degree of local control over the use and disposition of public and private land. Detti's project was bold in both its political presumptions and its planning details.

Detti entertained few illusions about the difficulty of achieving a plan that threatened so many entrenched interests. While La Pira sought backing among the DC's national leaders, Detti reached out to his old allies on the left and provided needed political support to the mayor. For a man of strong convictions, he proved a surprisingly supple politician. Overlooking long-standing differences, Detti advised La Pira to place Michelucci at the head of an architects committee that would rule on new construction projects. He cautioned La Pira to follow strict bureaucratic procedure in approving new construction projects. Detti even defended the mayor's beloved *case minime* before the city council as a necessary stopgap that successfully met the overwhelming need for housing in the early 1950s.[10]

The presence of Detti and his fellow Socialists in the junta had the welcome effect of defusing much Communist opposition. PCI Federation secretary Carlo Galluzzi defined the party's attachment as a "cautious" openness to political forces within both the PSI and DC that favored serious reform. The Communists remained skeptical about the coalition's ability to defuse the power of the DC right but would seize opportunities to advance their objectives through a loose collaboration with socially progressive elements in the city government.[11]

By 1961 Fabiani was openly pressing the point that the party needed to reshape its public image by achieving greater autonomy from the Soviet Union. Florence offered the PCI an opportunity to create a new relationship with the DC. Fabiani's sense of urgency grew as he began to fear that the center left formula would triumph on the provincial level, undercutting a key PCI power base. By 1962 the Communists informally provided La Pira with a friendly critique of his efforts.[12] The result was a PCI that was markedly less obstructionist and supportive of Detti's urban policies.

Detti's flexibility ended when he dealt with a local construction industry responsible for the degradation of Florence. When one builder approached him with a bribe offer, the new assessor of urban policy responded by targeting his illegal construction for demolition. Recognizing that a policy of widespread destruction was both politically dangerous and practically unrealistic, Detti pushed for a system of fines and higher licensing fees for those caught infringing zoning and construction regulations.[13]

Detti was equally firm on the basic elements of a zoning plan (PRG) for the city. In a 1963 essay entitled "The Difficult (*faticoso*) Salvage of Florence," the urban policy assessor commented that the lack of state support, the topography of the area surrounding Florence, the need for coordination with neighboring communes, the effects of fifteen years of unplanned reconstruction, and the historic and cultural importance of many existing buildings combined to severely hamper efforts to save the city. Urban plans needed to be detailed and precise in order to deal successfully with these problems.[14]

The first stages of drawing up a plan involved consultations with neighboring towns, a process made more difficult by Communist control of the vast majority of their governments. Detti then assembled a committee of experts to work out a plan. Its initial report was presented to both the national government and city council. The council appointed its own commission to oversee Detti's experts. After a long delay, the commission finally met in April 1962 to begin reviewing the draft PRG.[15]

Key to Detti's plans was a rapid legal expropriation of large tracts of privately owned land. At the beginning of the 1960s a construction boom was under way, and most Italian cities struggled to gain a measure of control over the private contractors who so easily evaded state supervision. They seized upon the PRG as the best tool for regulating and guiding construction. The Italian parliament came to their aid, passing the law of April 18, 1962, no. 167, which authorized new public housing projects and granted the communes the right to expropriate large areas for housing and related infrastructural improvements. The law obligated the communes to expropriate whenever they determined that a need for public housing existed. The following year, with the law of February 14, 1963, no. 60, parliament increased the pressure on local government to build by approving a new ten-year plan for public housing. Armed with these precedents, Detti planned to redirect development through large-scale expropriation on the periphery.[16]

The national and regional DC, representing large parts of the middle classes, balked at the Detti proposal both because of its immediate local consequences and because of the national precedents that such action would create. Moreover, the national DC was eager to see a new provincial airport placed in Prato, a party stronghold, while Detti insisted that S. Angelo Lecore was the only suitable site. Even the usually supportive Pistelli had doubts about some aspects of the Detti proposals. As a result, the DC provided a vague endorsement of Florence's PRG at the end of October 1962.[17]

In December 1962 Detti presented the city council with a plan that reflected his vision of Florence's future. He stressed that the new PRG be built on the most useful parts of the 1958 project: the movement of the provincial airport from Peretola, a reorganization of the city's rail service, changes in the location of the Rome–Florence autostrada, the creation of a commercial-industrial "port" outside the old city, and a careful restructuring of historic Florence to promote the tourist industry. The new PRG would stop rampant speculation through tight government control of available land while emphasizing the re-creation of desirable, multiclass homes in the center together with new parks, playgrounds, and other common areas. Transportation issues, including new roads, parking, mass transit, railroad relocation, and the construction of a provincial airport, were critical elements of a plan to shift industrial development and new housing progressing westward toward Pisa from the business zone (*porto*) along roads and railheads that tied together the economies of neighboring communes. Detti underlined the need for coordination with other provincial city administrations. He held out the hand of cooperation to the national government, corporations, and secure allies like the architecture faculty of the University of Florence.[18]

Detti's PRG, with its emphasis on local government leadership in development and its strict limitation on private involvement and initiative, was a typical expression of the ideals of social solidarity and local autonomy so central to the resistance and the Action Party. On the practical political level it was an open challenge to those elements of the middle class that had flourished as a result of the postwar economic boom, above all, the construction industry and its legal and political allies.[19]

The opposition was ready for a fight. In a December 28 statement to the city council, Artom attacked the fundamental premises of the PRG, arguing that it was a straitjacket on economic development and stressing that private capital would never accept the restraints that the plan imposed. The social engineering that Detti envisioned was unachievable because the city could not finance such an ambitious program.[20]

The Detti PRG won approval from the city council that evening as the PCI joined with the government to pass it by a large margin. Its impact was felt throughout Italy. The Detti plan was a powerful salvo in the battle over the future direction of Italy and a critical step on the path toward the creation of a center left coalition on the national level. Simultaneously, it hardened the battle lines between La Pira's administration and conservatives in Florence.

THE CENTER LEFT ADVANCES

The Detti plan attracted national attention for its intellectual precision and because it was launched at a moment of great difficulty for Italy's long-running political soap opera, the formation of a center left administration in Rome. Throughout 1961 and 1962 Nenni, Fanfani, and Moro inched toward an accord on Socialist participation in government. A potential new player appeared on the scene when Arthur Schlesinger, President John Kennedy's special assistant, began pushing the idea that the president intervene in support of the center left. The idea was mercifully buried by State Department bureaucrats but not before Schlesinger had created considerable confusion over U.S. policy and objectives.[21]

Nenni played the role of suitor, while Moro kept repeating that existing political problems made Socialist entry into power a difficult proposition. Fanfani again embraced the "opening to the left" in order to regain party leadership. The DC continued to insist that the PSI cut its remaining (primarily local and provincial) alliances with the PCI. Nenni assumed positions on foreign policy that distanced the PSI from the Soviet Union and in a 1962 *Foreign Affairs* essay finally embraced NATO. In the process of bringing his party to more moderate, pro-Western positions, Nenni irritated many on the PSI's left. They argued, correctly, that the DC was using the bait of political coalition to draw the PSI ever rightward, cutting it off from its historic bases of support.[22]

In contrast to Nenni, Moro and Fanfani placed consensus building within their party ahead of achieving the opening to the left. In January 1962, they succeeded in winning DC national congress approval for a gradual approach to a center left government. The DC would determine when the PSI met its criteria of suitability for partnership. In February, Nenni held talks with the two DC leaders that pinpointed areas of disagreement between the potential partners: the PSI's insistence on nationalizing key economic sectors, including electricity, the DC's opposition to the Socialists' proposals on education reform, and the personalities to be brought into government, an issue of particular concern to Moro because of its impact on party unity.[23]

Urban policy moved to the center of PSI-DC negotiations in mid-1962, when a DC minister, Fiorentino Sullo, introduced legislation that would have greatly expanded the powers of local government to expropriate land for urban renewal, handing the cities real control for development. Conservative reaction was ferocious. The Socialists adopted urban planning as their issue under the pressure of the party's left. Florence's PRG became a symbol of the major reforms that the Socialists and DC left hoped would emerge from a center left national government. It was a primary target for conservatives who hoped to blunt change.[24]

The La Pira administration increasingly found itself besieged from both sides of the political spectrum. While Florence's PCI continued to moderate its attacks and could be counted upon to support some reforms, its tolerance was limited by the concerns of national party headquarters. The success of the center left formula at Florence and its extension to a national government threatened to isolate the PCI.[25]

The La Pira junta got a foretaste of the type of opposition that the center left engendered in March 1961. Bands of neo-Fascist thugs, attending an MSI provincial congress, staged noisy demonstrations and physically attacked Florentines in an effort to intimidate the new government. La Pira, who displayed self-control and courage in confronting the Fascists, protested angrily to the central government about the lack of police intervention. He took full political advantage of the return of "squadrism" to bolster support for the center left.[26]

While the mayor produced a political success out of neo-Fascist violence, the episode underlined links between the DC right and the MSI that preoccupied Pistelli. However clumsily, the neo-Fascists were trying to exploit a glaring weakness of the center left: its lack of solid electoral support. An MSI city council member pointedly reminded the new junta that its two major parties, DC and PSI, had lost seats in the 1960 elections.[27]

The danger from the right was not limited to the MSI and DC dissidents. The Liberals formed a small, but effective and constitutionally legitimate, opposition. The junta's internal coherence was menaced by continuing mistrust between its two "Socialist" components. The PSDI's attitude toward the government was strongly influenced by a national party leadership, above all, Saragat, that remained ambivalent toward a center left on any terms but its own. Party leaders feared that they would either become a very weak junior partner in the center left coalition or be swallowed up by the larger PSI in a reunification. Saragat pressed Nenni to align the PSI with PSDI positions as the price for his support of a center left government. Personal ambitions also played a role in Saragat's diffidence. The PSDI leader wanted to cap his career as president of the republic. As chief of state, Saragat planned to mold a center left to his vision. In May

1962, Nenni's efforts to secure Saragat's election failed. Moro, always alert to the need to reinforce party unity, insisted on placing Segni, a confirmed enemy of the center left, in the Quirinal Palace. Saragat's wrath fell on both men and on Fanfani.[28]

The Social Democrats' anger extended to La Pira. In September they began to attack the coalition for its weak performance and suggested a "revision" of its membership. *La Nazione*, an ancient opponent of both La Pira and the center left, picked up the tempo of its attacks. In December, Gustavo Maier, leader of Florence's PSDI, resigned as assessor after a clash with La Pira over his administrative style. *La Nazione* got hold of copies of their correspondence and other internal documents, creating a major embarrassment for both men. Left and right took advantage to batter La Pira in the city council. The debate revealed major differences between PSI and DC on such critical issues as revenue and cooperation with the PCI. Despite the successful enactment of the Detti plan, Florence's center left began 1963 very much on the defensive.[29]

The La Pira junta's problems increased proportionally as the national center left took its last faltering steps toward realization. In March 1962, Fanfani formed a new government with a program of concrete reforms that enjoyed the external support of the PSI. It carried out most of the program, including the Socialist-inspired nationalization of the electric power industry. The DC continued to block PSI participation in government. Beset by powerful opponents inside church and party, Moro and Fanfani temporized while their personal and political differences grew. A frustrated Nenni, holding off a powerful internal opposition that comprised nearly 40 percent of the PSI membership, continued to push for a deal but won few concessions from either man.[30]

National elections in April 1963 were supposed to set the seal of popular approval on the center left. Instead, the DC and PSI suffered setbacks, while the Communists and the Liberals, the primary opponents of the opening, made strong advances. Fanfani became the scapegoat for defeat and resigned. Ironically, the increased size of the opposition made a center left government the only mathematical majority possible for the Christian Democrats. The DC put the brakes on both reform and the center left. Party warhorse Giovanni Leone took over as prime minister with a mandate to do nothing. When Sullo publicly raised the need for action on his urban reform bill, he got the sack.[31]

Nenni acknowledged that the election had been a severe defeat for which he had to bear responsibility within his party. Pointing to the blocked urban reform law and to the DC's readiness to gut its key provision, the section on expropriation, Riccardo Lombardi, leader of one of the party's major currents, complained that in his haste to close the center left deal Nenni was ready to offer too many concessions to the DC. Lombardi's revolt (June 17, 1963) forced the Socialist chief patiently to reknit his majority.[32]

Meanwhile, Florence's center left government ran aground in the face of stiff opposition from conservative interests. In a December 1962 letter, Pistelli remarked that La Pira's position within the DC continued to slip. The Florence

DC leadership was gradually turning against the mayor in spite of his proven ability to attract voters. La Pira had lost a number of key allies. Fellow Florentine and DC party president Adone Zoli was dead. Fanfani was losing influence even before the 1963 electoral setback. Mattei died in a 1962 airplane crash. A party decree forced Pistelli to resign as a city alderman.[33]

The parliamentary elections of 1963 were a severe blow to the Florence center left. The DC saw its share of the vote drop from 35.2 percent to 27.8 percent. In a candid postelection analysis, Pistelli warned that the defeat of the center left city administration was highly likely unless La Pira was able to mount a public information campaign that effectively countered *La Nazione*'s attacks. Failure to improve the junta's image would leave the La Pira administration caught between a hostile right and a well-organized PCI. To avoid defeat, the mayor had to energize and mobilize his Catholic voting base.[34]

La Pira responded to Pistelli's memorandum with a July statement before the city council outlining the objectives and achievements of his administration. The underlying theme of La Pira's talk was: We have a plan. He proceeded to list a number of significant achievements, large and small, beginning with the Detti PRG and including industrial expansion, reform of the schools, and public works. He underlined the junta's social and political vision, noting his frequent contacts with international leaders and the city government's promotion of major art shows and scientific and business congresses.[35]

The La Pira administration could claim other successes as well. It had tackled the increasingly pressing and costly traffic problem, creating more one-way streets to improve traffic flow, reducing parking to encourage drivers to use public transportation, reorganizing ATAF services to facilitate public access to the inner city, and encouraging the placement of many offices outside the old city. Assessor Rodolfo Francioni initiated studies that would create pedestrian zones through carefully planned restrictions on traffic and parking (*zone blu*), while Detti dealt with the equally difficult task of creating urban autoparks.[36]

Their efforts were essential because Florence in the 1960s was stricken by the boom in personal automobile ownership and use that affected all of Italy. The city was inundated by automobiles that carried two persons at a maximum. Historic piazzas were transformed overnight into massive car parks. Narrow medieval streets became more compact as Florentines parked their cars along the walls and on small sidewalks. City efforts to counter these trends, above all, through expanding public transportation, were costly and largely ineffective. Traffic grew, and so did the budget deficit.[37]

Other innovations included Pistelli's crackdown on building code violators, Detti's consistent efforts to preserve the architectural heritage and urban texture of Florence, La Pira's ultimately successful effort to liberate the Fortezza da Basso complex and its economic potential from the hands of the Italian army, improvements in the city's water and sewer systems, and the mayor's personal involvement in expanding tourism.[38]

The costs of these programs increased the junta's financial and political burden.

La Pira planned to pick up where he had left off in 1957, borrowing heavily from the state and pouring this money into a program of public works that would provide employment while creating the infrastructure to support industrial and service sector expansion. The mayor's response to critics was: Accept the debt and build a better city. Many critics were unconvinced. The Ministry of the Treasury put up stiff objections to further loans to the city, noting its already high ratio of indebtedness and its intention to use the majority of new loans for public works that brought no return on investment. Ignoring the opportuning of both La Pira and Prime Minister Fanfani, government ministers took the budgetary knife to Florence's requests and pared them down significantly. The city had to turn to the banks and even further increase its indebtedness. Municipalization of the gasworks, for example, cost 2 billion lire, borrowed from a private bank at 5.5 percent interest. The 1962 budget raised the deficit from 6.057 to 9.850 billion lire.[39]

While the members of the junta urged the mayor to find more sources of public support, the city's rising indebtedness triggered a hostile reaction on the right, including the conservative members of the DC. La Pira's expansive rhetoric fueled concerns. The mayor delegated most day-to-day responsibility for the operation of city government to the assessors. Turf battles flared between assessors with overlapping jurisdictions. A slowly moving city bureaucracy hindered the efficient functioning of services. La Pira continued to concentrate on setting out goals that went far beyond those of any other city administration in Italy. The notion of Florence as "mediator" between nations became the leitmotif of La Pira's center left period. He wrote Mattei that the city should be the testing grounds for developmental policies that could then be exported throughout the Third World. He proudly told the city council that its "acts . . . and . . . deeds provoke attention, resonance, and interest world-wide." In addition to the international congresses and his ultimately successful effort to capture the European University for Florence, La Pira promoted himself and Florence as envoys of peace, with a mission to settle conflicts between the Arab and Western worlds and between the two Cold War power blocs.[40]

The mayor's ambitious vision of his role and that of Florence had some internal political advantages. It appealed to deep-rooted local pride. However, the overall effect of La Pira's ambitious rhetoric was to create the image of a mayor out of touch with reality. The international aspect of La Pira's politics involved the city council in time-consuming debates about world affairs at the expense of local concerns. Ever more Florentines saw the mayor's grandiose projects as an unneeded burden on a city already deep in debt. Rogari and Artom of the PLI warned that deficit financing combined with continuing municipalization of public services was dangerous to hopes for careful urban growth and economic expansion. The opposition pounced upon these issues to discredit La Pira. "The mayor has given an address rich in fantasy—that is his peculiar quality even as an administrator," an opposition councilman scathingly remarked during a 1962 debate.[41]

Further weakening the mayor was a growing public perception, rooted in the *convegni* and La Pira's travels, that he had a blind spot toward the Communists. Marchese Emilio Pucci, a Liberal, complained that the mayor believed that Christ was the first Communist. The Social Democrats, too, were concerned about the mayor's flirtations with the left. Pistelli lamented La Pira's deep-rooted diffidence toward the United States. In 1964, the mayor visited the United States. Instead of seeking readily available private loans for his deeply indebted city, La Pira, Italy's king of deficit finances, rejected an offer of aid from Wall Street, telling his loyalists: "It's better to buy than to sell. We always have to be the creditors."[42]

The primary danger to La Pira came from within the Catholic movement. As early as the March 22, 1961, vote condemning Fascist violence, four DC councilers broke with the city administration, abstaining on the resolution because it enjoyed Communist support. Cardinal Dalla Costa was dead. His successor, Cardinal Florit, freed from the restraining hand of his predecessor, was openly hostile to La Pira. As long as Pistelli through alliance with the Fanfani faction controlled the DC's Florentine Federation, internal opponents would be at bay. The shifting nature of political alliances in Italy made retaining control difficult even for the astute Pistelli.[43]

Within the junta, divisions mounted. The PSI pressed for more innovative public programs and more public spending. PSDI aldermen, too, favored more spending for projects. The DC right, on the other hand, objected to both the new spending and the high degree of social planning that Detti's PRG entailed. The mayor's support for price controls, his willingness to put employment above all other economic priorities, and his tendency to support the interests of small shopkeepers against larger companies all carried a political price.[44]

The PCI, too, was modifying its attitude toward the city's center left. Its initially mild criticism aimed at driving La Pira toward more radical and costly innovation gave way to pointed attacks in the summer and fall of 1963 as Togliatti attempted to derail a national center left government. The Communists declared the La Pira junta a failure and excoriated the mayor for his creative financing. Pointing to its recent electoral successes, the PCI proclaimed that only its presence in a junta of the left offered the possibility of successful reform.[45]

The PCI hard line was most apparent where it did the most damage to the La Pira administration. An accord with neighboring PCI-dominated communes was critical to the success of the Detti PRG. In the spring of 1963, the Florence city council adopted its intercommunal plan. Communist administrations rejected Florentine approaches, while appeals for support to the PCI-dominated provincial government were unsuccessful.[46]

By the end of 1963, the opposition, aided by *La Nazione* and in a real sense by La Pira himself, had created a negative public image for the center left junta. Charges of fiscal irresponsibility and inefficiency were coupled with attacks on the supposed pro-Communist sympathies of La Pira and even claims that the mayor had failed to protect public morality. Continued squabbling within the majority reinforced the public perception that the center left had failed.[47]

Probably the most serious blow to the junta and its image was its inability to launch the Detti PRG. Final approval rested, as usual, with Rome. Opponents in Rome managed to bottle up the Detti plan for four years. Without government approval, the city could not begin the fairly extensive expropriation of lands central to Detti's concept. Other parts of the plan also were hamstrung at the national level. ANAS, the state roads agency, rejected Detti's proposal to move its Rome-Florence autostrada project farther away from the city. The state railways were equally resistant to Detti's plans for new stations and rail connections. Many Florentines became wary of the plan. Detti's architect son, Iacopo, commented years later that the plan would have put the city in a straitjacket: it was too detailed and offered too little space for organic development. Moreover, Edoardo Detti seriously underestimated the deleterious effects that mass tourism would have on the old city. His calls for a massive relocation of public offices to new zones of the city did not sit well with many central city shopkeepers. His plans for rehabilitation of the Campo Marte area led to a confrontation with its conservative DC alderman. Detti and Pistelli clashed over specifics such as the use of prefabricated school buildings. As resistance to implementation of the PRG grew, support for the La Pira junta fell.[48]

Detti and Pistelli recognized that the junta was dying slowly from the effects of its bad image and internal battles. Detti's solution, repeatedly pressed upon La Pira, was dramatic action on its programs, above all, urban reconstruction. Pistelli, while in accord, emphasized the need for a competent public relations program. He pushed La Pira into creating a monthly communal review to publicize the junta's accomplishments and began designing a confrontational strategy that would offer the mayor the chance to rebut his critics in public forums.[49]

THE BITTER END

The situation of the Florence junta worsened as a result of the completion of negotiations for a national center left government under Moro (November 1963). Nenni, determined to achieve the party's entry into government, accepted a schism as the price. A large and fairly influential part of the PSI's leadership and a smaller part of its base broke off to form the Proletarian Unity Socialist Party (PSIUP). Nenni's dependence on the DC increased, as did the probability of Socialist reunification with the more conservative PSDI. With the left wing of the new coalition weak, the position of reformers inside the DC became shaky. Sullo lost his leadership position in the Base current. Fanfani, always the opportunist, tacked rightward in an effort to create a majority within the DC and replace Moro as prime minister.[50]

With a weak center left in power in Rome, opponents of the La Pira junta stepped up their attacks, hoping to destroy a city government that had been in the forefront of political change in Italy. They claimed that La Pira would expand his coalition leftward to include the PCI, an idea that the mayor would certainly have rejected.[51]

La Pira, following Pistelli's strategy, presented a highly positive picture of the junta's work to the city council in November. The following month, he used the opportunity provided by the inauguration of a center left government in Rome to reorganize his junta. The Social Democrats quit. One rebel PSDI councilman remained in the junta, providing it with a single vote majority. Clinging to power, the junta faced the first of a series of crises that underlined its dependence on the central government. A January 1964 strike by communal workers forced La Pira to appeal to Moro for money to meet their demands. A strike of the milk transporters forced the city to turn to the prefect for assistance in supplying this essential foodstuff to its citizens. Later that year another Teatro Comunale budget crisis forced the city to go hat in hand to the national government for relief.[52]

The conservative opposition, spearheaded by *La Nazione*, continued to attack the mayor for his leadership style and his relations with the PCI. Some years later, La Pira remarked that the climate was so poisoned that had he been mayor in 1966, "They'd have accused me of creating the [flood]."[53]

The junta responded by advertising its public works and infrastructural programs. It kept up pressure on Rome for more economic assistance. However, La Pira was no longer in a position to triumphantly pull rabbits out of his hat. A new and unsympathetic group of DC politicians was in charge of party and government. Neither Prime Minister Moro nor party secretary Rumor was close to La Pira. On the local level only Pistelli and his "Forze Nuove" faction, about one-fifth of the federation, were solidly in La Pira's column. Another 20 percent of the DC was led by one of the mayor's committed foes, Edoardo Speranza. DC leaders complained that the mayor left them uninformed about policy. The mayor's fate increasingly lay in the hands of Fanfani's lieutenant, Ivo Buttini, whose relations with Pistelli went from warm to sour as Fanfani moved rightward.[54]

The crushing blow came in September 1964, when Pistelli died in an automobile accident. His death deprived La Pira of an energetic, sophisticated, intelligent, and politically attractive supporter who shared the mayor's concern about moral choices. Only a massive electoral triumph could keep his enemies within and outside the DC from wresting control of Florence from La Pira and his fellow reformers.[55]

The voters were in no mood to reward a badly divided center left for partially enacted reforms. The November 22, 1964, elections at Florence were a disaster for the center left. The electorate turned on both the DC and PSI. The Socialists lost two seats; the DC four. The PCI picked up two seats; the Liberals gained four. Mathematics ruled out both a center and center left majority. Simple addition pointed to a DC-PSI-PCI government, an idea that set off alarm bells in the headquarters of both the Christian Democratic and Social Democratic Parties in Rome.[56]

During the early 1960s the Christian Democratic Party machine tolerated La

Pira because of his attraction to voters in Florence. In December 1964, the mayor was a weight that they no longer willingly supported. The party's conservative majority recognized that backing the reforming mayor of Florence further would lead toward some kind of accommodation with the PCI. In turn, such an "opening" would have a major impact on national politics. They were unwilling to accept the consequences of a deal with the PCI and decided to get rid of La Pira as quickly as possible.[57]

The Social Democrats had strengthened their hand in local elections and through the December 1964 choice of their leader, Saragat, as president of the republic. Moro and Nenni joined forces to send Saragat to the Quirinale, blocking the ambitious Fanfani. Their accord spelled the political end for La Pira, a bête noire of the fiercely anti-Communist president.[58]

The PSI's attitude toward La Pira also changed as a result of defeat. The Socialists regarded the election as a major test for their party. Weakened by the 1963 split of their left and beaten in November 1964 elections, the Socialists made reunification with the PSDI and continuing membership in the national government their primary goals. The prospect of a deal between PCI and DC frightened the PSI's leaders, who foresaw their party's being squeezed out of power. Their readiness to sacrifice La Pira to the demands of Saragat and the DC's dominant right grew as the party's old guard laid responsibility for defeat on the ex-Actionists. Lelio Lagorio, the new Florence Federation secretary, backed by his predecessor, Luigi Mariotti, maneuvered to rid themselves of Detti and the former Actionists.[59]

Playing for time, La Pira resorted to a favorite tactic of avoiding city council sessions. On January 30, 1965, Lagorio opened the crisis of the La Pira junta with a letter to the mayor that demanded a meeting of the council within ten days. On February 9, the council, with Fabiani presiding, opened debate on election of a mayor. Lagorio proposed a minority government with a new mayor as the only way to head off a return to rule by the prefect. In this carefully choreographed scenario, the DC offered La Pira as its candidate with the objective of having him rejected. The council was deadlocked. A second city council meeting on February 15 produced a new mayor, Lagorio, when the Communists switched their votes to support him. The solution temporarily saved La Pira's candidacy. The DC was as unready to accept a Socialist-Communist deal as the Socialists were a DC-PCI pact. The Christian Democrats applied pressure at the national level to force Lagorio's resignation.[60]

The inability of local politicians to resolve the deadlock in Florence led to a meeting of the secretaries of the DC, PSI, and PSDI. They agreed on La Pira's replacement as part of a maneuver to freeze the PCI out of the Florence government. The agreement became public, and La Pira protested vigorously against this "betrayal," to no avail. Nenni commented that the PCI's support for Lagorio was a transparent attempt to force La Pira on their opponents and ruled out further alliances led by the "holy mayor."[61]

Further maneuvering followed. Moro suggested that La Pira return to power for two to four weeks to enable the three parties to craft a final solution for Florence as part of a deal for the formation of a new national center left administration. When the ex-mayor angrily rejected this role, the local political groupings went back to work, crafting a rather messy compromise that created a center left minority government under Lagorio. The new mayor won approval on March 10. The era of Giorgio La Pira was over. So was the city's experiment with reform government.[62]

La Pira's defeat was one of the first clear signs that the politics of social solidarity, ushered in by the resistance parties and hotly contested by propertied interests, had run its course. Italy's prosperity brought a renewed sense of individualism and, as La Pira and most on the left would have argued, selfishness. The welfare state that began to emerge as early as the 1950s and continued to grow for decades was primarily the product not of social consciousness but of pragmatic politics. While offering carefully crafted theories that aimed to disguise their patronage politics as the construction of a modern welfare system, the DC, PSI, and PCI all quietly built more extensive webs of clients through the use of public funds. Collecting and cementing votes, not careful reform, were the hallmark of the Italian welfare state. As the American scholar Judy Chubb explained in her study of Palermo: "There has been . . . a proliferation of welfare measures, sustaining levels of consumption. . . . At the same time mass clientelism has promoted the fragmentation of society. . . . The one stable point of reference is the party that holds power and thereby controls the distribution of pensions, subsidies and the like."[63] Chubb adds: "Italy is the classic example of economic and political dualism, an unparalleled example of internal dependency in which modernity and backwardness are inextricably intertwined."[64]

La Pira, Detti, and the other leaders of Florence's center left opposed this type of politics. For twenty years they fought to create a society that would meet the economic and spiritual needs of their fellow citizens. In spite of enormous opposition, these men of goodwill had succeeded, as Detti said, "*a meta*" (halfway). La Pira's public career was checkered with successes (Pignone, Galileo, public housing, food programs, public works, school construction) that benefited the city's poorest classes. He had done much to rebuild Florence's role as a center of intellectual activity through his support of the local publishing industry, scientific and cultural meetings, and his much criticized congresses. A latecomer to sophisticated urban planning, he gave Detti full support and played a key role in passage of the 1962 PRG.

While the Detti plan was too much the product of social engineering to fully translate into effective action, it spurred recognition by many Italians of the requirements of historic conservation and the need for careful zoning. Over the next quarter century, Florence would implement many of its elements on a piecemeal basis, and for more than twenty-five years it provided a guide for the expansion of the city.

Pistelli and Detti also stand out for the decency of their motivation and the idealism that they brought to the practice of local government in postwar Italy.

The generation that clustered around La Pira stood head and shoulders above their successors in terms of political vision and morality. They would be replaced by a generation of leaders whose political pragmatism translated into ever greater corruption. Florence would never again be so well led, and its weight in national political affairs declined precipitously after the first center left experiment.

NOTES

1. Tommaso and Iacopo Detti interviews, Florence, May 14, 18, 1993.

2. T. Detti interview, Mariella Zoppi, *Firenze e l'urbanistica* (Rome, 1982), pp. 82–84.

3. Piero Barucci, *Profilo economico della provincia di Firenze* (Florence, 1974), pp. 6, 14–16, 62, 64; Detti to Gabbuggiani, March 7, 1963, ALP, b 66, Comune di Firenze 1963, Detti to La Pira, June 8, 1963, ibid.

4. Palmiro Togliatti, *Togliatti e il Centro sinistra*, 2 vols. (Florence, 1975), 1: 719–38; *Rivelazione statistica*, p. 31; *Il Ponte*, June 1961, pp. 831–37; Pintacuda to La Pira, June 15, 1961, ALP, b 65, Comune di Firenze 1961.

5. Tiziana Borgogni, "Cronistoria delle amministrazioni La Pira," *Testimonianza* 21 (May 1978), pp. 280–81.

6. Davis Ottati, *L'acquedotto di Firenze dal 1860 ad oggi* (Florence, 1983), p. 288; Fioretta Mazzei, *Giorgio La Pira. Cose viste e ascoltate* (Florence, 1980), p. 99; La Pira to Andreotti, March 10, 1961, ALP, b 65, Comune di Firenze 1962.

7. Pella to La Pira, August 25, 1961, ALP, b 65, Comune di Firenze 1961; Taviani to La Pira, September 28, 1961, ibid.

8. Detti to La Pira, April 24, 1961, ALP b 65, Comune di Firenze 1961.

9. La Pira to Mattei, April 28, 1961, ALP, b 65, Comune di Firenze 1961; Amintore Fanfani, *Giorgio La Pira* (Milan, 1978), pp. 126–27; Statement by La Pira to National Conference of Urban Planners, October 1964, *Urbanistica* February 1965, p. 122.

10. Detti to La Pira, May 3, 15, 22, 1961, all ALP, b 65, Comune di Firenze 1961; ACC 1961, pp. 363–66.

11. "I comunisti e la giunta fiorentina," *Rinascita*, March 1962.

12. Malvezzi to La Pira, May 9, 1962, ALP. b 65, Comune di Firenze 1962; Orazio Barbieri, *La fede e la ragione* (Milan, 1982), pp. 158–59.

13. T. Detti interview; Detti to La Pira, September 4, 1961, ALP. b 65, Comune di Firenze 1961.

14. Augusto Boggiano, ed., *Firenze: La questione urbanistica* (Florence, 1982), pp. 299–308.

15. Ibid., pp. 319–38.

16. *Enciclopedia urbanistica*, 4: 244–45, 315, 322, 331, 705–7; Alex Fubini, *Urbanistica in Italia* (Milan, 1979), pp. 318–19; Michelle Achilli, *Casa* (Padua, 1972), pp. 16–17.

17. Detti to La Pira, April 7 and May 28, 1962, both ALP, b 65, Comune di Firenze 1962; Pistelli to la Pira, August 27, 1962, ibid.; Florence DC Provincial Committee to Detti, October 29, 1962, ibid.; Bisori to La Pira, June 15, 1961, ALP, subject file, b. 70, Aeroporto di Prato.

18. ACC 1962, 2: 1191–1209.

19. Marco Massa, ed., *Firenze* (Milan, 1988), p. 90; Philipp Duboy, ed., *Eduardo Detti, 1913–1984: architetto e urbanista* (Milan, 1993), p. 17; Zoppi, *Firenze*, pp. 89–91; Goffredo Nanni to La Pira, October 30, 1961, ALP, b 65, Comune di Firenze 1961.

20. ACC 1962, 2: 1296–1332.

21. Schlesinger, *A Thousand Days*, pp. 877–78; *Foreign Relations of the United States, 1961–1963*, vol. 13 (Washington, DC, 1995), pp. 826–29; Spencer Di Scala, *Renewing Italian Socialism* (New York, 1988), pp. 128–30.

22. *Foreign Affairs*, January 1962, pp. 213–23; Pietro Nenni, *Gli anni del Centro sinistra. Diari, 1957–1966* (Milan, 1982), pp. 181–82, 185, 188–89, 191–92; *Atti e documenti della DC*, Andrea Damiliano, ed., 2 vols. (Rome, 1968–1969), 1: 1165; Gianni Baget Bozzo and Giovanni Tassani, *Aldo Moro* (Florence, 1983), p. 71.

23. Nenni, *Gli anni*, pp. 191–93, 205–6, 209; Francesco Malgeri, ed., *Storia della Democrazia Cristiana* (Rome, 1987–1989), 3: 473–559; Nicola Pistelli, *Scritti e discorsi* (Florence, 1967), 230–32.

24. Fiorentino Sullo, *Lo scandolo urbanistico* (Florence, 1964), pp. 11–17, 20, 98–99, 117–48; Corrado Giustiani, *La casa promessa* (Turin, 1981), p. 62; *Urbanistica* 39 (October 1963), pp. 13–17; Luca Merli (Giovanni Di Capua), ed., *Antologia della Politica*, 4 vols. (Rome, 1973), 4: 98–103.

25. Togliatti, *Togliatti*, 2: 929–55, 1003–19, 1021–56, 1137–45, 1167–69.

26. Prefect to MI, March 12, 22, 1962, both AC/S, MI, Gab, Partiti politici, b 61, f. 195/P/31 MSI-Firenze; Press release, March 11, 1961, ALP b 74 Fatti fiorentine, personalissimi, La Pira to Gronchi, March 13, 1961, ibid. riservatissimi; La Pira to Scelba, March 17, 1961, ibid.; ACC 1961, pp. 23, 719.

27. Pistelli, *Scritti*, pp. 196–206; ACC 1961, pp. 8–11.

28. Nenni, *Gli anni*, pp. 208, 212, 216, 225–26, 272–73; Baget Bozzo and Tassani, *Aldo Moro*, p. 29; Tamburrano, *Storia*, p. 246.

29. ACC 1962, 2: 1182–91; ACC 1963, 1: 11–51; La Pira to Maier, January 11, 1963, ALP b 66, Comune di Firenze 1963; Zoppi, *Firenze*, pp. 88–89, 102–5; Borgogni, "Cronistoria," pp. 282–83; Nenni, *Gli anni*, pp. 209–10.

30. Nenni, *Gli anni*, pp. 246–47, 249–51, 260–61; Baget Bozzo and Tassani, *Aldo Moro*, pp. 60, 90.

31. Nenni, *Gli anni*, p. 285; Cyrus Sulzberger, *The Last of the Giants*, (New York, 1970), 1006–7; Baget Bozzo, *Moro*, pp. 66–67.

32. Baget Bozzo and Tassani, *Aldo Moro*, pp. 75–77; Leo Wollembourg, *Stars, Stripes and Italian Tricolor* (New York, 1990), pp. 88–89; Nenni, *Gli anni*, pp. 268–69, 272.

33. Ugo De Seviero, Gianni Giovannoni and Giorgio Giovannoni, eds., *La Pira sindaco*, 3 vols. (Florence, 1988–1989), 3: 155; Procacci to La Pira, April 19. 1961, ALP, b 65, Comune di Firenze 1961; Maltriani to La Pira, June 14, 1961, ibid.; Pistelli to Flochi, ibid.; Pistelli to La Pira, March 22, 1963, ALP, b 66, Comune di Firenze 1963.

34. Ballini, "Dinamica elettorale," Pier Luigi Ballini, Luigi Lotti and Mario Rossi, ed., *La Toscana nel secondo dopoguerra* (Milan, 1991), p. 371.

35. *La Pira sindaco*, 3: 225–40.

36. Francioni memorandum, November 19, 1962, ALP, b 65, Comune di Firenze 1962; Detti to La Pira, July 31, 1961, ibid., Comune di Firenze 1961.

37. Boggiano, ed., *Firenze: questione urbanistica*, pp. 309–18; Centro studi Pistelli, *Firenze uno due* (Florence, 1967), pp. 6, 37, 39–40; Fabiani, *Fabiani*, pp. 65–74.

38. Detti to La Pira, July 18, 1961, ALP. b 65, Comune di Firenze; Pistelli to La Pira, February 5, 1963, ibid.; Detti to La Pira, October 17, 1963, ibid.; La Pira to Andreotti, October 9, 1963, ibid.; La Pira to Congresso Turismo, c. February 24, 1962, ibid.

39. La Pira to Fanfani, August 8, 1961, ALP, b 65; Comune di Firenze 1961 lays out the mayor's program; Finance Ministry to Fanfani, July 6, 1961, ibid.; La Pira to Fanfani,

October 10, 1961, ibid.; Delle Fave to La Pira, October 12, 1961, ibid.; Gobbo to La Pira, April 20, 1961, ibid.

40. La Pira to Mattei, n.d., ALP, b 65, Comune di Firenze 1961; Pistelli to La Pira, July 13, 1964, ALP, b 66, Comune di Firenze 1964; Agnoletti to Aprioni, March 22, 1963, and Aprioni to Agnoletti, March 29, 1963, ibid.; Subject File, b 69 f Cantieri; Giorgio La Pira, *Lettere alle claustrale* (Milan, 1978), pp. 289–98, 410–39.

41. ACC 1961, 485–95; ACC 1962, 1: 562–74, 594.

42. Mazzei, *Giorgio La Pira*, pp. 103–4.

43. Giovanni Di Capua, *Pistelli ci disse* (Rome, 1971), pp. 43–44.

44. Maier to La Pira, May 7, 1962, ALP, b 65, Comune di Firenze 1962; Agnoletti to La Pira, June 17, 1963, ibid., b 66, Comune di Firenze 1963; *La Pira sindaco*, 3: 203–6.

45. ACC 1962, 1: 20–26; ACC 1963, 2: 762–78.

46. Zoppi, *Firenze*, pp. 102–5; Boggiano, ed., *Firenze: questione urbanistica*, pp. 319–38; Di Capua, *Pistelli*, pp. 184–85.

47. *Il Ponte*, December 1962, pp. 1579–1581; Florentine DC to La Pira, April 11, 1964, ALP Subject File, b 68, ATAF; Pistelli to La Pira, ibid.; b 66, Comune di Firenze 1963.

48. ACC 1962, 1: 408; ACC 1963, 1: 203; Detti to La Pira, February 3, 1963, ALP b 66, Comune di Firenze 1963; Detti to La Pira, March 5, 1963, ibid.; Pistelli to La Pira, June 4, 1963, ibid.

49. Detti to La Pira, June 8, 1963, ALP. b 66 Comune di Firenze; Pistelli to La Pira, June 3, 1963, ibid.; Pistelli to Nenci, June 30, 1964, ALP, b 66, Comune di Firenze 1964.

50. Baget Bozzo and Tassoni, *Aldo Moro*, pp. 52–53, 109, 111; Nenni, *Gli anni*, pp. 297, 302–5, 307–8.

51. "L. Svizzero" [pseudo], *La Pira e la via cattolica al comunismo* (Milan, 1964), pp. 15–17, 73–79; Baget Bozzo and Tassoni, *Aldo Moro*, pp. 108–9; Pistelli, *Scritti*, pp. 292–94.

52. *La Pira sindaco*, 3: 269–80; ACC 1963, 2: 1293–95; La Pira to Moro, n.d., but c. January 12, 1964, ALP, b 66, Comune di Firenze 1964; Francioni to La Pira, January 17, 1966, ibid.; Votto to La Pira, ALP, Subject File, b 70, Teatro Comunale; La Pira to Director General Italcasse, September 10, 1964, ibid.

53. Piero Meucci, *Giornalismo e cultura nella Firenze del dopoguerra 1945–1965* (Florence, 1986), pp. 95–96; La Pira to Fossombroni, December 12, 1962, ALP. b 65; Comune di Firenze 1962.

54. Pistelli to La Pira, June 1, 1964, ALP b 66, Comune di Firenze 1964; Detti to La Pira, September 18, 1964, ibid.; Pistelli, *Scritti*, pp. 207–8, 298–307.

55. *La Pira sindaco*, 3: 389–93; T. Detti interview.

56. Nenni, *Gli anni*, p. 416; *Il Mulino*, December 1964, pp. 1218–27; Baget Bozzo and Tossani, *Aldo Moro*, pp. 172–73.

57. G. Giovannoni, "I cento giorni di Firenze," *Politica*, March 1, 1965; Luciano Bausi interview, Florence, June 1, 1993.

58. Borgogni, "Cronistoria," pp. 284–86; Baget Bozzo and Tossani, *Aldo Moro*, pp. 177–78, 190.

59. Maurizio Degl'Innocenti and Stefano Caretti, *Il socialismo in Firenze e provincia* (Pisa, 1987), p. 185; M. Matteotti, "I socialisti al governo locale," *Mondo Operaio*, October 1964, pp. 9–12; Lelio Lagorio interview, Florence, October 4, 1995; T. Detti interview.

60. Lagorio to La Pira, January 30, 1965; ALP, b 66, Comune di Firenze 1965; ACC 1965, 1: 10–65; Lagorio interview.

61. La Pira to Rumor, February 18, 1965, ALP, b 66, Comune di Firenze 1965; La Pira

to Nenni, n.d. but February 1965; Fondazione Nenni, Archivio, serie C, Cartggio Nenni–La Pira; Nenni, *Gli anni*, pp. 453–54.

62. Nenni, *Gli anni*, pp. 455–58. ACC 1965, 1: 116–23, 130–34, 148–49, 154–65; Press release, February 28, 1965, ALP, b 66, Comune di Firenze 1965.

63. Judith Chubb, *Patronage, Power and Poverty in Southern Italy* (New York, 1982), p. 246.

64. Ibid., p. 251.

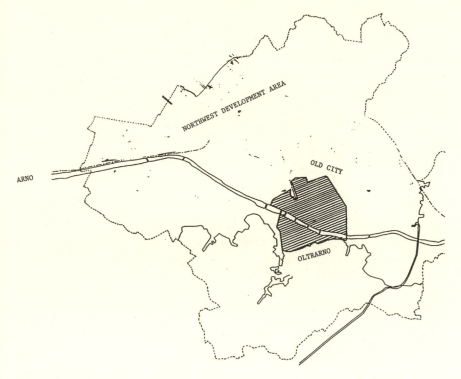

NORTHWEST DEVELOPMENT AREA

ARNO

OLD CITY

OLTRARNO

The City of Florence

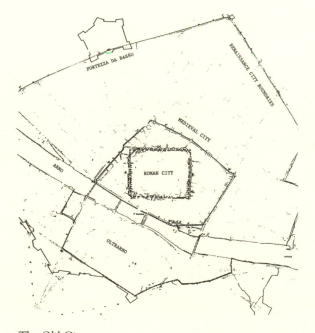

FORTEZZA DA BASSO

RENAISSANCE CITY BOUNDRIES

MEDIEVAL CITY

ROMAN CITY

ARNO

OLTRARNO

ARNO

The Old City

"Florence From Afar Seems Paradise" The City Seen From Poggi's Piazzale Michelangelo. Local artists capture the scene. (Photo by author)

Michelucchi's S. Maria Novella railroad station (center) one of the major projects of the Fascist era. (Church of S. Lorenzo in foreground, church of S. Maria Novella directly in front of station.) (Photo by author)

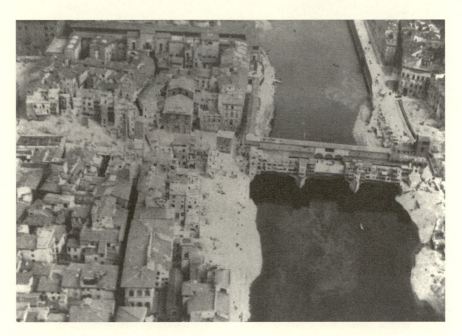

Florence at War: Aerial view of the Por S. Maria area, Fall 1944. (Istituto Storico della Resistenza in Toscana)

The Liberation of Florence: Partisans in action, August 1944. (Istituto Storico della Resistenza in Toscana)

City Divided: Liberated Florentines cross an Arno without bridges. (Istituto Storico della Resistenza in Toscana)

Modified *com'era* reconstruction: Por S. Maria. Note the pseudo-medieval lower parts of structures and modern construction of upper portions. A reconstructed medieval tower is in background. (Photo by author)

La Pira's Florence: a restored street shrine. (Photo by author)

La Pira's Florence: Apartment bloc in Isolotto. (Photo by author)

La Pira's Florence: Satellite cities. Florence (barely) seen from Isolotto. (Photo by author)

The Morning After: Piazza S. Croce in the wake of the November 1966 flood. (Museo di Storia della Fotografia Fratelli Alinari, Florence, Italy; Copyright Alinari/Art Resource, NY)

Palazzo di Giustizia: Its relocation has played a major role in urban planning disputes. (Photo by author)

Life on the periphery: Apartment blocs in the northwest zone of Florence. (Photo by author)

Traffic: The morning rush hour circles the old city in search of limited parking spaces. (Photo by author)

Piazza Repubblica. This large square with its monumental arch commemorating national unification incarnated the desire of nineteenth-century Florentine elites to achieve "modernity" by destroying the city's medieval heritage. (Photo by author)

Tourism: *Bancarelle* clutter Piazza Repubblica. (Photo by author)

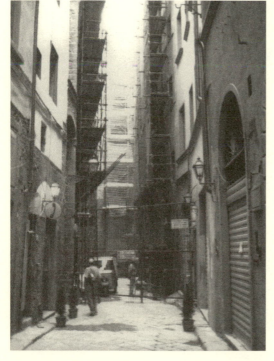

Terrorism: via Lambettesca site of 1993 bombing during early phase of reconstruction. (Photo by author)

Chapter 8

The Flood

On the fourth [of November] . . . an enormous flood occurred, covering the entire city and the plain of Florence, causing the death of many Christians and livestock, and the collapse of a large number of palaces, towers, and houses.

anonymous diary of the year 1333

October 1966. Italy's autumn rains were heavy and continuous. The Arno rose steadily. The overcast, the rain, and cool winds flowing off the Tyrrenian Sea made it a particularly cold early fall. Families and businesses stocked up on fuel oil and turned up their furnaces. The torrential rain that pelted Florence on November 2 continued throughout the next day with only a few brief pauses. In spite of rain and cold, the mood in the city was upbeat. November 4 was a national holiday. Vittorio Zumbo, a bookseller, drove happily into Florence that afternoon with a trunk full of his latest purchases. Exhausted but exhilarated, Zambo stacked his finds in the shop on via Verdi and headed home, planning to use his day off to catalog them. As shopkeepers locked up and headed home to enjoy a well-earned day off, Katherine Taylor, an American transplant, elbowed her way onto a bus filled with rain-soaked Florentines and headed back to a *pensione* on the Arno's banks. A small crowd filled the Verdi theater to watch Noah cope with the flood in John Huston's version of *The Bible*, while a concert in the Palazzo Vecchio's ornate Hall of the Cinquecento drew a group of hardy music aficionados. By early evening the city was semideserted; most Florentines preferred to wait out the rains in the warmth of their homes. Luciano Bausi, a Christian Democratic alderman, left a dinner meeting of the junta at Hotel S. Minerva and, after a brief stop at another dinner, headed home in the driving rain about 10 P.M. He planned an early start the next morning in order to reach Rome and a plane that would take him to a city planners meeting in Palermo. In Rome, Enrico Mattei, editor of *La Nazione*, was preparing for his trip home.[1]

Less than fifty miles away, at the point where the Arno hooks north, disaster was already beginning to play itself out. The plain of Arezzo was hit by major flooding. At the aptly named Gates of Hell, sites of the Levane and La Penna dams, about thirty-five miles south of the city, employees of the state electrical agency, ENEL, watched swelling water basins with mounting concern. By early evening the water was approaching the tops of the dams. Fevered calls to alert local authorities in Florence and request instructions followed. Sometime after 9 P.M., as the waters threatened to overflow the dams, ENEL's employees sounded a flood alarm as the preliminary to opening the dams. Shortly thereafter a further 13.5 million cubic meters of water joined the already flood-swollen river on its way to the sea. This knockout punch lurched downstream toward Florence.

While city officials watched the rising waters with apprehension, few locals seemed worried. "The Arno never floods," Taylor's landlady explained reassuringly. Elsewhere, however, the sense of security was fading. The rising river water, thoroughly mixed with a heavy, dark-brown mud and yellow fuel oil, picked up tree trunks, fuel drums, and all manner of smaller detritus as it roared through Tuscany. The storm reached unprecedented intensity. (In the twenty-four-hour period that began at 1 P.M., November 3, Florence was pelted by the equivalent of one-quarter its annual average rainfall.)

Around midnight a night watchman called owners of jewelry shops on the Ponte Vecchio to warn them that the waters would soon reach the floor level of their shops. Frightened shopkeepers galloped through the downpour to the bridge and hastily carried off precious stones and metals. Not far away, on via del Parione, the males of the Gucci clan, alerted to the danger by a relative, were hastily grabbing leather goods and other products off the shelves of their first-floor shop and carrying them upstairs.

The waters of the Sieve began to pour over their banks shortly after midnight. The two rapidly expanding rivers joined forces about twelve kilometers east of Florence, gathering further force from the heavy rains. At the western side of the city, the Mugione filled and began backing into the Arno at about 2 A.M., pushing over its banks and gradually covering the Cascina.

An hour later the Arno broke into low-lying Varlungo, a semiautonomous suburb of Florence. Around 4 A.M., a few volunteers appeared magically at the doors of the Uffizi and, joining the museum's skeleton force of night custodians, carried artworks to higher floors. Sixteen volunteers and custodians struggled valiantly with nearly 400 works stored in the basement or lying in lower-floor museum restoration shops.

Half an hour later, water entered the streets of the suburb of S. Donnino. Don Mantellassi, the parish priest, began ringing the church bells in an effort to alert the populace to the oncoming disaster. A few miles away, city officials debated whether to sound some sort of alert, then hesitated for fear of creating a murderous general panic. Mayor Bargellini stood along the banks of the river, observing the rising waters. His initial concern was for the safety of Ponte Vecchio. Few thought the seven-century-old bridge would withstand a combination of water pressure and the impact of uprooted tress and other massive pieces of debris.

Backed-up sewers began to flood the center of the city, disgorging their repulsive cargoes of filth. Between 6 and 7 A.M., as patches of clearer water heralded the arrival of the dam discharge, the Arno leaped over the last retaining walls and headed toward Florence's historic center. Once over the banks, the waters cascaded downward toward the heart of the old city. Don Gustavo Cocci, historian of S. Croce, opened the doors of the church about 6:30 P.M. and peered into the gloom. A wall of water was boiling toward the church. Aided by other early-rising Franciscans, Cocci vainly tried to shut the massive old doors. The raging waters flung them wide open, and the priests fled for safety along the nave, pursued by the Arno. Minutes later, as trattoria owner Gino Mugnaini sat peeling potatoes in his restaurant on via Giovanni da Verrazzano, he noted water seeping under the doors of his establishment. Looking down the street, he saw Piazza S. Croce under water.

By 7 A.M. the Arno was flowing throughout much of old Florence at speeds of over forty miles per hour. Water roared down the narrow streets, invaded basements, uprooted parked cars, and carried away the contents of homes and shops. Explosions erupted as the floodwaters reached lighted home furnaces, and pressure inside the sewer system blew the tops off manholes. Basic public services— lights, water, electricity—all failed within a few minutes. The 200 patients at the hospital of S. Giovanni di Dio lost effective medical assistance when the water knocked out their emergency generator. Inmates and guards at Murat and S. Teresa prisons sought safety by scrambling to rooftops. By 7:30 A.M. the Arno had thrust Florence back into the Middle Ages.

The river was equally merciless with the Oltrarno district. Following a gentle downward slope, the Arno rushed down the via Guicciardini, past the Palazzo Pitti along via Romana like an eight ball headed for a corner pocket. The pocket, Piazza S. Felice, nearly a quarter mile from the Arno's banks, inclines on two sides. Obeying the laws of gravity, the water banked right down the via Mazzetta to via S. Monaca, where it executed another right and headed back toward the riverbank, inundating Piazza del Carmine with its great Renaissance church as it passed. The returning waters joined forces with those pouring over the riverbanks east of the Ponte Vecchio to flood the low-lying zones of S. Frediano and S. Spirito. Further downstream, the Arno was turning the zones of Pignone and Isolotto into lakes.

Most Florentines became aware of the catastrophe as dawn broke. Many slept peacefully through the rainy night, awakening to find themselves isolated in man-made islands. As Bausi drove down toward the city center about 6:30, he noted the Arno's severe discoloration and the horrible smell coming from the river. Crossing the river at Ponte alla Carraia, he drove toward the train station. To Bausi's amazement, no one seemed aware of the danger lurking a few hundred yards away. Announcements of train delays and cancellations mounted, but it was business as usual for the station's porters, newspaper vendors, barmen, and railway employees. Abandoning his travel plans, Bausi headed toward Palazzo Vecchio to offer assistance to the city's administrators.

On the fourth floor of via del Presto, 2, a few blocks from the Duomo, Edoardo Detti's family awoke around 7 A.M. to shouts from a nearsighted grandmother. Looking down, the Dettis saw water everywhere. The phone rang. Tommaso's girlfriend was at Piazza Santa Maria Novella seeking help. By the time the two boys scampered downstairs, the water level was at their knees. Tommaso inflated a rubber boat, put it in the water, and glided down the narrow via del Corso to Piazza Repubblica and on to Piazza S. Maria Novella. He didn't find her. Heading back against the current, Tommaso fought a treacherous stream. Its dangerous eddies capsized his boat and threw him into the filthy waters.

Iacopo took his search for the missing girlfriend farther afield with an equal lack of success. He wandered around the city, skirting the Ponte Vecchio. Eventually, he came upon another young woman fleeing the rising waters. The two reached one corner of a flooding Piazza Duomo. On the other side, Marchese Emilio Pucci was improvising a safety rope to carry people across the piazza and toward higher ground. After assisting the woman to safety beyond Piazza S. Marco, Jacopo belatedly attempted to return home. The waters were too high. City telephones had long since failed, and after narrowly escaping drowning in one last effort to reach via del Presto, Detti headed for the safety of a friend's home in the hills. It was, he recalled years later, a great adventure for a sixteen-year-old.

Looking out the upper-story windows of his isolated Piazza Vecchio command post, Bargellini witnessed horrifying and astonishing sights. The swirling waters now reached the top of most ground floors and were carrying off anything that floated. Furniture, clothing, food, automobiles flew past city hall at speeds of forty-five miles per hour as did another, more horrible sight. A procession of bodies, some naked, some laid out in coffins, passed under the mayor's command post, as Florence's funeral parlors yielded up the dead to the river.

Here and there along the swelling canals of Florence, men and women clung to lampposts, while others sought safety from a steadily rising torrent on window ledges. One elderly woman lost her life when water shut her door and gradually filled her apartment. Frantic efforts by neighbors to cut through from the floor above failed.

City animals met varied fates. Birds housed in a shop in Piazza Castellani were chirping as the floodwaters approached. Silence followed quickly. Some dogs tried to swim with the current, usually unsuccessfully; others huddled with their families. Cats climbed ever higher on buildings in search of shelter. At the small city zoo in the Cascina, keeper Renzo Morozzi, alerted by the cries of frantic animals, overcame concern about dangers to the human population and opened the cages, allowing their inhabitants to scurry for safety. At the nearby hippodrome, groundskeeper Cesare Nesi faced a similar dilemma and arrived at the same solution for the horses in his care. Many animals failed to make their escape. Their bodies, along with those of numerous small mammals carried into Florence by the Arno, became a major public health problem.

By noon almost all of the historic center, the Cascina, and the majority of homes in zones lying along the Arno were under water. The Duomo and its surrounding piazza were under six feet of water. The raging waters ripped Ghiberti's bronze reliefs from the Baptistry's "Doors of Paradise." At Piazza S. Croce, the flood had reached a level of fifteen feet. The church of Santa Croce with its vast collection of masterpieces was inundated. A few hundred feet away, at the banks of the Arno, a treasury of books and manuscripts poured out of the National Library and headed into town. Many would pile into S. Croce. Ilaria Poggiolini's family drove from their home in the hills to Poggi's scenic Piazzale Michangelo to survey the scene. Incredulous, the little girl shouted: "Florence has become Venice."

Thousands of Florentines, isolated throughout the day in unheated apartment buildings, with no water, little food, and no means of communicating to the outside world, could only watch and wonder when and how assistance would reach them. Those with portable radios listened in shock as broadcast news reported only limited flooding in Florence. The sense of desperation rose as the waters continued to roar by, the rain poured down, and darkness approached. A few helicopters passed over the city unable to provide aid. Efforts to bring rescue personnel and supplies by boat were frustrated by the swiftness of the currents. Florentine government officials tried and failed to set up a line of communications through the Vasarian corridor. Tired, hungry, thirsty, the inhabitants of much of Florence settled into their beds that evening, frightened and deeply disoriented.

The water finally began a slow retreat after midnight, November 5. The rains let up. By dawn large sections of the city had been liberated from the Arno but not from its gifts: masses of oil-impregnated mud, battered cars, dead animals and men, raw sewage, tree trunks, furniture, foodstuffs, the telltale red bags filled with infectious hospital waste, books and artworks, all manner of detritus. Throughout that day and the next, the water receded, leaving more and more zones with the difficult job of digging out.

The destruction was impressive. Over 43,000 Florentines suffered flood damage. The 750 city piazzas and streets covered by the Arno were the home to 500,000 tons of oily mud. The flood's impact on Florence's cultural patrimony was overwhelming. Over 1,200 pictures, 1.2 million books, 400,000 newspapers, 60,000 journals, and 400,000 miscellaneous items at the National Library alone were damaged or destroyed. The archivio di Firenze lost 10 percent of its valuable manuscript collection. Thousands were homeless, 6,000 shops and 12,000 automobiles destroyed, and, most terrible of all, 121 citizens of the province, 31 from the city, were dead.

"FLORENCE, 5 NOVEMBER—YEAR ZERO"

A placard on one shop said it all: the year zero. Twenty-two years after the liberation, the citizens of Florence had to start all over again. They faced a rebuilding task much greater than that of 1944. The November deluge spread havoc from Venice in the northeast across Emilia and through Tuscany. Nearly a third of Italy claimed its share of emergency assistance from a government and national economy that were woefully unprepared to provide either immediate assistance or longer-term reconstruction aid. The outlook for recovery was grim on the cold dawn of November 5 as exhausted Florentines surveyed the damage and the horrible-smelling, disease-breeding carpet of petroleum-impregnated mud covering the city surface.

The administration of Piero Bargellini was singularly unequipped to deal with the disaster. A minority government, led by a popular political hack, it had displayed little initiative in its first months of administration, and, in fact, the mayor announced the junta's resignation just before the flood struck. Bargellini, author of children's books and a romanticized "history" of Florence, was a devoted right-wing Catholic whose political pedigree included a long flirtation with Fascism, a term as La Pira's assessor for culture, and a prominent role in the cabal that ousted the former mayor. Genial, well-spoken, a good writer, Bargellini's prestige rested on his repute as a staunch opponent of cultural innovation and as a promoter of tourism. His political ideas were as banal as his cultural views.[2]

Bargellini, the "mayor of the flood," would claim a position in the Italian Senate exactly one year later, surrounded by hosannas. This popular acclaim owed little to his performance during the disaster. The mayor failed to alert the city as the waters rose and isolated himself for hours in his Palazzo Vecchio command post during the flood. Fortunately for Bargellini, Florentine anger was directed at the national government. In the orgy of blame that followed the disaster of November 4, Aldo Moro emerged as the primary villain. Bargellini played the role of tribune of a sorely tried Florentine people with great skill.[3]

Bargellini was mayor because of the shipwreck of Florentine reform. La Pira completed his political immolation with an amateurish effort to mediate a peace settlement to the Vietnam War. Lagorio's minority government collapsed when the council majority rejected its budget. Dr. Adriano Monarcha took over as prefectural commissioner on November 16, 1965. This time, the interim government was just that. It governed long enough for the leadership of both DC and PSI to complete the purge of reformers in their ranks and then oversaw elections on June 12, 1966.[4]

The vote confirmed the Florentine electorate's inability to agree on public policy or a governing majority. The DC pushed Bargellini forward as its interim mayoral candidate, putting the final seal on its liquidation of La Pira and the left. The opposition taunted the "brilliant minds of . . . the center left [that] have given birth to a wonderful masterpiece: another minority government."[5]

The new junta, formed on the eve of summer vacations, was destined for a short life. Relations between its component parts were badly frayed. The mayor maladroitly courted a sulking La Pira, ratcheting up tensions within the DC. The Socialists mistrusted the DC right's leadership and the mayor. Bargellini and Lagorio, the PSI's leader, cooperated at drawn swords while the mayor found solace in long discussions with PSDI leader Gustavo Maier. DC-PSDI coopera-tion, always a source of irritation to the Florence PSI, was particularly aggravating at a moment when the two still competitive and mutually suspicious Socialist parties were moving toward national unification (October 30, 1966). For their part, Bargellini and other DC officials resented the continuing flirtation between the PSI and the Communists.[6]

Bargellini wisely avoided meetings of the city council or addressing major city problems. He tried to create the impression of action by holding frequent meet-ings of the junta and by maintaining a hectic schedule of museum and exhibition openings and other cultural events. The junta's meetings produced more intra-party friction than action. The Socialists withdrew from the government on September 30. After various last-ditch attempts to reconstruct a coalition, the junta's leading lights agreed to throw in the towel at a November 3 meeting. As the outgoing junta's members navigated from their meeting to their parked cars through streets that were becoming small lakes, the mayor laughed off one of the junta's few innovative projects, teasing urban planning assessor Bausi that his "Clean Florence" (*Firenze pulita*) initiative was an evident failure.[7]

Thirty-six hours later, *Firenze pulita* appeared to be an impossible dream. On the morning of November 5, those Florentines who could emerged from their homes to begin the daunting task of removing a mud carpet that in many places reached to their knees. The malodorous mudpack filled subsurface Florence: sew-ers, basements, storage areas, and its historic *buca*, the belowground restaurants that had been a city trademark for centuries.[8]

Florentines began to clean up their homes and shops. More mud and wreckage flew out into the already overwhelmed streets to await action by the city and state. Many shared the experience of Dario Frosecchi, a small shop owner: "I had to throw everything into the street and then see it all carried away . . . everything that permitted me to make a living."[9]

Florence was without food and water. Most people had only primitive tools, and hip boots, the most essential item for cleanup, were in short supply. The Florentines' proverbial ingenuity showed its bad side as a black market in boots and other cleanup supplies flourished. While desperate homeowners dug out, equally frightened shopkeepers from the suburbs struggled across the mudflats to reach their property and dig their way inside. City and national authorities or-ganized what assistance they could, bringing in water trucks, searching for food, setting up emergency kitchens and shelters. The Italian army sent in troops, trucks, bulldozers, and other heavy equipment, as they became available, to clear off the streets. The rescue of artworks commenced as soon as curators and vol-unteers could reach Florence's many galleries, churches, and other public build-ings.[10]

Key to the cleanup and recovery was the indomitable spirit of the citizens of Florence. Work proved to be the best cure for their initial psychological disorientation. Pluckier Florentines spiced their work with morale-enhancing gallows humor. Bargellini noted a few jocular signs on the walls of shops the morning of November 5. Powerfully aiding the recovery of morale was the work of the Italian and foreign student volunteers, "the Angels of the Mud" (*angeli del fango*), who began to appear in large numbers on November 6 and would stay on the front lines of the cleanup and recovery effort for months.[11]

Local institutions helped build the sense of community solidarity. Mattei and his fellow Florentine, Socialist minister Pieraccini, battled through the rain for hours, wandering through various flood-created detours to reach the city from Rome in the late afternoon of November 4. They immediately went to Palazzo Medici Riccardi and offered their assistance to the prefect. The city council met on November 6, and the parties unanimously pledged cooperation to Bargellini, who announced that the junta would withdraw its resignation to meet the crisis. *La Nazione*, a civic institution, had been flooded out of its just-completed offices. Utilizing the printing presses of *La Nazione*'s sister publication, *Resto del Carlino* of Bologna, Mattei relaunched the paper within a day, providing badly needed information and reinforcing the Florentines' sense of community and continuity. Cardinal Florit enlisted the city clergy in the cleanup effort, earning the affectionate nickname "the Cardinal with boots." Most importantly, Bargellini provided needed leadership for the cleanup effort. Coping with the disaster called for precisely the type of skills that he possessed: a flare for the dramatic gesture and an insider's ties to the DC leadership. Bargellini and the press corps toured the devastated city. He cooperated closely with provincial and national authorities and took on the politically rewarding task of loudly demanding immediate state assistance for Florence. The enormity of the disaster and of the initial cleanup operation created a short-lived political truce. The city's battling political factions submerged their differences to deal with immediate problems.[12]

The cleanup moved along briskly in the first few days on the basis of human muscle power and picked up speed as masses of mechanical equipment became available after November 10. Army bulldozers pushed the mud and detritus back into the river, a quick, but not necessarily safe, way to speed the cleanup. No serious disease outbreaks took place. Human remains were quickly recovered and buried. After depositing thousands of animal carcasses in a large pit in the Cascina, the army cremated them with flamethrowers before covering over the charred remains.[13]

By mid-November the first phase of the cleanup was over. Most Florentines had recovered physical control of their homes and shops. The mudpack was dissolving, and a majority of streets were passable. The next phase, the return of basic city services, centered around the difficult task of cleaning out sewers and subsurface structures. It was appalling work: the compacted, viscous, disease-bearing mudpack yielded its subsurface conquests only after great effort. The men of the Italian army and city workers, particularly the employees of ASNU, took the lead in the work. Simultaneously, the city began providing those services—electricity, water, buses, telephones, sanitation, medical and pharmaceutical assistance—needed to begin the reconstruction. Florentine self-discipline and the mudpack prevented the looting that frequently accompanies natural disasters.[14]

As in 1944, Florence signaled its symbolic rebirth with a performance at the flood-ravaged Teatro Comunale on November 27. The theater had felt the full force of the Arno. Its seating, scenery, electrical systems, and essential backstage equipment had been swept away as the river submerged this jewel of Florentine culture. The cleanup was rapid, and in spite of a lack of sets and seats a largely standing-room audience launched the 1966–1967 opera season with a performance of Monteverdi's *L'incoronazione di Poppea* twenty-three days after the disaster.

Notwithstanding the triumph at the Comunale, restoration of the city's vast cultural patrimony was a difficult and long-drawn-out process. In comparison to World War II, both the range and types of destruction were much greater. Wartime destruction had been limited to a small, although artistically critical, area near the waterfront. The flood of November 4 spread throughout the greater part of the old city. Few buildings were destroyed, but many were seriously damaged. German looters carried off many art treasures, but most were recovered intact. In 1966 hundreds of paintings and sculptures fell victim to indiscriminate floodwaters. Masterpieces like Cimabue's *Crucifixion* and Ghiberti's *Gates of Paradise* and many lesser works were destroyed or heavily damaged. Archives and early editions, which attracted little attention from rapacious Nazi dilettantes, perished en masse in November 1966. Millions of pages of retrievable books and manuscripts required immediate conservation measures to survive.[15]

The job facing restoration workers was extraordinarily complex. Paintings done on wood or plaster, marble, terracotta, and wood sculptures, various types of textiles, metalwork, vastly different paints, various types of paper—each required specially trained restorers. The experts had to be concentrated in Florence, housed, and paid. They required a variety of high-technology aids. The city was well positioned to attract help, but retaining it would require both money and imagination.[16]

The Italian state stepped forward with funding for restoration of works of art and reconstruction of the city's theaters. Supplementing Italian contributions, which included manpower and technical expertise as well as cash, were private donors from around the world. The Vatican sent a team of restoration specialists from its museum. Money and expertise arrived from other European states. However, the Americans held pride of place. An enormous outpouring of private capital and art restoration assistance arrived from the United States in the weeks immediately following the disaster. The Committee to Rescue Italian Art (CRIA), created by U.S. citizens determined to protect their cultural patrimony, was operating by mid-November and over succeeding years would funnel men, money, and material to the rescue and restoration efforts of Florence, Venice, and other Italian cities.

The first days of the restoration effort displayed both the great enthusiasm and concern of unprepared volunteers and the difficulties of leaving the job to non-professionals. Hundreds of young people lined the streets passing damaged volumes out of lower-story storage areas, peeling back waterlogged pages, and inserting tissue papers to assist the drying process. Many volumes were seriously damaged by the well-meaning efforts to pry them apart. Other enthusiastic volunteers raced to S. Croce and collected fragments of the severely damaged Cimabue *Crucifixion*. Equally enthusiastic Italian army troops overturned the metal plate on which the fragments were collected and washed them into the sewer system.[17]

By mid-November, Italian expertise and initiative joined with foreign financial and professional assistance to take control of the restoration process. Many of the world's best art conservation experts arrived to participate in a once-in-a-lifetime effort that would apply and increase their professional capability. Art conservation workshops sprang up throughout the city. The first steps in the two-decade-long process were under way. With each successive year the tenacity of the restoration teams paid greater dividends, and the techniques of restoration improved. Florentines, impatient to display the success of the recovery effort and attract tourism back, could scarcely hide their civic pride when the city's museums reopened for one day (December 22) to display the art already restored. The following March, the National Library gamely reopened its doors and proudly offered parts of its collections to scholars for renewed research.[18]

In spite of the evident success of the first stages of reconstruction, Florence was an angry city that winter. Isolated in their homes for hours or days, briefly cut off from the rest of Italy, Florentines had a strong sense of abandonment. The shock of isolation did not wear off easily. It was reinforced by a recognition that the damage was much greater than that of the war. Worse, the flood was an "act of God" that left most shop owners and householders with only limited insurance reimbursement. The privations of a city initially without heat, sanitation, adequate shelter, and food took a heavy toll on local morale. Florentine frustration and anger welled up against the national government. Bargellini's endless criticisms of the coverage that the state radio-television monopoly, RAI, gave Florence's disaster encapsulated this anger.[19]

Anger produced some positive reactions. Neighborhood councils arose spontaneously to claim a role in reconstruction planning. About 1,500 homeless Florentines took over vacant apartments in the Sorgane development and then organized to protect their new homes.[20]

A people educated to look to the national government for leadership were deeply disappointed by the limited assistance coming from Rome. "It's like September 8, 1943," was a popular refrain, as Florentines compared their "abandonment" by the Italian republic with that carried out by their former king.[21]

In fact, Moro and his cabinet colleagues recognized the breadth of the disaster immediately and struggled to deal with it, utilizing the very limited means at their disposal. Bargellini and his junta colleagues praised the cooperation that they received from central government officials, even while criticizing the limited assistance supplied. Goodwill was not the issue; the magnitude of the disaster was. Isolation had reinforced the Florentine tendency to look inward, forgetting that the disaster zone stretched for thousands of square miles and included many equally deserving and historic towns and cities, including a badly battered Venice.[22]

Like most governments, Italy's took only a passing interest in disaster relief, allocating its limited funds to a vast area of pressing needs: police, public health, schools, historic preservation, and infrastructural projects, as well as popular, employment-creating state industries. A disaster of the magnitude that struck northern Italy in the fall of 1966 simply was outside its experience, capability, or fiscal reserves. The Moro government recognized this and devoted its initial work to providing elementary assistance and to finding funds to assist the recovery. As a symbol of the concern of the national government, President Saragat visited Florence on November 6. His meetings with city and central government representatives helped to create a climate of intragovernmental cooperation. He immediately reported by telephone to the government, outlining Florence's needs and pleading for quick action. The president then accepted with grace abuse heaped upon him by crowds of hostile Florentines.[23]

The cabinet discussed the disaster and Florence's special needs at a twelve-hour marathon session that concluded in the early morning of November 9. Interior Minister Paolo Emilio Taviani's opening report was a truly bleak recapitulation of the damage done throughout the north. Over 110,000 soldiers and carabinieri were deployed to assist in relief efforts. The ministers discussed Florence's special problems, particularly the damage to its artistic treasures. After careful consideration of the possibilities, the government agreed to special taxes on gasoline to raise revenue combined with a tax amnesty for the stricken parts of the country.[24]

Major government-organized assistance arrived within two days. In the meantime, the ruling political parties, conscious of the need to create a positive image, jockeyed to assure that as much aid as possible passed through their patronage systems. The opposition, above all, the PCI, sought to extract political benefits from an assault on the government's conduct of relief efforts. In this supercharged atmosphere, the government got the worst of it in the press, in parliament, and in public opinion.[25]

The outcry for a scapegoat was inflamed by a general recognition that human factors were at work in Florence's and Italy's disaster. The primary culprit was the lack of soil conservation. More than a millennium of improper land use had deprived the entire region of natural defense against flooding. Here, responsibility could justly be shared among a citizen body and local governments that repeatedly violated both the law and common sense in their land management and successive national governments that failed to finance adequately the flood-control projects that parliament approved.[26]

A second, fixating issue for Florentines was ENEL's decision to release the waters behind the Levane and Le Penna dams. Conspiracy theorists, a breed always in oversupply in Italy, had a field day hypothesizing that malevolent intent, not human error, lay behind the decision of a few frightened state employees. They accused ENEL of falsifying its records and covering up the truth. Uncertainty about the time at which the dams emptied their reservoirs was grist for the mill of conspiracy. The state ordered an investigation, which proved inconclusive. The decision was clearly tragic in its consequences. Few Florentines found ENEL's explanations convincing.[27]

The national government came up short in a number of areas. Its limited funding and the large number of claimants meant that individual payments to victims were inevitably small, fostering great discontent. Bureaucratic delays in processing government aid were constant. Political infighting over policy and assistance distribution within the governing coalition and among the parties was vicious. An ambitious and still resentful Fanfani continuously undercut Moro's government. The costs of reconstruction narrowed Moro's already circumscribed ability to promote reforms in other areas. In addition to the physical damage that it inflicted on nearly one-third of Italy, the flood was a body blow to an already reeling center left.[28]

RECOVERY

Nothing displayed the toughness and adaptability of Florentines better than the speed and thoroughness of the city's recovery from the ravages of the 1966 flood. Individual initiative played the largest role in the recovery, but national and local government also contributed. By early December the cleanup essentially was over. Oil stains had largely disappeared. "It is as if Florence, which had been curled into a tight brown bun, were putting out the first edges of clean, colored petals."[29] Sunshine, warmer weather, and the reappearance of running water all improved morale.

The national government and the parties, with some prodding by local political figures, continued to show interest in Florence and its problems. Housing was the city's top priority. A 1967 census indicated that 40 percent of the city's population lived in houses damaged by the Arno. Low- and middle-income zones such as S. Croce and S. Frediano were particularly hard hit. A second and related priority was roads. The flood had left gaping holes in many city streets, had swept away parts of the roadway along the river and damaged a number of bridges. Many city streets had to be closed for months to facilitate extensive repairs. The water and sewer systems of Florence needed massive work. Tourism was at a standstill. "Foreigners," above all, the beloved and rich (or beloved because rich) Americans, had to be honored for their aid and enticed back to Florence. Bargellini emphasized this priority in declaring 1967 the "year of reconstruction." Finally, private businesses had to restock, repair, and reopen.[30]

The city's major problem was budgetary: how to pay for starting up Florence's economy. One useful source was funding from the United States. A majority of this money was earmarked for artistic restoration. However, Anglo-American groups in Florence supplied food and clothing to flood victims, and U.S. and British consular offices and churches collected cash contributions from abroad while U.S. business groups, practicing that particular American brand of enlightened self-interest charity, sent money to relaunch Florentine artisan industries.[31]

The greatest assistance that foreigners could provide was revitalizing the tourist industry. The Florentines worked feverishly throughout the winter of 1966–1967 to rebuild the necessary infrastructures of tourism. Cash contributions from abroad helped speed up the partial rehabilitation of museums, other architectural landmarks, and artworks. Larger, higher-priced (generally chain) hotels, favored by the well-heeled segment of U.S. tourism, quickly restored full services. The other classes of hotels and many *pensione* followed suit. By the spring of 1967 they were ready to receive guests.[32]

The spring season started off strongly, then tourism quickly fell off. By May, this essential building block of the Florentine economy was in the throes of a depression. News reports about the extent of damage and the difficulties of reconstruction discouraged travelers. Many foreigners and Italians delayed a visit to the city on the Arno out of concern for the recovery of its artistic heritage.[33]

While waiting for a tourist industry recovery that all judged too slow, city officials pushed forward with other recovery projects. Aided by a 2 billion lire grant from the state, city officials purchased 300 apartments for homeless victims of the flood. In February, the junta, with support from the PCI, passed a budget that pushed the city 100 billion lire further into debt as its part of reconstruction. In March, the Bargellini junta launched a "big cleanup" drive designed to improve the look of the city and reinforce its appeal to the tourist trade. Later the same month, the city council, in a display of self-confidence bordering on the absurd, voted to bid for the 1976 Olympic Games.[34]

Nenni visited Florence in April and came away impressed by the rhythm of reconstruction. Signs of recovery were everywhere: from freshly restuccoed buildings, to the massive traffic jams created by work in progress on roads and buildings. The state continued to provide new revenue that city leaders gladly accepted even as they publicly branded it inadequate. Local pride exploded in the fall when the city soccer club, La Fiorentina, won the Italian national championship.[35]

In a November 4, 1967, essay commemorating the disaster, *La Nazione*, Florence's primary font of "boosterism," celebrated the quick recovery of the city's industries. Even the paper admitted, however, that the situation of many Florentines remained bleak. Too many remained homeless or lived in flood-damaged units. Florentines complained that too much money was going to the artistic restoration projects and to rebuilding church properties. At the end of January residents of S. Croce demonstrated against the junta's insensitivity to their needs. Small-business people and homeowners resented slow government claims processing.[36]

The junta's decision to leave reconstruction largely in private hands and popular discontent with the national government's activities brought the issue of city planning back to center stage. Although politically marginalized, Detti, Ragghianti, and other urban planners continued to play an influential role in public life through their writings. The flood revealed major defects in the water and sewer systems. In May a major rainstorm backed up the entire system and left a carpet of one to six inches of water in lower-lying parts of Florence, damaging many newly rehabilitated structures. In June a second major storm caused new backups in the area around the Fortezza da Basso. A fortnight later, a third storm created more backups. In July a severe drought hit the province, and city officials found that they had inadequate pumping capacity. Heavy rains again struck in November with predictable results, this time on the city periphery.[37]

Pressing infrastructural projects included such perennials as the site for a city airport, new arterial highway construction, ATAF's deficit and ineffective services, the poor condition of city streets, mounting traffic, proper economic utilization of public historic buildings, flood prevention, and modernization of street lighting. Supporters of careful planning found an unexpected ally among elements of the Socialist Party.[38]

The Unified Socialist Party (PSU) was not so much unified as badly glued together. The arrangement that Nenni and Mario Tanassi signed in October 1966 foresaw a gradual, "organic" fusion of two parties that had been rivals for nearly twenty years. Inside the PSU, the old parties retained parallel organizational structures. While the party had a single "president" (Nenni), it possessed two secretaries with coequal powers, Francesco de Martino, a Nenni man, and Saragat's hard-nosed protégé, Tanassi. Nenni took on the unrewarding task of mediating between two antagonistic spirits. In the months between the signature of the accord for unification and the congress that finalized the deal, the depth of disagreement between the two wings of democratic Socialism became more evident and more public. As he had with the center left, Nenni nudged his colleagues forward to the goal of unity, heedless of the evidence that the marriage was unworkable.[39]

One of the key demands made by the former PSDI for unification was the elimination of PSI-PCI coalition governments on the local and provincial level, a strategy that would reduce the influence of the PSI component of the new party, especially in central and northern Italy. Even in areas where the PSI had customarily cooperated with the DC, insistence on the center left formula greatly reduced the Socialists' bargaining power. In Florence, where the local PSI regained some of its strength in spring 1966 elections, integration of the two Socialist parties went very badly. The two factions of the Unified Socialist Party divided over planning issues in the city council's first postflood sessions. Within two months of the formal unification of the party, the PSDI component of its Florentine Federation seceded and moved back to its old offices. Nenni intervened and patched over the quarrel; the leaders of both wings nursed their accumulated resentments.[40]

The DC watched the Socialist unification process with concern. Whether on the national or local level, a unified Socialist Party would have more weight within future center left coalitions and even have the option of forming a majority with the PCI. DC leaders readily exploited fissures within the PSU to weaken it. In February 1967, the provincial congress of the Florence DC fought over most issues but stood together on limiting Socialist access to patronage and power.[41]

One issue that accentuated fissions within the Socialist Party was urban planning. The PSI had purged the Detti-Codignola-Enriquez-Agnoletti group but retained a lively interest in planning. A group of young Socialist intellectuals, many trained by Detti at the University of Florence's school of architecture, became active in the party's ranks. Valdo Spini and Mariella Zoppi (Spini) were leaders in the new generation of urbanists. Vice Mayor Lelio Lagorio, the PSI faction's leader, provided carefully modulated support to them.[42]

On the other side of the unified party's gaping divide stood Maier and the PSDI veterans, who maintained their opposition to approaches associated with the La Pira junta.

The battle lines were drawn when, in March 1967, President Saragat signed the revised Detti plan into law. The PRG approved by the national government after four years of deliberation was a much modified version of the 1962 city council law. It scrapped plans for a new roadbed and a railroad station together with a number of proposed alterations in arterial access roads. It subjected the Detti zoning and development scheme to major variants, particularly in the definition of "historic zones." It threw out plans for conversion of many remaining military barracks and designated Peretola as the site of the city's new airport.[43]

Since taking office, Bargellini's junta, especially urban planning assessor Bausi, had undercut the PRG by granting zoning easements that effectively nullified parts of its grand design. The architects, urban planners, and others who had supported Detti made common cause with homeowners in areas like S. Croce. Planned reconstruction offered the best defenses against land speculation. Provincial officials who felt that the revised PRG offered inadequate solutions to the territorial issues like flood control joined forces with them in the battle against the junta's urban policy. Their ire reached new heights when the press revealed that Bausi had convened a restricted meeting of foreign urban planners to discuss city development.[44]

Bargellini and Bausi pressed on with their plans, confident that a crisis in the junta over urban planning served the DC's interests. Infuriated by the DC's open effort to exploit their divisions, the Socialists papered over their differences to demand a greater say in junta activities. The DC refused. Bargellini made the budget for 1968 an issue of confidence. The Socialists responded by withdrawing their support. The mayor resigned on November 4, 1967, putting the onus for ending his government of reconstruction on the PSU. Politics as usual had returned to Florence.[45]

NOTES

1. Sources for this description of the flood include: Tommaso and Iacopo Detti interviews, Florence, May 14, 18, 1993; Poggiolini and Luciano Bausi interview, Florence, June 1, 1993; Katherine Taylor, *Diary of Florence in Flood* (New York, 1967); Mario Chiesa, *Episodi della tragedia di Firenze* (Florence, 1967); Piero Bargellini, *La splendida storia di Firenze* (Florence, 1969); Guido Garosa, *L'Arno non gonfia d'acqua chiara* (Milan, 1967); Franco Zeffirelli, *Zeffirelli* (New York, 1986); a special issue of *Il Ponte*, December 1966; "Diario dell'Aluvione," *Politica*, November 15–December 1, 1966. The Enrico Mattei referred to in this chapter was not related to the late head of ENI.

2. Giovanni Spadolini, "Bargellini e Firenze" *NA* 115 (April 1980), pp. 313 ff. is a positive assessment. A negative picture emerges from Bargellini's "diary" in Pier Francesco, Listri, *Tutto Bargellini* (Florence, 1989) and Bargellini, *Splendida*; Gianni and Giorgio Giovannoni interview, May 25, 1993.

3. "Diario dell'alluvione," *Politica*, November 15–December 1, 1966.

4. Pietro Nenni, *Gli anni del Centro sinistra Diari, 1957–1966* (Milan, 1982), pp. 556, 568–73, 638; Remo Gianelli, "I gulli della Cascina," *Politica*, May 15, 1966; ACC 1965, 1: 644–61, 849–75; 2: 1464–84, 1787–1800, 2078–85; ACC 1966, pp. 7–15; *Rinascita*, May 22, 1965, pp. 8–9; Lagorio to Florentine Socialists, August 1, 1965, ISTR, Carte N. Traquandi, b 1, f Lega diritti uomo.

5. ACC 1966, p. 51.

6. Bargellini, diary, pp. 183–87, 203–4, 213–14, 225.

7. Ibid., pp. 223–27; ACC 1966, pp. 148–61, 175–81, 442–65; Luciano Bausi, *Il giorna della Piena* (Florence, 1987), pp. 5–6.

8. Piero Bargellini et al., *Firenze di domani* (Florence, 1967), 24–25; Bargellini, *La splendida*, 259; Zeffirelli, *Zeffirelli*, p. 221; Garosa, *L'arno non gonfia*, p. 71.

9. Chiesa, *Episodi*, p. 275.

10. Taylor, *Diary*, pp. 60–61; Bargellini, *La splendida*, pp. 260, 271–72; Chiesa, *Episodi*, pp. 156, 220, 311, 316; Mariella Zoppi, *Firenze e l'urbanistica* (Rome, 1982), pp. 115–18; Gerosa, *L'arno non gonfia*, pp. 42–43.

11. Bargellini, *La splendida*, pp. 261–62; Chiesa, *Episodi*, p. 59; "Diario dell'Alluvione," *Politica*, November 15–December 1, 1966; Greenfield, *Waters*, pp. 103–4.

12. Bargellini et al., *Firenze di domani*, pp. 22–23, 26; Bargellini, *La splendida*, pp. 273–74; Comunita di Isolotto, *Isolotto, 1954–1969* (Bari, 1971), pp. 121–22; 'Diario dell' Alluvione"; ACC 1966, pp. 468–72, 608–68; *Firenze domani*, p. 38.

13. Garosa, *L'arno non gonfia*, pp. 69, 95–96, 98; "Diaro dell'Alluvione."

14. Bausi, *Il giorno della piena*, p. 49; Davis Otatti, *Firenze pulita* (Florence, 1990), pp. 155–60.

15. *Firenze domani*, p. 139; "Saving the Libraries of Florence," *Wilson Library Bulletin*, June 1967, pp. 1035–43.

16. *La Nazione*, November 4, 1969.

17. Taylor, *Diary*, pp. 120–21; Zeffirelli, *Zeffirelli*, p. 222.

18. Taylor, *Diary*, p. 147; Greenfield, *Waters*, p. 109; *La Nazione*, January 9, February 27, April 13, June 16, 1967, January 19, 1978; Giuseppe Vedovato, *Difesa di Firenze* (Florence, 1968), p. 303; Sovraintendenza alle galarie di Firenze, *Firenze ristaurata* (Florence, 1972); *Holiday*, April 1967, pp. 29–40; *Time*, August 13, 1973.

19. Zeffirelli, *Zeffirelli*, p. 221; Chiesa, *Episodi*, pp. 110; *Nient'e successo*, pp. 16–20; "Dairio dell'Alluvione."

20. Comitato di quartieri di Brozzi and Centro studi Pistelli, *Cittadini senza piano, piano senza cittadini* (Florence, 1971), pp. 3–4; Gerosa, *L'arno non gonfia*, p. 103.

21. *Firenze domani*, pp. 69–74.

22. Bargellini, *La splendida*, pp. 269–70; Comune di Firenze, *Rassegna del Comune*, 1965–1968 (Florence, 1968), pp. 13–16, 19–21. T. Detti and Bausi interviews.

23. *Firenze domani*, pp. 27–29; Nenni, *Gli anni*, pp. 693–95; Zoppi, *Firenze*, p. 115; Bargellini, *La splendida*, p. 263.

24. Nenni, *Gli anni*, pp. 695–96; Minutes, November 8, 1966, AC/S, Presidenza del consiglio, verbali, b. 76; *Atti e documenti della DC*, 2: 2081.

25. *Firenze domani*, pp. 30–31; Nenni, *Gli anni*, pp. 697–698; *Atti e documenti della DC*, 2: 2082–83, 2087–89; *Rinascita*, November 12, 1966, pp. 5–8; ACC 1967, 1: 326–27.

26. Nenni, *Gli anni*, pp. 698–99; Giuseppe Tamburrano, *Storia e cronaca del centrosinistra* (Milan 1971), pp. 92–93.

27. Taylor, *Diary*, pp. 126–27.

28. Chiesa, *Episodi*, pp. 96, 279, 281; ACC 1966, pp. 632–33; Nenni, *Gli anni*, pp. 700–701; Minutes, November 17 and December 17, 1966, AC/S Consiglio dei Ministri, Verbali, b 76, *Politica*, November 15–December 1, 1966.

29. Taylor, *Diary*, p. 142.

30. La Pira to Paul VI, December 11, 1966, ALP. b 76, Alluvione, correspondenza; La Pira to Colombo, December 1, 1966, ibid.; *Reporter*, December 15, 1966; *La Nazione*, January 2, 8, 26, 28, 1967; *Rinascita*, January 10, 1967, pp. 24–25.

31. Taylor, *Diary*, pp. 122–23; *La Nazione*, January 5 and 12, February 5, April 7, September 6, 1967.

32. *La Nazione*, January 11, February 2, March 3, 1967.

33. *La Nazione*, January 14, 21, February 1, March 9, 26, April 7, 13, May 6, 27, 1967; Azienda autonoma di Turismo di Firenze, *Turismo a Firenze* (Florence, 1972), pp. 204–9.

34. *La Nazione*, February 3, 17, 25, March 11, 14. ACC 1967, 1: 98–108, 575–83.

35. Pietro Nenni, *I conti con la storia. Diari, 1967–1971* (Milan, 1983), p. 32; *La Nazione*, January 13, March 20, 23, April 22, May 20, 25, June 4, 16, July 11. *Rassegna del comune, 1965–1969*, pp. 77–79; Fondazione Olivetti, *Le regione e il governo locale*, 3 vols. (Florence, 1965), 1: 188–89.

36. *La Nazione*, January 30, February 1, 11, June 2, November 11, 1967; La Pira to Taviani, March 1, 1967, ALP, b 77, Alluvione, segnalazioni al minstro; *Yale Review*, Spring 1967, pp. 475–80; Chiesa, *Episodi*, pp. 80–81, 87, 119, 319–28.

37. *Firenze domani*, pp. 82–91, 94–105; *La Nazione*, May 17, June 10, 14, 20, July 26, November 6, 1967; *Regione*, p. 24.

38. *La Nazione*, March 2, 4, 6, April 24, May 21, 29, 31, July 8, October 6, 1967; *Firenze*, p. 60.

39. Nenni, *Gli anni*, pp. 609–10, 614, 639–40, 647–51, 687, 700; Nenni, *I conti*, pp. 9, 13–14, 36–37.

40. *Il Mulino*, September 1966, pp. 727–44; Nenni, *Gli anni*, pp. 639–40; Nenni, *I conti*, p. 57; *La Nazione*, January 5, May 16, 1967.

41. Nenni, *Gli anni*, p. 703; *La Nazione*, February 20, 1967.

42. Augusto Boggiano, ed., *Firenze: La questione urbanistica* (Florence, 1982), pp. 349–59.

43. *La Nazione*, March 12, 1967.

44. Boggiano, ed., *Firenze: questione urbanistica*, pp. 349–59, 382–84; *Politica*, January 15, 1967; *La Nazione*, May 12, July 14, 31, September 2, 1967.

45. *La Nazione*, July 19, 30, 31, September 11, 27, 28, 1967; ACC 1967, 3: 2722.

Chapter 9

Muddling Through: The Bausi Years, 1968–1974

They say that Florence has become a museum-city. Never, gentlemen.
City council debate, February 19, 1971

The University of Florence, a collection of semiautonomous schools whose deteriorating buildings dotted the old city, was a monument to an elite education system that had fallen out of step with the needs of an industrial society. By damaging buildings and destroying libraries and other research facilities, the flood exposed fully its backwardness. Student involvement in the cleanup and recovery provided a catalyst that simultaneously awakened youthful idealism and accentuated discontent with conditions at the university. A rapidly expanding student population organized to demand improved facilities and more control over the curriculum. The Detti plan with its concentration on improvements in the university physical plant became a rallying point for student political activism. In February 1967, university students went on strike. Ten thousand took to the streets in an impressive march to demand reforms and new facilities. The Bargellini administration praised their militancy and ignored their demands, no doubt hoping that the protest movement would wither away. Mass communications undercut this strategy. Florence's students were radicalized, organized, and aware that they were part of a movement that cut across national borders. Their leaders came largely from the highly politicized students of the School of Architecture, the home base of Edoardo Detti and his fellow urban planners.

In December 1967, following announcement of a government plan to place quotas on enrollment, Florentine students joined those in thirty-five other state universities in occupying classroom buildings in order to press their common and special demands. An influential minority of university professors supported their protest. After a month of increasingly tense, but peaceful, confrontation, the police began taking names of organizers in an apparent prelude to a crackdown. On the morning of January 30, 1968, a massive student protest march moved from its organizing point on via S. Gallo through the old city to Piazza S. Marco, seat of the university administration. Clashes between the police and students took place along the way. The march reached Piazza S. Marco around noon. Exasperated by the students' comportment, the police charged the crowd, releasing tear gas canisters. In the ensuing melee a number of students and policemen were injured. Faculty and students made common cause. University rector Giacomo Devoto led a mixed delegation of students and professors to the offices of the prefect to protest police brutality. The government's representative took a hard line, refusing to meet with the committee. By 8 P.M., students had occupied all university buildings. Devoto resigned.

As the occupation continued into February, students found strong support for their confrontation with the police and national government. The city council took their side. Florentine Socialist deputy Tristano Codignola, father of Italy's major educational reform law, denounced the clash as a "police riot." In response to student demands, the city government set aside 100 hectares for the construction of new science faculties, while private groups offered special training courses in the service industries. The occupation gradually ceased, and classes temporarily resumed. Further occupations, demonstrations, and confrontations would follow. Florence and Italy were entering a decade of protest and violence, the very difficult adjustment to the profound economic and social changes ushered in by the rapid industrialization of the 1950s and 1960s.[1]

THE POLITICS OF UPHEAVAL

The great wave of migration from the countryside that began in the 1950s slowly drew to a close in the late 1960s. The industrial boom that sparked it stumbled to a halt. The Organization of Petroleum Exporting Countries (OPEC)-generated "oil shock" of 1973 devastated a lagging Italian economy and began a long period of low growth and inflation. Unemployment and underemployment returned with a vengeance. The workers who had carried the nation to prosperity during the boom felt the full impact of hard times. They reacted by forcefully demanding a larger share of national income distribution. "Strikes, strikes, strikes. This is our daily bread," Nenni complained in his diary. Both the private sector and the Bank of Italy urged resistance to union demands; the DC, recognizing the power and anger of the workers, prudently surrendered. Corporate management, sensing its isolation, followed suit. The Workers' Rights Statute (1970) and the *scala mobile*, a wage indexation mechanism tied to the rate of inflation (1975), became the symbols of union power.[2]

Meanwhile, students flooded the universities as a result of reforms carried out in the early years of the center left experiment, which essentially opened higher education to everyone. They confronted antiquated and inadequate physical plants, a distant and generally uncooperative faculty, and out-of-date curricula.

Brought up in the Catholic or Marxist traditions of social solidarity, they found themselves in a competitive situation, almost totally lacking safeguards, and governed by the raw, humiliating patronage system of the "academic barons." Many abandoned the effort to win an education. Others sought to create security and a sort of "class" solidarity in student movements that confronted the barons and simultaneously challenged both Italy's ruling parties and the traditional opposition. The "movement" started among Catholic students in Milan in the mid-1960s. Within eighteen months it spread across the entire Italian university system. Strikes, marches, mass demonstrations, the occupation of university buildings, and teach-ins revealed the depth of student unrest.[3]

Efforts by their elders to channel youth protest into "useful" directions failed. The radicalization of students expanded into the middle schools. Protests increasingly turned to occupation of school buildings. Student unrest converged with protest movements outside academe. In Florence, Catholic students were drawn into common cause with rebellious parishioners in Isolotto who defied La Pira's old nemesis, Cardinal Florit, on issues ranging from discipline to liturgy. Throughout Italy, the students made common cause with angry, impatient workers. The war in Vietnam provided a catalyst for mobilizing the traditional left and radical youth against the policies of the United States.[4]

The student-worker revolt was evidence that the Italian political system was failing to deal with the problems of key members of its constituency. Neither the government nor the PCI had effective answers. Catholic and Marxist concepts of society, based on notions of party distribution of economic scarcity and the primacy of group rather than individual rights, were frontally challenged by the demands for self-enrichment coming from all sectors of society. A critical, if partially masked, change in the psychological outlook of the working class toward consumerism was noted with anguish by both Marxists and Catholics. Each sought, for its own reasons, to curb the transformation of Italy into a society where individualist values reigned. Communist spokesman Giovanni Berlinguer admitted party perplexity with the student protesters. The aging Pietro Secchia, with no evident sense of irony, complained to party secretary Luigi Longo that "extremists" were taking control of the working class. The party suffered a major defection within its own ranks when the "*Manifesto*" group of intellectuals broke with its iron discipline. The PCI was wounded by the Soviets' August 1968 invasion of Prague. Destruction of a reform movement within a "fraternal" Communist Party provided further evidence of the authoritarian political style of the Kremlin. The PCI's forceful denunciation of Soviet action only partially repaired the damage done to its image. Party paralysis in the face of unrest in working-class Isolotto underlined the calcification of the PCI on the local level.[5]

The DC was navigating changing social and political circumstances with equal difficulty. The center left experiment crash-landed in 1968. The collapse of La Pira's last center left government was a preview of the failure at the national level. By 1968, the voters were tired of an experiment that had promised so much and delivered so little. In May national elections, they swung to the right. The

DC shifted with them. Pushing Moro aside, Andreotti advanced, and the supple Fanfani reinvented himself as a man of order to become the strongest player within the DC. As social tensions mounted, the Christian Democratic Party came to the defense of existing social structure. Divorce was the symbol of this new policy. Moro's DC had looked the other way when parliament passed a divorce law. Fanfani's DC, with the full support of the Italian Church, decided to overturn the law, utilizing a national referendum.[6]

The DC displayed its customary resourcefulness in walking away from the wreckage of the center left. The PSI was the big casualty of the collapse of reformism. Nenni had staked his prestige and his party's future on the twin objectives of PSI participation in a reform government and reunification with the PSDI. He achieved the first in 1963 and the second in 1966. Successive Moro governments failed to produce significant reform, undercutting tenuous public support for the center left while Italy's two "Socialist" parties never achieved a real integration.[7]

In seeking a coalition with the DC and reunification with the Social Democrats, Nenni ignored the warnings of other party leaders that he was paying too high a price in concessions. Power, once achieved, became an end itself for an increasing number of Socialists, especially the younger generation. Saddled with a weak organizational base, they preferred to defer to the DC on specific issues rather than risk losing their patronage strongholds within the government.[8]

Even more devastating than the failure of the center left was the rapid collapse of Socialist unity. In December 1964, Nenni employed his formidable tactical skill to secure the election of his old rival Saragat as president of the republic. The PSI chief hoped to spur both reform and reunification. Saragat was an activist president, but not the type that Nenni envisioned. The new chief of state repeatedly utilized his powers to protect and advance the interests of his fellow Social Democrats, often at the expense of the Nenni Socialists.[9]

Lacking popular support, the PSDI had long been the quintessential party of government. It relied on control of patronage-distributing ministries to retain its small vote. Because it was an essential, if small, element in the majority coalitions through which the DC governed Italy, the PSDI was jealous of the entry of the larger PSI into the coalition. Fears of loss of power and identity grew as PSDI politicians faced integration with the larger party. Added to this were the mutual suspicions nurtured by two decades of rivalry. Nenni, in his role as president of a party with two coequal political secretaries, spent much of his time mediating between feuding former Social Democrats and Socialists.[10]

The "Unified" Socialist Party was an armed truce. In Florence, the expectation of national elections set off fierce infighting between the two wings of unified Socialism. The Tuscan Party had a hard time putting together a list of candidates for the 1968 elections because Nicola Cariglia (PSDI), a rising political star, demanded top position among the Senate candidates over the more popular and senior Mariotti (PSI). The PSI and PSDI components of the city council fought over whether to withdraw support from the junta. National party headquarters intervened speedily, resolving both issues in favor of the PSDI component. It ordered the PSI contingent to support the junta and sacrifice two of their best candidates: Tristano Codignola and Lelio Lagorio. The PSI faction complied with evident ill will.[11]

The elections of May 1968 were a disaster for the PSU. Nenni glumly surveyed a devastating personal defeat and lamented that the greatest problem facing Italy was the lack of an alternative to continuing with the center left politics that the voters had rejected. As long as the PCI was unacceptable to the DC and most voters as a coalition partner, no alternative majority existed. The center left staggered on, inflicting more political damage on the battered Socialists.[12]

Defeat was equally bruising for Florence's center left. Bausi's minority government depended on the support of the Liberals and *La Nazione*, two traditional opponents of the center left, for its survival. The junta collapsed in July 1968, when the Socialists demanded that it embrace a comprehensive reform program. A month later, Bausi formed another center left minority government.[13]

DC councilman Giancarlo Zoli blamed the junta's weakness on a hopelessly divided national PSU. Its PSI component split into contending factions. The PSDI current played off the divisions within the larger PSI faction, steadily whittling away Nenni's position. By early 1969, the party's president lamented: "I don't recognize it [the party] anymore." Riccardo Lombardi compared its savage infighting to tribal warfare.[14]

The partisan spirit dominated the Florentine PSI. Urban planning was the fulcrum of internal party discord. Lagorio supported youthful reformers, whose basic objective was enacting Detti's vision of urban development, against Mariotti. Both the DC and the PCI gleefully exploited Socialist divisions. In February 1969 opposition parties blocked approval of the center left parties' candidate for director of the Teatro Comunale. PSU headquarters, backed by PCI and PSIUP, offered the Socialist impresario Massimo Bogiankino as its candidate. The DC and right countered with Lagorio, the vice mayor and a Nenni supporter. Lagorio won election when seven of nine Socialist city council members abandoned party discipline. In Rome, the PSU's left-wing currents demanded both Lagorio's resignation and party withdrawal from the junta. Lagorio dutifully complied. The Socialists withdrew from city government only to return a few days later on the pretext of dealing with urgent communal business. A month later, the junta again collapsed, and the prefect appointed a special commissioner to carry the city to elections. Disagreements among the parties over an election date prolonged the life of this interim government for over six months.[15]

The Florence situation was an indicator of how profound divisions were within the PSU. Nenni continued his efforts to mediate among the warring factions. Saragat, calculating that his forces would do better on their own, was talking "divorce" and the re-creation of the PSDI. The rupture was consummated at a July national council meeting. Nenni's efforts to build a dominant position for the Socialists collapsed with the PSU. "The ruins of unification have fallen on me," he confided to his diary. "Burying me alive, the worst of all [fates]." The following year, Florentine voters rendered their judgment on Socialist unification in local elections. The PSI held on to five seats and emerged as the junior partner to the PSDI (six seats) in a series of center left governments that were marked by limited achievements and continuous internal bickering.[16]

In the wake of schism, the reborn PSI swung left. It took strong stands in favor of a greater government role in housing construction. Similarly, it helped father and then defended a mild, but politically divisive, law granting Italians the right to divorce. These issues made the survival of a center left even more difficult. Old Catholic allies of the PSI, like La Pira, followed the church on an issue of faith and stridently attacked the divorce law. Fanfani saw opposition to divorce as a lever to reaffirm DC control over Italian society. On social and political issues, the PSI was more frequently allied with the PCI than with its erstwhile governing partner.[17]

THE POLITICS OF BOOSTERISM

On both the national and local level the failure of Socialist unification removed the last barriers to a new and more devastating round of unguided development. Bausi took up Bargellini's mantle as chief spokesman for a series of grandiose projects. Most were never undertaken, but the heated debate that they provoked and the inaction that followed created a rationale for the continuation of unplanned growth. Detti and his fellow urban planners made one final, unsuccessful effort to foil them. Florence took giant steps toward becoming the "museum city"—a tourist playground whose center was increasingly depopulated—even as all concerned publicly lamented this development.

The post-1966 construction boom, fueled by easier availability of government funding, spread beyond the ravaged zones along the Arno, westward through and past Rifredi and to the south in the direction of the town of Galluzzo. Much of this building and rebuilding was unregulated. City fathers, in the La Pira tradition, were more interested in debating grandiose projects and international affairs. Beginning with the project for the 1976 Olympic Games in Florence, they discussed plans to create a "new Florence" whose economic base would combine more manufacturing industry with ever greater emphasis on tourism. Infrastructural projects such as an "international"-scale airport, fast train service that would link Florence with Milan and Rome, more bridges for traffic, a multistructure convention center, together with more housing, schools, and parks on the periphery, and efforts to attract major public and private corporations to set up shop were the key elements in successive Bausi junta programs. The Detti PRG was thrust aside as irrelevant.[18]

Civic boosterism was a natural outgrowth of the flood and largely successful recovery effort. The normally sober *Il Ponte*, a staunch supporter of the careful planning advocated by Detti, launched the Olympics in Florence idea in the days immediately after the disaster. *La Nazione*, always the city's primary font of boosterism, picked up and magnified the idea. The city DC then adopted it as part of a platform for a "new" Florence. City fathers never came forward with concrete plans. Florence was too small and its infrastructure too weak to house, feed, transportation, and entertain thousands of athletes and a million tourists simultaneously. Rome's despised bureaucrats recognized reality and mercifully killed the idea.[19]

The political impact of the Florence Olympics and other grandiose designs went far beyond the question of whether the city would host the games. Bausi believed that "[w]e are a city of the world mak[ing] us less a city of the region." Rather than cooperate with neighboring communes or the new regional government, Florence fought them for resources. The region, he recalled, was Florence's "natural enemy." This policy, he admitted years later, had a high cost for both city and region.[20] The civic boosterism evident in the city council's decision to fund a "history" of the flood and Florence's recovery was another part of DC strategy to claim priority on resources. Although the disaster spawned a cottage industry of books, city fathers wanted to get their version on record, one stressing Florence's grievances and heroic self-reconstruction. By handing the project to important local journalists, the city government effortlessly co-opted their support for its approach to reconstruction.[21]

The policy of going it alone carried serious consequences because the Bausi junta was singularly ill equipped to carry out "grand projects." He had no authority to raise money for such projects. Moreover, the new mayor led a contentious coalition that he described as "[s]ort of like one of those married couples that are always arguing and can't explain why." Quarreling Socialists and badly divided Christian Democrats had to confront a growing budgetary deficit, a hostile Communist opposition, discontented city employees, and contentious students. "I spent a lot of time in Piazza S. Marco," Bausi recalled a bit ruefully.[22]

Small, thin, dark-haired, this dapper lawyer was a master of the arts of conciliation. He tirelessly carried out the multiple public duties of the position, traveled abroad to attract attention to Florentine tourist industries, and carefully looked after the interests of the artisan component of the electorate. Bausi patiently endured years of Socialist infighting, irrelevant city council debates, and harsh criticism from within and outside his governing coalition to preserve the DC's predominant position in Florence. He presided over a period of uneven, but strong, economic growth and rising social and political tensions.[23]

The major accomplishment of the Bausi governments was undercutting the PRG of 1962 in the name of a new Florence. A series of congresses that began with an October 1967 meeting of modernist architects promoted the idea that Florence could deal with its problems only by growing out of them. Roberto Nardi (PSDI faction) labeled the Detti plan inadequate and out of touch with the realities of the postflood city and its growth. In April 1968, the city government announced that it was working on a new PRG. Bausi and subsequent city leaders would argue, with some justice, that by introducing modifications to the Detti plan they were simply trying to adjust to the realities of postflood development and the demands of Roman bureaucrats. The policy of redirecting the

Detti plan through a large number of small zoning variants had the ironic long-term effect of appearing to meet many of its stated goals (northwestern expansion, movement of commercial and government operations from the center, redirection of traffic) without achieving its major objective of orderly growth.[24]

The opposition, a coalition of urban planners and environmentalists connected with the advocacy group Italia Nostra (Our Italy) speedily organized and sought support on the left. Two junta proposals became the focus of opposition. It wanted to rehabilitate the Fortezza da Basso as a center for major business shows, including those of the increasingly important Florentine men's and women's clothing industry. It also wanted a general face-lift in the S. Croce zone. Over the next four years, Bausi and his allies pushed forward against a determined opposition. The Fortezza da Basso became part of a complex (including the new Palazzo dei Congressi) that promoted Florence's industries, while a massive new archives building went up on the periphery of the S. Croce neighborhood. Piazza S. Croce was repaved to serve as a parking lot.[25]

Bausi's victories were purchased at a high political cost. They drove a wedge between the DC and PSI that left the junta permanently destabilized. Urban planning and regional government were the issues that offered the PSI a chance to clean up and modernize its public image while claiming a central role in Florentine and Tuscan politics. Vice mayor Lelio Lagorio, in particular, tried to claim these issues for the PSI. Party rivals blocked these initiatives. The Social Democrats were closely aligned with the small contractors and real estate speculators who were the mortal enemies of urban reform. Socialist divisions caused the Bausi junta's collapse in early 1969. The PSI seized the urban planning issue after the 1969 schism liberated it from the Social Democrats. Attention to urban issues enticed a number of attractive younger people to the party and helped to improve its tattered image.[26]

A man of medium stature and streamlined, almost Oriental features, Lagorio possesses both cultivated manners and a gift for informality unusual in Italian politicians. He was the ultimate political pragmatist. The experience of the La Pira, Bargellini, and Bausi juntas taught him the limits of the center left formula, while the Florentine PSI's internal power struggle demonstrated the dangers of mixing ideology and politics. During his slow, but inexorable, rise to leadership of the Tuscan PSI, Lagorio shook off a number of setbacks. Once in control of the party, he imposed a platform emphasizing issues with appeal to a rapidly emerging new voting bloc, the middle-class technocracy. Recognizing that these interest groups were largely outside, and resistant to, traditional patronage networks, Lagorio sought their votes by embracing causes such as urban planning and regional government. The title of his quarterly review, *Citta e regione* (City and Region), nicely captured the prevailing enthusiasms of the early 1970s while showcasing rising Socialist intellectuals and "new thinking" about reforming Italy's dysfunctional political system. After winning election as president of the Tuscan region through hard-nosed bargaining with the PCI, Lagorio placed the numerically limited and organizationally weak PSI in a position to enjoy more or less permanent access to power. Coolly abandoning Cold War attitudes, he allied the Tuscan PSI with the Communists and began nudging the Florentine Party in the same direction. The ability to play off DC against PCI gave the Tuscan Socialists an ever greater role in local and regional politics.[27]

Regional and local autonomy became a major element in the national political debate of the late 1960s. The inability of the center left to carry forward a reform of Italian society and the perceived ineffectiveness of the national government's response to 1966s natural disaster, combined with its paralysis in the face of student revolts and subsequent labor unrest and burgeoning right-wing terrorism, sparked a search for some effective means to deal with Italy's problems. One part of the solution appeared to be delegating many administrative responsibilities (health, transportation, housing, tourism) to government bodies closer to citizens. The left fervently embraced the unfulfilled articles of the constitution (117–119) that called for creation of regional governments throughout Italy. The DC dragged its heels on regional reform to avoid the loss of power and patronage. A majority that included the PSI coalesced around regionalism as part of the solution to Italy's (and the Socialists') problems. In 1970 parliament finally passed enabling legislation, creating regional governments for all of Italy.[28]

The 1970 legislation was only the first step in a seven-year legislative process that produced a regional government system. In keeping with the centralizing philosophy that has dominated Italian politics since the eighteenth century, the parliament devolved powers to the regions but circumscribed them with various control bodies. It strictly limited the most fundamental of political powers: the right to tax. Lacking this power, the regions soon fell victim to Rome's party leaders and bureaucrats. Lagorio, who held a leading role in creating the regions, summed up their impact: "A great hope. A great illusion. It became a great disillusion. . . . The regions became big provinces," tied to Rome's purse strings rather than the independent, quasi-federal institutions that the reformers had envisioned.[29]

The debate over devolving power to the regions extended to the role of local government. It found particularly fertile soil in Florence, where indignation over postflood relief and reconstruction remained high. The city council sought a safety valve for public anger by formalizing the existing system of popularly created "local committees." These committees organized citizen participation in the first days of the cleanup and performed usefully in the reconstruction. The city council authorized twelve *consigli dei quartieri* (neighborhood councils), each containing at least one representative of each of the major parties and a chairman appointed by the mayor. Florentines ignored this poorly disguised effort to enhance party control at the expense of existing forms of grassroots democracy.[30]

The national government remained hostile to the concept of local autonomy. At the same time that it authorized the regions, parliament passed legislation further restricting the financial autonomy of the communes. Government ministries continued to intervene in matters of purely local interest. Local politicians of all factions complained about the oversight as well as government policies that placed unfunded mandates on already debt-laden local governments.[31]

The left insisted that enlarged regional autonomy was the first step in dealing with the problems of local government. The DC countered that regionalism was a mask for a PCI power grab and claimed that it was the true defender of local autonomy against the "centralizers" of the left. Lagorio complained that the government and the larger parties collaborated to starve the regions of funding.[32]

In Tuscany the debate over the role of regional government was closely connected with urban planning, above all, with housing issues. S. Croce, in the heart of Florence's historic district, was a focus of attention. Substandard housing was a major factor in its sharp demographic decline. A 1967 census found that 43 percent of S. Croce's citizens lived in homes damaged by the flood, that 76 percent lacked baths in their homes, and that 27 percent of the homes were without heating. More than 10 percent of S. Croce's homes were shared by two families, while an approximately equal number of homes lay abandoned.[33]

Parliament offered assistance in a 1967 act (No. 765), the so-called Mancini bridge law. Passed in response to the natural disasters of 1966, it placed major financial responsibility for urban development, particularly in costs of building supporting infrastructures, on private contractors, relieving the cities of a major income drain. The law would take effect in September 1968. Builders in Florence and other Italian cities used the interim period to take out record numbers of permits under the existing (the commune pays for infrastructure) system. Their maneuvers proved unnecessary when a court upheld their legal challenge to the law, voiding its provisions less than nine months after passage. Further, the court held that portions of the 1942 urban planning law dealing with zoning and expropriation were unconstitutional, reducing the limited control that local government could exercise over private construction.[34]

The court decision propelled Italy into a new round of battles over urban planning. The DC stood with private builders and landowners. Organized labor, whose political influence continued to grow, was committed to vastly expanding government-financed public housing. The PCI and PSI backed the unions. Urban planners and environmentalists, a growing force within the middle classes, were determined to halt the destruction of Italy's city centers. The PSI took up this banner. Carefully planned development became the coalition's battle cry.

A sense of urgency drove the coalition. "It was easy to get the feeling . . . that Rome was swiftly being submerged in a stone sea. Apart from the so-called historic center . . . 'the infamous outskirts' built during the past two decades—had become an ugly sprawl of unrelieved concrete."[35] GESCAL, the public housing authority set up by parliament in 1963 to replace INA-CASA, built just 40,000 new units in the first seven years of its existence, while private companies were putting up 1 million. The new and rehabilitated housing was usually out of reach of Italians of modest economic means. Tight credit was part of the problem. Rising construction costs, particularly for rehabilitation work, helped put housing out of reach for many. Evictions in the center were generally followed by reconfiguration of older structures for business occupancy rather than housing, further reducing the pool of available units. Many choice inner-city rehabilitation projects ended up in the hands of politically well-connected contractors. Finally, Italian landlords were reluctant to rent to their conationals. Faced with rigid rent control laws, they preferred short-term leases for well-heeled foreigners. Between 1969 and 1980 rental advertising virtually disappeared from Italian newspapers. For some years, the English-language Rome *Daily American* was the only paper in Italy listing property for rent in Florence.[36]

Housing shortages prompted mobilization on the local level by increasingly radicalized elements of the Italian public. Catholic and Marxist groups, operating outside traditional party lines, demanded greater local control over housing issues. Frustrated by Rome's inaction, political activists, exasperated home seekers, and hard-pressed renters occupied underutilized buildings, resisted evictions, and mounted rent strikes.[37]

Their actions produced results in the form of a 1971 law (No. 865) that returned some authority for urban planning and zoning to the cities while increasing local and regional control over the process of public housing construction. Ultimate decisions on funding remained in Rome. Nevertheless, the new law offered urban reformers a chance to regain a measure of control over development.[38]

As the battle over planning returned to the local level, the PSI–PCI regional government of Tuscany responded with a March 1973 law designed to coordinate planning between the region and communes and to encourage cooperation in planning among the communes. This last point was critical. As communes expanded, they needed to coordinate their plans for water, roads, and zoning in order to protect their mutual interests and keep their costs under control.

Surrounded by smaller, PCI-run communes, Florence's DC-dominated city council steadfastly avoided effective cooperation with its neighbors. Neighboring Communist city governments returned the hostility. As a result, the two sides never arrived at effective coordination of their common interest on issues such as transportation, water usage, flood protection, pollution control, and resource allocation. The Bausi administration used its expanded powers over urban policy to meet the demands of private developers for more construction permits. It employed a closed-bid system to limit access to many public contracts to its supporters. One critic defined urban policy under Bausi as government by zoning exemption.[39]

The strongest argument in favor of Bausi's embrace of unregulated growth was the sorry condition of the Italian national economy. The wave of strikes and other types of labor unrest that struck the country in the late 1960s continued unabated through most of the 1970s. Italian heavy industry was already losing competitive advantage when workers began to force wage and benefit concessions. It staggered under the weight of these demands and of a general downswing in the world business cycle. The first "oil shock" (1973) added further injury. Higher OPEC prices struck at the heart of Italian industry. For some years thereafter, growth in Italy's economy was confined to the service sector, above all, to tourism, transportation, and education.[40]

Florentine tourism became the industry that carried all others. Tuscan manufacturing was rooted in small business oriented to production for overseas markets. Florence was the showcase for its products. Foreign buyers and tourists familiarized themselves with Tuscan production in its capital. The link of the growth in other services with expanding tourism was equally evident. Bars, restaurants, hotels, food services, the clothing industry, jewelers, lawyers, and banks all rode the back of the tourist industry to steady expansion in the 1970s. In the late 1960s Florentine businessmen had recognized affluent youth as a major new source of revenue. Other fresh targets were Japanese tourists and the international convention trade. A major beneficiary of tourist sector growth was construction, particularly that portion operating in the old city. Growth in tourism also propelled new construction in nearby communes where service sector employees and workers in supporting industries found affordable housing.[41]

Tourism rewrote traditional political alliances in the city. Shopkeepers, historically strong supporters of urban planning, switched sides as they formed ties to their extraurban outsourcers. Both groups opposed any form of regulation. Within an expanding architectural profession, many found that their personal interest lay with the construction industry, not with their colleagues on the university faculties. Urban planning came under increasing attack from architects as an unrealistic holdover from Italy's collectivist past. Lawyers, another high-growth profession, supported the expansion-oriented industries that paid their retainers. A mushrooming banking sector was anxious to fuel further expansion by loaning money for development. Bankers worried that regulations would strangle profitability or create losses on investments. All of these groups pressed for expansion while giving little more than lip service to issues of common interest at the heart of urban planning. Bausi's approach to urban problems, with its stress on development and blind eye to illegal construction, served them well.[42]

The opposition was energized by the progrowth agenda of the junta. *Italia Nostra* decried the "museumization" of Florence that resulted from replacing housing units with shops catering to the tourists. The urban planners zeroed in on the uncoordinated nature of the postflood building boom, finding plenty of horror stories to illustrate their point that a policy of zoning by exemption, while highly profitable, was creating major immediate problems and placed the city in a straitjacket that would negate future efforts to resolve them. The Communist Party, always on the lookout for issues that would attract interclass support, joined in the attack, claiming that Florence's urban policies tilted economic development in favor of a minority at the cost of the interests of majority. Without a proper supporting infrastructure, they argued, the tourist industry would collapse under the weight of Florence's ever-growing army of visitors.[43]

The Bausi junta's systematic undermining of the 1962 PRG roused Edoardo Detti once again to join battle over the future of his city. Detti's loss of political influence inevitably brought with it discrimination against his work as an architect. In order to earn a living, he left Florence for commissions in other parts of the country. Embittered by his treatment at the hands of the political elite, Detti fought back in two ways. The publication of his *Firenze scomparsa* (The Florence We Have Lost, 1971), a richly illustrated, carefully researched history of the destruction of the city's architectural treasures, coauthored with his historian son, Tommaso, was designed to arouse both local and international interest in the fate of the city. Simultaneously, Detti organized an architects group, *Amalassunta*, to compete for the design and construction of the new university area on the city's northwest perimeter. Detti hoped that this project would set the pattern for overall development along the city's perimeter and link Florence into an intercommunal and regional development scheme.[44]

Detti received a sympathetic hearing, especially from outsiders, but failed to assemble the political support that he needed inside the city. The Bausi junta was committed to rapid exploitation of the land in the city's northwest. The PSI was in the hands of his enemies. While the PCI had cooperated with previous initiatives, city Communists, preoccupied with workers' housing, ignored his warning about the fate of the center.[45]

Florentine Socialists remained committed to the center left, permitting the PSDI and DC to alternate control of urban policy, guaranteeing a friendly hearing to local developers. Uneasiness with the direction that Bausi was taking, the city provoked a series of Socialist-created government crises. Only in 1973 did the party begin staking out a stronger position on urban-planning issues, bringing down another Bausi junta. Even then, the PSI opted for a further Bausi-led center left government. In the spring of 1974, the public shift toward the left became more evident, and the DC suffered a humiliating defeat on the divorce issue. The Socialists finally felt strong enough to break with the center left. In August, Bausi rang down the curtain on his six years as mayor.[46]

ADDING IT ALL UP

A 1974 article in *Architectural Review* praised the designs of some of the buildings erected in the wake of the flood but noted that no one was tending to Florence's major infrastructural needs. The city had no airport worthy of its tourist industry, had no real plans for road development, and had lost many of the architects and urban planners who once played prominent roles in its public life. A study published the following year by the Tuscany-Umbria section of Italy's National Urban Planning Institute echoed these criticisms, adding that the issue of placement of a railroad station remained unresolved after twenty years and that inner-city renovation occurred in an ad hoc manner that was destroying its livability. A senior Tuscan Christian Democrat expressed concern over the effect of unplanned development on the city's historic and cultural treasures and warned that the water and sewer systems of Florence remained totally inadequate to the needs of an expanding population. The travel magazine *Holiday*, while praising the economic individualism that stood at the base of the city's postflood "rebirth," chided the Florentines for their apparent indifference to their cultural patrimony and warned that pollution was becoming the greatest threat to the city's continued survival.[47]

Bausi responded that the critics overlooked the accomplishments of his administration because they were not well publicized. His assessor of urban planning argued that private capital was well on its way to achieving the objectives of the 1962 PRG, pointing to new housing, bridges, and roads and a reconstruction of the old city "on historic lines" as proof that the policy of leaving private firms a free hand worked.[48]

The city spent during the Bausi years, further running up its indebtedness. In six years, it put 15 billion lire into school construction, 4 billion into trash incinerators, 1.5 billion into hydraulic projects, another 3.3 billion in improved lighting, and 1.9 billion into public housing.[49]

The mayor could point to a number of individual projects launched by his administration, to the continuing economic growth of the city, and to success in winning state financing for city government programs of postflood reconstruction and economic development, above all, the creation of more public housing units. Bausi's administration trumpeted its support for the city's artisans and for the arts. He argued with some justice that his efforts to govern had been hampered by Socialist indecision and by frequent outbreaks of public unrest centered in the radical student body of the university's architecture faculty.[50]

Reliance on the private sector and uncoordinated responses to the city's growing infrastructural and ecological problems negated many useful individual actions. Housing, whether on the periphery or in the historic center, was a prime example of the effects of overreliance on individual initiative and lack of regulation by the city. The center was steadily depopulated of working-age inhabitants, the lower economic classes were driven further away, and new construction tended to be substandard, overpriced, and ugly. People who chose to live in the center found that many essential services had vanished. The emphasis on services required by tourists (food, souvenirs, newspapers) tended to produce the "museum city" atmosphere that most Florentines disliked.[51]

The city's response to its massive traffic and pollution problems was sporadic and often overly cautious. To its credit, the Bausi government took the first steps in regulating downtown traffic by creating "*zone blu*," areas of limited traffic circulation, and pedestrian-only streets. It set up special bus lanes, increased service and routes, installed traffic lights with pedestrian call buttons, attempted to direct more traffic on the city's major arterial roads, and built a new bridge (Ponte Verazzano) across the Arno, without mastering the problem. Resistance by shopkeepers scaled back various projects, and frequent bus strikes depressed ridership, while Poggi's nineteenth-century *viale* (boulevards) proved inadequate to the masses of cars that flowed on to them daily, spawning ever larger traffic jams. Plans for more parking garages or even a subway were discussed in council without action. The junta's actions were inadequate because the city government failed to place them in the context of a larger program designed to regulate growth and population distribution.[52]

The city misplayed the airport issue and failed to deal effectively with the question of linking Florence to the projected Milan–Rome express train line, the "*direttissima*." The city council debated the S. Giorgio al Colonica airport site for six years. Improvements to the Pisa terminal and the completion of a new superhighway between Florence and Pisa diminished the city's claim to an international airport. The private airline serving Peretola dropped its service, cutting off an important link with the rest of Italy. Florence, always seeking to accommodate tourism, wanted to route the *direttissima* into S. Maria Novella station. The state railway agency refused to consider the utilization of the station so far off the main line and insisted that only an upgraded and refurbished Campo Marte station would permit the projected supertrain to stop in Florence.[53]

Due to the initiatives of local merchants, tourism boomed through 1973. The opening of the "Palazzo dei congressi" complex, including the rehabilitation of the Fortezza da Basso, was a major, if controversial, achievement of the Bausi junta. The coalition parties fought over control of the Teatro Comunale. The quality of cultural events declined. Bausi admitted that the arts in Florence were having difficulties but pointed to rising ticket sales and laid part of the blame, justly, at the feet of the national government and contentious labor unions.[54]

Other problems plagued the tourist industry: prostitution, young thugs harassing and robbing tourists on the Ponte Vecchio, refuse in city streets and accompanying rat infestations, a polluted Arno, the museums' short opening hours, labor unrest at both artistic sites and hotels, and rising art theft.[55]

Evidence of the environmental decline of the city roused the concern of most Florentines. Tuscan ecologists pressed regional and national government for more laws to deal with problems of clean air and water. Lagorio's regional government was prepared to act, even where its legal role was restricted. The city's response was less impressive. It failed to meet antismog standards set by law, was indifferent to noise pollution issues, did little to deal with pollutants dumped into the Arno, failed to react to inspectors' warnings about the damage that traffic was doing to the stability of the Duomo, and promoted the use of massive smoke-belching incinerators to dispose of both trash and human waste at the cost of aggravating its relationships with neighboring communes.[56]

In spite of widespread agreement that Florence needed to confront the related issues of water supply and flood protection, city government was incapable of delivering anything more than short-term solutions. Dependence on Arno water had increased to 70 percent of total city requirements. Improved filtration units enabled Florence to increase its supply capacity by 15 percent in 1968, but this proved inadequate, as severe water shortages demonstrated the following year and again in 1971 and 1974. The riverbed was a prime breeding ground for hordes of mosquitoes that created summertime misery throughout the city. Other problems included salt deposits in water piping, unpleasant odors, low pipe pressure, and frequent water supply breakdowns. Much responsibility rested with the Italian government, which showed little interest in providing upstream basins and dams that would increase both water supply and safety from flooding. But infrastructural problems like inferior pipes and low water pressure were the city's responsibility.[57]

The historian who attempts to address the question of the success or failure of the Bausi government is faced with the age-old problem of judging whether the glass is half full or half empty. The city enjoyed a remarkable period of economic expansion. More Florentines took part in that prosperity than ever before. Tourists, whether foreign or Italian, continued to find Florence an attractive place to visit. Unfortunately, a significant number of citizens, above all, the elderly and the poor, failed to share in the benefits of growth. The cost of unregulated development was serious damage to the city's architectural and cultural patrimony and to its ecological balances. The city lacked a level of government involvement sufficient to protect it from the worst excesses of unplanned development while simultaneously leaving wide range to entrepreneurship. Admittedly, this is a difficult balance for any society to maintain and perhaps more so in an Italy, where government tends to be both ineffective and intrusive. Hanging over the Bausi junta is the sense of a major lost opportunity. Following the flood, Florentines displayed a strong sense of civic pride and unity. The disaster offered the opportunity to rebuild the city in such a way as to repair not only immediate physical damage but also the legacy of unplanned development of the immediate postwar era. Such a project required strong political leadership. Florence was in short supply. Bausi's junta operated to support, not lead economic development in Florence. While one major cause of this isolation was certainly the political weaknesses that derived from Socialist–DC infighting, the fundamental problem of the Bausi junta was a devotion to laissez-faire approaches in areas where private initiative was either ineffective or counterproductive. In the end, a policy of muddling through was insufficient to meet the city's needs.

NOTES

1. Giacomo Filardi and Alessandre Ammannati, *Universita da buttare* (Florence, 1974), p. 26; Carlo Bacci, Nicola Bovoli, Riccardo Marini and Giovanni Spinoso, eds., *Firenze: Piazza S. Marco 30 Gennaio '68* (Florence, 1968), for chronology; ACC 1968, 1: 303–4; Tristan. Codignola, *Scritti politici, 1943–1981* (Florence, 1987), 2: 605–608; *La Nazione*, February 1, 11, 1967, March 21, October 14, 1968.

2. Pietro Nenni, *I conti con la storia. Diari, 1967–1971* (Milan, 1983), p. 469; Silvio Lanaro, *Storia delli'Italia repubblicana* (Venice, 1992), pp. 279–80.

3. Robert Lumley, *States of Emergency* (London, 1990), pp. 54, 63–64, 66.

4. Bruno D'Avanzo, *Tra dissenso e rivoluzione* (Bologna, 1971), pp. 33–44, 69–79; *La Nazione*, June 5, October 10, November 15, December 8, 1968, March 1, 1969; Comunita di Isolotto, *Isolotto sotto processo* (Bari, 1971), pp. 12–16, 151–67; *Il cardinale contestato* (Rome, 1968), p. 8.

5. Giovanni Berlinguer, *Dieci anni dopo* (Bari, 1978), pp. 57, 136; Secchia, *Archivio*, pp. 712–13; Achille Occhetto, *A dieci anni dal '68* (Rome, 1978), pp. 81, 94; Giovanni Di Capua, *Un anno caldo* (Rome, 1970), pp. 6–7; *Isolotto: documenti*, p. 21.

6. *La Nazione*, March 31, 1969; Di Capua, *Un anno caldo*, pp. 149–56; Nenni, *I conti*, pp. 391, 538–39; "Un piano per la Toscana," *Politica*, April 7, 1974.

7. Giovanni Di Capua, *Verifica della repubblica* (Rome, 1972), pp. 21–23; Giuseppe Tamburrano, *Storia e cronica del centro sinistra* (Milan, 1971), p. 326.

8. Gaetano Arfe, "Alla fine di un anno difficile," *Mondo operaio*, December 1969; Di Capua, *Un anno caldo*, pp. 78–82.

9. Pietro Nenni, *Gli anni del Centro sinistra. Diari, 1957–1966* (Milan, 1982), pp. 401–2, 421–24, 432–33, 439–40.

10. Gianni Baget Bozzo and Giovanni Tassani, *Aldo Moro* (Florence, 1983), p. 240; Nenni, *I conti*, p. 16.

11. Nenni, *I conti*, pp. 168, 170; *La Nazione*, March 15, 16, 29, 30, April 10, 1968.

12. Nenni, *I conti*, p. 183; Tamburrano, *Storia e cronica*, p. 332.

13. ACC 1968, 2: 1557–73, 1580–81, 1720–39, 1756–67, 1788–89; *La Nazione*, July 3, 18, 25, 26, 27, 1968.

14. Nenni, *I conti*, pp. 220–21, 224–27, 231–33, 237–40, 288–89.

15. ACC 1969, 151–63, 328–43, 922–24; "Crisi anche a Firenze," *Rinascita*, March 7, 1969; *La Nazione*, March 5, 12, 25, April 29, September 8, 1969; Mariella Zoppi and Lelio Lagorio interviews, Florence, May 27, 1993, October 4, 1995.

16. Nenni, *I conti*, pp. 300, 321–25, 328, 337–38, 344, 348–50, 476, 486; *La Nazione*, July 4, 1969; Maurizio Degl'Innocenti and Stefano Caretti, *Il socialismo in Firenze e provincia* (Pisa, 1987), p. 185.

17. Michelle Achilli, *Casa* (Padua, 1972), pp. 15–16; Nenni, *I conti*, pp. 17–18, 244, 437; Baget Bozzo and Tassani, *Aldo Moro*, pp. 387, 441, 516.

18. *La Nazione*, December 8, 11, 1967, January 11, 1968; Mariella Zoppi, *Firenze e l'urbanistica* (Rome, 1982), pp. 118–27; *Notiziario*, April 1971, pp. 13–14, 25; May 1971, p. 24; July 1971, pp. 15–16; February 1972, p. 10; March 1972, pp. 3–8; ACC 1971, 1: 257–316.

19. Augusto Boggiano, ed., *Firenze: La Questione urbanistica* (Florence, 1982), pp. 428–36.

20. Luciano Bausi interview, Florence, June 1, 1993.

21. ACC 1968, 1: 375.

22. *La Nazione*, November 5, 7, 1967, January 31, June 2, 26, September 1, 1968; ACC 1968, 1: 613; Bausi interview.

23. Bausi and Lagorio interviews; Gianni Conti interview, Florence, May 26, 1993.

24. *La Nazione*, April 19, 20, 1968; *Firenze '80* (Florence, 1971), pp. 115–16, Zoppi, *Firenze*, pp. 118–27; Lagorio, Zoppi, Bausi, interviews; Valdo Spini interview, Rome, September 26, 1995.

25. *La Nazione*, April 23, July 10, October 12, 1968, March 19, October 7, 1970; *Il Mulino*, June 1969, pp. 630–35; *Firenze: questione urbanistica*, pp. 539–46; Zoppi interview.

26. *Firenze '80*, pp. 5–9; Nenni, *I Conti*, p. 426; Lagorio, Spini, and Zoppi interviews.

27. Giorgio Morales interview, Florence, October 4, 1995; Lagorio interview; ACC 1973, 1: 79–80; Di Capua, *Un anno caldo*, pp. 31–34.

28. Robert Putnam, *Making Democracy Work* (Princeton, NJ, 1993), p. 20; Percy Allum, *Italy—Republic without Government?* (New York, 1973), pp. 236–37.

29. *Citta e regione* 3 (1977), pp. 189–99; Allum, *Italy*, p. 233; Putnam, *Making*, p. 21; Lagorio interview.

30. ACC 1968, 1: 550–62; *La Nazione*, February 22, 1968; *La Politica*, March 2, 1969;

Comune di Firenze, *Rassegna del Comune, 1965–1968* (Florence, 1968), pp. 115–18; Augusto. Boggiano, ed., *Firenze: La questione urbanistica*, pp. 463–65.

31. *La Nazione*, June 26, 1968, November 21, 1970; ACC 1971, 3: 976–1017; ACC 1974, 1: 298–300; Bausi interview.

32. ACC 1971, 4: 1500–30; ACC 1972, 2: 490–532, 3: 1173–1212; "Un' attesa durate due anni, *Politica*, June 11, 1972; Giovanni Spadolini, "Le regioni: Una svolta," *NA* 107 (November 1972); Lelio Lagorio, "Le regioni tre anni dopo," *Mondo operaio*, June 1973.

33. Achille Ardigo, *Indicazioni e orientamenti sulle linee di ristrutturazione e di destinazione del quartieri di Santa Croce* (Florence, 1968), pp. 11, 13–15, 41, 44–45, 67.

34. Corrado Giustiniani, *La Casa promessa* (Turin, 1981), pp. 71, 73–74; *La Nazione*, July 9, 1968; Alex Fubini, *Urbanistica in Italia* (Milan, 1979), p. 275; Francesco Indovina, ed., *Enciclopedia urbanistica*, 4: 316–17, 711.

35. William Murray, *Italy, the Fatal Gift* (New York, 1982), p. 167.

36. Giustiani, *La Casa*, pp. 6, 89.

37. Andreina Daolio, *Le Lotta per la casa in Italia* (Milan, 1974), pp. 23–24.

38. "La patata bollente alle regioni," *La Politica*, April 2, 1972; Guistiniani, *Casa*, pp. 100–103.

39. Italia Nostra, Sezione di Firenze, *Restituzione di Firenze* (Florence, 1982), pp. 12–13; Zoppi interview.

40. Francesco Malgeri, ed., *Storia della Democrazia Cristiana* (Rome, 1987–1989), 4: 294–95.

41. Silvio Lanaro, *Storia delli'Italia repubblicana* (Venice, 1992), p. 291; *Manifatturiera toscana* (December 1975), pp. 9, 19–20, 32; Ferdinando Semboloni, *Appunti sulla topografia socile del centro storico di Firenze dal 1960 al 1981* (Florence, 1986), pp. 33–36, 52–55; *La Nazione*, October 24, 1968, January 29, 1969, March 26, 1970.

42. Zoppi, *Firenze*, p. 112; Semboloni, *Appunti*, pp. 52–55; Francesco Baglioni and Piero Passeri, *I viali di Firenze* (Florence, 1974), pp. 125–34; *La Nazione*, April 23, 1971; *Firenze: question urbanistica*, pp. 443–448; Valerio Paci, "La formazione del nuovo architetto," *Il Mulino*, October 1968; Carlo Cavalotti, "Appunti sulla cultura architetonica e urbanista italiana, 1945–1968," ibid.; Giuseppe Caronia, "Per una nuova legge urbanistica," *NA* 106 (June 1971); *Firenze '80*, pp. 49–61.

43. Italia Nostra, Sezione di Firenze, *Restituzione di Firenze*, p. 22; *Augusto Baggiano*, ed., *Firenze: La question urbanistica* (Florence, 1982), pp. 390–412, 437–40, 449–51, 466–73; Zoppi and Spini interviews.

44. Tommaso Detti interview (Florence, May 14, 1993); Phillipe Duboy, ed., *Edoardo Detti, 1913–1984: architetto e urbanistra* (Milan, 1993), pp. 17–18; Zoppi, *Firenze*, p. 136; Edoardo Detti, "Soluzione urbanistica," *Il Ponte*, December 1966.

45. T. Detti and Spini interviews; Zoppi, *Firenze*, pp. 22–23, 32; *Firenze: questione urbanistica*, pp. 498–99.

46. *Firenze: questione urbanistica*, pp. 453–55, 457–59; Paolo Bagnoli, "I giorni di Firenze (politica e cultura dal 1944 al 1974)," *Citta e regione* 7 (August 1981), pp. 172–73; Lelio Lagorio, "Esperienze regionale in tema di pianificazione territoriale," *Mondo operaio*, June 1971; Stefano Giacobini, "Burrasche su Firenze e dintorni," *Politica*, June 25, 1972; ACC 1973, 1: 18–20, 110–21; 2: 636–38; ACC 1974, 1: 381–95, 641–74; V. Spini, "Al commune di Firenze il colpo grosso non e riuscito," *Il Ponte*, October 10, 1973; *La Nazione*, September 11, 1970; *Citta e regione*, April 1975, p. 34.

47. "The New Architecture of Florence," *Architectural Record*, February 1974; *Firenze: questione urbanistica*, pp. 487–91; *Firenze '80*, pp. 91–106; *Holiday*, September 1969.

48. Comune di Firenze, *Rassegna di Firenze, 1965–1968* (Florence, 1968), pp. 3–4, 43–52.

49. ACC 1976, 1: 344–52; Comuno di Firenze, *Relazione sulla gestione Commissariale del Comune dal 29 aprile 1969 al 16 luglio 1970* (Florence, 1970), pp. 67–77; *La Nazione*, September 18, 1968, January 4, 1971, July 27, 1974; ACC 1972, 2: 533–51.

50. *La Nazione*, March 12, April 14, May 5, 26, June 13, September 30, October 3, 1968, January 5, 9, February 6, March 4, September 3, 1969, January 24, February 28, 1970, July 17, February 1, 9, 1971, August 27, 1974; *Rassegna del commune*, p. 7; ACC 1971, 5: 1980–2016; ACC 1972, 2: 625–62; ACC 1974, 1: 423–40; Zoppi, *Firenze*, p. 128; Giacomo Filardo and Alessandro Ammannati, *Universita di buttare* (Florence, 1974), pp. 8–10.

51. Indovina, *Risanimento*, p. 9; *Firenze '80*, p. 26; *Firenze: questione urbanistica*, pp. 441–42; Ardigo, *Indicazioni*, pp. 7, 9–10; PCI, *Firenze: inchiesta*, pp. 4, 12–15, 17–22, 25–27, 45; Spini interview; Iacopo Detti interview, Florence, May 18, 1993.

52. *Rassegna del Commune*, pp. 63–67; Commune di Firenze, *Progetto di massimo* (1967); ATAF, *Piano di sviluppo*, pp. 6–7, 27–28; ACC 1968, 4: 1468–90, 3294–3331; ACC 1971, 4: 1554–1603; ACC 1973, 2: 895, 925; Zoppi, *Firenze*, p. 138; PCI, *Firenze: inchiesta*, p. 31; Nicola Cefaretti and Morello Malaspina, *1865–1985. Centoventi anni di trasporti pubblica a Firenze* (Cortona, 1987), pp. 341–46; Indovina, *Risanimento*, pp. 34–37; Giorgio Simonici, "Trasporto e disegno urbano," *Il Mulino*, September 1969.

53. *Rassegna del commune, 1965–1968*, p. 131; ACC 1967, 3: 2782–85; 3: 3415–51; ACC 1968, 2: 2338–39; ACC 1973, 2: 855–57, 906–07; *La Nazione*, November 28, 1967; March 7, 1968; February 25, August 19, 1969; November 3, 11, 1970; February 18, March 6, April 8, June 13, 1971; June 10, 25, 1974; Bausi interview.

54. *La Nazione*, October 16, December 17, 1967; February 14, April 4, October 23, 1968; November 39, December 27, 1969; October 14, 1970; April 8, June 30, 1971; September 9, 1974; Egidio Mucci, "Henry Moore a Firenze," *Politica*, June 4, 1972; ACC 1974, 1: 25–62.

55. *La Nazione*, March 23, May 25, July 12, August 4, 7, 20, September 9, 27, 1968; May 27, July 3, 1969; March 3, November 7, October 28, 1970; March 25, 30, May 12, June 24, 1971; October 9, 1974.

56. ACC 1974, 1: 81–87; Furbini, *Urbanistica*, p. 19; *La Nazione*, February 8, July 12, October 22, 1969; January 30, 1970; January 8, February 3, 6, March 18, 1971; August 30, November 10, 20, 1974.

57. *Restituzione di Firenze*, pp. 4–5; *La Nazione*, November 12, 1967; May 31, December 19, 1968; January 2, October 8, 17, November 13, 1969; July 11, October 17, 1970; May 14, 1971; June 1, 7, 11, July 19, 1974.

Chapter 10

The Historic Compromise at Florence, 1975–1981

We aren't going to be the Trojan Horse of the Historic Compromise.
                                        Mario Bianco, PSI, 1979

A few years are insufficient to remedy and cover so many gaps.
                                Elio Gabbuggiani, PCI, January 1980

Slouching comfortably in one of the easy chairs in his well-appointed university office, former PCI alderman Giorgio Mori rattled off a series of causes for what he termed the "failure" of the Gabbuggiani junta. The Florentine PCI tried to expand beyond its traditional base of support by adopting programs that appealed to traditional Catholic voters. The junta offered a long-term program as if it could be put into place within months of the election. Then, of course, the PSI was a most unreliable partner. The Socialists abandoned all but the verbal pretense of being a working-class party and sought out a new electoral base that was profoundly opposed to the aims of the traditional left.[1]

PSI chief Lelio Lagorio simplified the issues. The PCI was a "long gray line" of administrators without a larger vision. The party was a threat because of its size and relentless hold on power. "In the end, the PCI tends to dominate what it controls." Florentine Socialists would not permit the Communists to devour them. "We have used our role—I would not always say . . . well—but used our power as a balancing party, pushing out [licenziando] the uncomfortable or inept ally."[2]

Caught between a PCI eager to build alliances to the Catholic political world and a Socialist Party determined to resist this grand alliance at all costs, the government of Elio Gabbuggiani was born with the most limited chances of success.

THE HISTORIC COMPROMISE

As center left collapsed, the PCI became an increasingly credible candidate for membership in Italy's national governing coalition. In 1968, the Italian Communists publicly criticized the Soviet invasion of Czechoslovakia. In 1969 the party's contending factions supported Longo's choice of the youthful Enrico Berlinguer as new deputy secretary and heir apparent to their ill leader. The small, slender Sard noble quickly became one of Italy's most admired politicians: a tireless worker, a cautious mediator, and, above all, a man who understood that the PCI had to embrace democracy and end the equivocations that had characterized its policies. Berlinguer's lack of flamboyance, his shyness, his apparent sense of the national interest created sympathy for him and his party that extended far beyond its normal supporters.[3]

Berlinguer's policy shifts were as drastic as the cautious Sard and his fundamentally conservative movement could endure. In the fall of 1973, he proposed that the DC and PCI join in a partnership to govern and reform Italy. The bloody overthrow of the leftist government of Chile provided the specific impetus for Berlinguer's "historic compromise" proposal. However, Berlinguer's proposal had roots in the resistance and the postwar national unity governments. He offered to bring the PCI-led portion of the working class into a governing coalition whose objective was gradually transforming Italy into an economically modern and socially equitable democratic state. The PCI's leader specifically ruled out an "alternative of the left," stating that a government coalition based on 51 percent of the electorate was insufficient. He called upon the other anti-Fascist parties to create a new relationship with a reformed PCI that would end its historic isolation. In the mid-1970s, he committed the party to maintenance of Italy's economic and security ties to the West.[4]

DC leaders like Moro recognized that the PCI's evolution toward democracy as well as its association with effective urban planning, good public transportation, well-managed public housing, and the promotion of small business expansion enhanced Berlinguer's claims to join a governing coalition.[5] Nevertheless, neither the DC nor the PSI rushed to embrace the PCI. Questions of power and of the division of government spoils were natural impediments. From a Socialist perspective, a historic compromise would totally nullify the party's role. Socialist hostility to the proposed PCI-DC marriage was consistent. Christian Democrats were genuinely skeptical about the depth of PCI commitment to democracy and the completeness of its break with the USSR. Moreover, alliance with the PCI would rob the DC of the political legitimacy that it derived from its role as the bulwark against Communism and threaten its internal unity. Seeking to calm their fears and cool opposition within his own camp, Berlinguer, ever the realist, announced that his party was in no hurry to enter a governing coalition.[6]

During the six dramatic years from Berlinguer's enunciation of the historic compromise strategy to the PCI's defeat in 1979 parliamentary elections, the initial positive political benefits that Berlinguer's offer created were erased as the implications of the historic compromise undercut support within the party and outside it. The serious damage done to the party's structure and its image was evident in cities like Florence.[7]

The PCI entered the 1970s with many unresolved structural problems. In spite of Communist rhetoric about sexual equality, women were underrepresented in its leadership. All sectors of the party demanded greater internal democracy. Recruitment lagged. By 1974, 61 percent of its national membership was over forty. In Tuscany, a bedrock of PCI strength, the figure was 65 percent. Pensioners and housewives filled its ranks, while worker and farm-laborer participation declined. The PCI had a hard time maintaining active sections and provincial organizations. The Communists were losing touch with Italian society.[8]

Economic and social change in the 1970s struck hard at the party's traditional strengths. On the intellectual level, Marxism was never more influential. However, the radical version of group that stood outside the PCI won the hearts and minds of the young. Most of them found the PCI decidedly staid. At the same time, the party's traditional hold on the working classes was undermined as Italians of all classes took advantage of inexpensive personal recreation opportunities. Television in particular broke down PCI control of after-work activities and at the same time had a central role in accentuating Italy's love affair with consumption. The acquisition of private property in the form of homes, cars, televisions, clothing, vacations, and furnishings undermined Marxism's collectivist values while accentuating individualism. Berlinguer did nothing to improve the PCI's image by making economic austerity a central theme of the Communist platform.[9]

Dogged by internal contradictions, the PCI tried to reassert its leadership role on the left and simultaneously push forward its claims to partnership in national government through successful administration of regional and local government. Partnered with the PSI on the local and regional level, the Communist Party hoped to carry out a reform of the state from below that ultimately would force the DC to invite it into national government. The PCI seized upon regional government and urban planning as key issues, threatening the PSI with the loss of its precarious political identity. The Socialist-Communist relationship became testy as they struggled over claim to these issues.[10]

In 1975 local elections, Italy's electorate swung left. PCI-PSI coalitions swept into power in all the nation's major cities, including such traditional bastions of conservative power as Naples, Palermo, and Rome. Florence was part of this trend. The DC, PLI, and PSDI all lost vote share and city council seats. The Social Democrats took a severe drubbing, losing half their votes and council seats. The Socialists advanced slightly, acquiring one seat. The Communists, with 41.46 percent of the popular vote and twenty-six seats, enjoyed a near majority. After complex negotiations, the PCI, PSI, and small Proletarian Unity Party formed coalition administrations at the regional, provincial, and local level.[11]

The Socialists extracted major concessions from the PCI in the division of local power, taking control of the assessorates of urban planning, decentralization, and communal planning, together with the prestigious Teatro Comunale directorship. Moreover, the PCI's very popular new mayor, the handsome Elio Gabbuggiani, limited himself to a general statement when the junta assumed office. Giorgio Morales (PSI), the assessor of decentralization, laid out the new government's program in a speech ten days later and then introduced the new team of assessors to the city council.[12]

Morales' statement set the tone for the left junta. It demanded both greater autonomy and more financial assistance from the national government to meet the needs of its citizens. The city would decentralize power through the creation of effective *consigli dei quartieri*, impose a more rational urban plan on Florence, end the era of laissez-faire development, and promote balanced economic growth. While encouraging tourism and artisan sector growth, the left proposed to attract technologically advanced industries to Florence and Tuscany to ensure growth and competitiveness. The city government's program, "Project Florence," would also address the chronic problems of the university while dealing forcefully with the city's indebtedness.

BOTTLED UP

The new junta inherited a massive debt. Opposition to its urban planning objectives included large sections of the construction industry, real estate interests, banks, and the legal profession. Opposition was powerful, well financed, politically well connected, and, since it frequently operated outside the law, very agile. The national government was (and would remain) in the hands of the DC. The local DC was full of fight. Youthful left-wing political extremists were ready to challenge the junta in the streets. Italy's national and local economies were developing in ways that operated against the left's plans for greater balance between industrial and service jobs and, thus, against its urban planning strategy.[13]

Relieved of the burdens of power, Florence's DC, with some help from the right, made city council meetings a battlefield. At the September 19, 1975, council session, Gabbuggiani urged the parties to deal with a series of pressing administrative issues to no avail. The opposition attacked the PCI city government for inviting representatives of East German regime, a major human rights violator, to attend the annual Festa dell'Unità. The opposition attacked PCI-PSI management of the Teatro Comunale for staging art with alleged totalitarian content. Gianni Conti, a rising star in DC local politics, dragged up examples of PCI behavior that, he claimed, had worked against Florence's interests under the center left, to justify Christian Democratic obstructionism. Gabbuggiani publicly bemoaned DC tactics. Thus encouraged, the opposition kept up the assault.[14]

The DC had an unlikely ally in the streets of Florence. The radicalization of Italy's youth continued across the 1970s. Many young Florentines abandoned legal forms of protest for violence. In April 1975 members of the "extra-parliamentary" left stormed a neo-Fascist party office near Piazza Independenza. Gunfire erupted later that night along the via Nazionale. One youth was seriously wounded and later died. Molotov cocktails flew as clashes continued. The culture of protest spawned a growing drug trade that, in turn, sparked a rise in common crime. Popular opinion, to some degree correctly, attributed the lawlessness to the ideology and permissiveness of the left. The left's standard reaction to violence was not deploying more police but proposing the creation of programs designed to deal with the "causes" of discontent.[15]

In attempting to deal with youth violence, to implement its programs, and to provide services to its constituents, the Gabbuggiani junta's basic problem was money. The tax policies of the national government, its willingness to place further unfunded mandates on the regions and localities, and the DC's political calculation that limiting local government funding in some sectors would undercut the left placed the government of Florence in serious straits.

The changing nature of the local economy magnified tourism's importance for the Florentine economy. Manufacturing jobs continued a steady decline that began in the 1960s, while service sector employment grew apace. New jobs, most linked to tourism, were frequently low-wage. They attracted a youthful migration from other parts of Italy. Florence's overall population aged, but a demographic blip of youth nineteen to twenty-four years of age found work in the city center's low-wage, dead-end tourist service jobs. These young people, together with a large pool of unemployed youths who also congregated in the old city, fueled crime, drug abuse, and the recruitment efforts of violent fringe political movements.[16]

Expanding tourism accentuated imbalances in the local economy. Florence's cost of living rose more rapidly than in other Italian cities, prompting Nuovo Pignone and Galileo to move their factories, while the city dropped from the twenty-eighth to the thirty-ninth position among Italian cities in per capita income.[17]

In trying to redress this imbalance, the city considered imposing an "obligatory loan" of 100 million lire on local business. It hoped to invest these funds in nontourism-related economic development. The need for employment-creating initiatives was underlined by stories such as the 391 people who applied for ten low-wage jobs in city kindergartens.[18]

The Gabbuggiani administration decided to approach its economic infrastructure problems with the development of a new PRG that would stress carefully regulated and limited growth and cooperation with neighboring communes. The DC attacked both the ideas of preferential treatment for some industries and cooperation with surrounding communal administrations. Laissez-faire growth remained its mantra.[19]

The first stage in advancing Project Firenze was securing state aid. By 1976 Florence's debt had reached 337 billion lire. Further loans and the authorization for increased indebtedness had to come from the state. Heavy communal indebtedness was Italy-wide. A financially hard-pressed Italian government was seeking foreign (American and German) credits to meet these and other shortfalls. Meanwhile, the debt-ridden city of Florence had to face up to realities:

reining in spending while it sought to improve its financial position through greater cost accountability and improved management. City plans for a five-year, 155 billion lire investment in Project Firenze quickly collapsed.[20]

Hamstrung by money problems and concerted opposition by the local DC, the Gabbuggiani junta did what it could to promote both change and public confidence. Neighborhood councils became a defining local political issue. If the government of Florence could launch them and maintain a high level of public participation in these institutions, it would underline differences between the Bausi and Gabbuggiani administrations. Grassroots political activity would presumably assist the city in containing the growth-at-any-price forces while it fought a comprehensive urban plan through the city council. It would reinforce the process of democratic legitimization that the PCI sought at all levels of politics.[21]

In April 1976 the Italian parliament passed a law (No. 278) authorizing localities to set up the neighborhood councils. The PCI and PSI had been campaigning hard for decentralization of many governmental functions, and the councils were designed to meet some of their demands. In May 1976 the city council approved rules for the operation of Florence's councils. The law divided Florence into fourteen neighborhoods. Elections for neighborhood councils took place November 28–29, with 82 percent of eligible voters participating. The left (PSI-PCI) won a majority in the overall voting, while the DC pulled slightly over one-third of the vote. The councils began functioning in January 1977 with the election of officers. Under terms of their charter, the new bodies had consultative privileges on the city plan, and education, zoning, and budget priorities. The city delegated control over medical services, child welfare, kindergartens and libraries, after-school activities, and certain public works projects to the councils.[22]

From the beginning the councils had considerable difficulty in providing services. Deliberate obstructionism by the DC added to their difficulties. The presidents of the new entities complained loudly about the red tape that they encountered at city hall, while praising Morales for his efforts to assist them. Members protested that their budgets and their powers were too limited. City efforts to satisfy their demands for greater autonomy took the form of increases in budget and the creation of civic centers to speed up bureaucratic procedures.[23]

By 1981 the neighborhood council experiment had petered out. In spite of Morales' leadership, popular participation in the councils, never robust, fell off dramatically. The neighborhood councils never took root in the rest of Italy. In 1980 only thirty-two Italian communes had functioning councils. Florence's city bureaucracy stymied local initiatives with a combination of inertia, hostility, and simple indifference. Bureaucratic opposition fostered widespread suspicion that the city was ignoring councils' needs. The DC exploited these discontents, claiming that the PCI deliberately limited the autonomy of the bodies. The answer to the neighborhood council's weakness, according to the Christian Democrats, was the introduction of the traditional patronage practices.[24]

Public safety issues were equally tough for the Gabbuggiani junta. Communists had great difficulty in confronting embarrassing ties of the left terrorists to Marxist ideology and the PCI. The DC ably exploited the issue, assisted by a series of terrorist actions directed at its offices and leaders. During the winter of 1976–1977, the city endured a wave of violent acts (twenty-three assaults on individuals, fourteen bank or post office robberies, and three jailbreaks). The crime wave coincided with another revolt at the Faculty of Architecture, building occupations, the virtual seizure of the Piazza S. Spirito area by nocturnal drug users, and a series of bombings. The police uncovered evidence that Florence was a major rear-area base for left-wing terrorist organizations. The Mafia reared its ugly head as police officials tried to suppress Sicilian-run gambling parlors. Right-wing extremists were also active. The DC remained a favorite target of both left and right extremists, who made thirty-one attacks on its offices and personnel.[25]

The city called on the prefect for more police and attempted to deal with the root causes of youth unrest. Following a strategy of conciliation rather than repression, the junta engaged in negotiations with left-wing ultras and in February 1978 agreed to host three days of "meetings" in Florence. Gabbuggiani ignored plentiful signs of public impatience not only with terrorists but with rebellious youths, their drug culture, and politicians who coddled them.[26]

On March 16, 1978, Florentines heard the stunning news of the kidnapping of Aldo Moro, president of the DC and chief artificer of partial Communist involvement in the national government. Berlinguer recognized that the PCI's credibility as a democratic movement as well as its continued participation in the governing majority depended on confronting terrorism. The PCI took a hard-line stance against any deals with the Red Brigades terrorists. The Florentine PCI and government, badly disoriented by Moro's kidnapping, followed suit.[27]

Moro's murder and the subsequent ouster of corruption-stained President Giovanni Leone were major blows to the DC. But, that ever-resilient party tightened its grip on power. The Communists were the major loser. Tarred by ideological association with the terrorists, the PCI never achieved credibility as a party of order. The Moro kidnapping became a catalyst for swelling voter discontent. Traditional Communist voters and recent supporters disliked the practical effects of collaboration with the DC. Realizing that national solidarity played into the hands of the Christian Democrats, Berlinguer forced a crisis in February 1979, extracted the PCI from its cohabitation with the DC, and set the stage for elections.[28] The voters punished the Communists, who dropped from 34 percent to 29 percent of the vote. The small parties recouped. Italy's ingenious politicians invented a new political formula, the Pentapartito (five-party coalition), a triumph of nonideological deal-making.

The Moro kidnapping was the turning point in the Italian state's battle against terrorism. Public tolerance for the terrorists vanished. Gradually, the state dismembered the terrorist cells while wiping out the larger groups of extra-parliamentary leftists who provided their seedbed and a layer of protective cover.

Sporadic acts of political terrorism continued in Florence until the mid-1980s.

Disaffected youth remained a major problem. As political activism lost much of its appeal, young people turned in growing numbers to drugs. Transvestite prostitutes and associated petty crime remained a major nuisance for both public order and the city's international image. The DC, PSDI, and the law-and-order parties of the right accused the junta of hiring too few police and "deprofessionalizing" them. The opposition had a field day when the city police struck for higher pay. The PSI joined the fun by breaking with the city government over drug policy issues.[29]

The junta was on equally slippery political footing as it attempted to deal with public housing issues. It engaged in unproductive negotiations with squatters occupying public and private apartments. Its efforts to increase the number of available rental units through rehabilitation and new construction came up short because of a combination of limited funding, bureaucratic delay, and the objections of private property owners.[30]

The junta's performance on quality-of-life issues also disappointed its backers. It failed to deal effectively with the pollution created by Bausi's massive incinerators. Nor was it able to get a firm grip on the city's water and sewer problem. Summer water shortages, river pollution, the lack of major flood control initiatives, and an aging water and sewer system all plagued the cash-short city administration. Socialist and Communist components of the majority fought over who should shoulder blame for the lack of progress in these areas.[31]

In the related area of traffic control, the junta did better but at considerable political cost. By 1981 Florence had a vehicular population of nearly 750,00 cars, trucks, buses, scooters, and motorcycles. Opposition from city merchants stymied plans for extension of environmentally sound ideas like *zone blu* for two years. Finally, beginning in mid-1978, the Gabbuggiani junta put into effect rules that doubled the area covered by *zone blu*, created pedestrian-only areas, and removed a major cause of both air pollution and structural damage from the city center: tourist buses. The opposition skillfully exploited discontent with these long-overdue measures. It was also able to play upon the inability of the city administration to come up with a solution to a chronic lack of public parking and with the shortcomings of ATAF bus services. However, the left performed a major service to the city with its programs. Subsequent city governments would expand upon traffic-free areas, increase *zone blu*, and add parking. The public gradually came to recognize the benefits of these actions. The Gabbuggiani junta won little credit for its foresight or courage.[32]

TOURIST BLUES

Following a brief recession in the mid-1970s, tourism was growing again. Since Project Firenze was not attracting industrial investment, tourism became even more central to the health of the local economy. The city could not promote a sensible program of urban development without confronting the tourist question.

Major infrastructure programs such as a new airport and high-speed rail found their prime justification in tourist sector growth.[33]

The city had a record 217 million visitors in 1975, but they were spending less and staying for shorter periods. Florence was becoming a one-day stop for large tourist buses that ran the main highways between Venice and Rome. Disgorging passengers in the morning, the giant buses lined up along the Arno's banks, waiting for their late afternoon departure. Lower-end tourism expanded, featuring people who consumed inexpensive fast food and cheap souvenirs. The offsetting spending of well-bankrolled Americans was in decline. Fewer were coming, and those who did spent less.[34]

To attract more big spenders, the city mounted major art exhibitions, attempted to improve merchant services, tried to publicize less-visited areas of the old city, and moved aggressively to attract convention trade. Florentine officials experimented with programs designed to attract tourists during the traditional off-seasons.[35]

In 1979 city officials suddenly realized that they had succeeded too well. Tourism was booming, and an overcrowded city strained to meet the needs of its visitors and citizens. Hotel rooms were in short supply throughout the summer. The visitors, at times, were not what the city wanted. Older tourists continued to spend less. The armies of youth who arrived were particularly short on cash and created all sorts of public nuisance problems.[36]

Expert predictions that tourism would double over the succeeding twenty years aroused Florentines to focus on defending their cultural patrimony. Businessmen complained about a lack of restaurants, perpetual traffic jams, deteriorating structures, and a paucity of cultural attractions for well-heeled visitors.[37]

Gabbuggiani headed off to the United States in an effort to attract back the big-spending Americans and produce new customers for Florence's traditional industries. The trip, one of the first made by Italian Communist officials to the United States, encouraged visits by U.S. buyers and won some press coverage. The following year, the mayor headed off to Tokyo to corral more Japanese tourism and trade.[38]

Reacting to reports of the weakened condition of the Duomo, the Rumor government appropriated a half billion lire to stabilize the Brunelleschi cupola in 1975. After the 1976 elections the money suddenly disappeared into another item of the national budget. Funding shortages stopped restoration work on national treasures such as S. Spirito, the Palazzo Vecchio, Teatro Goldini, the Villa Strozzi, and the Palazzo della Parte Guelfa.[39]

After considerable foot-dragging by the Italian state, work on these projects began or resumed. Time was running against the city. Anidride sulfide, a by-product of the automobile engine, was wreaking havoc on the facades of Florence's ancient architectural marvels. The effect of continuous traffic on buildings like the Duomo was the equivalent of a daily small earthquake. Other monuments like the elegant, eleventh-century church S. Miniato al Monte began to show signs of deterioration. Rockslides in an area around the Piazzale Michelangelo demonstrated the effects of centuries of human tampering with the environment.[40]

Concern about the effects of pollution cut across party lines and helped build a majority consensus for traffic restrictions. No such concord reigned in the area of cultural programming. Charging that the PCI-led government was attempting to impose Marxist cultural norms, the opposition somewhat contradictorily, but effectively, attacked the Gabbuggiani administration for failure to develop a systematic program. Once again the junta was hamstrung by a lack of cash and by the national government's dilatory approach to funding the long-promised European University. Gabbuggiani and his allies badly mismanaged the replacement of the director of the Teatro Comunale. The PCI's decision to follow DC patronage practices exposed it to charges of ignoring its reform platform and conspiring against cultural freedom. A massive 1980 show celebrating the Medici and sixteenth-century Florence and an agreement with the Moore Foundation to display some of the English sculptor's works permanently in Florence were among the junta's achievements.[41]

In 1981, the city suffered a tourist slowdown. Business fell by 15 percent in the first months of the year and remained depressed during the key spring and summer portions of the year. Businessmen blamed the city administration for failing to properly regulate services. Gabbuggiani offered a new package of infrastructural reforms to remedy the problems. In the short run, however, the city government had to rely on the interest of native son Giovanni Spadolini, the leader of the small Republican Party, who became prime minister on June 28, 1981, ending the DC's thirty-six-year hold on the position.[42]

If Florence were to maximize its tourist income, it had to build infrastructures capable of attracting a wealthier clientele. The Bausi junta had taken a major step in this direction by pushing forward the Palazzo dei Congressi complex. Gabbuggiani's administration poured funds into the rehabilitation of a number of larger central-city hotels. One key issue was speeding up travel time to Florence. City government and the business community agreed that a high-speed rail link with Rome and Milan that stopped in the heart of Florence (S. Maria Novella station), rather than on its outskirts (Campo Marte station), was essential. The state railway system continued to resist this costly project since it required major underground tunneling.[43]

Establishing a regular air link between Florence and the rest of Europe was another high priority for the Gabbuggiani junta and the business community. Regular service to the small, but close in, Peretola airport ended abruptly when Aerterrena airline folded in 1974, leaving two of its aircraft parked on the airstrip. Over the next five years, efforts to get Peretola back into service produced intermittent activity. The market existed, but a combination of bureaucratic delay, private start-up costs, a second bankruptcy, and infighting between the Socialist and Communist components of the city government undermined determined efforts to establish scheduled services.[44]

A PROJECT WITHOUT A PLAN

Ironically, a junta composed of Marxist parties failed to create a sense that it could develop and carry out a plan. The long-promised revision of the PRG languished for five years as the Gabbuggiani administration sought to find a formula that would win the backing of the business community. Mindful of Berlinguer's maxim that the left needed to create broad-based coalitions, the Communists were reluctant to adopt a confrontational approach on the central issue of planning. Instead, the party adopted a case-by-case approach to zoning that failed to win the trust of capital and exhausted the patience of many supporters.[45]

The PCI took power with a reasonable understanding of the problems that it would face. It hoped to use planning as a tool to restrain development and to rally public support for the notion that the common good should take precedence over individual interests. Environmentalism and historic conservation grew in popularity. The Communists and Socialists envisioned neighborhood councils, fully empowered regions, and intercommunal cooperation as the instruments by which to foster a consensus for carefully regulated growth. Finally, the left hoped that a reform of local administration would increase efficiency and build public confidence.[46]

Regionalism, like the center left, was an idea whose prolonged birth allowed the opposition ample time to weaken it. Asked about the regions in 1995, Lagorio gave a wan smile. They were a "great disappointment" that never got beyond the stage of becoming useful patronage machines. While spending approximately one-quarter of the national budget by 1980, the regions were unable to establish effective autonomy from the dictates of the central government and national party headquarters. Their role as a new layer of bureaucratic control frequently irked city administrators.[47]

The regions were contained because the DC made limited concessions under pressure from its temporary partner in government, the Communists. The PCI, with its own centralist prejudices and traditions, never pressed its early advantage in the way that regionalism's more enthusiastic supporters would have liked. Bettino Craxi, the PSI's new leader, embraced regionalism only so long as it smoothed his path to a rapprochement with the DC and then dropped the issue.[48]

The Gabbuggiani junta would have to act alone, and it needed to move quickly to reformulate an urban policy for Florence. Traffic and industrial pollutants were destroying its monuments. The aging portion of the city's population continued to cluster within the walls, where services were the weakest and housing inferior, for lack of affordable alternatives. Meanwhile, Florence's large student population was protesting its segregation in substandard classroom buildings inside the old city while demanding better scientific and library facilities.[49]

Initially, the junta tried to carry forward with Detti's overall conception, modified to take into account the changes imposed by the national government. This approach faced three serious problems. First, it was unsatisfactory to an important and vocal element of the PCI's supporting coalition, the urban planners and environmentalists who insisted that private investment was fundamentally harmful to the interests of the city. Second, the opposition parties, the DC, PLI, PSDI, and PRI, demanded that the junta produce an articulated program that would reduce public spending on real estate and emphasize private investment. Finally, a strong element within the PCI concluded that higher levels of private investment were indispensable if the city were to achieve its "modernization." By 1980, this faction had pushed the cautious urban planning alderman, Sergio Sozzi, out of power and sought to find a modus vivendi with the opposition and private industry.[50]

The PSI, too, had a more positive evaluation of private investment. However, the Socialists were unwilling to follow the PCI's lead. The PSI needed to differentiate itself from its larger and more powerful ally-rival. Urban planning was an area that offered the possibility of such a definition. The PCI was out of the national government, on the defensive, and had been signally unable to coordinate an urban policy on the local level. In late 1980, with local elections over, the time approached, in Lagorio's words, for the city to find "a new broom."[51]

THE PERILS OF REFORMISM

Gabbuggiani's government suffered the fate of many reform administrations. It assumed power by offering programs that required a certain type of national political climate. When the historic compromise failed to materialize, and terrorism issues undercut the PCI, local reformers lacked the weight to carry forward with a consistent program. Added to this were Gabbuggiani's political weaknesses. Florence's mayor was the classic "good" apparatchik. Courteous, well meaning, personally attractive, the *sindaco* lacked the ability to define issues or inspire respect in the opposition. In this he mirrored his party: the PCI offered competence but no real vision. As a result of these weaknesses, the PCI-led city government looked for compromise, generally settled for piecemeal reform, and after five years in power appeared to be an only slightly improved variant on the center left. Throughout Italy, PCI-dominated juntas of cities like Turin, Naples, Palermo, and Rome had their reform initiatives strangled in the cradle by a hostile national government and its local allies.[52]

In Florence, PCI administration was reasonably efficient. Party nominees, showing their customary flair for capitalism, did a good job running Fiorentinagas and other public enterprises. The city increased the number of classrooms, built new parks on the periphery, and rehabilitated the S. Lorenzo market. It modernized a number of hotels in the historic center and oversaw infrastructural improvements to inner-city gas, water, and electrical lines. A modern suspension bridge, Ponte al Indiano, linked Florence to the bedroom community of Scandicci.[53]

The stumbling blocks to more consistent performance were primarily financial. While the regions could contribute more, they, like the cities, remained tied to Rome's purse strings. Communist-Socialist administrations invested public money in infrastructural improvements such as roads, parks, illumination, sanitation, and culture to attract the private investment that would provide new jobs, an enlarged tax base, and expanded individual prosperity. They counted on cooperation between local government and private capital as a factor favoring carefully regulated new development. The model was imported from Bologna, where it had functioned well for over two decades.[54]

The left's tactical approach ran aground when business declined to invest in Florence. Corporations, with the backing of larger unions, demanded more exemption from city regulations than the Gabbuggiani administration was inclined to grant. At the same time, cooperation with neighboring "red" communes proved difficult to achieve. Ideologically similar city governments continued to disagree on a range of practical issues; from incineration to road planning, each sought its own advantage. Florence's neighbors resented the city's political and cultural preeminence and feared its ambitions as they had for 600 years.[55]

Thrown back on the mercy of a central government that had no desire to reward left-wing regimes and face massive demands for assistance from all localities, Florence lined up for its ration of aid. Big projects like a careful restructuring of the historic center were out of the city's economic reach. As interest groups pressed for attention, the city government reacted by granting a zoning variant here or constructing a public building there without any sense of planned integration. A highly vocal opposition, led by the DC's Gianni Conti, lambasted the junta for the lack of a comprehensive urban plan and charged that the city's poor were the primary victims of the left's mismanagement. Reflecting widespread disillusion with the junta's performance, Conti labeled the Gabbuggiani administration "six lost years." More ominously, Morales announced that his party was not wedded to alliance with the PCI and was ready to consider other alternatives. An increasingly aggressive, although directionless, PSI would dominate Florentine politics in the 1980s.[56]

NOTES

1. Giorgio Mori interview, Florence, May 20, 1993.

2. Lelio Lagorio interview, Florence, October 4, 1995.

3. Giuseppe Fiori, *Vita di Enrico Berlinguer* (Bari, 1989); Enzo Collotti, ed., *Archivio Pietro Secchia, 1945–1973* (Milan, 1979), pp. 510–12, 519–22; Pietro Nenni, *I conti con la storia. Diari, 1967–1971* (Milan, 1983), p. 286; Giovanni Di Capua, *Un anno caldo* (Rome, 1970), pp. 45–49; Cyrus Sulzberger, *An Age of Mediocrity* (New York, 1973), p. 688.

4. Pietro Valenza, *Il compromesso storico* (Rome, 1975), pp. 22–27, 45; Mori interview.

5. Valenza, *Compromesso storico*, p. 292; Francesco Malgeri, ed., *Storia della Democrazia Cristiana* (Rome, 1987–1989), 4: 551–55; Francesco Indovina, ed., *La citta occasionale* (Milan, 1993), pp. 19–20.

6. Malgeri, *Storia*, 4: 574; Giulio Andreotti, *Diari, 1976–1979* (Milan, 1981), pp. 141–42; Spencer Di Scala, *Renewing Italian Socialism* (New York, 1988), pp. 171–73, 177–78, 184; Nicola Gallerano and Marcello Flores, *Sul PCI* (Bari, 1992), pp. 68–70; Valenza, *Compromesso storico*, p. 293.

7. Gallerano and Flores, *Sul PCI*, p. 244; Geoffrey Pridham, *The Nature of the Italian Party System* (New York, 1981), p. 107.

8. Circular letter, February 14, 1971, ISRT, C. Collini, b 6, f "materiale PCI-Firenze"; Massimo Illardi and Aris Accornero, *Il Partito Comunista italiano* (Milan, 1982), p. 501; Pridham, *Nature*, pp. 51, 53, 65, 85–87; Gallerano and Flores, *Sul PCI*, pp. 132–33; Ghini, "Gli inscritti," in Massimo Ilardi and Aris Accornero, eds., *Il Partito Comunista italiano* (Milan, 1982), pp. 259, 271.

9. Patrick McCarthy, *The Crisis of the Italian State* (New York, 1997), Mark Gilbert, *The Italian Revolution* (Boulder, CO, 1995), ch. 5.

10. Pridham, *Nature*, pp. 231, 234; Elio Gabbuggiani interview, Florence, May 31, 1993; *Citta e regione*, July 1975, pp. 5–12; Vald. Spini interview, Rome, September 26, 1995.

11. *La Nazione*, June 17, 18, 27, 1975.

12. ACC 1975, 8–20, 48–52; ACC 1976, 1: 958–960; *La Nazione*, November 12, 23, 28, 1975; Spini interview.

13. Mariella Zoppi, *Firenze e l'urbanistica* (Rome, 1982), p. 160; Pridham, *Nature*, p. 222.

14. Gianni Conti interview, Florence, May 26, 1993; ACC 1975, pp. 350–57, 605, 691–778, 793–820, 973; ACC 1976, 1: 405; 2: 903–7, 971–73; *La Nazione*, July 6, 1977; Pridham, *Nature*, pp. 122–24, 139.

15. ACC 1975, pp. 438–46, 447; *La Nazione*, November 19, 1976, January 12, 1977; *Citta e regione*, October 1978, pp. 5–21; Ibid., February 1977, pp. 62–68; Pridham, *Nature*, p. 220; Mori, Gabbuggiani, and Conti interviews; *La Nazione*, April 19, 22, May 11, September 3, December 28, 31, 1975.

16. ACC 1976, 1: 477–82; *Il Ponte*, November 1981, pp. 1106–11.

17. *La Nazione*, June 19; August 18, 1980.

18. *La Nazione*, December 1, 1975, March 18, 1976; ACC 1976, 1: 477–82.

19. Comune di Firenze, *Piano intercomunale fiorentino* (Florence, 1979), pp. vii–viii; ACC 1976, 1: 184–97; Comitato Comunale Democrazia Cristiana, *Confronto su Firenze* (Florence, 1980).

20. ACC 1976, 2: 409–24, 573–74; ACC 1977, 1: 96–97; 2: 289–90; Andreotti, *Diari*, pp. 45–49; *La Nazione*, September 1, 1976; December 30, 1977; Comune di Firenze, *Firenze: Bilancio '76* (Florence, 1976), p. 31; *Il Mulino*, March 1982, pp. 271–303; *Citta e regione*, October 1978, pp. 40–47.

21. *La Nazione*, December 21, 1975; November 23, 1976; Fabrizio Borghini, *Il Circolo Vie Nuove di Firenze dal 1944 al 1974* (Florence, 1978), pp. 86–87; Comune di Firenze, *L'esperianza dei consigli di quartiere a Firenze*, 2 vols. (Florence, 1981), 1: 43–44, 46–47.

22. ACC 1976, 1: 27–31; Comune di Firenze, *L'esperienza dei consigli*, 21, 64–65, 122–27; *La Nazione*, November 28–29, December 1, 1976; January 3, 1977; Comune di Firenze, *Firenze: Consigli di quartieri* (Florence, 1976), pp. 46–64.

23. *La Nazione*, May 27, November 11, 1977; January 16, 1979; *Consigli*, pp. 48, 76.

24. Comune di Firenze, *L'esperienza dei consigli*, 2: 22–60; *Consigli*, pp. 66, 68, 79; ACC 1976, 1: 1146–51; ACC 1979, 1: 33–43; *La Nazione*, September 11, 1981, January 10–13, 15, 21–22, 1982; Giorgio Morales interview, Florence, October 4, 1995.

25. ACC 1977, 1: 118, 122–23, 160–72; ACC 1978, 1: 123–35; *La Nazione*, February 14, March 3, 6, April 4, 21, May 4, 27, July 26, September 23, October 2, 27, 1977; January 2, 15, 24, 1978.

26. ACC 1977, 1: 160–72; *La Nazione*, March 16, October 7, 1977; February 10–11, 1978; Giovanni Spadolini, *Diario dei dramma Moro* (Florence, 1978), p. 3.

27. Andreotti, *Diari*, pp. 150–51, 172–73, 192, 197–98, 232–33; Spadolini, *Diario*, pp. 8–9, 36; Gallerano and Flores, *Sul PCI*, pp. 242–43; ACC 1978, 1: 322–46.

28. Andreotti, *Diario*, pp. 307, 337.

29. ACC 1979, 1: 555–80, 804–05; 2: 219–28; *La Nazione*, June 1, July 1, August 3, November 15, 1978; January 2, April 20, September 4, October 4, 11, 1979; December 2, 1980; February 8, August 13, 1981.

30. ACC 1976, 2: 621–24; ACC 1977, 2: 576–78; ACC 1979, 1: 1309–48; *La Nazione*, February 20, July 22, 1976; September 17, 1977; November 18, 1978; Conti interview.

31. ACC 1976, 1: 160–61; ACC 1981, 1: 91–100; ACC 1982, 1: 138–58; *La Nazione*, February 18, September 4, 1976; April 15, December 11, 1977; July 3, 29, 1978; July 24, 1979; October 10, November 2, 6, 1980; February 26, March 13, June 5, October 1, November 4, 12, 1981; Zoppi, *Firenze*, pp. 178–80; *Citta e regione*, June 1975, pp. 5–53.

32. ACC 1978, 1: 989–1026; ACC 1979, 2: 640; Comune di Firenze, *La circolazione Stradale di Firenze* (Florence, 1950), pp. 4–7, 39–40, 51–54; Piero Forosetti, ed., *Vigili* (Florence, 1988), p. 45; *La Nazione*, October 25, November 7, 1975; January 21, 22, February 11, September 22, 1976; July 21, October 22, 1977; May 24, 27, June 27, July 5, November 11, 14, 21, 1978; October 25, 1979; April 4, May 7, July 1, 1980; January 22, May 20, June 4, July 18, December 13, 1981.

33. *La Nazione*, March 27, 1976.

34. *La Nazione*, February 26, March 23, 1976, March 7, August 1, 1977.

35. *La Nazione*, October 9, 1976; March 23, July 22, October 6, December 21, 1977.

36. *La Nazione*, March 1, July 22, August 8, 1979; March 19, 1980; January 6, 1981.

37. ACC 1981, 2: 1385–91; *La Nazione*, May 13, July 7, 1978; January 6, 18, August 8, 9, 1979; January 22, 24, March 25, 1980.

38. Andreotti, *Diari*, pp. 89–90; *La Nazione*, April 28, June 24, 1977; November 24, 1978.

39. *La Nazione*, December 4, 1975; April 8, September 7, 9, 26, October 5, 1976.

40. *La Nazione*, January 15, 1977; August 9, 1978, February 20, 1979; May 13, 1980; June 15, 1981; January 21, 1982.

41. ACC 1981, 2: 1077–80; *Il Ponte*, May 1981, pp. 394–96; *History Today*, December 1980, pp. 50–51; *La Nazione*, December 7, 1977; August 5, 1978; August 28, September 18, 1979.

42. *La Nazione*, March 19, April 22, June 27, September 9, 11, 13, 1981.

43. ACC 1975, pp. 122–24; Zoppi, *Firenze*, pp. 148–53; Comune di Firenze, *Firenze, Bilanco, '76* (Florence, 1976), 1976, p. 76.

44. *La Nazione*, February 7, 16, March 5, June 29, July 2, 13, 18, October 3, 31, November 30, 1975; January 3, 13, 28, March 12, April 7, 13, May 27, August 1, 6, 26, 1976, May 6, September 16, November 17, 1978; August 15, September 1, 5, October 9, 18, 30, 1979; March 4, May 5, 16, 1980; February 7, September 19, 1981; ACC 1976, 1: 835–41; ACC 1978, 1: 777–83; ACC 1980, 1: 953–57.

45. Marco Massa, ed., *Firenze* (Milan, 1988), p. 92; ACC 1981, 1: 313–18.

46. Firenze, *Firenze Bilancio '76*, pp. 41–46; Achille Ardigo, *Indicazioni e orientamenti sulle linee di ristrutturazione e di destinazione del quarteri di Santa Croce* (Florence, 1968), pp. 13–15; Comuni di Firenze, *Decentrimento e ristrutturazione nell'amministrazione comunale*, 3 vols. (Florence, 1980–1981), vol. 2.

47. Lagorio interview; Franco Bassanini, "Le regioni incompiute," *Movimento operaio*

30 (September 1977), pp. 15–22; *Il Mulino*, March 1980, pp. 217–45; Robert Putnam, *Making Democracy Work* (Princeton, NJ: 1973), pp. 21–23.

48. Lagorio and Morales interviews.

49. ACC 1976, 2: 20–27; *La Nazione*, July 11, 18, 23, 1976; January 5, 1978; February 28, 1980.

50. Conti and Mori interviews; Mariella Zoppi interview, Florence, May 27, 1993; Indovina, *La citta occasionale*, pp. 11–12, 19–20; Massa, *Firenze*, pp. 22–24.

51. Spini, Zoppi, Gabbuggiani, and Lagorio interviews; ACC 1976, 1: 354; *La Nazione*, January 5, 1978; *Mondo operaio* (March 1974), pp. 21–24; *NA* 113 (July 1978), pp. 317–22; *Il Mulino*, January 1983, pp. 42–59; Carlo Sorrentino, *Firenze* (Rome, 1990), p. 48.

52. Zoppi, *Firenze*, pp. 170–72, 179–80; Lagorio, Spini, Morales, Mori, and Gabbuggiani interviews.

53. ACC 1975, pp. 222–82; ACC 1976, 1: 945–46; Orazio Barbieri, *La fede e la ragione* (Milan, 1982), p. 299; *La Nazione*, July 9, 11, 1980.

54. Micali Osanna, Piero Roselli, and Giuseppina Romby, *Firenze tra passato e futuro* (Florence, 1976), pp. 3–8; Ardigo, *Indicazioni*, pp. 13–15; ACC 1980, 1: 931–53.

55. Zoppi, *Firenze*, pp. 166–67.

56. ACC 1976, 1: 894–95; ACC 1981, 1: 239–54, 313–18; Gabbuggiani and Lagorio interviews; Andreotti, *Diari*, 24–25.

Chapter 11

Who's in Charge? The Florentine *Pentapartito*

Culture is to Florence what oil is to Dallas. The problem is that we don't produce culture anymore . . . [and] . . . we are broke. We need private investment . . . to make things go forward.

Gianni Conti, 1993

In the spring of 1993, a few months after the collapse of his political career, former vice mayor Gianni Conti took a swallow of his *aperitivo* and ruminated on the problems of his city. Florence needed major infrastructural investments of the type made under Fascism when the railroad station went up and the first autostrada went into operation. Public investment of this level was inconceivable. Even if the money existed, the city was too divided along ideological lines to agree on what projects to pursue. The political class could not give a lead: it had a few first-class ponies but no real racehorses. Without leaders of higher caliber, Florence could not attract the trust of either Rome or the bankers. In addition to new leaders, Florence needed a renewal of public confidence in politics. The left a priori mistrusted any project tied to private capital. Florence's hardheaded businessmen rarely took the larger view that advancing the common interest would benefit them. The inability of the city to properly exploit its cultural heritage was one sign of its difficulties. The long saga of the development projects known as FIAT-Fondiaria that began during Conti's tenure as assessor of urban planning was another. Gazing wistfully at the Palazzo Vecchio, Conti made a rather weak profession of faith in the capacity of Florentines to meet their problems, paid his bill, and slowly walked away, merging into the sea of tourists lapping around Cafe Rivoire.[1]

CHANGING PARTNERS

Following the failure of the center left, the Italian Socialist Party wandered in the political wilderness for nearly a decade. Its leaders substituted tactical opportunism for vision and reaped a proper reward from a disillusioned Italian electorate. The party's share of the vote declined and would have fallen further if it had not enjoyed the patronage provided by membership in the national government. From the Socialists' perspective, it was unclear which of their principal rivals, the DC or PCI, was the greater threat. The Christian Democrats, at least, offered a limited share in power. The PCI's historic compromise strategy threatened to eliminate the PSI's political lifeline. Resentment against the Communists included another component: bitter memories of exploitation by the Stalinists in the postwar era, of Communist efforts to undercut the center left, and of the loss of the working classes to the better-organized, more ruthless Partito comunista.[2]

Bettino Craxi, the young, tall, bald, baby-faced, overweight secretary of the Milanese PSI, took over as national leader after the party's defeat in 1976 parliamentary elections. A Nenni protégé, Craxi brought a new generation of pragmatic, intensely anti-Communist leaders with him to power. He proved to be a political tactician of Machiavellian skill, quickly isolating and disarming the very party factional leaders who had installed him as secretary. He disciplined the PSI by ruthless use of patronage and his powers of expulsion. Initially, Craxi grudgingly accepted the PCI's leadership role on the left. Within a few years he was dueling the Communists for hegemony, arguing that the PSI represented the democratic and reformist Socialism that had triumphed throughout Northern Europe. Without a trace of irony, Craxi portrayed the PCI as an overdisciplined, Machiavellian party with leaders too close to the Stalinist past to be trusted. While never able to overcome the PCI's lead in organization or membership, Craxi revitalized the PSI and put it at the center of national politics. In 1983, he became Italy's first (and apparently last) Socialist prime minister. Four years of Craxi-led governments appeared to verify, partially, his claim to offer Italy a new type of government: pragmatic and decisive, with a sense of equity. The PSI's position at the polls improved.[3]

Craxi's anti-Communist policy was manna to the Florentine PSI. They chafed at the role of junior partner to the PCI and continued to resist Communist efforts to co-opt their issues, urban planning and regionalism. The Gabbuggiani administration's weak performance in both areas ignited frequent clashes within the junta. These tensions threatened to explode into full-blown crises on a number of occasions between 1977 and 1980. Codignola claimed that Gabbuggiani accomplished less than the Socialists won in collaboration with La Pira. Morales became a leading critic of the PCI's performance. With the PSI benevolently neutral, the local DC utilized issues like the installation of NATO missiles at Comiso and the presentation of honorary Florentine citizenship to Soviet dissident Andre Sakharov to harass and isolate the Communists inside the city coun-cil.[4]

In addition to its complement of tough-minded political pragmatists, the Flor-entine PSI was home to a number of young idealists who improved its badly tattered public image. The husband-wife team of Valdo Spini and Mariella Zoppi was particularly influential. Spini was brought up in the moral rigor of Walden-sian Protestantism. Honest, intense, and dedicated to public service, he supported Craxi in the hope of moralizing and reforming both the PSI and Italy. Zoppi, one of Edoardo Detti's students and eventually dean of the university architecture faculty, was a powerful voice in the urban planning debate. Her role as critic, her decision to teach rather than practice her profession, and quite possibly her sex contributed to much negative comment. Her publications, personality, and marital connection gave her plenty of weight in policy circles.[5]

Tensions between the coalition partners and DC attempts to woo the PSI back into an alliance intensified following June 1980 elections. The PSI emerged as the psychological winner by gaining an additional 2 percent of the total vote and two more seats on the city council. The DC tried to entice the PSI into a five-party coalition that would exclude the PCI from city government. Embold-ened by success, PSI Federation secretary Ottaviano Colzi demanded both the mayor's post and adoption of its reform programs as the price for PSI participation in any government.[6]

The Communists ridiculed Socialist demands and rejected the PSI's claim to the mayoralty. After drawn-out negotiations, the PCI presented Gabbuggiani as its candidate for mayor in July 1980. Colzi used the first session of the newly elected city council to announce the PSI's availability for another coalition and to outline its differences with the PCI. The Socialists abstained on the vote for mayor, forcing Gabbuggiani to wait through five ballots before he won election by a plurality. After renewed negotiations with the PSI, a chastened PCI rewrote parts of the junta program and agreed to hand the post of vice mayor to Morales.[7]

Revision of the Detti PRG was the major item of business that the second Gabbuggiani administration faced. The junta needed to address mushrooming economic and social problems created by tourism, including the fate of the his-toric center.[8]

The coalition partners had scarcely settled back into government when they began quarreling. In May 1981 the PSI and Social Democrats were badly tarred in the so-called P-2 (Propaganda 2) Masonic Lodge scandal. The lodge was ded-icated to the advancement and enrichment of its members—the business, polit-ical, and administrative elite that governed Italy. Grand Master Licio Gelli had elaborate plans for authoritarian rule. Subsequent investigations (in the Italian tradition) never satisfactorily clarified the degree of rank-and-file awareness of, or support for, Gelli's larger ambitions.[9] However, membership in the lodge by a good slice of Italy's political and administrative elite pretty clearly contravened the spirit, if not the letter, of the nation's constitution.

Florence has long been a center of Italian Masonry. In 1980 the city hosted forty-three lodges. By comparison, Rome, with six times Florence's population, had thirty-eight, and Milan had only twenty-one. The Masons were deeply embedded in Florentine political life and enjoyed particularly strong ties to the PSI and PSDI, two of the principal heirs to anticlerical traditions. In spite of church prohibitions, many Christian Democrats also were lodge members. Reputed Masonic ability to advance careers attracted self-promoters regardless of religious or party affiliation.[10]

The Communists exploited the P-2 incident for all its value, losing no opportunity to finger Socialists and Christian Democrats associated with Florentine lodges. PCI-PSI squabbles over the implications of Masonic Lodge membership impeded work on the city plan.

The Socialists, attempting to pay back the Communists for the P-2 embarrassment, joined the opposition to confront the PCI over Soviet human rights issues. They struck again in March 1982, when the PCI presented its nominee to succeed the Socialists' man, Massimo Bogiankino, as head of the Teatro Comunale. Under the complex rules of division of power, appointment of a replacement fell to the PCI, which nominated Mario Casalini. The Socialists, who were trying to stake out cultural policy as their political preserve, objected that the PCI's man lacked the prestige to succeed Bogiankino. The DC's Pallanti cheerfully reminded the council that battles over replacement of Teatro Comunale directors usually signaled the end of a coalition. When the minority offered Francesco Romano, the PSI gave its assent, and he was duly elected. Gabbuggiani offered his resignation. On March 30 the two parties patched over their differences. The PSI had again signaled its ability to block PCI plans. Colzi reiterated that the PSI was open to new alliances.[11]

Relations between the governing parties remained very tense during the remainder of 1982. The junta held together over a major package of improvements at Peretola airport but split over the site of a new airport. A month later, the two parties were at odds over a Rolling Stones concert. The PCI wanted to grant a permit for the popular English rock group; the PSI objected on environmental grounds. The PSI blocked the concert, only to be undercut by public criticisms from Venetian rock music enthusiast and Socialist minister of state participation Gianni de Michelis.[12]

The coalition parties briefly submerged their differences in midsummer, agreed upon a long-delayed zoning plan for the area vacated by the Galileo plant, and managed to offer a city budget that mirrored their March 1982 compromise program. Tensions further subsided when the junta's most active and effective critic, Christian Democrat Gianni Conti, announced that in line with directives from Rome, he was going to seek more cooperation in solving city problems.[13]

The truce broke down in the fall. The PCI-led junta had yet to come forward with a city plan. *La Nazione* went on the attack editorially, excoriating the junta for its inaction. Florence, like the rest of Italy, was in the grips of an economic downturn and accompanying job losses. The business community, especially its powerful tourist sector, complained about Gabbuggiani administration over-regulation.[14]

In December Communist–Socialist differences over urban planning brought down the Gabbuggiani junta. The Sollicciano prison complex was to be the most modern maximum-security facility in Italy. When it opened, the national government went back on its agreement to transfer the population from the aged Murat prison and close down that inner-city facility. The Socialists attacked Gabbuggiani's management of the prison construction, charging that the mayor and his party were at fault for missing the original completion date by nearly four years.[15]

THE MAN WITH A PLAN

On December 21, 1982, the mayor announced his resignation, laying blame for the collapse of the experiment in left-wing city leadership directly at the feet of the PSI. On January 2, the DC launched a public appeal to non-Communist city councilmen to join it in forming a government that excluded the PCI. Responding on January 4, Colzi told the city council that the Socialists, Social Democrats, Republicans, and Liberals were drafting a common platform of government and would present it within a fortnight. One of the two larger parties could then subscribe to it and create a new majority.[16]

A week later the four parties presented their candidate for mayor, the seventy-nine-year-old Alessandro Bonisanti, a popular Republican businessman and patron of the arts. With the backing of the DC, Bonisanti won the mayoralty from Gabbuggiani by a vote of thirty-two to twenty-four. The new mayor then threw the lay parties' plans into disarray by announcing that he would not accept the job until the majority that supported him agreed on a common program.[17]

Bonisanti's action forced the smaller parties and the DC back to the bargaining table to craft a program. The mayor-elect judged that a common desire for power would create the basis for a compromise platform. First, however, the parties had to go through a drawn-out and embarrassing set of talks that revealed how little they had in common on issues of public policy. Former prime minister Spadolini intervened to force the pace of compromise. Even so, the parties unveiled their program and agreement on the division of junta posts only on March 10. The *pentapartito* (five-party coalition) was a sign of the degree to which ideology was excess baggage in Italian politics.[18]

Unfortunately, the city faced a series of urgent problems that required a common sense of direction. Violence at a Florence–Rome soccer game underlined the degree to which sport had taken the place of politics as the escape valve for popular discontent. The plight of the inner city worsened. While the historic center vibrated with life, and its shops did record business, Florentines continued to desert it. Between 1953 and 1983, the historic center's population fell from 96,000 to 40,000. Basic services disappeared; rents rose. *Zone blu* and other forms of traffic limitation inexorably expanded, but so did pollution and its environmental effects. Florence suffered another acute water shortage in late July 1983. The drought continued into the late winter of 1994. The university pressed for better facilities, complaining about its overcrowded and dilapidated sites.[19]

Even the city's primary industry was a source of concern. The "knapsack" tourists who slept in parks and on city streets spent little and left behind major cleanup problems were a headache for city fathers. Florence's transvestites, with their growing clientele, spawned traffic jams, petty crime, and an unfavorable public image for the city as the European capital of a "different kind of love." Efforts to deal with these problems were costly and only partially successful. Meanwhile, the city's share of the convention trade, the most profitable segment of the tourist market, declined in the face of aggressive competition from cities like Milan.[20]

Even good economic news focused attention on urban ills. Regular flight service returned to Peretola. However, the airport's short runway limited the number and size of aircraft servicing Florence. Businessmen were particularly vocal with complaints about the difficulties of reaching the city in an expeditious manner. City merchants' newfound enthusiasm for further traffic limitations in the center, a product of their experience of the benefits of streets crowded with shoppers, threatened to strangle vehicular flow through the city.[21]

Florence would have to deal with these issues with reduced autonomy and contend with a powerful opposition party ready to block local initiatives. The PCI, representing over 40 percent of Florentine voters, was in no mood to accept the backroom deals that had ousted it or the leadership of the parties that engineered its political defenestration. From tourism to development policy, the Communists belabored the city government, demanding its resignation. The national government meanwhile straitjacketed local authorities with new legislation regulating city finances. The cash-poor Bonisanti administration had to raise sanitation services fees and real estate taxes, with predictable political consequences.[22]

The city administration was only beginning to confront these issues when Mayor Bonisanti died, and the majority began squabbling over a division of posts in a new junta. The Bonisanti government lasted long enough for Gianni Conti, the small, smartly dressed spokesman for the DC, to emerge as a major political factor. Conti had already established himself as the most persistent critic of the urban planning efforts of the Gabbuggiani junta. As assessor for urban planning in the Bonisanti junta, Conti began to shape an approach to the urban development problem that steered between the polar opposites of Detti's 1962 PRG and the laissez-faire of the Bausi years.

Conti got his political start in the 1950s as an aide to Giorgio La Pira. After giving him a brief, but highly educational, taste of the subtleties of the Roman bureaucracy, La Pira put his young assistant in charge of the city's road program. The job, Conti recalled, consisted in finding unpaved roads, an easy job in those days, and then seeing that they were asphalted. In securing funding for these projects, Conti furthered his education in the workings of the DC patronage machine. He also became interested in urban planning. Conti's January 1984 presentation on development policy stressed the use of government's planning powers to stimulate major private investment in Florence.[23]

Conti rejected the highly articulated type of plan that Detti had developed but recognized that Florence needed to have a systematic approach to its urban ills. The report listed twenty-eight specific projects that required attention. His technique was to take each problem separately, find a solution that fitted it, and then fit that solution into the larger mosaic by seeking zoning variants from the 1962 PRG. Revision by variant would avoid the time-consuming process of writing a new PRG. In a gesture to the left parties, the urban planning alderman pledged to seek neighborhood input on any zoning changes. Noting that the building code dated to 1931, Conti announced that a study group would recommend specific changes designed to bring it into line with technological improvements. In another gesture to the left, Conti reported that he had commissioned Detti to lead a panel charged with finding central city locations for the University of Florence's faculties. Finally, the assessor declared war on "nomads," groups that had occupied buildings and were exploiting city services without paying. Tough talk about law-and-order issues had a generally positive effect on the conservative element of the Florentine electorate.

Conti's plan for Florence was an example of the post-1976 Florentine DC rediscovery of La Pira. Placing itself securely in the political center, the DC announced that it would find a third way between the excesses of capitalist individualism and Marxist collectivism and stressed the unique role of Florence as laboratory for this experiment. Through Conti's plan the DC embraced the idea of Florence as an international meeting point for diverse cultures and a university city, placing itself in the forefront of new technologies and increased prosperity. By linking the university to Italian corporate development and giving a freer hand to the building industry, the DC offered a vision of a growth-oriented city that would avoid the worse excesses associated with past eras of expansion. It was an enticing vision: new housing, more jobs, and greater individual prosperity, with respect for the environment and consideration for the city's traditional economic bases, provided by a party that would borrow freely from the best parts of the programs of left and right and innovate in a caring manner reminiscent of Giorgio La Pira.[24]

Conti faced a tough sell. The Florentine PSI's young idealists saw Conti's proposals as a mask for uncontrolled development. Mariella Zoppi agreed that neither city nor national government had the resources to plan and carry out a major development scheme. However, based on past experience of the DC's style of urban planning, she doubted that the city government could provide the strong hand needed to restrain developers' headlong pursuit of profit.[25]

Moreover, Conti's stress on infrastructural development and his evident desire to free more of the city center to tourist industry activities left him open to charges of being the point man for another wave of profit-driven private development that would increase the imbalance between an already tourist-dominated center and the periphery with its population of native Florentines. Conti saw no alternative. Both Florentines and tourists needed breathing room. Removing city government to the periphery and surrounding it with new shops and housing would free up area for both parts of the local economy to grow. Retention of the "humanistic" faculties of the university in the center would provide a link between the two Florences.[26]

FIAT-FONDIARIA

Maneuvering to replace Bonisanti began within days of the mayor's death. Socialist Federation secretary Colzi claimed the position for his party. From Rome, Giovanni Spadolini announced that a Republican had to succeed a Republican. Craxi decided to heed the demands of his minister of defense. The Florentine PSI suffered an embarrassing public setback at the hands of its own leader, much to the delight of the PCI.[27]

Despite its strong showing in 1980 local elections, Florence's DC was in a relatively weak position as the parties maneuvered to select Bonisanti's successor. Christian Democracy had taken a beating in June 1983 national elections and surrendered leadership of the Italian government to Bettino Craxi. The Socialist leader recognized that he could not win more concessions from the DC without the threat of an alternative governing partner. In Florence, the PSI had the option to again swing left. The DC had to accept a mayor selected from the ranks of its coalition partners together with a limit on the number of junta seats that it held. After a month of negotiations, the five parties agreed upon a candidate, Republican Lando Conti, but lacked a program. In mid-April the Florentine *pentapartito* agreed on a program and offered full support to Conti.[28]

Initially, urban policy under the *pentapartito* was a continuation of the rather timid approach that had characterized the PCI-led Gabbuggiani regime. The major initiatives of the Bonisanti year were Gianni Conti's proposal to erect a second exhibition pavilion inside the Fortezza da Basso and build a parking garage under Piazza Independenza.[29]

Following up on his January 1984 commitment to more aggressive urban planning initiatives, Gianni Conti unveiled two large-scale projects that would ignite a decade-long political struggle. On July 9, Mayor Lando Conti presented proposals from the Fondiaria Insurance Company, the city's largest landowner, for a commercial and housing zone in the Castello area of the northwest quadrant of the city and a parking garage near Piazza Independenza. He then introduced a plan offered by the country's most important private employer, FIAT, for three construction projects. The most significant was to build an industrial park, shopping area, and housing complex in the Novoli area of the northwest. Mayor Conti refused to commit himself or the city government to support of the projects but carefully noted that these separate plans met long-standing city needs for parking, new hotels, and housing and, most importantly, would create new, high-wage jobs.[30]

Gianni Conti was less reserved. Bolstered by commitments from the two firms to follow the directives of the city government, Assessor Conti stressed that the two major plans would fulfill many of the objectives outlined in the 1962 PRG for development of the northwest zone of the city; readjust the balance in the local economy by bringing in jobs in the manufacturing and transportation industries; permit a better use of the area formerly occupied by the Nuovo Pignone plant; and offer the financing for preservation of the city's limited greenbelt. The assessor of urban planning indicated general support for the Fondiaria project while defining the FIAT submission as interesting but lacking sufficient detail. Conti informed the council that he had requested both corporations to provide the city with more detailed plans.[31]

The two projects nicely fitted Gianni Conti's definition of correct urban planning. The two offers, both privately financed, promised a more balanced economic development. Moreover, since they needed city approval, in theory, they guaranteed a high degree of local political control.[32]

The opposition was not convinced. In the first place, FIAT and Fondiaria were economic giants whose ability to influence decision making at the national level far exceeded that of Florence's city government. Second, the FIAT and Fondiaria offers appeared to be made on a take-it-or-leave-it basis that undercut city control over developers. Added to this was a deeply rooted mistrust of Italian capital that permeated the parties of the left. Zoppi remarked that the sudden, nearly simultaneous introduction of two plans that would essentially complete development of the city made urban reformers very suspicious. Florence was involved in a major confrontation between left and right that was more about cultural values and tactical political advantage than the projects' merits.[33]

In March 1985, Mayor Conti appeared before the city council, announced the junta's decisions on the FIAT and Fondiaria proposals, and simultaneously offered a preliminary project for a new PRG based on approval of these two plans. The meeting, the last scheduled before electors went to the polls, was the opening salvo of the upcoming election campaign. Conti added that both the city and PCI-PSI regional governments had approved the Fondiaria project and that FIAT's proposals met the criteria established by the regional government. Further, the city would move forward to find private financing for similar plans for the northeast quadrant. Finally, the mayor was able to report that Florence had assurances from FIAT that it would guarantee employment at specific levels as part of its project package.

The Communists lodged a number of specific objections regarding the environmental impact on neighboring communes and on older sections of the city and challenged the reliability of FIAT's employment pledges. One Communist councilman brushed aside the entire exercise, particularly the announcement of new jobs, as a clever election ploy by the *pentapartito*.

Gianni Conti responded that Communist criticisms were electorally motivated. The city was following Italian law; it was meeting a primary need for more housing; and it was achieving a number of the fundamental goals of the Detti plan. The Fondiaria project met Detti's vision for Novoli; the creation of a "polycentric" city was in lines with the objectives of the PRG; and the overall effect of the development would be to achieve the "metropolitan city" that the left endorsed.[34]

Councilman Pier Luigi Ballini introduced a resolution permitting the city to commission detailed impact studies of the two proposals. The PCI countered with a resolution that put a freeze on studies pending further discussion. The Communist motion lost by one vote. Balloting on Ballini's motion resulted in a tie, twenty-four to twenty-four, with one abstention. The left had achieved its immediate objective of blocking further action before elections. The vote as well as the heated public involvement were signs of a city deeply divided over the central question of large-scale private construction.

Florence's dilemma was two-pronged. In the first place, the city had failed to develop a detailed follow-up to Detti's general project. Twenty years of unregulated growth made many of Detti's objectives obsolete. Second, neither the city nor the national government could pay for major projects. The vibrant Italian economy of the mid-1980s was a private sector phenomenon. Public sector companies were largely inefficient and propped up by massive state subsidies. Private capital would dominate the next stage in urban development in Florence. The choice before Florentines was between large projects with a yet to be established degree of public regulation or the continuation of small-scale, largely unregulated urban creep, which had been the rule since the 1950s.[35]

In theory, Gianni Conti's program would permit development to take place with greater city supervision than had been the case for decades. The plan also handed large sectors of public lands to private contractors whose ability to develop the area independently of public control would increase as the project proceeded. Many, perhaps most Florentines were uneasy about replacing inefficient, but malleable, public investment with the better-organized and more ruthless private sector. The national ambivalence to the profit motive, nurtured by both Catholics and Communists, was manifest, as were widespread concerns about the impact on the city's delicate ecology.[36]

These cultural factors had a role in the defeat of the *pentapartito* in the June 1985 elections. The city government coalition headed into the elections with a mixed record. Local employment had grown during its term of office. Florence won a small battle for indirect European Community (EC) subsidies when the commission of the EC announced that the city would be home to its archives. The EC also selected Florence as its European Cultural Capital for 1986. The projected yearlong cultural programs would enjoy EC and Italian government financial support, would provide international recognition of Florence's cherished cultural status, and were a potential gold mine for the tourist industry. As the election campaign heated up, the *pentapartito* junta mounted a program designed to improve the overall cleanliness of the historic center and made a credit agreement with local banks that eased terms for loans to individual downtown restoration projects.[37]

The junta's public image needed a face-lift. Socialist Party secretary Colzi faced charges of bribe-taking resulting from city contracting agreements. A judicial investigation of contracting procedures for the rehabilitation of the Albergo Nazionale led to charges against two junta members. These cases reinforced charges that handing major urban projects over to private capital would result in large-scale profit-taking by a few and further corruption of politics.[38]

STALEMATE

The May 1985 elections intensified the stalemate over urban policy. Of the three major parties, only the PSI managed to hold on to its 1980 share of the vote but still lost two of its eight seats. The DC lost over 10,000 votes and two seats, while the PCI's support fell by nearly 4,000 and one seat. Among the smaller parties, the environmentalist "Greens" (Verde) attracted nearly 10,000 votes. They promptly refused to join a coalition with any of the major parties. The Republicans, too, advanced, while the Social Democrats lost nearly one-half of their voters. The Liberal vote was stationary. Since the election provided no clear indication of voters' desire, the Socialists and Republicans had a free hand to choose the next government of Florence. The options were a government with a fairly large majority with the PCI or a minority coalition with the DC.

Creating a coalition government was time-consuming. The PSI early ruled out a minority government with the DC. The party's left wing, led by reformer Valdo Spini, had outpolled Lagorio's pragmatists in total preference votes. Deeply suspicious of DC urban planning, they prefered a deal with the Communists. Negotiations with the PCI over program and assignment of posts dragged on. Meanwhile, the DC pressed its former partners to rejoin a *pentapartito* coalition, arguing that the PCI was badly out of step with Italian realities. After its summer adjournment, the city council met on September 16 and failed to reach agreement on a junta. With the European Cultural Year set to begin January 1, 1986, Florence desperately needed a government to organize its program. Progress toward an agreement was blocked by Socialist insistence on holding the mayor's position. The Republicans claimed the position for themselves. On September 23, the city council again met to elect a mayor and junta. The parties of the potential majority immediately asked for a three-hour adjournment to work out details on an accord.[39]

When the city council reconvened, Ballini made the DC's last appeal for the record, stressing the need to carry out Gianni Conti's urban planning initiatives and to set the year of culture program in motion. Valdo Spini responded that the new majority had not only a program but a candidate suited by experience to lead a cultural year: Massimo Bogiankino (PSI), the head of the Teatro Comunale and former director of the Paris Opera. With the combined support of the PCI and PSI, Bogiankino won election on the first ballot.[40]

NOTES

1. Gianni Conti interview, Florence, May 26, 1993.

2. Spencer Di Scala, *Renewing Italian Socialism* (New York, 1988), p. 173; Valdo Spini interview, Rome, September 26, 1995.

3. Spini interview; Lelio Lagorio interview, Florence, October 4, 1995.

4. ACC 1977, 2: 1099–1106; ACC 1979, 1: 516–17.

5. Iacopo Detti and Mariella Zoppi interviews, Florence, May 18, 27, 1993; V. Spini, "I socialisti e la questione morale," *Movimento operaio*, November 1981.

6. *La Nazione* June 11, July 4, 7, 1980.

7. ACC 1980, 2: 14–40, 75–88, 92–98; *La Nazione*, July 29, August 6, September 3, 1980.

8. ACC 1979, 1: 672–702, 865–70, 1003.

9. The wildly accusatory Anselmi report (1984) to Italy's parliament is a model of "*dietrologia*," the confounding national pastime of connecting the dots (evidence or what frequently passes for it in Italian judicial-political cases) into a vast web of conspiracy.

10. Partito Comunista Italiano, Federazione Fiorentina, Aspetti della presenza della massoneria a Firenze (Florence, 1983), pp. 9, 23–25, 101; *La Nazione*, May 22, 1981.

11. *La Nazione*, February 20, November 25, 1981; March 11, 31, 1982; ACC 1982, 1: 224–27, 380–83, 433–61, 526–43, 548–62.

12. *La Nazione*, June 1, 23, July 14, 1982.

13. ACC 1982, 2: 1328–29, 1460, 1505–9, 1519.

14. *La Nazione*, May 29, June 10, July 19, September 15, 1982.

15. ACC 1982, 2: 2353–64.

16. ACC 1983, 1: 49–55; *La Nazione*, December 29, 1982; January 3, 1983.

17. ACC 1983, 1: 68–87; *La Nazione*, January 13–14, 1983.

18. ACC 1983, 1: 117–33, 143–72; *La Nazione*, January 15, February 1, 2, 22, March 10, 1983.

19. *La Nazione*, March 29, April 8, 10, 13, May 5, 17, 24, June 22, August 1, October 12, December 8, 11, 13, 1983.

20. *La Nazione*, April 19, July 25, August 6, October 16, 1983.

21. *La Nazione*, July 6, 17, August 2, 1983; January 9, 1984.

22. ACC 1983, 1: 24–27, 394–98; 2: 947–80, 1350–51. ACC 1984, 1: 73–74; *La Nazione*, March 1, June 1, 2, 1983.

23. Conti's report is in ACC 1984, 1: 133–56.

24. See Democrazia Cristiana, *Confronto su Firenze* (Florence, 1980).

25. Zoppi interview.

26. Conti interview.

27. *La Nazione*, March 29, 1984; ACC 1984, 1: 276–88.

28. Franco Lucchesi, "Ancora qualche nuova su Palazzo Vecchio," *Il Governo*, June–July 1984; ACC 1984, 1: 320–21, 412–45; *La Nazione*, March 20, 27, April 13, 1984.

29. ACC 1984, 1: 412–45; Fabio Sforzi, "La citta allo specchio," *Il Ponte*, January 1988; *La Nazione*, January 18, March 5, 1984.

30. ACC 1984, 2: 934–37.

31. ACC 1984, 2: 937–41.

32. Conti interview.

33. ACC 1984, 2: 2075–85; Francesco Indovina, ed., *La citta occasionale* (Milan, 1993), p. 46. Zoppi, Spini, and Lagorio interviews.

34. The March 4 debate is in ACC 1985, 1: 719–40.

35. *Urbanistica,* November 1985, pp. 46–49; Marco Massa, ed., *Firenze* (Milan, 1988), p. 102.

36. *Urbanistica,* November 1985, pp. 50–65; Lagorio interview.

37. *La Nazione,* June 5; 8, 1984; April 27, 1985.

38. ACC 1984, 2: 1788; ACC 1985, 1: 360–73.

39. ACC 1985, 2: 11–63, 69–83, 89–112, 128–61; ACC 1986, 1: 200; Ennio Di Nolfo interview, Florence, April 8, May 17, 1993; Spini interview.

40. ACC 1985, 2: 168–232.

Chapter 12

City of Culture

For many [high-tech] is the only remaining hope for avoiding the reduction of the city to a museum.

La Nazione, May 28, 1987

Ennio Di Nolfo, professor of international relations at the University of Florence and member of the "12 Sages," the panel charged with planning Florence's 1986 self-celebration, minced no words in analyzing its "Year of Culture." The city had lost a chance to do something to strengthen itself for the long term with major infrastructural improvement projects. Pressed for time, short of cash, and under enormous pressure from the parties that had placed them on the panel, the *saggi* (wisemen) prudently decided that the city would go for the ephemeral. Art shows, cultural congresses, and some restoration projects in the inner city were all that Florence could produce for its abbreviated "year." The results were "mediocre." Once again, he added acidly, Florentines lived up to their reputation as people who "talk big and [then] do nothing."[1]

A CITY ON THE EDGE

Massimo Bogiankino's junta was a fragile pairing of Communists and the lay parties. Formed in September 1985 through a marriage of the Liberals, the two Socialist Parties, and the Communists, guided by a figure drawn from the world of high culture, and holding a one-vote majority in the city council, it had to deal with Florence's long-standing infrastructural problems and simultaneously create a program of events worthy of the European Community's designation of Florence as the "City of European Culture" for 1986.

Bettino Craxi, the PSI's prime minister-party secretary, personally selected

Bogiankino as mayor and then ordered the local party to enforce his pick as the price of collaboration with the PCI. By nominating Bogiankino and allying with the PCI, Craxi played divide-and-rule within the Tuscan PSI, cutting away at the power of Lagorio's faction and increasing that of his two rivals, Valdo Spini and Ottavio Colzi, in order to maintain a balance of power favorable to his continued control of the national party.[2]

The junta inherited a series of problems that it was ill equipped to handle. Florence's high unemployment existed alongside growth in the service sectors, particularly in the lower-wage and part-time areas. Galloping inflation widened the gap between haves and have-nots. Florence's already high cost of living continued to rise as both basic and discretionary consumption grew. Essential goods like food and fuels led the way in price growth. These costs hit hard at the fastest growing portion of the local population: the elderly. Marriages and births declined steadily; the number of elderly living alone expanded. They countered inflation by depleting their savings, reducing the money available locally for productive investment. The largest component of the elderly poor was rooted in the historic center, where they clung to rent-controlled housing while enduring the hollowing out of basic services.[3]

Inflation also hit business hard. Bankruptcy soared as the costs of commercial space rose by 300 percent between 1982 and 1987. By 1987, the city averaged one business failure a day. Meanwhile, the conversion of inner-city buildings from residential to office use continued. Ironically, the city had housing available on the periphery, but the rising costs of both public and private homes priced many out of modest apartments. The city and state invested in new units and in rehabilitation of older ones while regional and national government simultaneously enforced policies that drove up the number of evictions. At one and the same time, the city had over 12,000 families seeking housing and nearly 8,000 vacant units.[4]

Crime inevitably accompanied major economic inequality. Drug use continued to plague parts of the city, especially the S. Spirito zone. The Cascina was another area of high crime and drug use. "The streets are littered with disposable syringes. Sometimes one steps in vomit," one best-selling tourist guide reported.[5] By 1987 an average of 500 syringes a day were recovered from city streets and parks. Following hard on drug usage was the late twentieth century's plague, AIDS. By mid-1986 the city had 500 reported cases of AIDS. The disease spread among young drug users and homosexuals as the decade proceeded, straining public health capabilities and an already empty public treasury.[6]

In addition to the crimes against property and the petty theft associated with the drug culture, Florence faced sporadic problems with terrorists. In February 1986, Red Brigades terrorists assassinated former mayor Lando Conti for reasons that they alone could comprehend. As late as 1988 small bands of political fanatics disrupted the city with their random, but fortunately infrequent, attacks.[7]

Vandalism and hooliganism were on the rise. Monuments were frequent victims of bored youth, while violence at the city soccer stadium became epidemic.

One particularly obnoxious sociopath, the self-styled "Little Florentine Lighter," set fire to over 100 cars. The "Monster," a serial killer who operated in the lovers' lanes that surrounded the city, claimed eighteen victims between 1968 and 1986.[8]

Even with these problems, Florence did not approach the crime rates of other major Italian cities. Nevertheless, rising crime was a source of acute concern to most Florentines. Personal safety was especially critical to a city dependent on tourism. Mixed with the bad news about crimes against persons were statistical data about the rising number of Florentine businessmen under indictment for "victimless" crimes such as the production of phony brand-name goods, fake art scams, and tax evasion schemes. A March 1988 city survey found that 20 percent of Florentine shops openly flouted basic zoning regulations. Equally disturbing was evidence that the "Sicilians," the Mafia, had taken control of illegal gaming in Florence.[9]

The city's woes only increased when the state ordered the closure of its major waste disposal plant at S. Donnino in the spring of 1986. The incinerator-skyscraper, a landmark of the Bausi years of rapid expansion, was a massive producer of carcinogens. By mid-July 1986, the city was collecting approximately 400 tons of refuse a day without having any place to dispose of it. Only emergency measures prevented Florence from sinking in its own refuse. Meanwhile, trash collectors unions clashed with the city over benefits and struck. In May 1986 disgusted residents of the via S. Giovanni da Verrazzano collected their trash, wrapped it, decorated it with signs reading "A gift to the capital of culture," and dumped it in front of city hall. City efforts to deal with another disposal issue, throwaway plastics, were hamstrung by the courts. Automobile pollution continued to seriously imperil both public health and the survival of the monuments that made Florence one of Europe's great cities. Sensors on the Brunelleschi cupola demonstrated damage done to that monumental structure; the Ghiberti *Doors of Paradise* had to be removed due to the effects of car emissions.[10]

Tourism hit a down cycle in 1986. The U.S. clash with Libya combined with State Department warnings about the weakness of Italian antiterrorist precautions kept most Americans at home. "Alarm, the Foreigners Aren't Invading Us!" *La Nazione* headlined in June. U.S. visits dropped 60 percent in 1986.[11] Libya was not the sole culprit in the declining fortunes of Florentine tourism. City restaurants and hotels specialized in gouging the consumer. Florence acquired a reputation for poor service. It lacked hotels with large banquet and meeting facilities in the vicinity of its Palazzo dei Congressi-Fortezza da Basso complex. Sanitation, hotel, and hospital workers strikes plagued Florence.[12]

Aggressive advertising in the United States, special off-season discounts, and a reorganization of the tourist board produced positive results. By the end of 1988 the Florentine tourist industry was recovering slowly. However, the bankruptcy of ninety-one city hotels, including five "four-star" institutions, with 3,500 rooms, slowed recovery.[13]

In February 1986 the junta imposed a freeze on all new spending and began planning layoffs in anticipation of cuts in state subvention. The council faced the unhappy prospect of trimming 30 to 35 billion lire from the 1985 budget (of 135 billion) and simultaneously voting for new service fees to cover its operating expenses. Parliament's solution to lower state subsidies, the communal service tax increase (Tasco), would hit select types of property with rate increases from 46 to 148 percent of assessed value. Private homes, shops, and hotels were the big targets. The city announced big increases in the costs of public transportation to cover ATAF's yawning debt. The price that Florentines paid for water, sewer, sanitation, and natural gas would have to go up, while overall public services were cut. *La Nazione* playfully headlined "Watch Your Pocket [Tasca] Here Comes the Tasco."[14]

Florentine taxpayers might have accepted these increases with a bit less anger if the city was providing quality services. No one claimed that was the case. Expenditures of 46 billion lire for ASNU left Florence dirty. ATAF, 30 billion lire in debt, was the worst-run bus system in Italy. The city staggered under the burden of its own bureaucracy. In addition to ASNU and ATAF, it owned and managed La Pira's city pharmacy system and was a partner with private capital in seventeen service companies, including the gas company, the milk company, the airport, public illumination, parking, the fashion industry, training schools, the Palazzo dei Congressi, tourist information, and a business start-up project. The city council had authorized ten more mixed companies to manage sports facilities, wine promotion, tourist training, foreign commerce, and refuse disposal. Participation in cooperatives with neighboring communes further drained the public treasury. The city, one of Florence's largest landlords with some 2,000 properties, provided space to these mixed concerns and other businesses at a discount while renting some 300 separate properties for its own use at soaring commercial rates. The highly profitable "La Fiorentina" soccer club had a sweetheart deal on use of the Communal Stadium.[15]

City leaders talked wistfully of privatization. In truth, public employee unions were too strong, business interests were too well organized, and the overriding objective of all the parties was to collect votes by increasing services. The city would continue to expand its generally feeble public services. In November 1986, after considering its options, the junta used the visit of Prime Minister Craxi to introduce its basic fiscal plan: a request for more subsidies from the state.[16]

Florence continued seeking private investment as the best solution to its urban ills. Visions of clean, nonpolluting, high-tech industries danced in the heads and off the tongues of local politicians. Proponents of these ideas argued that the city's unique cultural heritage, if combined with some careful infrastructural improvements, would prove irresistible to companies seeking to invest. Implanting high-tech industry in Florence could reduce economic imbalances by providing employment to university graduates, revitalizing many service industries, and creating incentives for balanced redevelopment in the inner city. The city council passed legislation intended to attract high-tech investment, sought to protect its role as a major hub in the national railroad system, and urged the state and region to improve existing highway connections.[17] The Year of Culture and FIAT-Fondiaria initiatives played into the efforts of a debt-ridden city government to refurbish Florence's image and create new sources of capital investment.

YEAR OF CULTURE

The junta's 1985 decision to accept designation as the European City of Culture for the following year meant that Florence had to put on a costly program celebrating itself. Predictably, a major cultural program triggered conflict among the ruling parties since it involved large dollops of patronage. The Year of Culture threatened to sink Bogiankino's junta before it set sail. The Liberals, extremely uneasy over participating in a coalition with their Communist enemies, provoked a crisis over their desire to choose the new director of the Teatro Comunale. Patronage was at issue, and Bogiankino kept his coalition together with some pragmatic concessions involving public positions and moneys.[18]

In arranging a truce within the junta, Bogiankino utilized his knowledge of Italy's cultural scene. He came up with a compromise candidate for director. Giorgio Vidusso, a talented pianist and conductor and a native of Trieste, was unconnected with Florence's politically polarized cultural elites. Vidusso brought energy and creativity to his post. A year later, Vidusso dryly observed that the Milanese considered La Scala a temple, while the Florentines regarded Teatro Comunale as "an arena."[19]

Long a battleground of contending political factions and a primary source of patronage and prestige for the ruling coalition, Teatro Comunale, by the mid-1980s, was part of a national economic crisis of the arts. Production costs continued to rise. Major artists' fees skyrocketed. Unionized labor, both support staffs and musicians, demanded hefty pay and benefit increases. Government subventions rose but never kept pace with costs. On top of this, furious battles over questions of artistic direction pitted major cultural figures against one another. Strikes, resignations, canceled performances, and angry audience protests were a staple fare at the Teatro Comunale of the 1980s. Star conductor Riccardo Muti left the Maggio Musicale at the end of the 1983 season in protest. The following year modernist composer and PCI member Luciano Berio offered a series of updated versions of *Fidelio* and *Rigoletto*. Conductor Bruno Bartoletti and star baritone Piero Cappuccelli walked out after quarrels with director Yuri Ljubimov. Opening-night audiences showed up to lustily boo both productions. The 1985 Maggio was marred by management–union clashes. Its scheduled opening remained in doubt to the last minute.[20]

Battles between labor and management continued unabated during the winter 1985–1986 season. The unions demanded contracts similar to those of La Scala employees. Florentine administrators refused, noting that the Teatro Comunale was a distant fourth on the list of state-subsidized cultural centers. After a brief truce granted the newly appointed Vidusso, the union agitation forced cancellation of Berio's new opera, *Vera storia*. Vidusso resigned, then relented. The opposition presented a no-confidence against Bogiankino's junta. A last-minute compromise permitted the Maggio to begin and ultimately stage Berio's opera.[21]

In July 1986 the city closed the theater for major repairs to its public stairways and electrical system. Bogiankino first delayed taking action on Vidusso's reports on the deteriorating safety conditions at Teatro Comunale, then proposed working around them with a series of emergency measures such as closing off part of the theater. Ultimately, the Teatro's administrative commission (which included the mayor) had to take action. On July 11, it shut down the theater for an indeterminate period.[22]

Problems at the Teatro Comunale were only a part of the the 1986 cultural war in Florence. The major battle was the conflict over the European Year of Culture, specifically over its funding. In a December 20, 1985, ceremony in the Palazzo Vecchio's ornate Sala dei dugento (Room of the 200), Bogiankino officially inaugurated the Year of Culture by warning that many of the city's plans for the celebration would not be realized. A DC-controlled Ministry of Tourism and Spectacle delayed funding. On July 1, 1986, Bogiankino and an embarrassingly small group of European bigwigs presided over the first event of the year, now reduced to a semester, an open-air performance of Verdi's *Requiem* in Piazza Signoria.[23]

Viewed from the DC's perspective, the decision to slow down the flow of funding to Florence made eminent good sense. The Year of Culture offered the ruling junta major opportunities for patronage and prestige but also opportunity to fall on its face. By accepting designation as Europe's City of Culture at the last minute, the city government placed itself in a difficult position. It had to plan and implement a coherent program on the run. Even without funding delays, Florence would have been hard-pressed to mount a major program in the first half of 1986.

Designation as the European City of Culture necessitated the selection of a group of prestigious intellectuals to serve as advisers to the Commune. The parties made the choices. Half the Wisemen selections came from Rome, while local party organizations made the other half. Quite a few Wisemen had outstanding backgrounds. Vidusso, Carlo Ragghianti, and Alfonso Spadoni of Florence's Teatro La Pergola all had excellent credentials in the arts. The PCI nominated two distinguished historians, Eugenio Garin and Giorgio Mori. The Socialists' picks, dictated by Lagorio, included Di Nolfo. The Christian Democrats chose ineffectual warhorses. Age and illness reduced the involvement of Garin and Ragghianti. Alessandro Parronchi chose to limit his involvement to issues relating to literature. As a result the Wisemen were more compact and contentious.[24]

Bogiankino found out how contentious when the Wisemen began to meet in March. The junta offered a prepared program for the Wisemen to rubber-stamp. The mayor, claiming ex-officio membership, appeared at the group's first session prepared to guide their deliberations. The Wisemen rejected this claim, threw out the junta's program, and began writing a new one. Party pressures, prudence, and limitations of cash combined to keep the Wisemen under control, but, within the parameters imposed from Rome, they rewrote the city plan.[25]

The mayor had a particularly determined opponent in fellow Socialist Di Nolfo. Handsome, charming, deeply cultured, and extremely confrontational, Di Nolfo, a director of the Tuscan Regional Orchestra, commentator for *La Nazione*, and hard-line anti-Communist, viewed Bogiankino as little more than a front man for a number of his political and cultural "enemies," most notably, Berio, whose pet projects, by Di Nolfo's calculations, consumed half of the proposed Year of Culture budget.[26]

The combination of delayed financing and the Wisemen's rewriting of its program was a political black eye for the Bogiankino administration. To make matters worse, Socialists Morales and Bogiankino clashed publicly over plans for the cultural year program. The local Christian Democrats, led by their cultural expert, Pier Luigi Ballini, exploited the Wisemen's recommendations for all their intrinsic political value. The DC's position was simple. The city would adopt the recommendations of the *saggi*, or it would have no money to put on a cultural year program. As the city council battle over its program escalated, Bogiankino's junta scraped together 2.6 billion lire. Florence's elected leaders went to Rome in late May to demand autonomy in planning and the release of remaining governmental funds, only to be told to adopt the Wisemen's program.[27]

The standoff beteen the Tourism Ministry and the Bogiankino junta continued until June 9, when the city council, on a straight party vote, approved a program loosely based on the Wisemen's proposals. The Year of Culture would begin on July 1, and its major activities would open in September if the Ministry of Cultural Affairs came up with a promised subvention. Meanwhile, Socialist ministers in the Craxi government, led by Lagorio, got behind Florence's demands. The first performance of the Verdi *Requiem* took place three weeks later. Politically, the choice of a requiem was fitting. The cultural year had been truncated, the junta politically damaged, and its program gored by party infighting.[28]

The junta managed to best the *saggi* on a number of program selections and then stared down the national government, forcing it to cough up a promised 15 billion lire by the simple expedient of threatening to close down three months early. Eleven major programs were offered in September. They included exhibits of major European artists from the Middle Ages through Picasso and a couple of shows dedicated to contemporary painters and sculptors. The city council passed legislation authorizing the creation of a musical training institution, "Tempo reale," under the direction of Berio.[29]

The truncated Year of Culture was neither a total failure nor a great success. A few museums expanded opening hours. The money permitted some very useful repair work to architecturally significant buildings in the historic center. A number of banks, particularly the Cassa di Risparmio di Firenze, increased their civic involvement by funding special restoration projects and musical performances. The overall program was scarcely distinguishable from the sort of art shows that the city regularly supported. Some drew well. The contemporary art presentations attracted little attention. One critic summarized the overall program as heavy in "Pipobaudismo," a sarcastic reference to a popular television emcee. The city's decision to allow most galleries to close for the Christmas holidays brought the Year of Culture to a less than spectacular end. The regional government then put a damper on the larger objectives of the cultural year by denying funding to the Tempo Reale program.[30]

FIAT-FONDIARIA

The Year of Culture accentuated the deep divisions within the Socialist Party. The debate on the future of the city's northwest redevelopment uncovered the fissures among the parties of the junta and ultimately blew it apart. The issue of major infrastructural improvements moved to the center of public debate. In addition to the proposed development projects of FIAT and Fondiaria, the airport question remained unresolved. Florentine businessmen insistently pressed for improvements at the Peretola facility, particularly a longer second landing strip, arguing that regular business flight schedules would give a needed spark to the local economy. The related issue of vehicular traffic simultaneously moved to center stage.[31]

Cesare Romiti, FIAT's managing director, arrived in Florence on January 14, 1986, to win the new junta to plans for a "21st Century Florence." The key elements of the FIAT offer were to transfer its spare parts plant to another part of Novoli and to construct a large office building to house the courts and supporting staffs of Florence's massive legal administration together with a major new public park, bank, and hotel and new roadways. FIAT, Romiti explained, was not expanding into the real estate business. It believed that Florence was the ideal place to build its state-of-the-art spare parts plant and was ready to help the city reach its objectives in exchange for agreement to host the new plant. "We aren't in any hurry," Romiti told *La Nazione*. "We can even wait 500 years."[32]

Romiti undoubtedly left Florence feeling that FIAT would have its new plant site in a good deal less than five centuries. The Bogiankino administration was cautiously favorable to the FIAT project and to its Fondiaria twin. *La Nazione*, reflecting its habitual boosterism and the views of large segments of the business community, kept up a drumbeat in favor of the two projects. In March the city and regional governments agreed to move forward with both. City officials held talks with other major corporate employers, seeking to fold them into a development plan that would retain their plants and jobs in Florence.[33]

The junta speedily backtracked as the infrastructural problems associated with FIAT-Fondiaria became clear. Chief among these was the impact that new road construction would have on an already chaotic traffic situation. Environmental and urban planning groups objected that the project would accelerate the hollowing out of the old city and that the proposed buildings were just more cement monstrosities. Opponents centered their fire on La Fondiaria, pointing to an increasing "foreign" presence in this old Florentine company. The Milan-based chemical giant Montedison already owned 38 percent of the company. The possibility that outsiders with little sense of the city's needs or history would dominate the northwest redevelopment became a useful tool for opponents of the FIAT-Fondiaria project. The Communists began to back away from their cautious approval of FIAT-Fondiaria.[34]

In April 1986, the junta, seeking political backing for FIAT-Fondiaria, opened a city council debate on Florence's future. The opposition pointed out the weakness of the Bogiankino junta's commitment to FIAT-Fondiaria, belaboring the PCI for its tepid support in hopes of forcing a government crisis. The council discussions displayed unanimity on the principle of city control over whatever redevelopment took place. After four months, a majority coalesced around FIAT-Fondiaria that included both the junta parties, the DC and the PRI. The opposition, led by the Greens, offered over 800 amendments to the legislation, authorizing negotiations with the two business giants to no avail. On July 26, 1986, the city council approved a plan and sent it to the Tuscan regional government for its review. FIAT-Fondiaria appeared to be back on track.[35]

In a classic understatement, *La Nazione* observed: "While it leaves the man in the street quite indifferent . . . [FIAT-Fondiaria] inflames politics."[36] Redevelopment of the northwest aroused the passions of the elites that dominate politics, the press, and the intellectual establishment. When the Tuscan region blocked further action by the city on the grounds that its plans had not been coordinated with surrounding communes, the conflict over the northwest's future again exploded. A November 1986 protest signed by nine major city intellectual figures announced a new phase in the battle. Simultaneously, *Il Ponte* published a long and thoughtful essay by economist Giacomo Becattini entitled "A Design for Florence," arguing that the FIAT-Fondiaria question was the third and final chance for postwar Florentines to determine the future of their city. While reconstructions after the disasters of 1944 and 1966 were more dramatic, the city's present emergency was as profound. The final design of the northwest was probably Florentines' last chance to determine whether their city would be livable. The project would foreclose future growth while it simultaneously determined the utilization of Florence's historic center. The northwest development would have an equally profound effect on the economic future of Florence. Increasingly, the city functioned on two levels. It was an international center for tourism, and it was the central market for the specialized Tuscan economy. Keeping these two roles in balance would be critical. If Florence failed to nurture its regional ties, it faced reduction to the position of a "museum city," totally dependent on tourism.[37]

Writing a few months later in *Il Ponte*, Paolo Baldeschi widened the debate. Besides FIAT-Fondiaria, the city and its government had to make decisions on other "major projects," including the location of the new technical campus of the university, roads, the airport, commercial developments, parking garages, and inner-city restoration projects. Land utilization in itself was insufficient as a guide to urban policy. Florentine leaders needed to consider the sort of economy that they hoped to nurture in the context of the national and international division of labor, integrating Florentine industries with larger economic units. The city's major strength was its position at the hub of a number of major communications links. It needed to attract private investment and to adopt a more cooperative approach to neighboring cities. Florence's future was clearly linked to the growth of a vibrant service sector economy. Public-private cooperation on development issues could reverse the decline of the historic center and promote the economic well-being of all Florentines.[38]

As long as the junta lacked a common position on FIAT-Fondiaria, debate continued, and the divisions within city government festered. The opposition effectively attacked the Bogiankino administration, pointing to its inability to merge the widely divergent views of Communists and Liberals. Bogiankino's junta was weak, opponents charged, because it stood for nothing but the division of spoils. A discontent business community joined in this criticism, as did many intellectuals. In mid-1988 city merchants staged a three-day "blackout" of their shops to protest the junta's failure to resolve the pressing issues of rail links, parking, and the airport. National elections in 1987 profoundly upset the balance between the PCI and PSI, to the latter's favor. While this development temporarily strengthened Bogiankino, it laid the groundwork for further problems between the junta's two major components. The cooperation between Morales (PSI) and Ballini (DC) on cultural matters became increasingly close, laying groundwork for a future Socialist–Christian Democratic rapprochement. The Socialists continued fighting among themselves and then were embarrassed by yet another scandal involving bribes to their leadership. "Milan has fog, Venice high water, and Florence has Bogiankino's junta," *La Nazione* complained.[39]

While the junta delayed action, FIAT mobilized its mighty public relations machine to move its plan along, supported, as always, by *La Nazione*. The car company provided a more detailed plan that it hoped would answer some of its critics' objections. It suggested folding its project into Fondiaria's, abandoning Novoli as a development site in a successful ploy that aroused local citizens groups and increased pressure on the city to accept FIAT's initial proposals.[40]

A January 1988 special edition of *Il Ponte*, dedicated to the development debate, offered city political leaders a chance to set out their views. A number of city planners rushed to the defense of the FIAT-Fondiaria concept, attacking its critics as ivory tower academics. Giovanni Koenig underlined a critical point in the thinking of supporters of big firms' northwest development schemes, pointing out that only large corporations were capable of financing major urban development.[41]

The missing voice in the debate belonged to the city's largest political party. The PCI was consistently of two minds about FIAT-Fondiaria. Its older leaders, happy to be back in power, insisted on the need to sustain Bogiankino's junta by backing FIAT-Fondiaria. They agreed with the general thrust of the two northwest development projects, favoring fine-tuning to achieve PCI political objectives. A younger group of party leaders was strongly opposed. They recognized that major change was on the way for the Communist Party. Soviet leader Michael Gorbachev's perestroika program of reforming the corrupt Soviet state challenged the legitimacy of all Communist movements as had no events since 1956. Although the PCI was by far the most liberalized Communist Party, it could not escape the impact of perestroika. It needed to come to terms with its ambiguous past; it needed to find new issues and create new coalitions; and it needed to thoroughly remake its public image. Two decades of an increasingly cozy cooperation with the DC and big business weighed heavily on the party. It had lost credibility with large segments of youth and with intellectuals. Building its bona fides with the ever-expanding element of the Italian electorate alienated from traditional politics was critical to a party whose working-class base was eroding.[42]

The party's newly elected secretary, Achille Occhetto, sensed the need for rapid and deep change in the PCI. FIAT-Fondiaria presented him with an opportunity to begin the work of redefinition. The project had come under heavy fire from environmentalists, one of the groups that Occhetto was seeking to attract to the PCI. On the evening of June 26, 1989, Occhetto called PCI headquarters in Florence and instructed the local party leadership to withdraw its support for FIAT-Fondiaria.[43]

Occhetto's phone call sparked an immediate crisis. The Communist secretary had undercut the PCI's representatives on the junta and effectively placed the Florentine party in receivership. The Socialists asked for the resignation of the PCI assessor of urban planning, Stefano Bassi. Although Bogiankino rode out the first shock waves, withdrawal of PCI support for FIAT-Fondiaria meant the end of his career as mayor. Shortly thereafter Bogiankino suffered a heart attack and resigned. Giorgio Morales took over as mayor and leader of a junta that clearly had no future.[44]

With elections scheduled for the spring of 1990, the parties used the intervening months to strengthen their ties to traditional constituencies and approach new ones. The first Morales junta was distinguished more by creation of the groundwork for a new alliance between the PSI and DC than by any significant innovation. Taking a strong stand for public order and merchants' interests, Morales sent the police into downtown Florence to clean out the mainly Somali street vendors who clogged its major streets. The mayor and his activist assessor of culture, Valdo Spini, came up with a 300-million-lire project to infuse the local economy with new vitality. Plans for a program of infrastructural improvements designed to support the 1990 World Cup were bandied about. The Socialists left open the possibility of a new coalition with the PCI, but their natural ally was Gianni Conti's DC. The mayor and Conti shared similar views on FIAT-Fondiaria. Conti spoke of his desire to "develop the discourse interrupted in . . . 1985." A PCI that had been discredited by its own national leadership was an inviting target for both parties.[45]

ON THE MOVE

In spite of the city's multiple problems, Florentine elites entered the 1990s in an optimistic mood. The Year of Culture had been modestly successful. Fighting over FIAT-Fondiaria obscured Florence's attractiveness to major investors. Finally, the city appeared to be making major progress against one of its longest-standing problems, its traffic chaos. "Firenze s'e desta," (Florence Is on the Move), suggested *Il Ponte*, a weathervane of Florentine cultural-political life.[46]

By 1986 local politicians were in substantial accord that dramatic steps would be needed to end the inner city's environmental crisis. Traffic was literally drowning the city. Florence enjoyed the unhappy distinction of the highest per capita ownership of cars in Italy, one for every two residents. Its public transportation system was inferior; it had few police assigned to traffic control; and it faced a daily invasion by 40,000 persons seeking to reach downtown employment. Florence's rush hour traffic left 80,000 liters of pollutants in the air every year. Traffic chaos cost commuters 300 billion lire a year in repairs and upkeep. Violations of traffic regulations by desperate drivers seeking to reach parking and their jobs averaged three per year per vehicle. Inside the city of Florence 4,842 accidents left forty-four dead and 4,711 injured.[47]

Supported by the city's powerful labor unions, political leaders drew up plans for expanding *zone blu* and pedestrian-only zones and for rerouting traffic approaching the historic center. More circumferential roads, more peripheral parking garages, the reintroduction of nonpolluting electric trams, and more efficient buses were other key elements in city planning.[48]

In July and August 1986, as most Florentines headed off for the annual summer vacation, the city introduced expanded *zone blu* and new traffic directional patterns. The experiment worked well, but nervous city fathers backed off in early October, replacing full-time *zone blu* regulations with a nighttime-only version. Traffic assessor Adalberto Scarlino (PLI) explained that the city lacked the funds to pay for policing a strict traffic limitation policy but pledged that the junta would introduce the new system on a full-time basis at the beginning of 1988.[49]

The Liberal assessor of traffic had a hard time rounding up a junta majority for further restrictions. A decision on further limiting traffic was postponed to the spring of 1987, when Scarlino found himself the target of an opportunist DC, a PSI that judged his plan extreme, and, ironically, an environmental left that complained that his proposals did not go far enough.[50]

La Nazione swung strongly behind the idea of further limitations. It conducted polls showing massive citizen support, editorialized for increased *zone blu*, organized a conference on transportation alternatives, and provided Scarlino with favorable coverage. Supported by an unlikely coalition of environmentalists, business, the Automobile Club of Italy, the smaller parties, and *La Nazione*, Scarlino secured enactment of a plan that reduced or eliminated traffic in large portions of the old city.[51]

In mid-1987 the Bank of Italy authorized a number of local banks to provide financing for a joint city–private enterprise venture in the construction of new parking garages. Realization of the program would be a long and tormented process, but Florence was taking an important step toward providing alternatives to the use of the private automobile inside the city. In another notable initiative to reduce pollution and traffic, the city council (March 1987) reduced by two-thirds the number of gas stations operating in and around the city.[52]

By early 1988, *La Nazione*, at least, was ready to proclaim the *zone blu* a "real revolution" and hymn the restoration of cleaner air and a more visible Florence. Its polls showed two-thirds of Florentines backing *zone blu*. The junta, with the PCI and PSI now solidly behind the idea, expanded limited traffic zoning (ZTL) to an even larger part of the city. Initially, the council voted for a one-week experiment, but under pressure from environmental interests, the Bogiankino government pushed through legislation making it permanent for almost all the old city.[53]

Reaction from a strong component of inner-city merchants was speedy. They protested, threatened to shut their shops, and found support for demands for a reduction in the ZTL from within the junta. The smaller parties objected to the plans of Scarlino's successor, Graziano Cioni (PCI), to further expand ZTL. Socialists fought among themselves, while Bogiankino backed his assessor of traffic. The strength of inner-city business opposition led *La Nazione* to qualify its support.[54] Florence's stop-and-start style of traffic regulation was again operating. Nevertheless, the Bogiankino junta made major progress in conserving the city center, and the merchants would discover with time that business was as good with ZTL as before.

YEAR OF SOCCER

Another critical element in providing a balanced transportation system was the introduction of parking garages located on the periphery of the old city that offered alternatives for drivers headed to their place of employment. After depositing their cars in near-in parking garages, Florentines would have the option of public transportation or a relatively easy walk to their jobs.

The opportunity for a major program of parking garage construction arose as a result of Italy's successful bid to host the 1990 "World Cup" soccer play-offs. As one of the world's premier tourist attractions, Florence could count on a large influx of well-heeled foreign and Italian fans to fill its coffers. The national government, eager to reap prestige and tourist dollars, pledged major investment in infrastructural improvements. The city offered its plans for a complete overhaul of the stadium and better parking garages together with other long-term programs.[55]

Planning for stadium expansion began in earnest in 1986. In late December, the Italian parliament allocated 620 billion lire for stadium improvements. Between 30 and 40 billion would go to Florence. In February 1987, the city council approved a stadium upgrade. In August, the city appropriated 66 billion lire in matching funds for the project.[56]

The stadium work was completed shortly before the World Cup games began. The ambitious parking garage program lagged far behind. By the time that the teams took to the field at Stadio Comunale, only one of the projected garages was completed. A second, astride Piazza Independenza, began operating in the early 1990s but was underutilized by Floretines, who complained that it was too far from the city center to be an attractive alternative to driving into town. Moreover, judicial inquiries into contracting for the garage raised questions of corruption within the city government.[57]

World Cup play in Florence went off successfully. Italy's failure to qualify for the finals, while a most serious blow to the national image, did not affect the orgy of profit making that accompanies World Cup competition. Unfortunately, the World Cup also emphasized the disturbing realities of 1980s Florence. The "touristification" of the inner city's economy intensified, and the decline of its resident population continued. Between 1981 and 1991, approximately 100,000 Florentines left their city, usually for nearby and less crowded communes. Demographers confidently predicted that 40,000 more would follow suit by 2000. The city's tax base declined as its infrastructural problems grew. The divorce between the "real" Florence of working citizens and the "tourist" Florence of pizzerias, museums, and hotels accelerated. By the end of the decade Florence was following, albeit at a considerable distance, the path laid out by Venice, Italy's foremost "museum-city." The divorce between the historic center and the life of the province was accelerating.

NOTES

1. Ennio Di Nolfo interview, Florence, May 17, 1993.

2. Di Nolfo (May 17, 1993) and Lelio Lagorio, Florence, October 4, 1995, interviews.

3. Marco Massa, ed., *Firenze* (Milan, 1988), p. 66; Statistical data from *La Nazione*, January 9, 23, April 29, July 23, August 26, 30, September 25, November 1, 5, December 21, 1986; January 18, February 17, March 12, June 6, 26, 1987; April 6, 1988.

4. *La Nazione*, September 17, 1986, November 20, 1987, January 24, 1988. Housing data, ibid., January 31, February 21, June 20, August 3, 5, 1986; January 22, June 18, July 8, July 30, 1987; May 6, 1988.

5. Barbara Grizzuti Harrison, *Italian Days* (New York, 1989), pp. 159–60.

6. On drugs: *La Nazione*, February 4, 8, 20, July 23, 24, November 5, 1986; May 26, September 12, October 2, 6, 1987; on AIDS, ibid., December 28, 1985, January 1, July 17, 1986.

7. *FBIS Daily Report, Europe*, May 8, 1990; NA 121 (April 1986), pp. 96–101; *La Nazione*, February 11, 1986, May 14, June 7, 1987.

8. *La Nazione*, September 10, October 2, 1985; January 4, April 1, 22, August 17, October 14, 1986; *The European*, May 25–27, 1990; *Time*, March 24, 1986.

9. *La Nazione*, January 23, 1986; January 4, 18, May 12, 24, July 21, 1987; March 17, 1988.

10. *La Nazione*, April 1, May 15, July 15, 18, September 9, 12, November 19, 21, December 10, 11, 13, 16, 1986; January 15, May 19, 20, 24, June 2, 4, 11, October 3, 1987; February 3, 1988.

11. *La Nazione*, February 23, April 17, 19, June 21, August 3, September 10, November 19, 1986; January 18, 1987.

12. *La Nazione*, January 28, March 6, August 27, November 12, 1986; May 19, 1987.

13. *La Nazione*, September 24, 1986; April 21, June 23, November 18, 21, 1987; March 18, May 3, April 26, June 21, 22, 1988.

14. *La Nazione*, February 4, 7, 8, 1986; ACC 1985, 2: 897–925.

15. *La Nazione*, January 3, 8, March 14, 1986; January 7, May 20, 1988; Comue di Firenze, *Attivita di formazione professionale dell'amministrazione comunale* (Florence, 1987).

16. *La Nazione*, October 3, 8, November 7, 15, 1986; April 4, 1987.

17. Massa, *Firenze*, p. 38; *La Nazione*, December 27, 28, 1985; January 2–3, June 29, 1986; July 5, December 4, 1987; January 20, 22, February 6, March 6, 1988.

18. *La Nazione*, December 27, 1985, January 10, 31, February 1, 27, June 4, 1986.

19. *La Nazione*, January 15, February 11, April 27, 1986; March 8, 1987.

20. *La Nazione*, April 27, 1986; *New York Times*, August 9, 1987.

21. *La Nazione*, April 30, May 1, 3, 1986.

22. *La Nazione*, May 21, July 16, 1986.

23. ACC 1986, 2: 465–67; 3: 2059–91; Marcello Vanucci, *Storia di Firenze*, 6 vols. (Rome, 1988), 6: 94; Giorgio Morales interview, Florence, October 4, 1995.

24. Di Nolfo interview, May 17, 1993; *La Nazione*, March 22, 1986.

25. ACC 1986, 1: 465–74; Di Nolfo interviews, April 8, May 17, 1993; *La Nazione*, February 23, March 22, 25, 1986.

26. Di Nolfo interview, April 8, 1993; for his judgment of Bogiankino, *La Nazione*, September 21, 1986.

27. ACC 1986, 1: 495–529, 535–85; 2: 1326–1331, 1558–72; *La Nazione*, March 5, May 9, 21, 24, 27, 30; June 5, 6, 10, 1986.

28. *La Nazione*, April 24, June 10, 25, July 1, 4, 1986; Lagorio interview; Giorgio Mori interview, Florence, May 20, 1993.

29. *La Nazione*, July 10, August 10, 29, September 16, 1986.

30. Valdo Spini interview, Rome, September 26, 1995; Mori and Morales interviews; *La Nazione*, February 27, December 16, 24, 1986; January 3, 14, March 7, 1987; *Il Ponte*, November–December 1986, pp. 143–48; Di Nolfo interview, May 17, 1993.

31. *La Nazione*, December 27, 1986; January 20, July 14, 1987.

32. *La Nazione*, January 15, 1987.

33. ACC 1986, 1: 387; *La Nazione*, January 14, March 11, 1986.

34. *The Economist*, October 18, 1986; *La Nazione*, April 1, 4, 9, August 14, 1986; *L'Unita*, March 30, 1986.

35. ACC 1986, 2: 1015–21, 1211–32, 1250–85, 1293–1321; 3: 2139–2288; *La Nazione*, July 26, 30, 1986; Iacopo Detti interview, Florence, May 18, 1993.

36. *La Nazione*, May 6, 1968.

37. *La Nazione*, November 14, 1986; *Il Ponte* November–December 1986, pp. 6–14; ibid., May–June 1987, pp. 41–48; Cf. Giorgio Mori, ed., *Storia d'Italia dall'unita ad oggi: La Toscana* (Turin, 1986), pp. 869–97.

38. *Il Ponte*, March–April 1987, pp. 43–55.

39. ACC 1986, 4: 2701; ACC 1987, 1: 201–3; *La Nazione*, April 4, June 10, September

21, December 16, 1986; February 3, June 18, 28, 30, July 3, 9, 31, September 6, 16, 17, 22, 1987, January 27, February 6, 7, June 8, 24 (quote), 1988.

40. *La Nazione*, March 12, December 6, 8, 11, 17, 1987; February 16, March 16, April 23, 1988; P. Baldeschi et al., *Citta fine millenio* (Milan, 1990), p. 85.

41. *Il Ponte*, January 1988, pp. 9–12, 125–35, 171–87, 205–9.

42. *La Nazione*, April 20, 1988; Mark Gilbert, *The Italian Revolution* (Boulder, CO, 1995), pp. 67–75.

43. *La Nazione*, April 14–15, 1988; *La Gazzetta*, April 13, 1989; Francesco Indovina, *La citta occasionale* (Milan, 1993), pp. 83–84.

44. *L'Unita*, June 28, 1989; *La Nazione*, June 28, 30, 1989; *La Repubblica*, June 29, 1989.

45. *La Repubblica*, February 15, 1990; *L'Unita*, June 26, July 5, 1990; *Urbanistica informazioni*, 1990 n. 109; *Il Governo*, September–October 1989, pp. 11–12; Morales interview.

46. "Firenze s'e desta," *Il Ponte* 44 (January 1988).

47. *La Nazione*, December 19, 1985; January 4, 25, 30, 1986.

48. ACC 1986, 2: 1737–41; *La Nazione*, January 8, February 23, March 29, April 23, 30, May 25, June 11, 1986.

49. *La Nazione*, July 11, October 2, November 4, 1986; ACC 1986; 4: 3208.

50. ACC 1987, 2: 972–1064; *La Nazione*, October 25, November 18, 1986.

51. *La Nazione*, November 29, December 6, 11, 13, 1986; February 15, March 14, 28, April 5, 16, May 12, June 12, 21, 1987.

52. *La Nazione*, January 4, June 26, July 1, September 26, October 16, December 11, 1987.

53. *La Nazione*, January 16, 17, 19, February 20, 24, 25, 26, March 1, 1988.

54. *La Nazione*, March 12, 13, 18, 22, April 19, June 21, December 5, 1988.

55. *La Nazione*, May 14, 1988.

56. ACC 1987, 1: 433–459; *La Nazione*, April 19, December 31, 1986; August 6, 1987; July 23, 1988.

57. Morales and Lagorio interviews.

Chapter 13

The Party's Over

After Milan, the climate in Italy and Florence too is [one] of general crimin-
alization of all public administrators.

Giorgio Morales, June 1992

In December 1992, the Arno rose menacingly, overflowing the plain near Pisa
and coming within inches of inundating Florence. Six months later, investigating
magistrates informed Mayor Morales and his assessor of the environment that
they were targets of a probe into presumed mismanagement of the city during
the near flood. In June 1993, the mayor and assessor appeared at the baroque
Palazzo di Giustizia in Piazza S. Firenze to take up the difficult task of defending
their conduct during a hypothetical disaster. This improbable summons was one
of thousands that rained upon the political leaders of Italy during a three-year
period between 1992 and 1995. Many were fully justified. Others were simply
politically motivated attacks by a part of the magistracy that was in headlong
pursuit of its own agenda for restructuring a very corrupt Italian state. The effect
of this Niagara of investigations was to freeze the normal political and administrative processes. The direction of the Italian state fell into the hands of the
magistrates and an activist president.[1]

THE MAN FOR ALL SEASONS

The May 1990 election for city council gave few indications of the political
earthquake that would shake Italy two years later. The former PCI, which lacked
a new name but was clearly moving toward a social democratic identity, dropped
from 39.9 percent of the vote (twenty-five seats) to 32.5 percent (twenty-one
seats). The PSI, however, gained litle at the expense of its longtime rival. The

Socialists advanced modestly, capturing an additional 1 percent of the vote (13.3 percent) and gaining two seats in the city council. With nine aldermen, the Socialists were well positioned to reassert their claim to the mayor's post. The DC held its own, the same number of seats (seventeen) and almost the same percentage of the popular vote. The smaller lay parties generally held stable, with the PRI gaining one seat. The Green Party failed to win a council seat.

Carefully playing off the PCI and DC, the Socialists carved out an accord for a five-party coalition that gave them the mayor's position. The DC's bid for five assessorates, including urban planning, culture, and public instruction, was blocked by a stronger PRI that demanded and got the urban planning post. To compensate the Christian Democrats, Conti became both the vice mayor and assessor of culture. The new city government, *Unita* tartly noted, had an agreement on division of posts and promised to come up with a program later. Morales presented his team to the city council in September. The junta could count on thirty-two votes for its majority.[2]

Even the opposition admitted that Morales, whom *Unita* sarcastically dubbed "the man for all seasons," was an unusually capable politician. Square-jawed, with a curly mop of receding gray hair, the stylishly dressed, suave Morales projected a relaxed confidence. Florence's mayor was a superb mediator who held his disparate coalition together for five years in spite of political scandal and the demise of his own party. DC assessor Ballini recalled that the political scandals buffeting Italy from the spring of 1992 actually strengthened Morales' hold. As the major parties dissolved, personal relationships became key. Morales excelled at building and maintaining these ties. As Italians loudly demanded the end of *clientelismo* (patronge politics), the business of government moved forward, utilizing a jury-rigged patronage system without the parties.[3]

The new junta started out under a cloud. Morales received an *avviso di garanzia* (notice of investigation) from the public prosecutor in September 1990. The charge was favoring business partners of the lady with whom he lived. Morales' protested his innocence and secured a vote of confidence from his junta allies. Morales' personal problems were only part of the junta's headaches. The new city administration was divided on urban policy. Urban planning assessor Franchini engaged in a running feud with Lele Tiscar (DC), the assessor of housing, over new apartment construction. The junta faced a fierce political assault from the former Communists, who accused it of "assassinating" the aggressive extension of *zone blu*. Short of cash, the junta had to take the politically unpopular decision to raise service fees on schools, museums, recreation facilities, and water in October 1990.[4]

Urban planning continued to divide not only the government but the junta's largest party. Conti's opponents within the Florentine DC, including the communal party secretary, Vittorio D'Oriano, exploited the differences between Francini and Tiscar to mount an assault on the vice mayor. Protracted infighting within the regional and local DC became so intense that it menaced the stability of the junta. The Tuscan DC's seven identifiable factions, hungry for patronage after nearly five years in the opposition, battled over the division of spoils of government.[5]

The Florentine PSI's always-tenuous unity unwound over the desire of factional chief Alberto Magnolfi for a seat in parliament. Magnolfi's challenge disrupted the delicate balance that Tuscan party secretary Riccardo Nencini had arranged between the Spini, Colzi, and Lagorio factions. Nencini warned Magnolfi: "Anyone not with me is against Bettino [Craxi]."[6]

The maneuvering of the junta's major parties brought down the wrath of Florence's archbishop, Cardinal Silvano Piovanelli, who denounced the arrogance of power, *clientelismo*, and amoral pragmatism of the ruling parties in a June 24 homily at the Duomo. Florence's cardinal attributed the decline in public morality to the continuing infiltration of the Masonic lodges into the ruling parties. Piovanelli pleaded with the DC to reform itself.[7]

Morales already had in hand a piece of legislation designed to give the appearance of rendering local government more open, efficient, and responsive to citizen needs. "The Constitution (Statuto) against Bad Government and Bad Service" offered citizens the right to instigate investigations of city government operations through the collection of 5,000 signatures on a petition. It created a public defender's office to oversee the city bureaucracy. The law increased the mayor's powers to take independent action. Warmly supported by the PSI, which drafted it, and hotly opposed by the DC, the bill finally passed the city council in October after Morales kept the lawmakers in continuous session and threatened to resign.[8]

The new law won considerable support in the press. However, Cardinal Piovanelli was more in step with public discontent than the politicians. Power games, not reform, occupied Florence's governing parties, which brushed aside his complaints about Masonic influence. The parties proceeded confidently because of the evident and growing weakness of the opposition. The ex-PCI, now officially renamed the Democratic Party of the Left (PDS), was in the midst of a deep crisis. Achille Occhetto had acted courageously by pushing the party to a rapid transformation in 1989. By 1991, the former Communists were in the midst of a painful divorce. Occhetto and his advisers accepted the loss of a minority of party leaders and members as part of the price for taking a major step toward democratic legitimization. They did not count on the defectors being capable organizers or on the continuing appeal of their views to a large slice of the rank and file.[9]

The defectors' new party, Rifondazione comunista (PRC), was a blend of old-time Stalinists, various radicals, idealists, nostalgics, and contrarians. In Tuscany, this mix of elements organized efficiently. By mid-1991, PRC had its own provincial organizations and was poised to mount a serious challenge to the PDS in 1992 parliamentary elections.[10]

The PDS meanwhile attempted to renew both itself and its public image, introducing greater internal democracy, redefining itself as a party of the moderate left, and challenging the PSI for political space. The Florentine PDS lost

40 percent of its card-carrying members in a single year. The local party's financial condition worsened dramatically, forcing it to sell off its headquarters building and close its major cultural operation, the Istituto Gramsci. As spring 1992 parliamentary elections approached, the PDS was too weak to effectively challenge the ruling coalition.[11]

The end of the Cold War in 1989–1991 had a significant psychological impact on Italian voters. The collapse first of the Berlin Wall and then of the Soviet state cut away one of the principal justifications for continuing rule by DC-led coalitions. Public discontent with the governing parties was a long-standing fact of Italian life. The upheavals of 1968–1969, the terrorism of the 1970s, and the rise of special interest and regional parties in the 1980s all testified to this unhappiness, as did the declining vote of both the DC and PCI. In 1992, voters tested the waters of new politics in larger numbers. Then, in an unexpected, but well prepared, assault, the nation's judiciary brought down the parties in a matter of months. Constructing a system to replace *partitocrazia* (party rule) proved more complex.

Following the elections of April 1992, the old parties thought that, with necessary adjustments, they could ride out the electorate's anger. Three major protest parties, the Northern Leagues, the Sicily-based Rete (Network), and the PRC, collected over 16 percent of the popular vote and sent 101 deputies to parliament. The DC lost twenty-eight seats and nearly 5 percent of its national electorate. The PDS, as expected, suffered a savage defeat, losing seventy seats in the Chamber of Deputies and nearly one-third of its voters. On the other hand, voters only lightly punished the PSI, which lost just two seats, and rewarded the Liberals and Republicans with six extra seats each. The Social Democrats held their own, losing one seat.

Public prosecutors in Milan, rather than the voters, delivered the deathblow to the Italian "First Republic." In February, the Milan prosecutorial pool arrested a local Socialist politician named Mario Chiesa. Chiesa ran a series of profitable scams, passing some of the money back to the local party machinery. Scandals of this sort dotted the postwar history of Italy. The Socialists had an unequaled record of involvement in them. Late in lining up at the trough of public graft, they seemed intent on compensating by developing the most voracious appetites. Previous scandals ran a prescribed course of revelation, press comment, and eventual burial (*archivazzione*) at the hands of senior officials.

This time things would be different. Italian magistrates form, by constitutional design, a unique corporation. Constitution makers tried to shelter the administration of justice against political interference by creating the self-governing board, the Supreme Council of the Magistracy (*Consiglio superiore della magistratura*). The parties easily infiltrated both the Supreme Council and the working level of the judiciary, while the magistrates created factions among themselves. Nevertheless, the magistrates possessed a strong sense of corporate identity together with long-nurtured grievances against a political class that openly flouted the law. This hostility was fully reciprocated by most politicians, who viewed a majority of public prosecutors as political hatchet men.[12]

The prosecutors of the Milan magistrates pool used the months after Chiesa's arrest to carefully build up a case against the local Socialist Party organization. Exploiting preventive detention laws that permitted them to apply extreme psychological pressure, the magistrates extracted a detailed confession from Chiesa and assembled impressive documentation and the testimony of other witnesses. Shortly after the elections, the Milan pool unveiled its "Clean Hands" (*Mani pulite*) operation. The case hinged on the operations of Milan's Socialist Federation but also clarified the agreements by which governing and opposition parties divided the graft.

The Milan investigation broke at the psychologically perfect moment. Public anger at the parties boiled over as revelations of the degree of corruption and graft mounted daily. The Italian media, particularly the press, were largely in the hands of a few businessmen who profited from cooperation with the parties but also nurtured strong resentment against being forced to pay bribes and were genuinely concerned that Italy's international competitiveness and their personal futures were imperiled by the *partitocrazia*'s practices. Television, although largely controlled by the parties or the Socialists' ally, Silvio Berlusconi, was filled with managers and journalists who nurtured their own grudges or speedily realized that their individual survival would depend on an ability to break their ties with disgraced parties and politicians. The media's contribution to *Mani pulite* was enormous. By fully and dramatically reporting the daily flow of new revelations and by glamorizing one Milan magistrate, Antonio Di Pietro, the media fueled public indignation and accelerated the process of the collapse of the party system.

By late summer 1992, the Milan investigation had widened, and magistrates in other regions were eagerly moving on parallel cases. The election of a new president opened deep wounds in the DC and broke the already shaky alliance between Craxi and Prime Minister Giulio Andreotti. DC Secretary Arnaldo Forlani resigned, and the ineffective, reform-minded Mino Martinazzoli replaced him, ensuring that the Christian Democratic Party would be paralyzed at the most critical moment in its history. The terrifying murders of two outstanding anti-Mafia magistrates, Giovanni Falcone and Paolo Borsellino, stoked public anger at the long-standing ties of the ruling parties with organized crime. The magistrates of *Mani pulite* created a focus for this anger: Socialist Party leader Bettino Craxi.

The Milan case was built on a universally accepted view: nothing happened inside the PSI without Craxi's approval. The Socialist leader's passion for control had been amply demonstrated during his fifteen years as PSI secretary. Moreover, Milan was not only Craxi's home base but a family fief. Craxi's son, Vittorio, was Milan's party leader; Craxi's brother-in-law was Milan's mayor. The *Mani pulite* pool convincingly demonstrated that Milan's corruption was part of a national system of bribery run out of PSI headquarters. In June 1992, President Luigi Oscar Scalfaro informed Craxi that his bid for another term as prime minister was out of the question. In February 1993, the besieged Craxi finally resigned as PSI secretary. The Socialist Party began to disintegrate. The Christian Democrats followed.

Neither Florence nor Tuscany was untouched by the shattering events of 1992. The results of the April 1992 elections in Tuscany more or less replicated national results. The PDS was severely cuffed by voters. A majority of its lost voters passed to the PRC. The Socialists and Christian Democrats also slid backward, while the Republicans and Liberals advanced. Neither of the major protest parties of 1992, the Leagues or the Rete, had solid roots in Tuscany. Their combined vote was a puny 7 percent of the total. Voters were unhappy with the parties but had yet to discover an acceptable alternative.[13]

"After Milan," Morales commented, everything changed. In June Gianni Conti received an *avviso di garanzia* indicating that he was being investigated for possible illegal business connections. He had ridden out a similar notification two years earlier. With *Mani pulite* revelations filling the daily press, Conti recognized that he had no alternative but to resign from the junta and as vice mayor within hours of receiving the notification. Coming within days of the resignation of another assessor, Sandro Barcali, over policy disagreements, Conti's departure began a period of intense political turbulence in Florence. The governing parties collapsed, battling continued over public policy, and Morales held firmly to the helm, carrying out the threat-promise, made to a journalist of *Unita*, to govern until his mandate expired in 1995. "We're a tough bunch of guys, we're clean, and we hang in there" a satisfied Pier Luigi Ballini chuckled some years later.[14]

The DC's remnants put a new face on their party representation. Ballini, a squeaky-clean, devout Catholic, took over Conti's position as assessor of culture. Giovanni Pallanti became vice mayor. Twenty-eight-year-old Lapo Pistelli, the son of La Pira's ally Nicola, joined the aldermen, succeeding Ballini at public instruction. Pistelli was the point man for a new generation of Catholic idealists who were forcing their way into leadership of the Tuscan DC. Their slogan, *La Repubblica* suggested, was "Elect us and we'll liquidate the DC." As it turned out, they were not needed.[15]

The Socialists were not so fortunate. By October 1992 Morales had recognized that Craxi's efforts to ride out the political storm were bringing the party down with its leader. With polls showing half its electorate abandoning the Florentine PSI, the mayor delivered his message in an October interview with *L'Unita*: the PSI's leader had to step aside. In the stampede to distance themselves from Craxi, Morales found himself in the company of such former loyalists as Nencini and sometime critics like Lagorio. Desperate to present the face of reform, the old guard then united with internal reformers to elect labor leader Giorgio Benvenuto party secretary. The effort to project a new face for the PSI fell victim to the subsequent maneuvers of Craxi and his followers. The Tuscan Party received another blow when public prosecutors indicted the region's former president, Maurizio Marucci, and thirteen others on charges of siphoning off funds from the Bilancino dam project. In addition to producing cheaper energy, the dam

was to protect Florence from the threat of major floods. Further arrests and in-
dictments followed. By mid-1993, the Florentine PSI had evaporated.[16]

WHAT KIND OF CITY?

The collapse of the old parties was only one reason that the Morales junta
operated with its back to the wall. The national economy took a nose dive shortly
after it entered office. Cash shortages mounted. Growth in the tourist industry
stalled. Ugly racial incidents marred the city's international image. In spite of
this, Morales and company made major decisions that would have enormous
impact on the city's future. The junta advanced traffic planning, and it reached
agreement on the FIAT-Fondiaria issue.

The Occhetto veto put FIAT-Fondiaria on ice for nearly two years. With
Conti back in the junta, these issues were bound to be resurrected. Both FIAT
and Fondiaria had utilized the intervening period to address their plans' overall
impact on the city. By 1991, the two economic giants each had detailed plans
and well-financed public relations operations.[17]

The political and economic situation favored approval of the two development
projects. With the PDS effectively neutralized by internal problems, the PSI and
DC were able to make a deal that permitted each party to gain one of its major
objectives. The worsening condition of Florence's economy made the prospect
of new jobs nearly irresistible to politicians and large segments of the electorate.
FIAT and Fondiaria ratcheted up pressure on the city government by acquiring
property near Florence with the unstated objective of building on these alternative sites.[18]

The basis for a FIAT-Fondiaria accord was the junta's decision to enlarge the
runway at Peretola. City Socialists pressed hard for this improvement against the
opposition not only of the PDS but of their own party at the regional government
level. Expansion of the runway was part of a deal that saw the Aga Kahn, the
owner of both Meridiana airlines and the CIGA hotels group, locate his operation in Florence. It permitted Peretola to greatly expand its flight services. Florence and other Tuscan city governments agreed to integrate service at Pisa and
Peretola, placing the two airports under a single management. Finally, the accord
on Peretola widened the split between the environmentalist and growth factions
within the PDS, keeping that party on the defensive, to the satisfaction of the
majority.[19]

The junta also made progress on outstanding urban projects. It separated negotiations on the FIAT and Fondiaria projects. Discussions with FIAT continued
during 1990; those with Fondiaria ceased after the Occhetto veto. In January
1991 Fondiaria and the city resumed their talks. Meanwhile, the governing parties faced off on the future of the FIAT proposal. Urban assessor Franchini isolated and defeated Conti with the aid of the vice mayor's old nemesis, fellow
Christian Democrat Vittorio D'Oriano. When the Socialists threw their weight
behind Franchini, he was able to introduce a new version of the Novoli project

as part of a broader draft of a new PRG. The new Novoli plan, which FIAT accepted, reduced the total land open to development and guaranteed that the automaker would make a considerable investment in infrastructure improvements as well as handing over gratis to the city the land needed for the construction of a new courts building. Pushing aside the opposition of environmentalists and the PDS, the junta parties gave the Franchini scheme unanimous approval in May 1991. Two months later they approved the accord with FIAT. This time the PDS softened its opposition, leaving Italia Nostra and other environmentalists in the lurch. A new PRG had been launched successfully, Franchini proclaimed.[20]

Approval of a new PRG and the Novoli project took place against the background of efforts to improve Florence's relationship with its neighbors. Accord on Peretola was the first step. In 1990, Italy's parliament passed a new law (number 142, June 8, 1990) designed to expand the financial and political autonomy of the communes. Cities were to draw up their own basic law and to enjoy expanded powers over revenue. The law also provided for the creation of "metropolitan areas," governmental bodies that would carry on the functions of both provincial and communal governments in areas of high population density. The province of Florence was designated a metropolitan area, and local administrators were instructed to come up with a working plan to coordinate their approach to issues such as roads, public transportation, the protection of cultural resources and the environment, water and sewer systems, waste disposal, public health, and economic development. Citizens of the former province would elect a metropolitan government comprising a mayor, junta, and council.[21]

Metropolitan government was designed to deal with some of the more serious problems facing local authorities in the traditional Italian manner: creating a more centralized administration. Since the communes frequently failed to cooperate, a higher governmental authority would unify their approach to local problems. In effect, the metropolitan governments subtracted from the localities the autonomy that the rest of the law was designed to provide.

In the specific case of Florence, the creation of a metropolitan area threatened the independent authority of a large number of communes. The Tuscan region would define the boundaries of the metropolitan area. Two alternative schemes emerged. The "donut," or life preserver (*ciambella*), solution would create a reduced area consisting of Florence and the neighboring communes of Sesto Fiorentino, Scandicci, Fiesole, and Bagno a Ripoli. The second, or "Big Florence," scheme would expand the metropolitan city north and northwest into the hills and along the Arno to bring together the manufacturing centers of Pistoia and Prato with their major marketplace and include most of Florence's bedroom communities.[22]

The Big Florence idea made good sense economically but presented two problems. The proposed metropolitan area would flow over the boundaries of Florence Province, necessitating parliamentary action to modify law 142/90, and it faced the unrelenting hostility of the government of the city of Prato. The Pratese announced plans to utilize other provisions of Law 142/90 to create their own province.[23]

On February 28, 1991, the mayors of Prato and Florence met for the first time in thirteen years to discuss outstanding differences. The two city leaders found little common ground beyond agreement on enlarging Peretola and on placing part of the University of Florence in Prato. Emblematic of their disagreement was Florence's plan to build a new museum of modern art in Rifredi. The Pratese, who had only recently inaugurated the Pecci Center for modern arts, accused the Florentines of plotting to further monopolize culture and tourism. The Pratese also wanted a bigger slice of the convention market. The two sides found no common ground on the metropolitan city issue.[24]

The deadlock over the metropolitan city issue deepened as the regional government bowed to Prato and scrubbed the idea of a Big Florence. Instead it proposed a confederated metropolitan area (Pistoia, Prato, and Florence). The parties of the Morales junta fought over the definition of the metropolitan area. The regional PDS favored the Tuscan government proposal; the local PDS opposed it. Administrators from Florence joined with those from other "metropolitan areas" to denounce the whole idea as a sham that would subtract autonomy from their cities. Recognizing that Grande Firenze was unattainable, Morales endorsed the *ciambella* concept in the hopes of increasing the city's control over its problems. Even this solution was out of reach. Tuscany's smaller communes rejected all the proposals, and the metropolitan area project was frozen while city and regional leaders looked for a compromise. Prato established its separate province.[25]

Meanwhile, the Morales administration approved a new PRG for Florence. Franchini and his consultant on planning, Marcello Vittorini, doggedly pushed forward against the usual combination of political maneuvering and public division to carry the new city plan to a 1993 vote. Simultaneously, the city took some important new steps in controlling its traffic problems.

By 1991, the Detti plan was more a memory than a guide to development. The 1962 PRG was so amended by zoning exemptions that it had long ceased to be anything other than a totem that progrowth and conservation forces waved at each other. Even after the Morales junta, in November 1990, directed Vittorini to draft a new PRG in the shortest time possible, he and Franchini continued to rely on further zoning exemptions to lay the basis for a new plan.[26]

Although Vittorini announced that the zoning variant permitting the Novoli project to go forward would be the "last" amendment to the existing PRG, he was back in November 1991 with a second major zoning exemption, the Special Plan for Housing (*Piano straordinario della casa*), which authorized the city to construct 550,000 square meters of new public housing (1,700 units).[27]

Vittorini's plan called for the distribution of the new public housing units throughout the city. Its small projects were ideal for rewarding private contractors for their political support. By June 1992, the special plan was the target of judicial investigations, centering on Vice Mayor Conti. Public housing was caught up in a series of contradictions that plagued city policy. Evictions continued to rise as Morales pressed for more public housing to meet the crisis. At the same time that the city was talking about privatizing services, it placed higher fees on home-owners and cut back on many existing functions.[28]

Political upheaval, protest from environmentalists, and splits within the junta over related policy issues slowed down Vittorini, who finally presented his PRG draft to the city council in late 1992. The Vittorini plan offered special treatment for the city's historic center, defined as the areas surrounded by Poggi's *viali*. It set out sixteen areas scattered beyond the *viali* (and one inside the historic district alongside the train station) that were formerly occupied by factories as "reurban-ization" projects. Nine other parcels of land would be dedicated to new building. These included Peretola and the Castello zone owned by La Fondiaria. The FIAT zone remained a separate development project. Three new parks would go up along the city periphery. Three subway lines would connect the outer parts of the city with its principal train stations and with S. Maria Novella. One of these lines would pass through the historic center. A long tunnel would connect auto traffic between the Novoli zone and the Campo Marte district, reducing the strain on urban streets. The city's convention facility would be expanded by the crea-tion of an "exchange park" next to the existing Palazzo congressi-Fortezza da Basso complex. S. Maria Novella station would be converted into a massive transportation museum. Underground high-speed trams were to link the city's new principal railheads, Campo Marte and Castello. Finally, a "Musical Pole" dedicated to education and performances, housing a new Teatro Comunale, was to go up at Porta a Prato close to the old city and the convention zone.[29]

As critics noted, the Vittorini plan said little about the future utilization of the inner city. It did not presume any improvement in cooperation with neigh-boring communes, nor did it attempt to take into consideration the ultimate impact of Florence's designation as a metropolitan city. These issues, particularly the pressing questions related to traffic control, were largely left to the city's latest "*mago*" (wizard), the German planner Bernhard Winkler. Plans for the FIAT project were in the hands of the company's major architect-planner, Leon Krier. The Fondiaria project could expect similar autonomy. Vittorini had set out to provide a framework that would respect the uncertainties of politics and the realities of limited budgets. Even so, the plan's future was problematic.[30]

The great unanswered problem was the fate of the inner city. The Vittorini plan followed Detti in supporting movement of many city offices from the historic center to the northwest (Novoli or Castello). Detti had foreseen the replacement of these offices with a balance of tourist services and homes. Thirty years later, that concept had fallen by the wayside, the victim of the inflationary impact of tourism. Moving city and state offices and education facilities from the center opened the way for a greater expansion of tourist activities and supporting service sector businesses, above all, banks. The center was already denuded of artisans, who had fled its skyrocketing rents. Moving government out would further fence off the inhabitants of Florence from the city's daily average of 12,000 visitors.

"What kind of urban planning is that?" demanded an anguished Fioretta Mazzei, a former council member.[31]

The answer that most city government members gave was that they were responding to political reality. Youthful reformist councilman Giacomo Billi commented that the city supported FIAT-Fondiaria because only private capital could spark growth in a city that was rapidly losing its population. The companies had money; the city had control of the land. It exchanged part of its control for cash infusions into its economy. Assessor Pier Luigi Ballini was equally frank. The tourist industry was lagging. The city had to find ways to reanimate it or face major losses in revenue. This meant widening the Peretola airport runway to attract more and larger planes. It meant concessions to the Aga Khan, who claimed to be taking a financial bath by putting his airline's headquarters in the city. It also meant devising new schemes to further swell the number of tourists daily visiting the city. Too much of Florence's economy depended on tourism to place any barriers to its continued expansion.[32]

PAINTING THE CITY BLUE

Traffic patterns in Florence change with remarkable speed, Ballini explained, unable to contain a smile. Sometimes streets that are one-way north suddenly become one-way south. "It all depends on whether we use an English or German planner. One drives on the right and the other on the left side. So they organize the flow in different directions."[33] The Morales junta chose a German whose responsibilities included not only arranging traffic flow but reorganizing the bus services, enlarging the ZtL, mapping out a parking system, and protecting the environment of the city. The Winkler plan for traffic was as important as the Vittorini PRG proposal in determining Florence's future viability.

The magician would be working with a weak hand. His selection was made at the insistence of the soon-to-evaporate Socialist Party. Moreover, the city had limited control over its traffic and environmentally related problems. Existing Italian law on environmental protection lacked enforcement provisions. Florence could not pay for a large-scale replacement of its primary pollution producer, ATAF's buses, or build transportation alternatives. The Vittorini PRG's plans for a subway were dropped in late 1992 after the city computed the cost. Efforts to limit access by car to the old city met with limited success. Florentines still preferred to put their famed ingenuity to work dodging rules and finding scarce parking rather than in devising and using other means to enter the historic center. Serious smog problems forced the city to declare a state of emergency in December 1992 and again in early 1993, banning cars from the center for four days.[34]

After prolonged study, Winkler swung into action in January 1991. Aided by city officials, he conducted a survey of vehicular use in the old city. The ten-day survey, released in May of that year, showed that, on average, nearly 270,000 vehicles (85 percent cars) entered the city during the morning rush; approximately 278,000 vehicles (89 percent cars) fled at night. To reduce this crush, Winkler proposed to create attractive alternatives in the form of improved bus services, to offer parking around the periphery, and to block off enough of the city center to make traveling by car positively unappealing. The issue was not simply one of long delays but public health. The right of personal mobility had to be modified to respect the right to life. Added to this, of course, was the continuing damage that automobile pollution and vibrations were doing to Florence's antiquities.[35]

Further complicating Winkler's task was the evident difficulty of creating sensible traffic flow in a city with few large thoroughfares. Placing large sections of the city under traffic flow restrictions or closing off sectors of the historic center meant figuring out how to direct cars, buses, and trucks to their goals without increasing both delays and pollution. Electrified mass transit, whether in the form of a subway or trams, was years away. Florence had no existing rail rights of way on which to build. Everything would have to begin from scratch in a city where even minor construction created massive problems for commuters. The 1990 World Cup had revealed all the delays that a highly politicized public contracting system created.[36]

In October 1991 Winkler laid out his plans. The first stage would be an enlargement of *zone blu* to include parts of the *lungarni* together with the gradual replacement of inner-city buses with small electric units (minibuses) and the simultaneous reorganization of inner-city bus lines. Piazza Duomo would become a pedestrian-only zone. Over the longer run Winkler foresaw the extension of ZTL to the entire historic center, including the Oltrarno, with special zoning for the area around S. Maria Novella.[37]

The difficulty, Winkler acknowledged, was the degree of political support that he could round up. Traffic Alderman Paolo Cappelletti (PSI) enacted major parts of the Winkler plan by the end of October, turning the Duomo into a pedestrian island, limiting traffic around its periphery, and expanding *zone blu* to the *lungarni*. However, Cappelletti balked at extending ZTL to cover the entire old city. ATAF liked little in the Winkler proposal and prepared to fight.[38]

ATAF had its own plan, "Metrobus 2000," to counter Winkler's projects. Shortly after Winkler presented his proposals for reorganizing service to the historic center, ATAF's president, Felice Cecchi, launched a counterattack, calling for the reopening of the Piazza Duomo to bus traffic and for redesign of the No. 15 route within the old city. The bus service remained in chronic debt, but Cecchi had ambitious plans for reorganizing ATAF, controlling any future high-speed mass-transit service, creating links with public and private transportation companies in the Tuscan region, and loosening the commune's control over his agency. Exploiting prevailing public discontent with public services and making an interpretation of the intentions of Law 142/90 designed to appeal to the DC and PDS, Cecchi offered to attract private capital into partnership while avoiding the full-scale privatization of ATAF that was anathema to both Marxists and Catholics. Cecchi's distaste for direction from the city administration exploded over the Winkler plan. In a particularly intemperate letter to the city council, he claimed parity with Assessor Cappelletti in matters relating to ATAF routes and services. He then poured ridicule on both the assessor and Winkler for their stress on using smaller vehicles in the old city.[39]

Initially, Winkler and Cappelletti were able to carry the junta along with their proposals. ATAF's effort to reopen the Piazza Duomo was a poorly thought-out power play that could only bring the agency into public discredit. Polling data consistently showed that public approval of *zone blu* had grown with experience. Moreover, the transportation agency's political sally was launched after a winter and spring of alarming press reports over the dangerous effects of automobile pollution on public health. ATAF's counterattack collapsed, but Cappelletti and Winkler had lost political capital.[40]

Winkler, *L'Unita* commented in late April 1992, had a fairly easy time of it during his first three years as Florence's "wizard." The city was without ideas and surrendered itself to the judgment of the German expert, who wisely absented himself most of the time. Winkler's period of grace was over. The PDS paper charged that the absentee planner had become the convenient tool of a faction within the junta led by Cappelletti. "Everyone cites Winkler, but there's no trace of the professor," the paper continued, calling for the city council to resume its legal role of "disciplining" the magician's proposals.[41]

On April 30, Winkler made a disastrous public appearance before Lapo Pistelli's transportation committee. The professor appeared overwilling to make concessions and gave imprecise answers. Winkler, *La Citta* acidly commented, appeared more the sorcerer's apprentice than the expert, implying that Cappelletti was the real author of his plans.[42]

At the April 30 hearings and in subsequent press interviews, Pistelli leveled a devastating attack on both Cappelletti and Winkler. According to Pistelli, Winkler's decision to limit his initial proposals to the inner city had the effect of impeding work on the PRG since planners wanted to know what the traffic flow would be before locating specific projects. Pistelli was very upset by the German professor's decision to carry out the majority of his work in Munich. His infrequent visits to Florence were dramatic, the Catholic reformer charged, and politically well timed but left the professor cut off from the realities of Florentine life. The result, Pistelli concluded, was a traffic plan that failed to deal with Florence's problems.[43]

Morales, who appeared to see *zone blu* as the most effective way to nudge traffic out of the center at low political risk, sensed that the prevailing political winds no longer favored Cappelletti and his *mago* and subtly abandoned them and their plans. In December 1992, the mayor removed restrictions on traffic that had been triggered by another bad bout of pollution. He then convoked Cappelletti and Cecchi to his office to announce that the city would commit the majority of its traffic resources to preventing a recurrence of these problems, immediately reorganizing its bus services. The president of ATAF was to take the lead in developing a plan.[44]

Two months later the Morales junta rewrote Cappelletti's plan for a city subway system, substituting a project for energy-efficient trams always favored by
Cecchi. The assessor of traffic resigned immediately. Winkler was quietly sent
packing.[45]

WAITING FOR GODOT

By the spring of 1993, Italy was deep in the crisis of its political class. Its
traditional governing parties were dissolving with amazing rapidity. Public spending was drying up as the national government, led by technocrat Carlo Azeglio
Ciampi, attacked a major source of party wealth and corruption. The Cappelletti–
Winkler initiative with its plans for heavy investment in new infrastructure and
rolling stock was partially a victim of changing national political priorities. Cappelletti's effort to end-run the democratic process with the aid of a prestigious
international expert enjoyed a fairly long run of success and produced some
notable results. The part of the old city breathing cleaner air was notably increased. ATAF was pushed toward the acquisition of vehicles that would create
fewer pollutants. The aging buildings of the center would suffer less seismically
caused structural damage from smaller buses.

In addition to furthering the city's commitment to a cleaner environment, the
Morales junta concluded basic agreements with both FIAT and Fondiaria that
set the seal on urban development for the next decade. These deals recognized
the weakness of the Italian state and economy. The city would exercise controls
over the expansion process, but private capital would set its pace and draw the
profits from its investment. The social welfare experiment begun in 1945–1946
had run its course. The Italian state had overspent; the corruption and arrogance
of its parties destroyed the credibility of the state as a principal actor; the parties
that had supported and nurtured the state-led economy had crumbled.

Sitting amid the ruins of the party-state of the "First Republic," one could
describe both the causes and the extent of the collapse. What sort of replacement
system Italy needed was a good deal less clear. New political leaders were ready
with a variety of plans for rebuilding the state. Umberto Bossi, the raucous tribune
of the Lega Nord, demanded either the outright partition of the nation into three
republics or, at the minimum, the creation of a "federal" system that would
empower the regions at the expense of the national government and would favor
the rich and economically advanced north at the expense of a south that in
Bossi's mythology was the root of all national evils. Mario Segni, the conservative
political reformer, offered a quick fix in the form of electoral reforms that would
create a bipolar political system. Segni's emphasis on political engineering
blithely ignored many of the nation's deep-rooted economic and social problems.
The old parties eagerly leaped on the electoral reform bandwagon, hoping to find
salvation in rigging a new voting system.[46]

Meanwhile, the judicial process continued inexorably to sweep away the old
leaders and old parties. The Tuscan regional government collapsed in the spring

of 1993 in the wake of investigations of the Fiditoscani, the regional investment agency. The Christian Democrats went to war with themselves over internal reform. Investigation centering on the dam at Bilancino drove the last nail into the political coffin of the DC's once-powerful political secretary, Arnoldo Forlani.[47]

In mid-1993, Italy entered a new phase of its postwar political development. Having shed its old parties and leaders, it remained imprisoned in the constitution of 1946 and lacked a consensus for changing the basic document. Calls for a new constituent assembly arose regularly and were regularly ignored. Electoral engineering, rather than basic reform, was the rallying cry of elites who wanted a painless exit from the nation's profound social and political problems. While its discredited governing parties worked out a new law, the Italian electorate searched for a leader who offered a positive vision of the future for a society awash with corruption and economic failure. The left optimistically awaited its moment to lead. The right desperately searched for a knight to save it from the dragon of "Communism."

NOTES

1. *La Nazione*, June 25, 1993.

2. *L'Unita*, July 7, 17, 19, 1990; Francesco Indovina, ed., *La citta occasionale* (Milan, 1993), p. 90.

3. Interviews with Ennio Di Nolfo, May 17, 1993, and Pier Luigi Ballini, May 16–17, 1993; *L'Unita*, July 7, 1990.

4. *L'Unita*, September 7, 12, 15, October 26, 27, November 4, December 21, 1990; Indovina, *La citta occasionale*, p. 67.

5. *La Nazione*, April 5, 8, 23, May 26, July 1, 16, 1991; *La Gazzetta*, April 2, 8, May 13, 14, 26, July 17, 1991.

6. *La Nazione*, September 23, 26, 1991.

7. *La Repubblica*, June 25, 1991.

8. *La Repubblica*, October 15, 19, 1991.

9. Martin Bull, "Whatever Happened to Italian Communism?" *West European Politics* 14 (October 1991); Mark Gilbert, *The Italian Revolution* (Boulder, CO, 1995), ch. 5; cf. David Kertzer, *Politics and Symbols* (New Haven, CT, 1996).

10. *La Repubblica*, February 13, July 13, 1991; *La Gazzetta*, June 27, 1991.

11. *La Repubblica*, March 1, September 10, 1991; *La Nazione*, July 21, 1991; *La Gazzetta*, July 13, 1991.

12. Ballini interview, March 8, 1993.

13. *La Nazione*, March 27, 1992; *Panorama*, October 11, 1992.

14. *L'Unita*, June 21, 1992; Ballini interview, May 16, 1993.

15. *L'Unita*, June 23, 1992; *La Repubblica*, May 5, 1993.

16. *L'Unita*, October 15, 27, 1992; January 31, February 14, 1993; *La Repubblica*, May 5, 25, 1993; *La Nazione*, May 14, 1993.

17. Francesco Indovina, ed., *Citta fine millenio* (Milan, 1990), pp. 104–22; Indovina, ed., *La citta occasionale*, pp. 26, 82.

18. Marco Massa, ed., *Firenze* (Milan, 1988), pp. 64–65; Indovina, ed., *La citta occasionale*, pp. 55–56, 65.

19. *La Repubblica*, September 17, December 31, 1991; *La Gazzetta*, September 17, 1991; *La Nazione*, January 17, 1991.

20. *La Repubblica*, January 16, 17, April 17–18, 1991; *La Nazione*, April 2, July 2–3, 1991; *La Gazzetta*, May 24, 1991.

21. G. Speranza and L. Tramontano, *L'ordinamento delle autonomie locali* (Naples, 1992).

22. *La Nazione*, February 19, 1991.

23. *La Repubblica*, January 10, 1991; *La Nazione*, January 10, February 19, 1991.

24. *La Nazione*, March 1, 1991; *La Repubblica*, March 1, 1991.

25. *La Nazione*, February 20–21, March 7, April 7, July 10, 12, 21, 1991; *La Repubblica*, April 16, August 10, October 29, 1991.

26. Iacopo Detti interview, May 18, 1993; *La Gazzetta*, March 7, 1991.

27. *La Repubblica*, June 12, 1992.

28. *L'Unita*, September 25, October 3, November 7, 25, December 1, 10, 1992; *La Repubblica*, November 17, 1991.

29. Francesco Papafava, ed., *Firenze: Introduzione* (Florence, 1993), pp. 37–52.

30. *La Repubblica*, April 29, 1993; *L'Unita*, January 22, 1993.

31. Fioretta Mazzei interview, Florence, May 19, 1993; J. Detti interview; Indovina, *La citta occasionale*, pp. 53–54; Massa, *Firenze*, pp. 133, 139–141.

32. Giacomo Billi interview, Washington, DC, April 23, 1992; Ballini interview, May 16–17, 1993; Carlo Sorrentino, *Firenze* (Rome, 1990), p. 21.

33. Ballini interview, March 8, 1993.

34. *L'Unita*, February 21, 1991; October 15, December 12, 27, 1992; January 14, 1993; *La Repubblica*, May 15, October 3, 1991.

35. *La Nazione*, May 12, 1991; *L'Unita*, January 31, 1991.

36. *L'Unita*, January 31, 1991; statement by Lapo Pistelli, July 12, 1991; CTDP, Dossiers, Traffic; parcheggio.

37. *La Repubblica*, October 30, 1991.

38. *La Repubblica*, November 20, 1991; "Promemoria Piano Winkler," [1992]; CDPT, Dossier, Trasporti.

39. Cecchi's comments, January 1992, April 29, 1992, letter to the city council are in CDPT, Dossier, Trasporti.

40. *La Repubblica*, January 12, March 18, April 24, 1992; *La Nazione*, February 8, March 18, April 22, 1992; *La Gazzetta*, March 9, 1992. *L'Unita*, March 10, April 29, 1992.

41. *L'Unita*, April 29, 1992.

42. *La Citta*, May 1, 1992.

43. *La Repubblica*, May 1, 1992.

44. *L'Unita*, December 24, 1992.

45. *L'Unita*, February 9, 10, 12, 1992; Comune di Firenze, "Rete di metropolitana leggera," May 1992, CDPT, Dossier, Trasporti.

46. *La Nazione*, May 28, 1993.

47. *La Repubblica*, April 20, May 11, 20, 27, 1993.

Chapter 14

Conclusion: Penelope's Spindle

Local Government in Italy is a great paradox. In no European national state are the local differences in language, cultural traditions and economic conditions so great as they are in Italy. At the same time the system of government is unquestionably the most highly centralized and bureaucratized of any European state, designed to give the national government control over even the most minute aspects of local affairs. Local government in Italy has been a matter of great discontent since the very beginnings of the present national state and is destined to be a matter of primary importance in the impending political reconstruction of Italy.

Department of State, 1944 report

Achille Occhetto's June 26, 1989, telephone call to the Communist Party's local leadership opposing the FIAT-Fondiaria project ruptured decades of accord among Florence's major parties on the need for the city to follow a strategy of growth. Torn between its Marxist ideology and its pragmatic need to win elections, the PCI had always been the most ambivalent supporter of the growth strategy. Its successor, the PDS, emerged from the tempest that swept away its main competitors as Italy's largest party and strongest supporter of careful management of existing resources. Gradually, patiently, the PDS knitted together a coalition of Marxists, environmentalists, survivors of the Socialist debacle, and moderate reformers who wanted to halt the cycle of expansion that had changed the face of Florence after World War II. In 1995 and 1999, this coalition won city elections. Whether it could save a divided city from the worst excesses of a half-century of rampant development remains an unanswered question.[1]

A NATION DIVIDED

By 1995 the public outrage that gave such a powerful initial push toward major reform of the Italian state was notably diminished. The heroes of the first stage of the overthrow of the old regime, the magistrates, repeatedly overstepped the bounds of judicial restraint, creating widening cynicism about their objectives. Further, as the investigations expanded, average Italians started to ask whether their concrete interests might be damaged. Local and national elections in 1993 and 1994 channeled off a great deal of the enthusiasm for new faces and gave legitimacy to a new political leadership. In the spring of 1994, Italians placed their future in the hands of a "new man," television mogul Silvio Berlusconi, and a group of parties untouched by the scandals of the old regime, only to see these new leaders fall back into the worst practices of the old regime. The voters' choice fell on a three-party coalition of center right parties, campaigning as the "Freedom" and "Good Government" poles. Umberto Bossi, leader of the anti-Rome Lega Nord, one of the victor parties, celebrated his success by openly maneuvering for choice ministerial posts in the new cabinet. Berlusconi, the telegenic prime minister and leader of the Forza Italia movement, seized control of the public television networks, gaining a near monopoly over the primary source of public information, while blithely ignoring conflict-of-interest issues. He then attempted to quash ongoing judicial investigations of his business empire under a rather transparent guise of protecting civil liberties. The third coalition partner, Gianfranco Fini, concentrated on giving his "post-Fascist" party, the Alleanza nazionale, a new public image but stumbled over his own statements about the historical roles of Mussolini and Fascism. Within months the partners in this uneasy coalition were at each other's throats, and in a replay of the political practices of the "First" Republic, Bossi overthrew Berlusconi in December 1994.

The forces favoring limited reform, whose champion was the Christian Democratic president of the republic, Luigi Oscar Scalfaro, moved into the void created by Berlusconi's debacle. A "presidential" government, enjoying the support of the recently defeated left and Bossi's *Lega* and staffed by a group of conservative "technicians" led by Berlusconi's former treasury minister, Umberto Dini, governed Italy for the next sixteen months. Following in the steps of two previous "technical" governments, the Dini cabinet took some essential and politically difficult decisions on economic retrenchment and pension reform.

National elections in April 1996 revealed an Italy profoundly divided over the issues of political reform. Neither the victorious coalition of the center left nor the narrowly defeated center right of Berlusconi and Fini possessed any internal accord on the way to remake the Italian state. Bossi offered only his customary fuzzy, contradictory, and demagogic remedies for the ills of the Italian state. Ill-suited for the hard task of governing, this raucous podium-pounder soon committed his movement to the path of "secession," disregarding the evidence that the overwhelming majority of the citizens of the north (Padania to Bossi) had no intention of following him and the dangers to public order that his actions created. A series of electoral setbacks eventually led him to reverse course, reembrace "federalism," and reknit his alliance with Berlusconi.

A CITY DIVIDED

The political deadlock was equally great at the local level. At the beginning of the *tangentopoli* ("bribe city") scandal, reformers pushed through a basic change in the administration of local government: direct election of mayors. Concentration on electoral reforms spoke volumes about the mind-set of the intellectuals who spearheaded reform efforts in 1992–1993. They wanted to avoid involving the Italian public in hard and divisive decisions about the nature of their state by facilitating a change in the governing class. Ample polling data demonstrated that Italians yearned for major constitutional change in the spring of 1993. The reformers offered largely symbolic ones and eschewed serious systemic overhaul.

Timid reformism meant minimal progress in dealing with the root problems of the Italian constitution. In the case of local government, direct election of mayors gave greater prominence to the activities of the mayors of major cities like Milan, Naples, Rome, and Palermo, as well as historic curiosities like Venice. The first citizens of Italy's cities had a louder voice in the political debate and used it. A "party of the mayors" emerged, making frequent appearances in Rome's piazzas and in the press. A number of these mayors, most notably, Naples' Antonio Bassolino, made headlines with their aggressive and at least partially successful attacks on the ills that plagued their cities. However, they left unresolved the basic problem of distribution of power between central government and localities, especially the question of taxation authority. The *sindaci* failed to press the case for greater independent taxing power, evidently preferring to demand a larger share of Rome's resources rather than to confront the political risks of assuming more extensive responsibility for both taxing and spending decisions.[2]

Meanwhile, the decline of Italy's cities continued. "Once Italian cities were very beautiful," columnist Francesco Alberone lamented, "not only the famous [ones] . . . also the smallest centers." The postwar economic expansion had put an end to that: "A sea of apartment buildings, offices, factories, shopping centers have made our cities as ugly as in the rest of the world." Responsibility, Alberone concluded, rested squarely on Italians:

Postwar Italy, the Italy we see, has been built by Italians. Planners, engineers, architects who were trained in our schools and our universities. It has been commissioned by private citizens [and] by democratically elected politicians, and it has been supervised by building commissions [and] the Superintendent of Fine Arts.[3]

Nowhere was the decline more evident or the paralysis of leadership more clear than in Florence. Gianni Conti, a spokesman for pro-growth forces in the city, analyzed the paralysis of urban politics, laying blame on anti-growth forces:

There are those who work by day to build the city of the future. And there are those who work by night to undo it all. It's a kind of Penelope's spindle. . . . [Florentines] don't do anything to protect the values of the Renaissance . . . [or] give a European and modern character to the city.[4]

Lagorio expressed puzzlement at the vehemence with which the opponents of growth had fought efforts to build a "new Florence." Noting that many were students of Edoardo Detti, he explained in injured tones that he and other Florentine politicians had simply tried to carry out Detti's vision with the modifications imposed by changing times and the different sociopolitical makeup of the city.[5]

Florence's (and Italy's) urban woes were rooted in the nation's division into hostile ideological camps that canceled out each other's major initiatives. These camps cut across party lines. The continuing stalemate over urban policy favored private developers who exploited their own political ties to ignore the law and create "new" cities on the outskirts of medieval towns. The continuing attraction of "modernity," defined in terms of bigger buildings, wider roads, and more personal conveniences such as the automobile, weakened the ability of urban planners to offer long-term solutions to mushrooming city ills. The planners, who normally came from the left, offered tightly constructed and logically exclusive solutions that were at once too utopian and too restrictive of personal liberty to appeal to voters. Compromise rarely came easily to 1960s Marxist visionaries or 1990s "Greens."

Both the urban planners and the Greens reflected nagging concerns that many Italians nurtured about the price of "modernity." While reluctant to abandon any of the freedom that prosperity granted them, many Italians were awake to the degradation that their personal independence, perhaps best symbolized in the automobile, had created. The majority were willing to accept limits on their freedoms if government applied them with equity and if they produced positive environmental benefits. Public support for ideas like ZTL and pedestrian-only zones was consistently high. Proposals for restrictions on tourists also won support. From 1989 on, the PDS in coalition with a number of small parties actively sought to capitalize on these concerns. As the PDS abandoned its Marxist ideology and moved to the center, it placed greater emphasis on careful management of existing patrimonies while deferring "big" projects.

In the spring of 1995 Florentines went to the polls to directly elect a mayor. Mayor Morales broke with the remnants of the Socialist Party to present himself as the candidate with a proven vision of private sector-driven, government-regulated expansion. He offered an impressive record of activities designed to foster that growth: agreements with FIAT and Fondiaria, laws to extend the airport's runway for use by larger jet aircraft, enactment of a new PRG, expansion of ZTL, an accord on a high-speed railroad, and completion of two parking garages. The mayor made the completion of a subway system the centerpiece of his campaign platform, turning the mayoral elections into a referendum on growth. Powerful local economic interests lined up behind him. Meridiana Airways' owner, the Aga Khan, supported the mayor's reelection. Berlusconi's Forza Italia announced that it would back his bid, and the former prime minister appeared at one of Morales' rallies to endorse the mayor and play on a favorite common theme: the peril to Florence and Italy posed by the "Communists" of the PDS.[6]

In April 1995, Mario Primicerio, La Pira's former aide, the candidate of a coalition stretching from the PDS to the heirs of the DC, won easily, capturing 59.9 percent of the popular vote. Organization, Morales felt, decided the outcome of the election. However, the mayor's decision to turn the election into a referendum on growth was equally significant. Signs of public exhaustion with the side effects of growth were manifest. In January 1995, Cardinal Piovanelli publicly complained that the glut of tourists was sinking the city and suggested limiting the number permitted to enter its churches and museums. A year later the Primicerio junta imposed a special tax on tour buses seeking to park in the city and limited their number to 150 a day. In a separate initiative supported by the new junta, hotel owners attempted to reduce spring scholastic tours by offering discounts on lodgings during the winter months.[7]

Public impatience with costs of growth was equally visible in a growing irritation at the *roma* (gypsies) and other vagrants whose criminal activities were no longer restricted primarily to tourists. Primicerio championed both a crackdown on crime and efforts to "integrate" the *roma* and others into Florentine life. In practice, efforts to integrate the "extracommunitarians" into Florentine social structures foundered on public hostility and continuing migrant misdeeds.[8]

Doubts about continuing strategies to foster growth were fed by aggressive reporting on cozy city government–business alliances. Many important local businesses were not paying their water bills. The city turned an apparent blind eye and simultaneously sold off various pieces of prime real estate to meet its debts. La Fondiaria, whose building projects were supposed to bring more employment, announced that it would be laying off workers.[9]

Florence's nation-leading monthly inflation was a direct result of the city's most important "growth" industry, tourism. Its citizens' tax bill continued to rise inexorably as the state and city reached into their pockets to pay for a tourist-friendly environment. Environmental degradation and crime grew, particularly in zones inhabited by Florentines. The progressive hollowing out of the city population, a development directly linked to growth strategies, meant that Florence had Italy's third largest population of people over sixty-five years of age. Nearly one in four Florentines had passed this important social and economic threshold.[10]

Florence was a city in decline: abandoned by its working-age population, overrun by tourists, short of cash, unable to deliver adequate services to its remaining inhabitants, and quickly running out of options for dealing with these serious problems. After forty-five years of a mixture of unrestrained and semicontrolled growth, Florence was traveling the path already trod by Venice, albeit in a slower and less dramatic way. The city center remained beautiful, and Florence's principal monuments seemed to be surviving the worst effects of pollution. The great art collections housed in its museums were intact. The ongoing closure of the city to motor vehicles and lack of major industries prevented the wholesale ecological disaster that visited postwar Venice. The population decline might level off, and demographic realities would eventually reduce an over age population. The tourists would still come in millions to enrich Florentine businesspeople. However, the city was paying a high price for this prosperity. It had been unable to find a political solution to its problems of growth and preservation. As a result, Florence had become two cities whose tenuous link was the daily passage of a part of its working force from the outer community into the inner city. The old city was a museum. The ring of development surrounding the city center, particularly the northwest corridor, was an increasingly degraded living zone, offering few attractions to its inhabitants. Its fate was decoupled from that of "old" Florence. A government situated in the historic center had failed conspicuously either to preserve the old or to carefully build the new. Neither the region nor the national state was in a position to provide meaningful aid to Florence, and past experience suggested that neither had the vision to deal effectively with the difficult problems that Florence offered. The task facing reformers was indeed daunting.[11]

NOTES

1. Giorgio Morales, *L'assedio de Firenze* (Firenze, 1995), pp. 11–16; Giorgio Morales interview, Florence, October 4, 1995; Di Nolfo interviews, Florence, April 8, May 17, 1993; Pier Luigi Ballini interviews, Florence, March 8, May 16, May 17, 1993; Conti interview, Florence, May 26, 1993; Leilo Lagorio interview, Florence, October 4, 1995.

2. *Corriere della Sera*, November 18, 1995; Valdo Spini interview, Rome, September 26, 1995; *Unita*, September 29, 1995; *La Repubblica*, September 30, 1995.

3. *Corriere della Sera*, July 10, 1995.

4. Conti interview.

5. Lagorio interview.

6. *La Nazione*, March 1, April 19, 21, 1995; Morales interview; *Corriere della Sera*, March 28, 1995; Morales, *Assedio*, pp. 103–24.

7. Morales interview; *La Nazione*, January 31, 1995; *Corriere della Sera*, August 30, 1995, April 4, 1996; *International Herald Tribune*, May 30, 1996; *La Repubblica*, October 4, 1995.

8. *La Nazione*, September 6, 1994; *La Repubblica*, October 3, 4, 6, 1995; *Washington Post*, October 15, 1995.

9. *La Nazione*, September 29, 1994, March 2, April 21, 1995.

10. *La Nazione*, January 25, 1995; *La Mattina*, September 29, 1995; *Corriere della Sera*, June 17, 1995; *La Repubblica*, October 4, 1995.

11. Michael Spector, "A Sinking Feeling," *New Yorker*, July 22, 1999; "La nueva Venecia?" *El Pais* Digital (Madrid), July 5, 1999.

Bibliography

ARCHIVES

Archivio Centrale dello Stato, Rome
     Records of the Presidenza del Consiglio dei ministri
     Records of the Ministero dell'Interno
     Records of the Ministero della Pubblica Istruzione
     Records of the Ministero del Tesoro
     Records of the Ministero dell'Industria e del Commercio
Archivio di Stato di Firenze
     Records of the Prefettura di Firenze
Archivio Storico del Comune di Firenze
     Atti del Consiglio
     Atti della Giunta
     Gabinetto del Sindaco
     Ufficio Legale
Centro Toscano di Documentazione Politica, Florence
     Subject Files (Dossier)
     Press Files (Stampa)
Fondazione Giorgio La Pira, Florence
     Archivio La Pira
Fondazione Pietro Nenni, Rome
     Archivio Nenni
Istituto Gramsci, Rome
     Archivio del Partito Comunista
       Records Pertaining to the Federazione Fiorentina
Istituto Storico della Resistenza in Toscana, Florence
     Carte E. Enriquez Agnolotti
     Fondo P. Calamandrei

Fondo Collini
Fondo Comitato Toscano di Liberazione Nazionale
Carte Fasola
Fondo F. Lombardi
Carte M. A. Martini
Fondo A. Medici-Tornaquinci
Fondo F. Rossi
Carte N. Traquandi
Library of Congress, Washington, DC
W. Averell Harriman Papers
Clare Boothe Luce Papers
Lyndon B. Johnson Presidential Library, Austin, TX
National Security File: Country File, Italy
Special Head of State Correspondence
National Archives of the United States, Washington, DC
General Records of the Department of State
Records of Department of State Diplomatic and Consular Posts
Records of the Allied Control Commission (Italy)
National Gallery of Art, Washington, DC
Papers of Frederic Hartt

OFFICIAL PUBLICATIONS

Archivio di Stato di Firenze. *L'archivio di stato di Firenze e gli archivi toscani dopo l'inondazione del 4 novembre 1966.* Florence, 1967.

Azienda Autonoma del Turismo di Firenze. *Turismo a Firenze.* Florence, 1972.

Comune di Firenze. *ATAF, Piano di sviluppo aziendale.* Florence, 1968.

———. *Attività di formazione professionale dell'amministrazione comunale.* Florence, 1987.

———. *Cascine.* Florence, 1992.

———. *La circolazione stradale di Firenze.* Florence, 1950.

———. *Decentramento e ricostruzione nell'amministrazione comunale.* 3 volumes. Florence, 1980–1981.

———. *L'esperienza dei consigli di quartiere a Firenze.* 2 volumes. Florence, 1981.

———. *Firenze/Bilancio '76.* Florence, 1976.

———. *Firenze: Consigli di quartiere.* Florence, 1976.

———. *Firenze per Giorgio La Pira.* Florence, 1978.

———. *Firenze nella vita e nell'opera, 1951–1956.* Florence, 1956.

———. *Firenze: Note di storia e di urbanistica.* Florence, 1977.

———. *Firenze: Rassegna del Comune, 1944–1951.* Florence, 1951.

———. *Firenze: Rassegna del Comune, 1951–1960.* Florence, 1960.

———. *Firenze: Rassegna del Comune, 1965–1968.* Florence, 1968.

———. *Firenze: Rassegna del Comune, 1975–1980.* Florence, 1980.

———. *L'inquinamento delle acque.* Florence, 1971.

———. *L'opera ritrovata.* Florence, 1984.

———. *Piano intercomunale fiorentino.* Florence, 1979.

———. *Progetto di massima per la ricostruzione del sistema del traffico nel centro storico.* Florence, 1967.

————. *Progetto urbanistico della mobilita di Firenze*. Florence, 1993.

————. *Proposta di legge speciale a favore di Firenze*. Florence, 1954.

————. *Proposta per un sistema integrato della infrastruttura di trasporto*. Florence, 1980.

————. *Rapporto sull'economia fiorentina e sull'occupazione*. Florence, 1989.

————. *Regolamento per il consiglio comunale*. Florence, 1989.

————. *Relazione sulla gestione Commissariale dal 31 ottobre 1974 al 25 luglio 1975*. Florence, 1975.

————. *Relazione sulla gestione Commissariale del Comune dal 29 aprile 1969 al 16 luglio 1970*. Florence, 1970.

————. *Relazione statistica per il piano intercomunale*. Florence, 1962.

————. *Statuto*. Florence, 1987.

————. *Studio per il riordino della circolazione e della sosta nel centro storico*. Florence, 1980.

————. *Tossicodipendenza*. Florence, 1990.

Comune di Firenze, Consiglio di quartiere No. 2. *L'Arno in restauro*. Florence, 1988.

Comune di Firenze and Provincia di Firenze. *Firenze 11 agosto 1944–1964*. Florence, 1964.

Consiglio Nazionale delle Ricerche. *Ricerche relative al recupero dei dipinti danneggiati dall'alluvione di Firenze nel 1966*. Rome, 1972.

Ferrovie dello Stato. *Programma direttiva per l'area fiorentina*. Rome, 1992.

Ferrovie dello Stato di Firenze. *Ricostruzione di linee ed impianti ferroviari eseguiti dalla sezione lavori di Firenze dalla Liberazione in tutto il 1947*. Florence, 1948.

Istituto autonomo per le case popolari della provincia di Firenze. *Bilancio consultativo dell'esercizio*. Florence, 1969.

Ministero dell'Interno, *Le leggi elettorali comunale e provinciale*. Florence, 1954.

Partito Comunista Italiano, Federazione Fiorentina. *Resoconto dell'VIII Congresso provinciale*. Florence, 1954.

Sovrintendenza alle gallerie di Firenze. *Firenze restaurata*. Florence, 1972.

PUBLISHED DOCUMENTARY COLLECTIONS

Absalom, Roger, ed. *Gli alleati e la ricostruzione in Toscana*. 2 volumes. Florence, 1988.

Aiazzi, Giuseppe, ed. *Narrazioni istoriche delle piu considerevoli inondazioni dall'Arno*. Verona, 1967.

Amministrazione provinciale di Firenze. *Mario Fabiani*. Florence, 1975.

Andreotti, Giulio. *Diari, 1976–1979*. Milan, 1981.

Batelli, Giuseppe, ed. *Lorenzo Milani alla mamma*. Genoa, 1990.

Berlinguer, Giovanni. *Dieci anni dopo*. Bari, 1978.

Biocca, Dario, ed. *A Matter of Passion*. Berkeley, 1989.

Boggiano, Augusto, ed. *Firenze: La questione urbanistica*. Florence, 1982.

Calamandrei, Franco. *La vita indivisibile*. Ed. R. Bilenchi. Rome, 1984.

Calamandrei, Piero. *Diari, 1939–1945*. 2 volumes. Florence, 1982.

————. *Lettere, 1916–1956*. Florence, 1968.

————. *Scritti e discorsi politici*. 2 volumes. Florence, 1966.

————. *Uomini e citta della resistenza*. Bari, 1977.

Casoni, Giovanni. *Diari fiorentino, giugno–agosto 1944*. Florence, 1946.

Codignola, Tristano. *Scritti politici, 1943–1981*. 2 volumes. Florence, 1987.

Collotti, Enzo, ed. *Archivio Pietro Secchia, 1945–1973*. Milan, 1979.

Collotti, Enzo, et al., eds. *Ferruccio Parri. Scritti*. Milan, 1976.

Colombo, Furio, ed. *In Italy*. New York, 1981.

Damiliano, Andrea, ed. *Atti e documenti della Democrazia Cristiana*. 2 volumes. Rome, 1968–1969.

De Gasperi, Alcide. *Lettere al presidente*. Ed. C. Belli. Milan, 1964.

De Gasperi, Maria Romana. *De Gasperi scrive*. 2 volumes. Brescia, 1974.

De Luna, Giovanni, Piero Camilla, and Stefano Vitali, eds. *Le formazioni GL nella Resistenza*. Milan, 1985.

De Siervo, Ugo, Gianni Giovannoni, and Giorgio Giovannoni, eds. *Giorgio La Pira Sindaco*. 3 volumes. Florence, 1988–1989.

Di Capua, Giovanni. *Un anno caldo*. Rome, 1970.

———. *I professorini alla costituente*. Rome, 1989.

———. *Verifica della repubblica*. Rome, 1972.

Favilli, Giovanni. *Prima linea Firenze*. Milan, 1975.

Galloni, Giovanni, ed. *Antologia di Iniziativa*. Rome, 1973.

———. *Una proposta culturale della Democrazia Cristiana*. Rome, 1976.

Glisenti, M., and Leopoldo Elia, eds. *Cronache sociali*. 2 volumes. S. Giovanni Valdarno, 1962.

Gonella, Guido. *Cinque anni al Ministero della pubblica istruzione*. Volume 3: *Arte, cultura, storia*. Rome, 1982.

Greppi, Luciano, ed. *Il compromesso storico*. Rome, 1977.

Gronchi, Giovanni. *Una politica nuova*. Rome, 1955.

———. *Una politica sociale*. Bologna, 1962.

———. *Per la storia della Democrazia Cristiana*. Bologna, 1962.

Jemolo, Arturo Carlo. *Anni di prova*. Vicenza, 1969.

———. *Italia tormentata, 1946–1951*. Bari, 1951.

———. *Questa repubblica*. Florence, 1981.

La Pira, Giorgio. *Lettere a casa*. Milan, 1981.

———. *Lettere a Carmelo*. Milan, 1985.

———. *Lettere alle claustrali*. Milan, 1978.

———. *Lettere a Salvatore Pugliatti, 1920–1939*. Rome, 1980.

Libro Bianco sulle Officine Galileo. Florence, 1959.

Martinelli, Renzo. *Il fronte interno a Firenze*. Florence, 1989.

Masini, Pier Carlo, and Stefano Merli, eds. *Il socialismo al bivio*. Milan, 1990.

Merli, Luca [Giovanni Di Capua], ed. *Antologia della Base*. Rome, 1971.

———. *Antologia di Politica*. 4 volumes. Rome, 1973.

———. *Antologia di San Marco*. Rome, 1972.

Moro, Aldo. *Al di la della politica e altri scritti*. Rome, 1982.

Mortimer, Raymond, ed. *The Passionate Sightseer*. New York, 1988.

Nenni, Pietro. *Gli anni del Centro sinistra. Diari, 1957–1966*. Milan, 1982.

———. *La battaglia socialista per la svolta a sinistra nella terza legislatura*. Milan, 1963.

———. *I conti con la storia. Diari, 1967–1971*. Milan, 1983.

———. *Tempo di guerra fredda. Diari, 1943–1956*. Milan, 1981.

Pasolini, Pier Paolo. *Scritti corsari*, Milan, 1990.

Piccioni, Attilio. *Scritti e discorsi*. Florence, 1967.

Pistelli, Nicola. *Scritti politici*. Florence, 1967.

Quasimodo, Salvatore. *Salvatore Quasimodo-Giorgio La Pira Carteggio*. Milan, 1980.

Ragionieri, Ernesto and Luciano Gruppi, eds. *Palmiro Togliatti. Opere*. Volumes 5, 6. Rome, 1967–1984.

"Il Regno." *Isolotto*. Bologna, 1969.

Romita, Giuseppe. *Taccuini politici, 1947–1958*. Milan, 1980.

Salvemini, Gaetano. *Lettere dall'America*. 2 volumes. Bari, 1967–1968.

Santi, Piero. *Diario, 1943–1946*. Venice, 1950.

Saraceno, Pasquale. *Gli anni dello schema Vanoni*. Milan, 1982.

Secchia, Pietro, ed. *Il partito comunista italiano e la guerra di liberazione, 1943–1945*. Milan, 1973.

Secchia, Pietro, and Filippo Frassati, eds. *La resistenza e gli alleati*. Milan, 1962.

Spadolini, Giovanni. *Diario del dramma Moro*. Florence, 1978.

Spini, Valdo. *Intervista sul Buongoverno*. Ed. M. Griffo. Florence, 1994.

Sulzberger, Cyrus. *An Age of Mediocrity*. New York, 1973.

———. *The Last of the Giants*. New York, 1970.

———. *A Long Row of Candles*. New York, 1969.

Taylor, Katherine. *Diary of Florence in Flood*. New York, 1967.

Togliatti, Palmiro. *Togliatti e il Centro Sinistra*. 2 volumes. Florence, 1975.

U.S. Department of State. *Foreign Relations of the United States*. Volumes relating to Europe, 1952–1963. Washington, DC, 1977–1995.

Vanoni, Enzo. *La politica economica degli anni degasperiani*. Florence, 1977.

Villani, Giulio, ed. *Giorni di guerra*. Florence, 1992.

Zoli, Adone. *Discorsi parlamentari*. Rome, 1989.

MEMOIRS

Andreotti. Giulio. *Concerti a sei voci*. Rome, 1945.

Barbieri, Orazio. *La fede e la ragione*. Milan, 1982.

Baroni, Bruno. *Messaggio speciale—l'Arno scorre a Firenze*. Florence, 1981.

Bausi, Luciano. *Il giorno della piena*. Florence, 1987.

Chiesa, Mario. *Episodi della tragedia di Firenze*. Florence, 1967.

Comnene, Nicholas. *Firenze Citta aperta*. Florence, 1945.

Devoto, Giacomo. *La parentesi*. Florence, 1974.

Dini, Alfio. *La mia pietra*. 2 volumes. Livorno, 1985.

Gonella, Guido. *Con De Gasperi nella formazione della DC*. Rome, 1978.

Hartt, Frederic. *Florentine Art under Fire*. Princeton, NJ, 1949.

Kiel, Hanna. *La battagia delle colline*. Florence, 1986.

Lizzadri, Oreste. *Il socialismo italiano dal frontismo al Centro Sinistra*. Rome, 1969.

Mazzei, Fioretta. *La Pira. Cose viste e ascoltate*. Florence, 1981.

Morales, Giorgio. *L'assedio di Firenze*. Firenze, 1995.

Moretti, Mario. *Brigate Rosse*. Milan, 1994.

Occhetto, Achille. *A dieci anni dal '68*. Rome, 1978.

Pajetta, Giancarlo. *Il ragazzo rosso*. Milan, 1983.

Pertini, Sandro. *Quei giorni della liberazione di Firenze*. Florence, 1983.

Piccardi, Leopoldo. *A dieci anni dalla battaglia di Unita Popolare*. Rome, 1968.

Roasio, Antonio. *Figlio della classe operaia*. Milan, 1983.

Romita, Giuseppe. *Dalla monarchia all repubblica*. Milan, 1973.

Saccenti, Dino. *Memorie*. Florence, 1981.

Sullo, Fiorentino. *Lo scandalo urbanistico*. Florence, 1964.

Valenzi, Maurizio. *Sindaco a Napoli*. Rome, 1978.

Wollembourg, Leo. *Stars, Stripes and Italian Tricolor*. New York, 1990.
Zeffirelli, Franco. *Zeffirelli*. New York, 1986.
Zoli, Adone. *Acqua limacciosa sotto "Ponti sul Arno."* Florence, 1959.

INTERVIEWS

Giovannoni, Gianni and Giorgio, Florence, September 26, 1991; May 25, 1993.
Ballini, Pier Luigi, Florence, March 8, May 16, May 17, 1993.
Billi, Giacomo, Washington, DC, April 23, 1992; Florence, May 19, 1993.
Bausi, Luciano, Florence, June 1, 1993.
Conti, Gianni, Florence, May 26, 1993.
Detti, Iacopo, Florence, May 18, 1993.
Detti, Tommaso, Florence, May 14, 1993.
Di Nolfo, Ennio, Florence, April 8, May 17, 1993.
Gabbuggiani, Elio, Florence, May 31, 1993.
Lagorio, Lelio, Florence, October 4, 1995.
Mazzei, Fioretta, Florence, May 19, 1993.
Morales, Giorgio, Florence, October 4, 1995.
Mori, Giorgio, Florence, May 20, 1993.
Spini, Valdo, Rome, September 26, 1995.
Zoppi, Mariella, Florence, May 27, 1993.

BOOKS AND ARTICLES

Achilli, Michele. *Casa*. Padua, 1972.
Adams, John, and Paolo Barile. *The Government of Republican Italy*. Boston, 1961.
Adamson, Walter. *Avant-Garde Florence*. Cambridge, MA, 1993.
Allum, Percy. *Italy—Republic without Government?* New York, 1973.
———. *Politics and Society in Postwar Naples*. Cambridge, 1973.
Andreotti, Giulio. *De Gasperi e la ricostruzione*. Rome, 1974.
———. *De Gasperi visto da vicino*. Milan, 1986.
———. *La Democrazia Cristiana, 1943–1948*. Rome, 1975.
Antonielli, Antonello. *Giorgio La Pira*. Florence, 1987.
Ardigo, Achille. *Indicazioni e orientamenti sulle linee di ristrutturazione e di destinazione del quartieri di Santa Croce*. Florence, 1968.
Associazione per la difesa delle arti minori. *L'artigianato fiorentino del legno nel suo valore storico e nella sua attuale dimensione*. Florence, n.d.
Bacci, Carlo, Nicola Bovoli, Riccardo Mariani, and Giovanni Spinoso, eds. *Firenze, Piazza S Marco, 30 Gennaio 68*. Florence, 1968.
Bagatti, Fabrizio, Ottavio Cecchi, and Giorgio Van Stratten. *Autobiografia di un giornale*. Rome, 1989.
Baget Bozzo, Gianni. *L'elefante e la ballena*. Bologna, 1979.
———. *Il partito cristiano e l'apertura a sinistra*. Florence, 1977.
———. *Il partito cristiano al potere*. 2 volumes. Florence, 1974.
———. *Tesi sulla DC*. Bologna, 1980.
Baget Bozzo, Gianni, and Giovanni Tassani. *Aldo Moro*. Florence, 1983.
Baglioni, Francesco, and Piero Passeri. *I viali di Firenze*. Florence, 1974.

Bagnoli, Paolo. "I giorni di Firenze (politica e cultura dal 1944 al 1974)." *Citta e regione* 7 (April, June, August 1981), pp. 72–97, 211–42, 149–79.

Baldeschi, P., et al. *La citta fine millenio.* Milan, 1990.

Baldesi, Piero. *Un'esperienza liberale.* Livorno, 1985.

Ballini, Pier Luigi, Luigi Lotti, and Mario Rossi, eds. *La Toscana nel secondo dopoguerra.* Milan, 1991.

Bandettini, Pierfrancesco. *La popolazione della Toscana dal 1810 al 1959.* Florence, 1961.

Baraldi, Alessandro. *I contratti dei comuni.* Florence, 1964.

Barbieri, Orazio. *Giuseppe Rossi.* Milan, 1989.

———. *Ponti sull'Arno.* Rome, 1975.

———. *I sopravvissuti.* Milan, 1972.

Bardazzi, Silvestro. *Ipotesi di citta.* Florence, 1990.

Bargellini, Piero. *La splendida storia di Firenze.* 4 volumes. Florence, 1969.

Bargellini, Piero, et al. *Firenze domani.* Florence, 1967.

Bartole, S., et al. "Le regioni, le provincie, i comuni." In Giuseppe Branca, ed., *Commentario della Costituzione.* Bologna, 1985.

Bartolini, Roberto. *Florence and Its Hills.* Florence, 1953.

Bartolotti, Franco, and Alberto Tassinari. *Immigranti a Firenze.* Florence, 1992.

Barucci, Piero. *L'artigianato in Toscana.* Florence, 1969.

———. *Profilo economico della provincia di Firenze.* Florence, 1974.

Batisti, Gino. *Bilancio.* Florence, 1991.

Battaglia, Rosario, Michela D'Angelo, and Santi Fedele, eds. *Il Milazzismo.* Messina, 1980.

———. *Lo sviluppo economico in Toscana.* 2 volumes. Florence, 1975–1976.

Becattini, Giacomo, and Marcello Rossi, eds. *Firenze s'e desta.* Florence, 1988.

Bernabei, Domenico. *Giorgio La Pira.* Rome, 1985.

Biblioteca Civica di Schio. *Testimonianze nel centenario della nascita del cardinale Elia Dalla Costa.* Schio, 1972.

Biblioteca Nazionale Centrale di Firenze. *La Biblioteca Nazionale Centrale di Firenze dieci anni dopo.* Florence, 1976.

———. *Il quartiere di S. Croce e la Biblioteca Nazionale.* Florence, 1976.

Bilenchi, Romano. *Amici.* Torino, 1976.

———. *Cronache degli anni neri.* Rome, 1984.

Binazzi, Andrea, and Ivo Guasti, eds. *La Toscana nel regime Fascista, 1922–1939.* 2 volumes. Florence, 1971.

Bobbio, Norberto. *Ideological Profile of Twentieth Century Italy.* Trans. L. Cochrane. Princeton, NJ, 1995.

Boccia, Lionello. *Firenze, illuminazione pubblica e ambiente urbano.* Florence, 1983.

Boiardi, Franco. *Dossetti e la crisi dei cattolici italiani.* Florence, 1956.

Borghini, Fabrizio. *Il Circolo Vie Nuove di Firenze dal 1944 al 1974.* Florence, 1978.

Borgogni, Tiziana. "Cronistoria delle amministrazioni La Pira." *Testimonianza* 21 (May 1978), pp. 270–290.

———. "Il PSI a Firenze tra il 1956 e il 1960: alla ricerca di un'identita autonomista." *Citta e regione* 7 (December 1981), pp. 251–71.

Borselli, Giuliano. *Bargellini.* Florence, 1976.

Bortolotti, Lando. "Libri recenti sulla storia urbana di Firenze." *Storia urbana* (July 1977), pp. 247–263.

Braunfels, Wolfgang. *Urban Design in Western Europe.* Chicago, 1988.

Brucker, Gene. *Firenze 1138–1737.* Milan, 1983.

Bull, Martin. "Whatever Happened to Italian Communism?" *West European Politics* 14 (October 1991), pp. 96–120.

Calamandrei, Piero, ed. *Commentario sistematico alla Costituzione italiana*. 2 volumes. Florence, 1950.

Calandrone, Giacomo. *Gli anni di Scelba*. Milan, 1975.

Camerani, Sergio. *Firenze dopo Porta Pia*. Florence, 1977.

Canosa, Romano. *Storia della magistratura in Italia*. Milan, 1996.

Cantagalli, Roberto. *Storia del fascismo fiorentino, 1919–1925*. Florence, 1972.

Capitini Maccabruni, Nicla. "La municipalizzazione dei servizi a Firenze tra le fine dell'Ottocento e gli inizi del Novecento." *Storia urbana* 6 (July 1982), pp. 95–110.

Cappelletti, Ugo. *Firenze citta aperta*. Florence, 1975.

———. *Firenze in guerra*. Florence, 1984.

Il cardinale contestato. Rome, 1968.

Carlino, Salvatore. *Il senso della storia negli scritti di Giorgio la Pira*. Florence, 1990.

———. *Storia e testimonianza*. Florence, 1990.

Carocci, Guido. *Firenze scomparsa*. Rome, 1979.

———. *Il mercato vecchio di Firenze*. Florence, 1975.

Casani, Tito. *Elia Dalla Costa*. Florence, 1972.

Cassigoli, Renato, ed. *Il servizio del gas nella resistenza*. Florence, 1984.

Cassigoli, Renato, and Milly Mostardini. *Un'idea di citta per il duemila*. Florence, 1988.

Casula, Carlo. "Lo scioglimento della sinistra cristiana." In P. Scoppola and F. Traniello, eds., *I cattolici tra fascismo e democrazia* (Bologna, 1975), pp. 299–359.

Causarano, Pietro. *Una rilettura della vicenda Fiat-Fondiaria*. Florence, n.d.

Cavallina, Gianni. *Firenze universita e centro storico*. Florence, 1976.

Ceccarelli, Paolo. *Risanamento e speculazione nei centri storici*. Milan, 1974.

Cefaratti, Nicola, and Morello Malaspina. *1865–1985. Centoventi anni di trasporti pubblici a Firenze*. Cortona, 1987.

Centro Toscano di documentazione politica and Progetto arcobaleno. *Guida al volontariato fiorentino* Florence, 1992.

Centro Studi Nicola Pistelli. *Firenze uno e due*. Florence, 1967.

Chubb, Judith. *Power, Patronage and Poverty in Southern Italy*. New York, 1982.

Ciuffoletti, Zeffiro, Mario Rossi, and Angelo Varni. *La Camera del Lavoro di Firenze*. Naples, 1991.

Cochrane, Eric. *Florence in the Forgotten Centuries, 1527–1800*. Chicago, 1973.

Collini, Cesare. "Il Partito Comunista nella provincia di Firenze." Typescript, n.d.

Colombo, Furio, ed. *In Italy*. New York, 1981.

Comitato Comunale Democrazia Cristiana. *Confronto su Firenze*. Florence, 1980.

Comitato di quartiere di Brozzi and Centro Studi Nicola Pistelli. *Cittadini senza piano, piano senza cittadini*. Florence, 1971.

Comitato regionale Toscano per il trenteniale della resistenza. *Il clero toscano nella resistenza*. Florence, 1975.

Comunita di Isolotto. *Isolotto, 1954–1969*. Bari, 1969.

———. *Isolotto sotto processo*. Bari, 1971.

Consiglio, Alberto. *Il presidente Gronchi*. Genoa, 1962.

Conti, Giuseppe. *I tributi comunali e provinciali*. Florence, 1969.

Contini, Giovanni. *Memoria e storia*. Milan, 1985.

Convegno per il centenario della Casa Editrice Leo Olschki. Florence, 1987.

Coppetti, Marcello, and Franco Vaselli. *Giorgio La Pira—Agente d'Iddio*. Milan, 1978.

Corsani, Gabriele. "Giuseppe Poggi e il viale dei colli a Firenze." *Storia urbana* 16 (July 1992), pp. 37–58.

Cresti, Carlo. *Firenze, capitale mancata*. Milan, 1995.

Cresti, Carlo, and Silvano Fei. "Le vicende del 'risanamento' del Mercato Vecchio a Firenze." *Storia urbana* 1 (April 1977), pp. 99–127.

Cresti, Carlo, and Gabriella Orefice. "Caratteri sociali, situazioni ambientali e piani di risanamento del quartiere d'Oltrarno a Firenze." *Storia urbana* 2 (September 1978), pp. 181–207.

Daolio, Andreina, ed. *Le lotte per la casa in Italia*. Milan, 1974.

D'Avanzo, Bruno. *Tra dissenso e rivoluzione*. Bologna, 1971.

Degl'Innocenti, Maurizio. *Le sinistre e il governo locale in Europa*. Pisa, 1984.

Degl'Innocenti, Maurizio, and Stefano Caretti. *Il socialismo in Firenze e provincia*. Pisa, 1987.

De Grand, Alexander. *The Italian Left in the Twentieth Century*. Bloomington, IN, 1989.

De Luca, Giuseppe. "La costituzione della rete autostradale italiana. L'autostrada Firenze-Mare, 1927–1940." *Storia urbana* 16 (April 1992), pp. 71–126.

De Luna, Giovanni. *Storia del Partito d'Azione*. Milan, 1982.

Democrazia Cristiana. *Confronto su Firenze*. Florence, 1980.

Denzer, Peter. "Notes from a Flood Journal." *Yale Review* (Spring 1967), pp. 475–80.

Detti, Edoardo, with Tommaso Detti. *Florence That Was*. Florence, 1970.

Di Capua, Giovanni. *Le chiavi del Quirinale*. Milan, 1971.

———. *I professorini all costituente*. Rome, 1989.

———. *Nicola Pistelli*. Florence, 1969.

———. *Pistelli ci disse*. Rome, 1971.

———. *Processo a De Gasperi*. Rome, 1976.

Dickens, Charles. *Pictures from Italy*. London, 1989.

Dieci anni del piano regolatore di Roma. Rome, 1972.

Dieci anni dopo, 1945–1955. Bari, 1955.

Di Loreto, Pietro. *La difficile transizione*. Bologna, 1993.

Di Nolfo, Ennio. *Le paure e le speranze degli italiani*. Milan, 1986.

Di Scala, Spencer. *Renewing Italian Socialism*. New York, 1988.

Domenico, Roy P. "America, the Holy See and the War in Vietnam." In P. Kent and J. Pollard, eds., *Papal Diplomacy in the Modern Age* (Westport, CT, 1994), pp. 203–19.

Drake, Richard. *The Aldo Moro Murder Case*. Cambridge, MA, 1995.

———. *The Revolutionary Mystique and Terrorism in Contemporary Italy*. Bloomington, IN, 1989.

Duboy, Philippe, ed. *Edoardo Detti, 1913–1984: architetto e urbanista*. Milan, 1993.

Esposito, Rosario. *La massoneria e l'Italia*. Rome, 1979.

Facolta di architettura dell'Universita di Firenze. *Gli impianti sportivi nel comprensorio Firenze e Pistoia*. Florence, 1968.

Fanelli, Giovanni. *Firenze*. Bari, 1980.

Fanfani, Amintore. *Giorgio la Pira*. Milan, 1978.

Fasola, Cesare. *Le gallerie di Firenze e la guerra*. Florence, 1945.

Fei, Silvano. *Firenze 1881–1898*. Rome, 1977.

———. *Nascita e sviluppo di Firenze citta borghese*. Florence, 1973.

Filardi, Giacomo, and Alessandro Ammannati. *Universita da buttare*. Florence, 1974.

Fiori, Giuseppe. *Il Venditore*. Milan, 1995.

————. *Vita di Enrico Berlinguer*. Bari, 1989.

Firenze, materiale e colore. Florence, 1986.

Firenze '80. Florence, 1971.

Firenze. Studi e ricerche sul centro antico. Pisa, 1974.

Fondazione La Pira. *La Pira Oggi*. Florence, 1983.

Fondazione Olivetti. *La regione e il governo locale*. 3 volumes. Florence, 1965.

Forosetti, Piero, ed. *Vigili*. Florence, 1983.

Francovich, Carlo. *La resistenza a Firenze*. Florence, 1975.

————. *Storia della massoneria in Italia*. Florence, 1974.

Frankel, P. H. *Mattei*. London, 1966.

Frei, Matt. *Getting the Boot*. New York, 1995.

Fried, Robert. *The Italian Prefects*. New Haven, CT, 1963.

Frullini, Giovanni. *La liberazione di Firenze*. Milan, 1982.

Fubini, Alex. *Urbanistica in Italia*. Milan, 1979.

Galante Garrone, Alessandro. *Calamandrei*. Milan, 1987.

————. *L'Italia corrotta*. Rome, 1996.

Gallerano, Nicola, and Marcello Flores. *Sul PCI*. Bari, 1992.

Galli, Gianni. *Ha difeso Pignone*. Florence, 1984.

Galli, Giorgio. *Fanfani*. Milan, 1975.

————. *La sfida perduta*. Milan, 1976.

Galli, Giorgio, and Paolo Fracchi. *La sinistra democristiana*. Milan, 1962.

Gargani, Alessandro. *Ciao Firenze*. Florence, n.d.

Garosa, Guido. *L'Arno non gonfia d'acqua chiara*. Milan, 1967.

Giannetti, Vincenzo, and Rodolfo Vedovato. *S. Frediano*. Florence, 1986.

Giannuli, Aldo, ed. *La nuova legge per l'elezione dei sindaci*. Rome, 1993.

Gilbert, Mark. *The Italian Revolution*. Boulder, CO, 1995.

Ginsborg, Paul. *L'Italia del tempo presente*. Turin, 1998.

Giuntini, Andrea. *Dalla Lyonnaise alla Fiorentinagas*. Bari, 1990.

Giustiniani, Corrado. *La casa promessa*. Turin, 1981.

Gobbi, Grazia, and Michele Di Sivo. "Edilizia popolare a Firenze, 1915–40." *Storia urbana* 4 (April 1980), pp. 67–99.

Goldthwaite, Richard. *The Building of Renaissance Florence*. Baltimore, 1980.

Gonella, Guido. *Luci ed ombre della esperienza costituzionale*. Florence, 1978.

Gori, Riccardo. *Storia di 'Societa', 1945–50*. Verona, 1981.

Gorresio, Vittorio. *L'Italia a sinistra*. Milan, 1963.

Grassellini, Emilio. *Firenze*. Florence, 1984.

Grassi, S. "Giorgio La Pira alla costituente." *Testimonianza* 21 (May 1978), pp. 240–66.

Gundle, Stephen, and Simon Parker, eds. *The New Italian Republic*. London, 1996.

Harrison, Barbara Grizzuti. *Italian Days*. New York, 1989.

Herder, Harry. *Italy in the Age of Risorgimento*. London, 1983.

Herderson, Gavin, ed. *Augustus Hare in Italy*. New York, 1988.

Hibbert, Christopher. *Florence*. New York, 1993.

Ilardi, Massimo, and Accornero, Aris, eds. *Il Partito Comunista italiano*. Milan, 1982.

Indovina, Francesco, ed. *Dal blocco dei fitti all'equo canone*. Venice, 1977.

————. *La città fine millennio*. Milan, 1990.

————. *La città occasionale*. Milan, 1993.

————. *Enciclopedia di urbanistica e pianificazione territoriale*. 8 volumes. Milan, 1984–1988.

————. *Esperienze di pianificazione regionale*. Padua, 1967.

————. *Lo spreco edilizio.* Padua, 1973.

Inghirami, Francesco. *Bibliografia storica della Toscana.* 2 volumes. Bologna, 1983.

Innamorati, Serena. *Mario Fabiani.* Florence, 1984.

————. *Per l'unita della resistenza.* Milan, 1990.

Innocenti, Piero. *L'industria nell'area fiorentina.* Florence, 1980.

Intellettuali di frontiera. 2 volumes. Florence, 1985.

Invito, Giovanni, ed. *Novecento. Minore.* Lecce, 1977.

IRPET (Istituto Regionale per la Programmazione Economica in Toscana). *Intervento pubblico e politiche del territorio nel nuovo ordinamento di governo locale.* Florence, 1991.

Istituto Gramsci Toscano. *I compagni di Firenze.* Florence, 1984.

Istituto di studi politici economici e sociali. *La qualita della vita a Firenze.* Florence, 1993.

Italia Nostra. Sezione di Firenze. *Restituzione di Firenze.* Florence, 1982.

Jentlesone, Bruce. *Pipeline Politics.* Ithaca, NY, 1986.

Kerzer, David. *Politics and Symbols.* New Haven, CT, 1996.

Klein, Rich. "The Florence Floods." *Natural History* (August 1969), pp. 46–55.

Kogan, Norman. *The Government of Italy.* New York, 1962.

Lanaro, Silvio. *Storia dell'Italia repubblicana.* Venice, 1992.

Lancisi, Mario. "La Pira e la sinistra DC di Pistelli." *Testimonianza* 21 (May 1978), pp. 311–25.

Lane, Ron. "Giorgio La Pira." *Forepoint* (Summer 1994), pp. 28–30.

Lange, Peter, George Ross, and Maurizio Vannicelli. *Unions, Change and Crisis.* New York, 1982.

La Pira, Giorgio. *La attesa della povera gente.* Florence, 1977.

————. *La casa comune.* Florence, 1979.

————. *Le citta sono vive.* Brescia, 1978.

————. *I prinicipi.* Florence, 1955.

————. *Premesse della politica e architettura di uno Stato democratico.* Florence, 1978.

Leom, Sandro. *La formazione del pensiero politico di Giorgio La Pira.* Florence, 1991.

Leonardi, Robert, and Douglas Wertman. *Italian Christian Democracy.* New York, 1989.

Lepre, Aurelio. *Le illusioni, la paura, la rabbia.* Naples, 1989.

————. *L'occhio del Duce.* Milan, 1992.

————. *Storia della prima repubblica.* Bologna, 1993.

Lewis, R.W.B. *The City of Florence.* New York, 1995.

Listri, Pier Franceseo. *Tutto Bargellini.* Florence, 1989.

Litchfield, R. Burr. *Emergence of a Bureaucracy.* Princeton, NJ, 1986.

Locke, Richard. *Remaking the Italian Economy.* Ithaca, NY, 1995.

Lopes Pegna, Mario. *Quattro novembre 1966.* Florence, 1971.

Lugli, Antonio. *Giorgio La Pira.* Padua, 1978.

Lumley, Robert. *States of Emergency.* London, 1990.

Mafai, Miriam. *Dimenticare Berlinguer.* Rome, 1996.

Maffei, Gian Luigi. *La casa fiorentina nella storia della citta.* Venice, 1990.

————. *La progettazione edilizia a Firenze.* Venice, 1981.

Malaparte, Curzio. *Maladetti Toscani.* Florence, 1991.

————. *La Pelle.* Florence, 1959.

Malgeri, Francesco. *La sinistra cristiana, 1939–1945.* Bescia, 1982.

————. *Stato e Chiesa in Italia.* Rome, 1976.

————, ed. *Storia della Democrazia Cristiana*. 5 volumes. Rome, 1987–1989.

Mangalaviti, Lirio. *Gaetano Pieraccini*. Florence, 1980.

————. "Gaetano Pieraccini e il socialismo autonomo fiorentino, 1947–1953." *Citta e regione* 7 (February 1981), pp. 177–86.

Maranini, Giuseppe. *Governo parlamentare e partitocrazia*. Florence, 1950.

————. *Storia del potere in Italia*. Florence, 1967.

Maranini, Giuseppe, et al. *Aspetti di vita italiana contemporanea*. Bologna, 1957.

Margiotta Broglio, Francesco, ed. *La chiesa del Concordato*. 2 volumes. Bologna, 1983.

Martini, Mario. *La missione sociale e politica della Democrazia Cristiana*. Rome, n.d.

Martini, Maurizio. *L'industria manifatturiera toscana*. Florence, 1975.

Massa, Marco, ed. *Firenze*. Milan, 1988.

Matelli, Giuseppe. "L'edilizia popolare in Italia." *Citta e Regione* (January 1977), pp. 80–89.

Mazzei, Fioretta. *Giorgio La Pira Cose viste e ascoltate*. Florence, 1980.

Mazzoni, Andrea. *I vigili del fuoco a Firenze*. Florence, 1992.

McCarthy, Benjamin. "Return to Florence." *National Geographic* (March 1945), pp. 257–96.

McCarthy, Mary. *The Stone of Florence*. New York, 1963.

McCarthy, Patrick. *The Crisis of the Italian State*. New York, 1997.

Melchionda, Roberto. *Firenze industriale nei suoi incerti albori*. Florence, 1988.

Merli, Gianfranco. *Don Angeli e i cattolici democratici in Toscana*. Rome, 1978.

Meucci, Piero. *Giornalismo e cultura nella Firenze del dopoguerra, 1945–1965*. Florence, 1986.

Mezzani, Donatella. *La discriminazione politica e sindacale nelle fabbriche della Provincia di Firenze dal 1948 al 1966*. Florence, 1983.

Miller, James Edward. "Roughhouse Diplomacy: The United States Confronts Italian Communism, 1944–1958." *Storia delle relazione internationale* 5 (Fall 1989), pp. 279–311.

————. *The United States and Italy 1940–1950*. Chapel Hill, NC, 1986.

Mola, Aldo. *Storia della massoneria italiana dalle origini ai nostri giorni*. Milan, 1992.

Molajoli, Bruno. *Firenze salvata*. Turin, 1970.

Montanelli, Indro, and Mario Cervi. *L'Italia degli anni di fango*. Milan, 1993.

————. *L'Italia degli anni di piombo*. Milan, 1991.

Morales, Giorgio, Giuseppe Longo, and Marcello Stefanini. *I consigli di quartieri*. Rome, 1980.

Morgan, Philip. "I primi podesta fascisti, 1926–1932." *Storia contemporanea* 9 (June 1978), pp. 407–23.

Mori, Giorgio, ed. *Storia d'Italia. Le regioni dall'Unita a oggi. La Toscana*. Turin, 1986.

Mori, Grigorio, and Piero Roggi. *Firenze 1815–1945*. Florence, 1990.

Murray, William. *Italy, the Fatal Gift*. New York, 1982.

Nencini, Franco. *Florence*. Florence, 1967.

Le officine Galileo. Florence, 1985.

Orfei, Ruggero. *L'occupazione del potere*. Milan, 1976.

Orfice, Gabriella. *Da Ponta Vecchio a S. Croce*. Florence, 1992.

Osanna, Micali. *La citta desiderata*. Florence, 1992.

Osanna, Micali, Piero Rosseli, and Giuseppina Romby. *Firenze tra passato e futuro*. Florence, 1976.

Ottati, Davis. *L'acquedotto di Firenze dal 1860 ad oggi*. Florence, 1983.

————. *Firenze pulita.* Florence, 1990.

————. *Fuochi di gioia ed oltre.* Florence, 1989.

————. *Il ventre di Firenze.* Florence, 1988.

Ottone, Piero. *Fanfani.* Milan, 1966.

Palla, Marco. "Firenze del periodo fascista." *Storia urbana* 1 (July 1977), pp. 187–220.

————. *Firenze nel regime fascista.* Florence, 1978.

Paoletti, Paolo. *Il ponte a Santa Trinita.* Florence, 1987.

Paoletti, Paolo, and Paola Torrini. *Firenze anni '50.* 2 volumes. Florence, 1991.

Papafava, Francesco, ed. *Firenze: Introduzione.* Florence, 1993.

Parenti, Gabriele. *ACLI e sindicato a Firenze negli anni 1945–1950.* Florence, 1986.

Partito Comunista Italiano, Federazione Fiorentina. *Aspetti della presenza della massoneria a Firenze.* Florence, 1983.

————. *Per un nuovo tip di sviluppo economico; per la piena occupazione in provincia di Firenze.* Florence, 1973.

Pasolini, Pier Paolo. *Scritti corsari.* Milan, 1990.

Perrone, Nico. *Mattei.* Milan, 1989.

Pieroni, Piero. *Firenze, gli anni terribile.* Florence, 1970.

Pietra, Italo. *Mattei.* Milan, 1987.

Pinzauti, Leonardo, ed. *Firenze nel dopoguerra.* Milan, 1983.

————. *Il Maggio Musicale Fiorentino dalla prima alla trentesima edizione.* Florence, 1967.

Pizzinelli, Corrado. *Scelba.* Milan, 1982.

Pombeni, Paolo. *Le Cronache sociali di Dossetti.* Florence, 1976.

————. *Il gruppo dossettiano e la fondazione della democrazia italiana, 1938–1948.* Bologna, 1979.

Pope-Henessy, John. "Flowers of Florence." *New York Review of Books* (June 24, 1993), pp. 42–44.

Pozzana, Giuseppe. *Tra pubblico e privato.* Florence, 1985.

Pridham, Geoffrey. *The Nature of the Italian Party System.* New York, 1981.

Princivalle, Senio. *Guida amministrativa per sindaci, assessori e consiglieri comunali.* Florence, 1970.

Provincia di Firenze. *Contro ogni ritorno.* Florence, 1972.

Putnam, Robert. *Making Democracy Work.* Princeton, NJ, 1993.

Quaranta, Italo. *Il bilancio comunale.* Milan, 1972.

Ragni, Luciano. *Ieri e oggi della camera di commercio fiorentina.* Florence, 1975.

Rainero, Enrico. *Firenze.* Florence, 1986.

Ranney, Austin and Giovanni Sartori, eds. *Eurocommunism.* Washington, DC, 1978.

Recupero, N., F. Leonetti, and F. Fiorani. *La polemica Vittorini-Togliatti e la linea del PCI nel '45–47.* Milan, 1976.

Redazione Fiorentina dell'Unita. *La cultura a Firenze.* Florence, 1962.

Regione Toscana. *La Toscana e i suoi comuni.* Florence, 1985.

Reps, John. *The Making of Urban America.* Princeton, NJ, 1965.

Riccardi, Andrea, ed. *Le chiese di Pio XII.* Rome, 1986.

Ristori, Renzo, ed. *La camera di commercio e la borsa di Firenze.* Florence, 1963.

Rochat, Giorgio, Enzo Santarelli, and Paolo Sorcinelli, eds. *Linea gotica 1944.* Milan, 1986.

Roggi, Piero. *I cattolici e la piena occupazione.* Milan, 1983.

Romano, Sergio. *Tra due repubbliche.* Milan, 1995.

Romero, Federico. *Emigrazione e integrazione europea, 1945–1973.* Rome, 1991.

Rossini, Giuseppe, ed. *Alcide De Gasperi e l'eta del centrismo.* Rome, 1990.

————. *Democrazia Cristiana e costituente nella societa del dopoguerra*. Rome, 1980.

Rotelli, Ettore. "Le trasformazione dell'ordinamento comunale e provinciale durante il regime fascista." *Storia contemporanea* 4 (March 1973), pp. 57–121.

————, ed. *La Ricostruzione in Toscana dal CTLN ai partiti*. 2 volumes. Bologna, 1980–1981.

Russo, Alfio, ed. *La Nazione nei suoi cento anni, 1859–1959*. Bologna, 1959.

Sabbatucci, Giovanni, ed. *Storia del socialismo*. Volumes 5, 6. Rome, 1981.

Salvati, Mariuccia. *Stato e industria nella ricostruzione*. Milan, 1982.

Santa Croce nel '800. Florence, 1986.

Scarpari, Giancarlo. *La Democrazia Cristiana e le leggi eccezionali*. Milan, 1977.

Scoppola, Pietro. *Gli anni della costituente fra politica e storia*. Bologna, 1980.

————. *Dal neoguelfismo alla Democrazia Cristiana*. Rome, 1957.

————. *La proposta politica di De Gasperi*. Bologna, 1977.

————. *La repubblica dei partiti*. Bologna, 1991.

Scoppola, Pietro, and Francesco Traniello, eds. *I cattolici tra fascismo e democrazia*. Bologna, 1975.

Seacrest, Maryle. *Being Bernard Berenson*. New York, 1979.

Secchia, Pietro. *I comunisti e la insurrezione, 1943–1954*. Rome, 1973.

————. *Il Partito Comunista Italiano e la guerra di liberazione, 1943–1945*. Milan, 1973.

Sechi, Salvatore. *Dimenticare Livorno*. Milan, 1985.

Semboloni, Ferdinando. *Appunti sulla topografia socile del centro storico di Firenze dal 1960 al 1981*. Florence, 1986.

Sestan, Ernesto, ed. *Convegno su Gaetano Salvemini*. Milan, 1977.

Snowden, Frank. *The Fascist Revolution in Tuscany, 1919–22*. New York, 1989.

Sorrentino, Carlo. *Firenze*. Rome, 1990.

Spadolini, Giovanni. *Firenze mille anni*. Florence, 1977.

Spark, Penny. "A Home for Everybody: Design, Ideology, and the Culture of the Home in Italy, 1945–1972." in Z. Baranski and R. Lumley, eds., *Culture and Conflict in Postwar Italy* (London, 1990), pp. 225–41.

————. *Italian Design*. New York, 1988.

Speranza, G., and L. Tramontano. *L'ordinamento delle autonomie locali*. Naples, 1992.

Spini, Giorgio, and Antonio Casali. *Firenze*. Bari, 1986.

Spini, Valdo. *Viaggio dentro le istituzioni*. Milan, 1992.

Spini, Valdo, and Mariella Zoppi. *Firenze*. Florence, 1975.

Studio d'arte Il Moro. *Firenze/Ricerca*. Florence, 1985.

Studi storici sul centro di Firenze. Bologna, 1978.

"Lo Svizzero" [pseud.]. *La Pira e la via cattolica al comunismo*. Milan, 1964.

Taddei, Francesca. *Il Pignone di Firenze, 1944–1954*. Florence, 1980.

Tamburrano, Giuseppe. *Dal centrosinistra al neocentrisimo, 1962–1972*. Florence, 1973.

————. *Pietro Nenni*. Rome, 1986.

————. *Storia e cronaca del centrosinistra*. Milan, 1971.

Tarchi, Marco. *Cinquant'anni di nostalgia*. Milan, 1995.

Tassani, Giovanni. *La cultura politica della destra cattolica*. Rome, 1976.

————. *La terza generazione*. Rome, 1988.

————. *Vista da sinistra*. Florence, 1986.

Taurini, Giampoalo. "La Pira e il dissenso cattolico fiorentino." *Testimonianza* 21 (May 1978), pp. 326–37.

Teodori, Massimo. *Costituzione italiana e modello americano*. Milan, 1992.

Terra, Dino, et al. *Firenze '80*. Florence, 1971.

Tomasetti, Fabio. "Trasporti pubblici nella citta e nel territorio di Firenze, 1860–1915." *Storia urbana* 3 (January 1979), pp. 115–62.

Toniolo, Domenico. *Il compromesso storico*. Rome, 1981.

Trotta, Giampaolo. *Monticelli*. Florence, 1987.

————. *Il prato d'Ognissanti a Firenze*. Florence, 1988.

————. *Varlungo e Rovezzano*. Florence, 1988.

Tutaev, David. *The Man Who Saved Florence*. New York, 1966.

Twain, Mark. *The Innocents Abroad*. New York, 1990.

Valenza, Pietro. *Il Compromesso Storico*. Rome, 1975.

Vanucci, Marcello. *L'avventura degli stranieri in Toscana*. Aosta, 1981.

————. *Storia di Firenze*. 6 volumes. Rome, 1988.

Varni, Angelo. *La CGIL regionale toscana*. Florence, 1981.

Vedovato, Giuseppe. *Difesa di Firenze*. Florence, 1968.

Venti firme per Firenze. Florence, 1980.

Ventura, Francesco. "Genesi e progetti di un ingrandimento di citta nella prima meta del '800: Il nuovo quartiere presso il Fortezza da Basso di Firenze." *Storia urbana* 9 (October 1985), pp. 47–66.

Vezzosi, Elisabetta. "La sinistra democristiana tra neutralismo e Patto Atlantico." In E. DiNolfo, R. Rainero, and B. Vigezzi, eds., *L'Italia e la politica di potenza in Europa* (Milan, 1988), pp. 195–221.

Villani, Giulio. *Il vescovo Elia Dalla Costa*. Florence, 1974.

Vitta, Cino. *Giunta provinciale amministrativa*. Milan, 1907.

Webster, Richard. *The Cross and the Fasces*. Stanford, CA, 1960.

Weinberg, Leonard. *The Transformation of Italian Communism*. London, 1995.

Willan, Philip. *Puppetmasters*. London, 1991.

Zampella, Frida. "L'amministrazione Fabiani, 1946–1951." Tesi di lauria, University of Florence, 1986–1987.

Zoppi, Mariella. *Firenze e l'urbanistica*. Rome, 1982.

Index

Action Party (PdA), 4–5; and reconstruction, 21–22; and resistance, 4
Agnoletti, E. Enriquez, 76
Andreotti, Giulio, 103, 141–142, 209
ANPI (National Partisans Association), 91
Artom, Eugenio, 23, 41, 106; comments on La Pira, 76
ATAF (Florence City Agency for Trams and Buses), 17, 38–39, 76, 134, 192, 216–217

Badoglio, Pietro, 3–4
Ballini, Pier Luigi, xi, 184, 185; on city urban plan, 215; and cultural affairs, 178; on Morales junta, 210; on traffic patterns, 215
Bargellini, Piero, 59; as administrator, 126–127, 130–133; character, 126; and Detti plan, 135; and 1996 flood, 123–124; resignation as mayor, 135
Bausi, Luciano: assessor of urban planning, 121, 123–124, 127, 135; elected mayor, 144; impact on Florence, 166, 168; leadership analyzed, 151–154; objectives, 145; and tourism, 150; urban projects, 144–145, 149–150
Berenson, Bernard, 22
Berio, Luciano, 193–195

Berlinguer, Enrico: described, 160; and Moro kidnapping, 165; strategy, 160–161
Berlusconi, Silvio, 209, 222, 225
Bianchi Bandinelli, Ranuccio, 22
Bilenchi, Romano, 35, 88
Bogiankino, Massimo, 143, 178; Craxi's role in election, 189–190; elected mayor, 185–186; FIAT-Fondiaria issue, 196–199; mayor (1985–1989), 189–193, 200–201; resignation, 199; and Year of Culture, 193–196
Bonisanti, Alessandro: death, 180; election as mayor, 179; problems facing administration, 179–180
Bonomi, Ivanoe, 16
Bossi, Umberto, 218, 222–223

Calamandrei, Piero, 24, 76
Case minime, 58–59
Chiappi, Armellini, 4
Christian Democratic Party (DC), 4, 5, 15, 23, 31, 32; collapse, 209–210; cooperation with communists and socialists, 24; and Historical Compromise, 160; and local government, 26; relations with Vatican, 24–25, role in political system, 26–27

Codignola, Tristano, 76, 140, 143

Colzi, Ottaviano, 177, 182, 185, 190

Com'era reconstruction: debate over, 22–23, examples, 43, 61

Conti, Gianni, 171, 185; assessor of urban planning, 179–182; bids for cooperation with PSI, 178; FIAT-Fondiaria plan, 182–184, 199; forced to resign, 210; on problems of Florence, 175; and socialists, 199; vice mayor, 206, 213; views on growth, 223–224

Conti, Lando: mayor (1983–1985), 182–185; murder, 190

Corriere di Firenze, 32

Craxi, Bettino: control over PSI, 182, 189–190; and corruption, 209–210; rise and strategy, 176

Dalla Costa, Elia, 5, 36, 77, 80, 111; anti-Fascism, 2–3; and La Pira, 53, 55, 71; support for "open city," 6

DeGasperi, Alcide, 24–26, 62, 70–72; and DC left, 50–52; defeated, 62

Democratic Party of Left (PDS): creation, 207–208; electoral strategy, 221; 1992 elections, 210

Detti, Edoardo, xi, 59, 76, 115, 124, 139, 170; assessor of urban planning, 103–106, 109–112; attempts to forward 1962 urban plan, 150–151; characterized, 101–102; contrasted with La Pira, 101; on La Pira's urban management, 94; purged by PSI, 135; view of La Pira, 101–102

Detti, Iacopo, 112, 124

Detti, Tommaso, 124, 151

Devoto, Giacomo, 140

Dini, Alfio, 75–76

DiNolfo, Ennio, ix; and Bogiankino, 195; member of the "12 Sages" (Wisemen), 189, 194–195; on the Year of Culture, 189

Dossetti, Giuseppe, 49–50, 52–53, 79

ENEL (State Electric Agency), role in 1966 flood, 122, 131–132

Fabiani, Mario, 33, 53, 79, 88, 91; administration of Florence, 36–41; anti-

Stalinism, 36; cooperation with La Pira, 39–40; cultural programs, 40–41; elected mayor, 32; head of provincial PCI, 78; 1951 elections, 55; political views, 35–36, 41; president of province of Florence, 56; tourism policies, 39–41; urban planning, 41–44

Fanfani, Amintore, 50, 102, 106; and center left, 86, 89–92; DC party secretary, 63, 69–70; prime minister (1960–1963), 93, 103; prime minister (1958–1959), 91–92; and public housing, 51–52; regains leading party role, 142; ties with La Pira, 56, 63, 84, 103

Festa dell'Unita, 77

FIAT-Fondiaria plans: and Bogiankino junta, 193, 196–199; L. Conti junta supports, 183; and Morales junta, 211–212, 214–215; projects described, 182; relationship to Detti plan, 183–184

Florence: airport requirements, 95, 105, 153, 168, 211, 215; city government's economic role, 192; declining population, 202; drugs and AIDS, 190; environmental problems, 167–168, 191; European Cultural Capital, 184–185, 193–196; German occupation, 3–6; liberation 9–10; looted art, 7–8, 21; metropolitan government issue, 212–213; neighborhood councils (*consigli dei quartieri*), 147, 164; 1996 flood described, 121–125; 1976 Olympic Games bid, 144–145; "open city" issue, 6–8; optimism regarding future, 200–201; outlook at end of 20th century, 225–226; post-flood reconstruction, 127, 133; "Project Firenze," 163, 166; prostitution 19–20, 166; traffic restrictions (ZTL and *zone blu*), 152–153, 166, 200–201, 215–218; traffic usage, 43, 60, 95, 109, 152, 166–167, 200, 215–218; traffic woes, 200–202; wartime destruction, 9–11; youth culture and violence, 162–163, 165–166, 190–191

Florit, Ermenegildo, 71, 111; conflict over Isolotto, 141; and 1966 flood, 128

Fortezza da Basso-Palazzo dei Congressi complex, 146, 168, 191

Gabbuggiani, Elio, 159; elected mayor, 162; forced from power, 178–179; mayor (1975–1980), 162–166; performance evaluated, 170–171; reelection as mayor (1980), 177; tourism, 166–168; transportation issues, 168; urban plan, 166–167, 169–170, 177
Galileo Optics, 19, 72, 74, 91
Gronchi, Giovanni, 69, 92–93

Hartt, Frederick, rescue of Italian art, 20–21

Italian Communist party (PCI), 31; bid for Historic Compromise, 160–162; Cold war policies, 33–34; confronts future, 199; effects of de-Stalinization, 88–91; and FIAT-Fondiaria, 198–199; governs Florence, 32; 1956 elections, 77–78; 1960 elections, 96; postwar position, 15; relations with Soviet communism, 33; role in ouster of La Pira, 114; role in resistance, 4–5; transformation to social democratic party, 205–207; weaknesses, 170; and youth unrest of 1970s, 141
Italian elections of 1948, impact, 34
Italian Liberal Party (PLI), and La Pira, 76–79
Italian Social Movement (MSI), violence in Florence, 107
Italian Socialist Party (PSI), 4, 31; abortive reunion with social democrats, 142–144; balancing role in Florentine politics, 177–179; center left project, 83–93; collapse, 210–211; Historical Compromise issue, 159–160; internal problems, 75–76; joins PCI to govern Florence, 32; and 1956 elections, 77; relations with PCI, 33–35; revival, 176–177; splits weaken, 33–34
Italy, constitution, 25–26

Lagorio, Lelio: mayor (1965), 114–115, 126; on communist-socialist relations, 159; political views and character, 146–147; on regionalism, 146–148, 169; vice mayor (1965–1967), 126–127,

143, 146; and the Year of Culture, 194–195
La Nazione, 3, 35, 143, 191–192; on Bogiankino junta, 198; and FIAT-Fondiaria, 196–198; and 1966 flood, 128, 133; opposes Gabbuggiani junta, 178; opposes La Pira, 79, 111, 113; on traffic limitation, 200–201
La Pira, Giorgio, 19, 27, 180; achievements, 74–75; and the Americans, 61–62, 111; anti-Fascism, 3–4; attacked by Vatican, 90; campaign for mayor (1951), 53, 55–56; career collapses, 126; causes of fall, 115; center left issue, 62–63, 68–70, 73–80, 83–85; characterized, 49, 74, 101; creation of Italian democracy, 24; culture 61, 68; and Detti, 101; and Galileo crisis, 91; international affairs, 51, 68, 77, 94, 110–111, 126; mayor (1951–1956), 57–62; mayor (1956–1957), 83–85; mayor (1961–1964), 102–113; moves toward cooperation with PCI, 111–113; negotiations for junta, 96–97; 1956 elections, 77–80, 83; 1960 elections, 96; 1964 elections, 113–114; ouster, 114–115; Pignone crisis, 67–68, 71–73; political ideas, 49–55; political style, 56; relations with Florentine PCI, 57, 63, 69, 73, 77–78, 91, 104; tourism, 61, 68–69; views on communism, 55; views on urban planning, 54, 59–60, 76, 103; vision of Florence, 54–55
Longo, Luigi, 73
Luce, Clare Boothe, 62, 84

Maggio Musicale festival, 5, 40, 69, 85, 193
Maier, Guido, 85, 127
Mani pulite (Clean Hands): discussed, 209–210; effects, 209, 222–223
Marinotti, Franco, 72
Mariotti, Luigi, 75, 114, 142
Masonry: P-2 Lodge scandal, 177–178; role in Florence, 177–178, 207
Mattei, Enrico (ENI), 67–68, 72, 102–103, 109–110
Mattei, Enrico (publisher), 122, 128
Morales, Giorgio: character, 206; cooperation with DC, 198; decentralization is-

sue, 162, 164; elected mayor (1989), 199; infighting in coalition, 206–207; mayor (1990–1995), 206–207; mayor following 1990 elections, 205–206; 1995 campaign, 224–225; and PCI, 176; traffic problems, 215–218; urban planning, 211–215
Mori, Giorgio, 159
Moro, Aldo, 50, 106, 142; and center left, 92, 97; DC secretary, 89, 92; Historic Compromise, 160; kidnapping, 165; and La Pira, 114; 1966 flood, 130–132; prime minister (1963–1964), 112–113
Musco, Gianfranco, 42
Mussolini, Benito, 2, 7

Nazione del Popolo, 32
Nenni, Pietro, 24, 52; meetings with La Pira, 89, 96–97; opening to left, 75, 86–89, 93–94, 96–97, 106–107, 108, 112; reunification with social democrats, 107–108, 134, 142–144
Nuovo Corriere, 32, 34–35, 55, 88
Nuovo Pignone, 72–73

Occhetto, Achille: and FIAT-Fondiaria, 199, 211, 221; PCI secretary, 199, 207
Orebaugh, Walter, 20, 31–32, 36

Parri, Ferruccio, 15, 25
Paterno, Giulio, 15–17
Patriotic Action Groups (GAP), 4–5
Peretola airport, 95, 168, 211, 214–215
Piano Regolatore Generale (PRG): 1949 version, 43–44; 1958 version, 94–96; 1962 version (Detti Plan), 103–106, 108, 111–112, 115, 135, 144–145, 169–170, 177, 183–184; 1992 version, 213–215
Pieraccini, Gaetano: mayor, 10; reconstruction, 17, 21–22
Pignone, 5, 19, 67–68, 71–74
Piovanelli, Silvano, 207, 225
Pistelli, Nicola, 70, 79, 90, 92, 103, 107–108; and center left, 107–109, 111–113; death, 113
Pius XII, Pope: anti-communism, 32; op-

poses center left, 84; opposes De-Gasperi, 62; views of La Pira, 71
Ponte alla Vittoria, role in reconstruction politics, 22
Ponte S. Trinita: destruction, 9; reconstruction, 20, 42, 60–61, 95
Ponte Vecchio, 21; escapes destruction, 9; and 1966 flood, 122–123

Ramat, Raffaello, 84–85, 93
Regional government: reforms, 146–148; shortcomings, 169
Romita, Giuseppe, 23, 25
Romiti, Cesare, 196
Roncalli, Angelo (Pope John XXIII), 84
Rossi, Giuseppe, 31

Salazar, Lorenzo, 85, 94–95
Saragat, Giuseppe, 86, 89, 107–108, 114, 142
Scelba, Mario, 53, 57
Secchia, Pietro, 90, 141
Spadolini, Giovanni: and Florentine local politics, 179, 182; prime minister, 168
Speranza, Edoardo, 84, 90
Spini, Valdo, and PSI, 177, 185, 190
Stalin, Joseph, 33, 87–88, 91
Sullo, Fiorentino, 107–108, 112

Tambroni, Ferdinando, 93
Tanassi, Mario, 89
Teatro Comunale, 2, 5, 20, 69, 113, 153, 168, 178, 193; destruction, 5; disruption at, 193–194; 1966 flood, 129; political role, 178; reconstruction, 40
Togliatti, Palmiro, 24, 33, 35; on economic "miracle," 102; opposes opening to left, 87–88, 90–91, 111; views of DC left, 50–51
Tuscan Committee of National Liberation (CTLN): decline of influence, 15–17; interparty relations, 4–5, 7; liberation of Florence, 8–10; occupation authorities, 16, 21; organization of resistance, 4; preservation of arts, 21; reconstruction, 21–22; relations with allied purge of fascists, 16

Unita Popolare, 76; merges with PSI, 90
United States, role in Florence's recon-
struction, 18–19
Uomo qualunque, 32

Vanoni, Enzo, 50, 75
Votto, Parise, 40, 69

Winkler, Bernard, 215–218
Wolf, Gerhardt, 6–7

Zoli, Adone, 32, 79, 109
Zoppi, Mariella, xi; FIAT-Fondiaria,
183; and PSI, 177; urban planning,
181

About the Author

JAMES EDWARD MILLER is a scholar with the European Studies Program of the Foreign Service Institute.